BUYWAYS

Cultural Spaces series, edited by Sharon Zukin

Other titles in the series:

BUYWAYS

BILLBOARDS, AUTOMOBILES, AND THE AMERICAN LANDSCAPE

CATHERINE GUDIS

ROUTLEDGE   NEW YORK AND LONDON

A volume in the *Cultural Spaces* series, edited by Sharon Zukin.

Published in 2004 by
Routledge
29 West 35th Street
New York, NY 10001
www.routledge-ny.com

Published in Great Britain by
Routledge
11 New Fetter Lane
London EC4P 4EE
www.routledge.co.uk

Library of Congress Cataloging-in-Publication Data.

Gudis, Catherine.
    Buyways : billboards, automobiles, and the American landscape / by Catherine Gudis.
        p. cm.
    ISBN 0-415-93454-0 (alk. paper) – ISBN 0-415-93455-9 (pbk. : alk. paper)
    1. Advertising, Outdoor–United States–History–20th century. 2. Billboards–United States–History–20th century. 3. Consumption (Economics)–United States–History–20th century. 4. Automobile travel–United States–History–20th century. I. Title.
    HF5843.G84 2004
    659.13'42–dc22   2003017457

FOR MICKEY

CONTENTS

INTRODUCTION

**The highway has become the buyway. There is a highway greater than
Broadway, Fifth Avenue or Main Street. It includes them all. It is the road
that the public travels. It is millions of miles long. And billions of dollars are
spent because of what the public sees when it travels this buyway.**

  This is the Rue de la *Pay*.

–Advertisement, *Poster,* December 1923

By the second and third decades of the twentieth century it had already become
obvious that the car was here to stay and that it would forever alter our daily lives.
As the car came to be a routine part of the American way, the highway also
became more than merely a route to be traveled. Among other things, the road
now comprised a boundless marketplace "millions of miles long" and billions of
dollars strong that with every year burst farther out of its traditional confinement
within town and city boundaries. Broadway, Fifth Avenue, and Main Street might
once have been the commercial centers for business and trade, but in the age of
the automobile all highways were now destined to serve that function. The highway had become the "buyway" (fig. 1).

  To entrepreneurs, real-estate developers, city boosters, nature enthusiasts,
and even urban and regional planners, cars and highways were opening up the
countryside as a new location for all kinds of businesses, industries, residences,
and leisure pursuits. While in the previous century the lines put down by railroad and streetcar companies defined commercial and residential development, it was the areas between and beyond these old delineated routes that
began to look gilded when seen through the eyes of the twentieth-century

Rue De La Pay

THE HIGHWAY
and THE BUYWAY

The highway has become the buyway. There is a highway greater than Broadway, Fifth Avenue or Main Street. It includes them all. It is the road that the public travels. It is millions of miles long. And billions of dollars are spent because of what the public sees when it travels this buyway.

This is the Rue de la *Pay*.

Here outdoor advertising pays and pays and pays.

O-double-A is a useful institution to advertisers because, among other reasons it understands the geography and the psychology and the buyology of this Rue de la Pay.

OUTDOOR ADVERTISING AGENCY
OF AMERICA, INCORPORATED
Successors to Ivan B. Nordhem Co.
8 WEST FORTIETH STREET, NEW YORK
CHICAGO   PITTSBURGH   DETROIT

*Poster
Advertising*

*Painted
Displays*

1. Advertisement for the Outdoor Advertising Agency of America, 1923.

prospector. The whole countryside seemed ripe for development. Indeed, over the course of the twentieth century, the American landscape would bear virtually untrammeled commercial decentralization. It began in the 1920s at the fringes of cities and towns, and grew farther still with the aid of 1930s highway developments, until the decentralization tendency reached a frenzy in the 1950s and 1960s when the interstate highway system extended its broad asphalt fingers across all of America, linking countryside to cities and clogging all with automobile congestion.

Today we generally identify commercial sprawl with cars, roadways, and retail developments, but what of the visual features that involve more than steel, concrete, and asphalt? What of the pictures, forms, and words that populate the strip and the city, and that turn even the remotest highway with a billboard into a location of market relations? Integral to both the changing American landscape and to the diffusion of the market so that it is now placeless, decentralized, and sojourning along every road has been the business of outdoor advertising. For advertisers, the highway itself comprised a new "Rue de la Pay" consisting of just about any road anyone dared to travel. Today, advertisements, automobiles, and highways are so omnipresent that they hardly give us pause to notice. Yet it took all three, growing together, to decentralize the market so that it is now virtually everywhere. In so spreading the market, these forces have altered the ways we experience very basic things, including nature, the landscape, community, images, words, architecture, and even abstract space and time.

People often ascribe the spread of commercial strips, suburbs, and sprawl to the period after World War II, and when they do they also leave out the influence of the outdoor advertising industry.[1] In fact, the surge for sprawl came earlier, after World War I. It was immediately accompanied by advertising, and was often led by it. The outdoor advertising industry, like many industries, grew and rationalized itself with such speed that a mere decade after the Treaty of Versailles the American landscape was well on its way to the dissonance of signs and patchwork of buildings and spaces we know today. Outdoor advertisers aided this process in several unique ways. They recognized that the commercial audience, unlike that of print media, was in motion. Rather than rooted to places of dense commerce or population, markets themselves moved, following audiences who now traveled in increasingly diverse directions. Logically, then, outdoor advertisers concluded that signs and markets ought to follow these audiences. As outdoor advertisers came to see drivers and passengers as mobile markets, they worked to make the automobile trip itself a commercial experience aimed to help motorists consume more. Reasoning that advertisements at the side of the road were as fitting a view as the natural environment, billboard operators even infiltrated geographical arenas that did not yet have other forms of on-site commerce (such as stores and gasoline stations). There they hawked tangible goods and services available down the road. They also sold ideas that small towns and businesses were prone to appreciate—namely, the benefits of car travel, attention to localities otherwise less distinguishable without signs, and, of course, tourism, a simple commercial means by which drivers could consume the landscapes and places beyond the billboards. In time, these silent signs of commerce came to hold the space for the development of more stores and services.

In all of these ways—by construing their market as mobile, by reinforcing the tourist enterprise of experiencing the landscape as a series of views to be consumed before passing on, and by physically marking the natural environment with the signs of commerce that laid the way for on-site businesses—outdoor advertisers altered the physical locations and the perceptual understanding of not only the marketplace but public space. Since outdoor advertising occupied private property but broadcast across public rights-of-way, it raised questions regarding ownership of the road, the roadside, the broadcast space around it, and whose interests should prevail in controlling the use and appearance of what many presumed to be public space. Advertisers and their audiences struggled to answer these questions and to define the natural and commercial uses and values of the roadside environment.

Just as different interests and groups have shaped the landscape, so have various factions and constituents molded the outdoor advertising industry. As the industry grew more organized in the twentieth century, its standards and practices were often responses to the criticisms of its most vocal and organized audiences. The ways the industry has defended itself legally and politically have followed a pattern of call and response, with perhaps a whispered aside or backroom political deal to sidestep the most demanding issues at hand. Nevertheless, to say that advertisers and audiences simply held polarized views or that they stuck to their discrete roles or economic positions as, respectively, producers and consumers, is simply incorrect. The billboard industry began to self-regulate and to deal with consumer groups starting in the late nineteenth century, and they continue to do so today. Advertisers are not, after all, above being consumers or constituents. They too are travelers and residents of the roads that bear the signs of their art and commerce, just as they are also consumers of advertised goods. There is no neutral place to stand outside of the market, and we do well to remember that the most diverse groups and interests—from politicians and planners to developers, merchants, and advertisers, to ecotourists and commuters—all participate in building America as a network of buyways.

Although this study attempts to consider the views of diverse producers, distributors, and consumers of outdoor advertising, it is hamstrung by the historical record left behind, which is weighted heavily toward two primary groups: big outdoor advertising companies and their most strident opponents. Like many who have looked at advertisements retrospectively, I must invoke the apology that it is difficult to know just what the full range of audiences thought of the ads they saw (if they thought anything at all), or how their viewing of the ads affected their actions. Whether the ads worked or not (i.e., whether people bought the products because of the billboards they saw) cannot be my concern, though outdoor advertisers made great claims about their success and superiority to other methods and advertising media. I refer to such claims in these pages only to ascertain what members of the industry believed to be true about their work, not to confirm or deny that these claims were true.

That is to say, my point is not to determine the effectiveness of advertising, and it is not to pass judgment on an industry. This is not a practical book nor is it strictly a business history. Rather, I seek to determine, since the advent of the automobile, the cultural implications of the market on our built and natural environments and, therefore, on our experiences of these most basic facts of daily life. The implications of the mobile market are vast, I think, and, according to one advertiser's boast, they ought to be evident to anyone who will take a look around, excluding the bedridden and the blind.

Buyways is organized around the themes of production, distribution, and consumption, in that order. After an overview of billposting before the common use of cars, the first part of this book examines the rise in billboard advertising after World War I by considering the production of both mobile audiences and advertisements. America became "a nation on wheels," and advertisers tried to imagine the new mobile audiences and to communicate with them. Advertisers also attempted to produce the new mobile audiences as commodities to be sold to big business, and to turn the highways through which these audiences traveled into corridors of consumption. As part of the project to foster mass consumption, outdoor advertisers promoted a culture of mobility and tapped the traditional American mythology of the freedom of the open road. They helped construe automobility as the American Dream on four wheels, a key to the

American Way. Part one explores the formal and conceptual strategies advertisers employed to foster the culture of mobility, and it describes the development of an aesthetics of speed specific to the billboard and aiming to appeal to fast-moving audiences without requiring much of them by way of attention, literacy, or thoughtful consideration. The development of the billboard and the diffusion of the marketplace—not to mention the growing rapidity with which audiences in the age of cars, movies, radio, cartoons, and tabloids now expected to receive information and entertainment—ultimately urged the use in advertising of both stereotypes and logos, both among the most important design revolutions of twentieth-century propaganda and publicity.

By imprinting the landscape with the signs of commercial exchange, outdoor advertising distinguished itself from other media, such as print and radio. The second part of this book examines its unique distribution, the placement of advertisements along highways. This section shows how outdoor advertising helped to decentralize the city and fill the countryside with national advertising campaigns as well as retail establishments and potential customers. As the billboard industry evaluated its distribution of billboards and the audiences for them, advertisers realized that their market was not determined by political boundaries such as city and county lines or central business districts. It is for similar reasons that this study, too, cannot be bound by traditional borders. Some readers may wish to learn more of regional history, but I have concluded, along with outdoor advertisers themselves, that their audiences were more flexible than traditional markers of space could contain—they were markets in motion whose travel paid little heed to older precincts of space and time. Recognizing this, advertisers predicted and promoted new commercial developments far from traditional business centers. They did this partly through theatrical displays and an architecture of mobility that acclimated motorists to an exurban culture of spectacle and an auto-oriented consumer landscape, where drivers were encouraged to window shop right through the windshield. Thus outdoor advertisers helped develop fringe areas, laying the pavement for the birth of the commercial strip and the urban sprawl that exploded in the late twentieth and early twenty-first centuries.

That highways would turn into buyways and country roads into "ribbons of gold" was the utopian vision of outdoor advertisers. To others, however, this was a dystopia and a nightmare. Critics felt that markets ought not mix with Mother Nature. Thus, the third part of this book analyzes audience responses to outdoor advertising—in a word, *consumption*. It focuses on the roadside beautification attempts of civic reformers, and looks at the deeply gender-divided "billboard war" that pitted female roadside reformers against male out-door advertisers. While the "scenic sisters," as they were called by admen, wished to rid the public highway of the signs of commerce, their billboard "brethren" asserted their private right to commercial broadcasting across public space. Ultimately, their war contested whether Americans ought to preserve certain spaces from the domain of business and of markets. This section reviews the philosophies and aesthetics of each side and analyzes their competing—though often complementary—visions of the American pastoral ideal. It portrays the billboard war as a battle over aesthetics, access, economics, and the physical location of markets, and is as much about class ideals as it is about cultural conflict. Part three concludes by describing the swan song of the scenic sisters, Lady Bird Johnson's efforts to pass the 1965 Highway Beautification Act (HBA), which limited and called for the removal of many billboards, junkyards, and roadside stands along the newly constructed interstate expressways. The HBA marked the legal culmination of the billboard war, but has not resolved the continuing conflicts between advertisers and their audiences.

The concluding chapter shows some ways in which the mobile market and its concomitant trail of advertising have influenced more recent decades. The asphalt paths of highway systems and the speed of its automotive travelers raise questions regarding changing forms of visual communication, access to public space, and the aesthetic value of natural and built environments. As the conclusion suggests, in the twenty-first century new electronic telecommunications technologies, which often use the metaphor of the highway to represent cyber-audience mobility, take the challenges of the scenic sisters to new extremes as the lines between private and public space blur along with what constitutes the public sphere and public discourse, while issues of speed, decentralization, and mobility intensify along the new virtual buyway, the Internet. *Buyways* thus traces the century-long development of our spatially dispersed landscape of concrete and electronic highways and the advertisements that wrap around them, and ponders the implication of these landscapes, not so much for markets, but for the people that markets are meant to serve.

CHAPTER I

BEFORE THE CAR

As industrial America grew, so did advertising outdoors. Handbills and broadsides for farm machinery, auctions, runaway slaves, stagecoach schedules, and theatrical performances had long fluttered on the walls outside inns and taverns. By the time of the Civil War, banners and posters for circuses and other celebrations comprised a good portion of the finery draping city buildings, past which might rattle a flamboyantly decorated advertising wagon. Painted patent medicine ads screeched their messages from rocks, trees, and fences. Gaslit signs illuminated blocks of New York City. To the titillation of many, sandwich men paced the streets with signs hung over their shoulders and display cases, hats, or other objects perched upon their heads.[1] "Never a brick pile rises in any part of the city," someone noticed in 1867, "but it is covered almost in a night with the fungus and mould of hot notoriety-hunting."[2] Growing cities became embroidered with the handiwork of the billposter and his minions, whose overlapping, multilayered mixed messages offered ephemeral companionship to the brick and mortar of rising buildings. These ads served as an apt symbol for burgeoning commercial culture as well as for the constant change and instability characteristic of the rapidly expanding and increasingly heterogeneous metropolis.[3]

New York journalist George Foster, in his popular 1850 account *New York by Gas-light*, was among those who commented on the mutability of the messages that plastered the city, which served less as a testament to the poetry of advertisers than to the battles between billposters. On the "calicoed surface" of the Park Theater, for instance, one could read "interminably from the handbills lying like scales . . . one upon another" something that went like this: "'Steamer Ali–Sugar-Coat–and Pantaloons for–the Great Anaconda–Whig

Nominations–Panorama of Principles–Democrats Rally to the–American Museum'–and so on."[4] Any one message was lost in the cacophony (fig. 2). The well-coated wall was the result of billposters' efforts to lighten their loads of paper and to beat their competitors at the same game.

The billposters' ad-hoc practices and competing claims to space meant that no available surface was sacred, and even a wall freshly papered with bills seemed to beg to be anointed by the next fellow's paste brush. Even the Memorial Presbyterian Church in New York was forced to publish a special newspaper notice admonishing the billposter who insisted upon covering the church's own posters for their fair.[5] The internecine struggles of the billposters were legion, and, as one paper explained, "it took a husky man to keep his bills in sight" for more than a few hours (fig. 3).[6] Before the 1870s it was unheard of to lease or rent space and, even after, such practices constituted only a fraction of the business. It was even more rare for a lease to go uncontested. Such was the case in the fierce rivalry between the Brooklyn billposters and former partners "Big" John Kenny and Thomas Murphy in the late 1870s. It started casually enough, with one billposter placing lecture bills over the other's theatrical posters, both claiming their right to that site. Competition soon escalated, so that "[w]hen the employees of one firm spotted a bill posted by the other, they tore it down and trampled it in the dust. . . . Bill Boards were smashed and so were heads." Kenny's men were known to "decorate the eyes" of Murphy's, according to the *Brooklyn Eagle*, but they did so with less than full mouthfuls of teeth, courtesy of Murphy's men. By the time Kenny and a henchman were sentenced to the state penitentiary, iron bars, clubs, and even an ax had been called into service, along with the usual paper and paste pot of the billposter's trade.[7] The story of these gentlemen unfortunately does not end here. For Kenny, jail did have a palliative effect, for upon his release he reunited with Murphy, restoring their partnership and fortifying them both against their four or five remaining rivals.[8] But even this hopeful reconciliation and girding of forces could not ensure the success–or health–of both men, as we will soon learn.

The billposters' brawls as well as their copious "snipes" and "daubs"– terms used to describe the pasting of half sheet (twenty-eight inches by twenty-one inches) or smaller bills on ash cans, telegraph poles, and other spaces, and larger posters on walls or fences without permission–both became part of the street life and the spectacle of the city. They were, after all, heirs apparent to none other than entertainment impresario P. T. Barnum, who, thirty years before circulating his circus caravans and advance cars of billposters across

2. "The Bill-Poster's Dream," 1862. Lithograph by B. Derby.

3. "The Battle of the Billboards," c. 1909. Cartoon drawing by Foster Follet.

the country, had promoted his American Museum with a range of outdoor advertisements, including banners, men carrying signs through the streets, and staged street events to lure bystanders into his establishment.[9] Crowds often formed around the battling billposters, too, as they did for the poster war between the Empire and the Novelty Theaters in New York. As each sought to "outdo each other in securing telegraph poles for advertising purposes," audiences goaded them on, until, finally, as newspapers reported, "Something like a fistic encounter took place between the rival posters and their followers." Not until police were installed to uphold an existing ordinance prohibiting the posting of signs on telegraph poles did the ruckus halt, at least temporarily.[10] The law had also stepped in some years before, when the same two theaters battled over the telegraph poles on Broadway. In that case, James Johnson and Michael Dempsey, both prizefighters in the employ of the Empire Theater, lighted upon William Boehm putting up bills for the Novelty. What, then, did these gentlemen do? "They knocked [Boehm] down, emptied the pail of paste over him and then, when he regained his feet, chased him down the street."[11] Suffice it to say that the organization, professionalization, and rationalization of the billposting industry still had some way to go.

Advertising space was not yet construed as real estate. Outdoor advertising was still considered a public spectacle that encompassed all imaginable territory, from chimney tops to curbstones, and from romantic glens to roadside rocks. There was no more tranquil joy for the billposter, said *Harper's Weekly*, than in billing and rebilling the common ash barrel, padding it with paste and paper until its obese form was broader than it was long. Indefatigable, the billposter worked under cover of night, hardly sleeping so that he could put up the gigantic bills "which cover fences and sides of houses."[12] Few paid regard to the inviolability of private and public property. Overnight the visual landscape of the city itself could be transformed, as in New York in the late 1860s, when the construction of the new elevated railways meant that as fast as the pillars for tracks and risers for stairways went up, they were slathered in paper and paste.[13] The platforms helped bring advertisements to new heights, as billposters scrambled to cover chimneys and church steeples with bills to be seen from the "el." Not all riders might see such ads, though, since after the tops, sides, and interiors of the trains were filled with advertising signs, the windows began to be covered with them, too.[14] Not all practices were even so civilized. One enterprising but morbid billposter in Pittsburgh gained a billposting record "second to none" by posting a half-sheet on the "carcass of a horse while the body was still warm."[15] Another painted on the fence of a cemetery,

"Use Jones's bottled ale if you would keep out of here."[16] Every space was fair. Looking to the heavens, some predicted that "[s]oon it will be possible to project from an electrical machine at night advertisements on the clouds."[17]

Most outdoor advertisers planted themselves more firmly on earth, where nature itself could serve as ample canvas for the sign painter's craft. In the 1860s and 1870s, the heyday of patent medicines in the United States, even sparsely settled areas (especially those in view of railway lines or steamboats) sported white-painted rocks, trees, and bluffs boasting the benefits of such nostrums as St. Jacob's Oil; Buchu (recommended for everything from syphilis to rheumatism); Jones's Tonic ("a Sure Cure for Paralysis, Vertigo, Insomnia, Jim Jams," etc.); and a variety of "Anti-bilious Pills." Despite the passage of laws in several states in the 1870s prohibiting landscape advertising, over the next few decades an even greater variety of signs graced nature. In the 1880s, the Bull Durham tobacco company hired four sets of painters to decorate good rocks and barns across the nation. Mail Pouch chewing tobacco competed with them for barns starting in 1897. The trademarked bull and pouch found themselves in good stead with huge notices not only for "snake oils" (as the patent medicines came to be known) but for plasters, powders, soaps, polishes, hair dyes, chewing gum, and a variety of cigars and cigarettes.[18]

When novelist William Dean Howells wrote in 1884 of the king of mineral oil paint, Silas Lapham, who saw nothing "so very sacred" about the rocks along a river to prevent him from painting them with ads in three colors, he did not exaggerate.[19] Lapham compared well to real historical actors, such as P. H. Drake, who had an entire mountainside forest chopped down "so Pennsylvania Railroad passengers could read about Plantation Bitters in letters four hundred feet high." Drake had nothing on Sam Houghteling, cofounder in 1870 of the first nationwide paint service (Bradbury and Houghteling), who once boasted "I've painted on rocks while standing up to my neck in water" and "put the name of 'Vitality Bitters' on Lookout Mountain." Speaking of his exploits after nearly thirty years in the business, Houghteling, by then a millionaire known as "Hote," continued to brag: "'I guess I have desecrated more nature than any man in the United States." "And what of it?" he said. "There's not a town or village I ain't been into." Hote's greatest caper was to paint a gargantuan sign for St. Jacob's Oil on a rock across from one of Niagara Fall's prime vistas. Such ads galvanized the New York State Legislature to regulate landscape advertising on government property, and by the first years of the twentieth century, public lands around the falls were wiped clean, although painted ads still loomed on nearby private property. Still, some could not help but admire Hote's pluck. Without naming names, *Scribner's* magazine published an article about the painter's "handiwork high up on the colossal escarpments of Echo Cañon; again on the somber granite of the cliffs of Weber; further west on the arid rocks of Humboldt; even on the forlorn wigwams of the Piutes, straggling over the fallow desert, and continuing over the Sierras and down the golden valley of the Sacramento—sign after sign high above the levee, and often in position the manner of reaching which was inexplicable."[20]

Like the New York City sign painters whose work blocked the streets with curious onlookers, and like the rural billposters who were followed by gaping country boys wherever they went, Hote often gathered a crowd of both admirers and detractors. Yet, like others who succeeded in the business, he was both fleet of foot and had the gift of gab, able to lull the farmer or the nature seeker into seeing the value of his artifice and to then beat a hasty retreat.[21] Proper permissions or payments for the use of private or public properties were not, in other words, priorities. Farmers whose barns were in need of a good, protective coating of paint gladly loaned their spaces for free, though those who held out might get a pocket watch or a magazine subscription as payment.[22] Rarely was money exchanged or leases signed.

Sign painters and billposters sometimes followed practices established by the circus and theatrical managers they often worked for and offered show tickets to property owners who allowed the use of their space. In fact, the extensive distribution of circus tickets and theater passes (giving way to the phrase "papering" the house) led to its own underground economy. Unscrupulous billposters would trade their supply of tickets for tobacco and alcohol. Theatrical props were borrowed in exchange for tickets. Keepers of coal yards and owners of fenced vacant lots could get two theater tickets for every night of the season, while any business with its ash barrel out front could acquire tickets as well. With all of these tickets in circulation, avid theatergoers could easily and cheaply feed their habit through the illicit trade in "billboard tickets." It was enough of a problem that when theatrical managers discussed starting a union in 1891, they resolved, among other things, to "restrain the growth of the pernicious system of lithograph and billboard passes."[23]

From around the 1790s on, circuses, traveling menageries, and theatrical performers (who were among the earliest and most extensive users of outdoor advertising) had advertised with handbills and small posters that relied heavily on text, a few stock images, and just one color of ink. As the size and extent of the shows expanded in the nineteenth century, so did the means to market the events, especially as the printing trade expanded in step with show business.[24] New technologies of cheaper forms of woodblock printing that permitted larger sizes and more illustrations and colors; then stone lithography, whose multicolored prints best captured the tones and clarity of oil paintings; and, finally, mechanized, high-speed printing presses and paper-folding equipment led to the creation of bigger and more spectacular posters. Prior to these developments, circus and theater bills might measure twelve or eighteen inches long and include a black-and-white woodcut portrait of the proprietor or an actor, but now they featured dramatic scenes or performances that a patron could expect to see at the show, presented in four colors. Until they became more affordable in the last few decades of the 1800s, color or chromolithographs for advertising were generally limited to one-sheet prints (twenty-eight inches by forty-two inches–the size of the lithographic stone, which became a standard measure for posters), which hung in shop windows.[25] Thereafter, a world of color and imagery exploded onto the public landscape. In 1878, when Strobridge Lithograph Company of Cincinnati, one of the premium show printers in the country, exhibited its first twenty-four-sheet lithographed poster, "Eliza Crossing the Ice," from the traveling show of *Uncle Tom's Cabin*, public interest was "so great that the Mayor was obliged to call out extra police to handle the crowds." For years after, audiences continued to thrill at the colorful pictures of Eliza leaping over the floating cakes of ice to escape the bloodhounds (fig. 4).[26]

To audiences unaccustomed to seeing a range and vitality of colors in print, the posters comprised an awesome sight, particularly as competing showmen–including the Barnum and Bailey, W. W. Cole, and Sells-Forepaugh Circuses, as well as Buffalo Bill's Wild West Show–upped the size and drama year after year, with forty-eight-sheet, sixty-four-sheet, and one-hundred-sheet posters, some in six and eight colors (fig. 5). The Ringling Brothers Circus even constructed a 357-sheet display in Chicago, 25 feet high and 120 feet long.[27] While the size and colorful dramatic pictorials of the circus postings were surely impressive, most overwhelming was their quantity and repetition scattered around a town, sometimes leaving barely even a window uncovered. Special bills, banners, and streamers were produced to fit every nook and cranny, big and small, narrow or wide. A special advertisement called a "rat sheet" or a "flaming poster" was sometimes used to paste over competitors' signs and to defame rival companies, a practice not limited to circuses.[28] It is no wonder that Barnum and Bailey distributed nearly 1.5 million sheets of posters for its 1888 season alone, or so they professed. Local papers argued

4. "Uncle Tom's Cabin," c. 1899. Courier Lithograph Company, Buffalo.

5. Billposters were hired to paper all available surfaces and, often, to distribute circulars, samples, or programs such as those for the Wild West Show at the 101 Ranch, Ponca City, Oklahoma.

over how many sheets a show had used for their city, with numbers ranging from five thousand to eighty thousand. Rival firms competing to create the largest displays and billposters, with their boasts of six hundred or even one thousand sheets pasted in a day, fed the frenzy.[29] Typically, fifteen to twenty-five billposters were employed per season. They rode in gaily painted advance cars thirty days ahead of the circus and covered with their posters up to forty-five miles around the town at which the show was scheduled to stop. Literally tons of paper and paste were consumed.

Such excesses were not reserved for the circus. Fairs and traveling theatrical performances also advertised with thousands of sheets of paper, though their changing repertoire of troupes and events meant that they could not achieve the kind of national brand-name marketing blitz that accompanied the yearly extravaganzas of the biggest circuses.[30] Even the Salvation Army, in what was described as an "unusual contract" undoubtedly influenced by the publicity dictum "to bill it like a circus," hired the American Advertising and Bill Posting Company of Chicago to post 24,000 half-sheet, 1,000 eight-sheet, and 200 twenty-five-sheet posters in 1894.[31] Even when employed for other purposes, the billposting practice revealed its roots in show business, and the expansion of theaters and circuses over the course of the nineteenth century greatly contributed to its growth. When our sometime criminal billposter John Kenny first started his work in 1860, the bulk of his business did not come from Brooklyn, his home, which did not yet have a theater, but from across the river, in New York City, the location of numerous playhouses.[32] During the theatrical season of September to May, traveling shows would supply local theaters with playbills and posters. Theater owners, in turn, would hire young gentlemen like Kenny or send their stagehands out to post the city. For the other weeks of the year, during down times, theaters would accept other commercial advertisements.[33] Many billposting companies started as offshoots of theaters and opera houses, and were aimed to serve them first and foremost. Some kept growing, buying more theaters and renting more billboards.[34] The two industries were inextricable. It made sense, then, that *Billboard Advertising,* the first outdoor advertising trade journal, started in 1894 by the son of Cincinnati printer William Donaldson, was devoted to the interests of showmen, and included lists of fairs, information on circuses, and regular features on theatrical posters.[35] Theaters essentially controlled outdoor advertising.

A fundamental development for the billposting industry came with the novel idea to formally lease space on which to advertise, and to construct special boards on which to do so. The demands of circus advertising helped pioneer such practices since, after every other available surface in a city or town was covered, special structures had to be erected to accommodate their huge displays.[36] The first recorded instance of such a specially built and leased hoarding for outdoor advertising was in 1869, while the New York City Post Office was under construction. The building contractor had the bright idea to lease the long-spanning fence that surrounded the site, but ended up selling the space for a modest fee to someone who knew little about billposting and who had trouble finding paying clients. Although George Rowell, one of the nation's first advertising agents, covered the entire length of three sides of the fence with posters for his firm, the project failed and the lease was rescinded when the rights of the contractor to sell the space were questioned.[37] Still, the idea was good. If billposting was to develop as an independent business of a proprietary nature, it would require some legal claim to advertising space. As individual painters and billposters such as Kenny and Murphy and O. J. Gude in Brooklyn, Kissam and Allen in New York City, and Thomas Cusack and R. J. Gunning in Chicago began to form their own companies in the 1870s (by which time there were an estimated 275 such firms, each counting between two and twenty employees), they also began to construct their own boards on which to paste bills—hence the name *billboards*.[38]

The formation of billboard companies and their more formal claims to urban and rural space meant that outdoor advertising had begun to carve out a legitimate place in the rapidly changing commercial landscape of the industrial age. Rather than being a mere overlay to other businesses and buildings, now permanent and semipermanent structures were devoted to the signs of commercial development. Like the buildings rising in growing metropolises, billboards contributed to the accretion of commercial centers and formalized the incursion of pictures and texts in the public sphere.

The business of Henry William Walker, a Detroit sign painter and billposter, narrates the way in which the billboard business participated in spatial changes of the built environment. Henry followed his brother John's footsteps in the business he had begun in 1850 by posting bills on the rough walls of businesses and along the fences flanking the wooden sidewalks in downtown Detroit. But Henry literally aimed higher: once he had established his business, he gathered up some old piano boxes and used them to build extensions above the six-foot fences that enclosed vacant lots in the area. By the 1890s, he was leasing space and building special boards for both posters and paint.[39] As the city grew, with larger commercial buildings rising higher in the sky, so did Henry's boards grow upward with double- and even triple-decker panels paralleling the multiple stories of adjacent structures. The same story could be told about the firm Siebe and Green (later called Foster and Kleiser) in San Francisco, American Advertising and Bill Posting in Chicago, and Van Beuren and Company in New York.[40] In each of these cities and in many more across the nation, advertising extended the skyward reach of construction, especially in the first years of the 1900s, with rooftop signs, now illuminated with electricity, creating a new spectacle and skyline (figs. 6–7; also see fig. 48).

Until the 1900s the use of billboards remained an uneven and unchecked practice, especially since it involved a capital investment and billposting had heretofore required only minor outlays. Billboards thus remained insubordinate to "as-chance-may-have-it" snipes and daubs, which did not guarantee

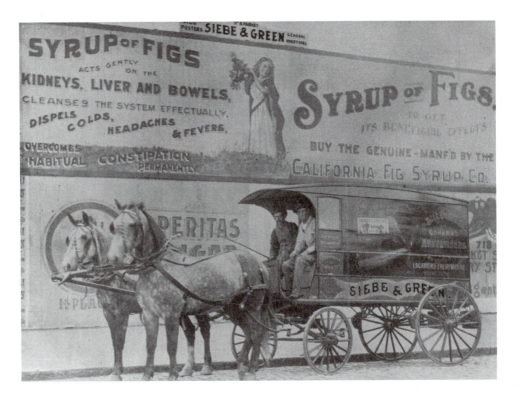

6. Siebe and Green Bill Posters, Eleventh and Market Streets, San Francisco, 1897.

that a message would be visible for any given amount of time. The only promise to an advertiser was that the paper would be posted or the signs painted, and even that promise was often unfulfilled. In contrast to newspaper advertising where results were easily verified, advertisers could either follow the billposter at work (and some did), or they had to operate on good faith that their advertisements would be posted as promised. Common indeed were stories of the billposter who made bonfires with the paper he was to post, or who found "how much easier it was to make an affidavit than to pass a number of days painting and placing signs." After all, "it was all the same to the advertiser, for he knew no different."[41] Thus, the character and reliability of the billposter often became an issue, as advertisements for their services also suggest. The W. W. Cole Circus called for billposters only "of established and untarnished reputation," while others made sobriety the primary issue, exhorting that "lushers" and "laggards" need not apply.[42]

The rough-and-tumble world of the brawling billposters and their grudge matches, covering each others' signs as fast as they could be pasted did not help to burnish the reputation of the industry. Their antics were always well

7. The architecture of the Hotel Metropole is barely visible beneath the theater posters and rooftop signs, 42nd Street and Broadway, New York, 1909.

reported. Poor John Kenny, whose unhappy story we must now conclude, had the misfortune of yet more newspaper notoriety when he was arrested again in 1871 for election fraud. His many tangles with the law while he had feuded with Thomas Murphy, his sometime rival billposter and his sometime partner, only foreshadowed his final dramatic denouement, in which he was found guilty of murder and sentenced to life in prison. But even iron bars could not keep him out of the public eye, as newspapers regaled in his final story of jailhouse suicide in 1883 via a smuggled gun. In subsequent years, Kenny's brothers continued to make headlines with their own threats against the now-successful and well-heeled Thomas Murphy, who, by 1900 had become the third largest outdoor advertiser in the country.[43] This was no way to run a multimillion-dollar industry. The time had come to shape up.

The first tenuous step to turn billposting into a respectable profession came in 1872, when eleven concerned billposters decided to form the International Billposters' Association of North America, the first association of advertisers in the country. One of the association's first unanimous resolutions was that "this Association deprecate the malicious covering of bills to gratify private animosity of opposing billposters and that we will endorse no bill poster guilty of this offense."[44] The organization remained woefully incapable of solving the problems of the billposters' brawls, and dissolved after a dozen years. It had little influence, except to sow the ground for later developments.[45]

The redundantly named Associated Billposters' Association of the United States and Canada, formed in 1891, found greater success. First among its goals was to formalize and standardize the practice of billposting, and to do so nationally. Among the early accomplishments of the group was to grant franchises to billposters—one per city—and to establish standard rates for posting. Within a decade, standardized sizes and billboard structures had been adopted.[46] In addition, members could not accept advertising contracts from nonmembers and, starting in 1900, could not accept advertising through agencies, but only through solicitors authorized by the association. This meant that when Artemas Ward, the renowned advertiser of Sapolio cleanser and an early and consistent user of poster and streetcar advertising, approached billposters to request their services at *his* standard rates (lower than those established by the association), members were enjoined to refuse. Members were, similarly, warned through a postcard mailing from the association that the O. J. Gude Company, which had contracted with Adams' Tutti Frutti Chewing Gum, might be contacting them to get a break in the posting price. Likewise, when

Sam W. Hoke, who ran a sign and poster business in New York but was not a member of the Billposters' Association, approached another member with a contract to post Royal Baking Powder advertisements in his locality, the member was, again, ordered to refuse.[47] Initially, nonmembers might have had a competitive advantage in this game, but they lacked the clout that the association had rapidly gained through its publicity and oversight of the industry. The Billposters' Association assured advertisers that their members were the only ones able to provide reliable and certifiable billposting services. They followed through on this promise, first by having members pledge with bonds that they would fulfill contracts for billposting, and then by penalizing those who reneged on contracts.[48]

Association clout also meant that it exerted pressure on competing billposters to resolve their differences. In New York and Chicago, member companies who held the association franchise for each city faced rivals that were quite substantial in scale and revenue. Yet within a short time, the association and its board of directors had helped negotiate the mergers of the biggest players and the subsequent incorporation of smaller companies as well.[49] Though participants hesitated to call their combinations a trust, others in the industry had no such qualm. Gaylord Wilshire, the owner of a billposting company who went on to develop much real estate in Los Angeles and for whom Wilshire Boulevard is named, unabashedly mounted a campaign within the association to forthrightly reduce all competition. "In the days when a bucket and brush represented the capital stock of a billposting plant it was a personal question, and a billposting war was a series of street brawls," he said. "To-day it has developed into a capitalistic enterprise, and the weapons of the capitalist must be used. The most modern and by far the most deadly product from the armory of capitalism is the trust, and we must adopt it or perish like the red man with his bow and arrow against the frontierman's rifle."[50] Despite the romantic language, billposters had joined the ranks of industrial capitalism.

By 1909, the organization took final steps to obliterate the ad-hoc practices of as-chance-may-have-it or unprotected postings. Members could post ads only on spaces that they owned or leased, and they were required to provide clients with contracts for "listed and protected showings," a kind of proof of exactly where and for how long the advertiser's posters would be displayed. No other posters could be assigned to that location. Thus did the association attempt to end the battles among billposters.[51] It also was establishing a legal basis for billposting as a legitimate business, with claims just as rightful as other owners and renters of property. In this way it professionalized the industry while it rationalized advertising services and spaces.

As the industry consolidated, its ties to show business were strained. *Billboard Advertising*, the magazine of both advertising and show business, noted that the nature of postings was changing as greater numbers of general advertisers began to vie with theaters for use of the boards. No longer was it sufficient to put commodity advertisements in leftover theater ad spaces. Billposting companies scrambled to build more boards and to wrest from theaters the locations they dominated, while theatrical managers wondered if they should all join forces to regain control from the billposters.[52] Simultaneously, the Billposters' Association believed that theater owners were slowing the industry because theaters had only a secondary interest in billposting. There was also increasing public opposition to lithographic posters for burlesque and other shows that depicted scantily clad women. Those that considered themselves "legitimate" theaters (rather than purveyors of burlesque), or who wanted to appear as such, debated the values of outdoor advertising entirely, and refrained from using poster advertising for some of their more elegant shows, thus giving billboard companies a chance to swoop in and claim those unused spaces. Most of those theater proprietors changed their minds when they realized the disadvantage unless all competitors similarly refrained.[53] But it was too late, and theaters were never able to recoup their lost advertising space from the billposting companies. Whereas in the 1880s theatrical advertising constituted 80 percent of the billposting trade, by 1905 it represented only 20 percent.[54] By the first years of the 1900s, the theater business itself waned with the rise of movies, while the billboard business grew in inverse proportion.[55]

Even *Billboard Advertising* could not weather these changes; in 1895, the magazine had been declared the official organ of the Associated Billposters' Association, but that relationship lasted roughly seven months. When the journal began to report controversies within the association, especially the strong-arm tactics of its leaders in reducing competition, and when it gave equal time to nonmembers and to the competing trade associations they were forming, the association severed ties. *Billboard*, as the magazine was called starting in 1897, was now deemed by the association to be the official "gazette of 'grafters,' 'fakirs' and 'fair followers.'"[56] Increasingly, it devoted less attention to billposting and more to show business. Today *Billboard* continues as the bible of the music industry.[57] To replace *Billboard*, the Billposters' Association started its own journal in 1896, the *Billposter*, whose editorial content was overseen by directors of the association and was devoted "exclusively to the interests of general outdoor advertising." Aptly, an early issue bore the slogan, "you stick to me, and I'll stick to you."

By the turn of the century, use of outdoor advertising grew, but so did advertising more generally, as a greater range of companies began to see its value. So it was that by 1908, according to outdoor advertising industry estimates, 8.5 million linear feet (nearly 1,610 miles) of billboards spread across the country.[58] The Billposters' Association played no small part in ensuring the windfall. By systematizing the services of its members and driving out of business those that did not comply, it made the billposting business more agreeable to far more national manufacturers (plate 1). Companies such as Coca-Cola, Heinz, and Campbell's Soup soon discovered that outdoor advertising was a cheap and effective means of introducing their trademarks to a national audience.[59] When Nabisco launched its brand new packaged product, Uneeda Biscuit, in 1899, with one of the largest national campaigns to that time, the company forced N. W. Ayer and Son, the advertising agency handling the account, to include painted signs and billboards. Though Ayer had long expressed his personal distaste for the outdoor medium, his agency set up its own division to handle outdoor advertising for clients.[60]

Some believed that the new interest in billboard advertising was directly related to the rise in the art poster, which had been inspired by advances in lithography that made the printing of color and pictorial imagery more precise and affordable. As article after article recounted, the artistic advertising poster had European origins. In France it emerged with the exuberantly animated Parisian belles that adorned the music hall posters of Jules Chéret and Henri de Toulouse-Lautrec and in England it came with the shockingly exotic renderings of Aubrey Beardsley and the flat expanses of color in the book and magazine poster advertisements of the Beggarstaffs (James Pryde and William Nicholson). These impressed American illustrators such as Will Bradley (who was dubbed the "American Beardsley"), Maxfield Parrish, and Edward Penfield, not to mention the collectors for whom the advertising poster itself became the object of consumption. The artistic poster also drew attention to its creator, who was generally a freelance illustrator rather than an employee of the lithography house. Commissioned mainly by high-end publishers and by a few companies such as Victor Bicycles, the posters were small in format (nineteen inches by fourteen inches) and were posted mostly indoors or sold directly to collectors (plate 2). Despite their celebrity, they were never the stock and trade of billposting companies.[61]

Most billposting industry commentators viewed the art poster as an odd-ity and a fad; they failed to understand its merits and scoffed at its pretensions. "It is not original, it is not beautiful, and it certainly is not artistic," one wrote. Only those with "an o'er-weening fondness for the weird and fantastic took it up," claimed another critic, who added that the American iteration of the art poster movement had "succeeded in producing results far more hideous and soul disturbing than anything their transatlantique confreres ever dreamed of." Others pointed to the art poster's commercial failing, since "more often than not there was no sales message and no relation of the picture to a selling point." Still, few denied that the effect of the poster craze was beneficial to the billposting industry. Collectors, exhibits, and newspaper commentaries "directed public attention to the advertising value of the bill boards so forcibly and effectively, that they . . . enjoyed a boom such as they have never experienced heretofore."[62]

The American poster craze of the 1890s coincided with the rise of vocal opposition to billboard advertising as an immoral and corrupting influence, far from an artistic expression worthy of collection. Though theatrical posters were targeted specifically, the increasing use of images of women in a variety of advertisements was central to the debate.[63] American show posters, in contrast to the demure collectible art posters by Bradley and others, were revealing and exuberant in both their color schemes and animation of their female subjects. Like the burlesque shows they advertised, these posters focused on the display of women's bodies. "It is urged that these theatrical posters which show various lithe-limbed and full-chested young women, dressed in decidedly brief skirts and very décolleté waists, corrupt the boys and girls who pause, with their fondness for gaudy pictures, to gaze at them as they pass," one Sunday school group complained.[64] No good could come of such "highly colored caricatures of the female body," claimed a group of crusading clergymen; "[they] stand for nothing but obscenity, and appeal only to prurient tastes."[65] The clergymen referred not just to show posters but to advertisements for all sorts of commodities. Long-time president of the Society for the Prevention of Vice, Anthony Comstock; the Women's Christian Temperance Union (WCTU); and various women's clubs joined the fray, criticizing not just the indecency of scantily clad women on the posters, but the very onslaught of colors and pictures presented in the public realm and the effect this would have on the taste and manners of the populace—especially those most susceptible to its influences: women, children, and the masses of new immigrants.[66]

From New York to Chattanooga, billposters were actually hauled off by police for their hand in putting up "indecent" pictures.[67] Some billposters in the West responded by clothing over the most offensive areas of their posters by pasting "over the stockings of skirt dancers and Amazons" small bits of paper bills, but quickly found that practice "irksome."[68] In Boston, theater managers were ordered by their board of aldermen "to tone down their representations of women in tights and skirts," though the board could not agree on what constituted a "proper" poster. Nor could other groups charged with the task of drafting local ordinances ever determine precisely what constituted immoral depictions; the public regulation of private morality was proving to be more difficult than reformers had imagined.[69]

Newspapers and the trade magazine *Printers' Ink*, which represented the interests of advertising agents and print media, regularly excoriated the use of lithographs of their outdoor advertising competitors on the grounds that they were crude, lurid, and ineffective in conveying the advertisers' message. The educated public, the journal asserted, could not be moved by "grandiloquent appeals or glaring pictures."[70] In this they cast their lot with critics and reformers of outdoor advertising, who based their arguments on both aesthetic and intellectual distinctions. Those of the class who read newspapers were bound to remain unmoved by posters, so their well-being was not at issue. But then there were those who were incapable of understanding anything but lurid pictures and colorful slogans on posters, and they needed protection. Print media also argued that outdoor advertising put the reputation of all advertising in jeopardy, both because of its appeal to immigrants and illiterates and because of its cheapening of civic beauty with lurid images and gaudy colors.

At first the billboard and theatrical trades dismissed these critics, labeling them "prurient preachers and spouting spinsters," and declared that these had garnered attention solely due to "the cupidity and malice of the publisher" rather than the legitimacy of the claims.[71] But soon the Billposters' Association took notice. As municipal art societies, the WCTU, and the American Civic Association became organized and national in scope, so the Billposters' Association hastened to regulate itself, standardize, and promote the industry on a national level. In response to the charges of immoral advertising content, the association imposed penalties on members who posted any paper carrying sensational or suggestive titles and content and warned lithographers and theater owners to "use their influence to end the use of objectionable posters on billboards."[72] When Massachusetts and Pennsylvania passed laws forbidding posting on public property without the consent of the owner, the association was steps ahead. It had already required membership to obtain permission from property owners.[73] And, as courts resolved cases regarding the safety haz-

ards of billboard structures, the association unveiled new plans for a standardized billboard structure that would replace rough-hewn plywood hoard-
ings with sturdier steel billboards.[74] Though the association fought the challenges to the industry with batteries of lawyers, it also used self-reform and
abundant promotion of those internal reforms to quell criticism and to pre-
empt more invasive governmental regulation. Their self-regulatory zeal had
multiple aims: to weed out billposters who gave the industry a bad name, to
convince critics that the mainstream business of billboard advertising operated
on the right side of the law, and to ensure the goodwill of the public. The billboard industry had turned its sights on the consumer, and begun to recognize
the importance of public opinion. It sought to prove that the industry had
come a long way from the ad hoc, anarchic, and sometimes violent practices
of its nineteenth-century forebears.

Other branches of the advertising industry were similarly engaged in self-
regulatory and self-promotional efforts at the turn of the century, as they
organized clubs and associations, rationalized their business, and sought to
mitigate public criticism that advertising was untruthful and unproductive,
adding cost but no value to products.[75] Advertisers accepted without resistance
the passage of the Pure Food and Drug Act of 1906, requiring accurate package labeling, and self-initiated a "truth in advertising" movement in 1911 aimed
both to rid the industry of the "bad apples" that spoiled the reputation of
advertising at large and to stave off the external threat of government regulation. Equally important was the articulation of the benefit of advertising to
industry, to the economy, and to society itself. Advertising might be costly, but
it was not wasteful, said promoters.[76] As an efficient sales medium, advertising
allowed manufacturers to expand their production and thus reduce prices. Just
as important as the benefit of advertising to the economic arena was its cultural role. As Boston department store magnate Edward Filene said, advertising served as an educational and civilizing force, "teaching the masses not
what to think but HOW TO THINK, and thus to find out how to behave like
human beings in the machine age."[77] Other proponents of advertising also
claimed that "the right kind of advertising, the advertising of the right kind of
goods, is one of the great factors of civilization."[78]

No event contributed more to the selling of advertising as a legitimate profession and a public service than World War I, which gave advertisers the
opportunity to connect their rhetoric of economic and civic utilitarianism to
patriotism and allowed them to prove the value of advertising as a centralized
force in mass persuasion that could sell the idea of democracy. It also came to

awaken in business the realization that advertising could play a role in promoting not just individual products but more abstract things—even the corporation itself. Most important, the wartime activities of advertisers granted them entry into the most exclusive fraternity—the federal government—and no more authoritative endorsement for legitimacy could be had than that.

The advertising industry did not wait for America's declaration of war to mobilize its forces. In April 1916, Herbert S. Houston, president of the Associated Advertising Clubs of the World, and Barney Link, a director of the Poster Advertising Association (as the Associated Billposters' Association was renamed in 1912), called members of the art, design, and advertising communities to arms. What the country needed now, they said, was national industrial preparedness. What better way to send the masses the message than with advertising? Before an audience of artists and illustrators, most with minimal experience in poster production, Link, then one of the largest individual owners of billboard locations in the country, gave a rousing speech and made an ambitious offer: "If you distinguished artists will give us the product of your varied talents, the poster men of America will display it from New York to San Francisco. . . . If you will give us now a store of war posters calling the nation to arms, we will, on the possible outbreak of war, put them on 50,000 poster boards in this country in twenty-four hours."[79] His was no empty promise, and it dramatized—and advertised—the great strides in the organization of billposting as an industry.

Outdoor advertisers were well situated to fulfill Link's promise. In 1912, the association formally established an education committee whose task was to create a central network for public service campaigns using open advertising space. They kicked it off in December 1913 with the circulation of ten thousand color lithographs of a Nativity scene, and at Christmas time every year thereafter, through at least World War II, this image graced billboards across America. General Ulysses S. Grant, the Boy Scouts of America, and the merits of churchgoing were among the symbols of moral rectitude that filled the boards of 1914.[80] Critics were rightfully skeptical of this "sudden spasm of virtue among the billposters" and ridiculed the efficacy of advertising spiritual uplift and civic education, especially when it was "sandwiched in between 'Special Holiday Rates,' vaudeville screams in brief attire, and hair tonic that [would] make a billiard ball look like a baby doll."[81] Nor would such critics be convinced when, in 1914, both the U.S. Army and the U.S. Navy made liberal use of outdoor advertising for recruitment purposes. J. Horace McFarland, president of the American Civic Association, went straight to President William Howard Taft with his complaint that the government only demeaned itself when it made use of billboards, but his outcry was not heeded.[82] He couldn't know that in the coming years, the government as well as many service organizations would become the biggest patrons and boosters of billboard advertising.

Nearly a year after Houston and Link called their meeting of advertising men, America had entered the European war. Within weeks, President Woodrow Wilson issued an executive order establishing a Committee on Public Information (CPI), headed by progressive-minded journalist and muckraker George Creel, to rally Americans to war and to use the most modern means of mass persuasion to do so.[83] The CPI was a propaganda bureau aimed to reach all Americans and to infiltrate all arenas of their lives. Its very existence testified to the recognition by America's political and business leaders of the importance of public opinion and the techniques of manipulating it through images, text, and moving pictures. As Creel later acknowledged, the committee's task was to coordinate an advertising campaign writ large, incorporating spoken and printed words, posters, paintings, motion pictures, and every possible means of public spectacle.[84]

As the mechanisms for wartime publicity geared up, many outdoor advertisers and artists donated space and services, but other advertisers hung back, still uncertain about the role to be assigned to advertising. *Printers' Ink* ran editorials questioning the requests for free advertising space being made by defense organizations. If manufacturers of munitions were to be paid for their products, why shouldn't "the manufacturers of advertising space be paid for the products of *their* factories?" Although advertisers did end up donating their services and advertising space (outdoor advertisers to the tune of $1.5 million) the question remained: Was this not a failure to recognize advertising as a commodity, and a mark of how little it was valued as an industry?[85] With the CPI's formation of the Division of Pictorial Publicity, headed by famed illustrator Charles Dana Gibson, and the Division of Advertising, run by leading advertising agent William D'Arcy, these issues receded. The prestige these divisions offered, the access they granted advertisers to members of congress and other political figures, and the effusive praise that was heaped upon them by such luminaries as Bernard Baruch, Herbert Hoover, William McAdoo, General John Pershing, and Woodrow Wilson, offered a different kind of payment.[86] In the words of William D'Arcy, advertising had been "made an arm of our Government."[87] As such, while advertisers were doing their job to publicize government, government was, in turn, doing the same for advertisers. This kind of power and publicity money alone could never buy.

For outdoor advertisers, wartime use of their medium meant more than a boost in legitimacy. It meant a reversal of losses they had experienced at the hands of reformers and municipal lawmakers who, in the preceding few years, had succeeded in galvanizing opposition to billboard advertising and passing ordinances in several cities restricting billboards to industrial and commercial areas. With the onslaught of wartime publicity, such restrictions were rendered moot.[88] The idea to "bill it like a circus" was back, with over a million advertising handbills and stickers pasted along building facades, fences, subway entrances, and other surfaces to promote wartime recruitment alone.[89] Some twenty-eight million posters selling five series of Liberty Bonds were distributed to cities and towns across the United States, while combined campaigns for the war effort, including the Food Savings campaign, the Red Cross campaign, and others reached upwards of forty million posters (fig. 8). Designed by well-known illustrators such as Howard Chandler Christy, James Montgomery Flagg, Charles Dana Gibson, Neysa McMein, Herbert Paus, and Joseph Pennell, these posters covered churches, libraries, courthouses, city hall grounds, and other properties where commercial posters were generally banned.[90]

The poster presentations often took center stage, quite literally, as the novel antics of the billposter again, as in its nineteenth-century incarnation, drew curious crowds. In this case, the objects of their attention were even more spectacular, as when the billposter was comedian and movie star Fatty Arbuckle, or when the sign painters were artists James Montgomery Flagg or Henry Reuterdahl perched on scaffolding high above the steps of the U.S. Subtreasury building or the New York Public Library.[91] Events like these augmented the legitimacy of the poster artist and his art. This was work on behalf of the government and its people, important and practical rather than merely an act of aesthetic whimsy.[92] At the same time, the work was granted the status of high art, as exhibitions devoted to World War I poster publicity were hosted even by the Metropolitan Museum of Art. The artistic advertising poster that had moved collectors and museums at the turn of the century had been resuscitated, only now it had the power of patriotism behind it. As Creel said, the posters not only "stirred" nationalism, but "awakened in the public mind the importance" of the poster to art and education.[93]

The war also accelerated another poster trend of previous years—namely, the consideration of the consumer as an irrational and impulsive individual rather than a reasonable one. Wartime poster manuals instructed artists that good illustrations should be directed to emotional, not intellectual, faculties. As Gibson explained, "One cannot create enthusiasm for war on the basis of

8. Women help paste up poster for the Fourth Liberty Loan, New York, 1918.

practical appeal." Rather, the artist must "appeal to the heart."[94] Artists worked with symbols more than with facts. The sternly authoritative Uncle Sam wagging an accusatory finger, soldiers in combat, and women with outstretched arms or in allegorical roles as the Pietà, Liberty, Columbia, or Joan of Arc, were among the images deployed to tug at the heart and to elicit emotions, mainly those of shame, fear, duty, and reprobation (see fig. 8, plate 3). But such ad hominem approaches were objectionable to some critics; one explained that "the most successful advertising phrases of the past have not been hortatory, but gently winning. We were not commanded to sit up and bite a biscuit, but were persuaded that we really needed a biscuit."[95] Others bemoaned the infantalization induced by many of the posters, in which popular characters of magazine illustrations seemed to have strayed out onto the street. The Arrow Collar Man now wore a sailor's suit, the Gibson Girl marched for the Food Savings Campaign, and the Christy Girl went "speeding a Liberty Loan." These offered "puerile assurances" rather than the "eloquence of poetry." "The war poster, if it is worth anything, must be something more than that," complained a disappointed critic who felt that poster designers had wasted an opportunity to create a new and more powerful avenue of advertising art. The poster should, he said, "compel the multitude to think as well as to look, to learn that war is a serious matter."[96] But these objections were, for the most part, drowned out by the chorus of praise with which even the most desultory war posters were met. Indeed, the approach exemplified by the war poster was what would define the coming decades of advertising production, in which thinking was subordinated to sentiment, and reasoning became but a lowly misfit to the instinctual appeal.

Posters commissioned by governmental agencies and service organizations were not the only ones to employ the rhetoric of patriotism or the imagery of wartime defense. Many regular commercial advertisements came to include tag lines at the bottom of their campaigns exhorting people to buy Liberty Bonds or merely using scenes of fighting soldiers to fuse the ideas of consumerism and citizenship. Wartime messages suggested that patriotism and the fulfillment of civic duty could be purchased along with, or just like, any other commodity. In some cases, as with goods not available during the war, the company continued its billboard campaigns anyway in order to keep their product in the public eye. The same was true for other firms that had turned their plants over to defense production or were merely trying to prepare for increased competition in the postwar period.[97] Manufacturers had discovered that advertising was not merely a means of selling goods; it could create markets rather than merely enhance them, and it had a larger public relations value too, in "correcting misapprehensions" and "reducing friction with customers." After the passage of the War Revenue Tax in 1917 companies were even more likely to use advertising, since it was a way to spend excess profits that would otherwise be taxed.[98]

The cooperative spirit between government and business during the war also directed attention to the construction of highways, which was greatly aided by the passage of the Federal Aid to Roads Acts of 1916 and 1921. This, of course, was a godsend to outdoor advertising. World War I thus served as a massive and comprehensive promotional campaign for the field of advertising at large, and for outdoor advertising especially. The previous decades of conflict with both consumers and other branches of the advertising business had been smoothed by wartime requisites, while the billboard industry had entered the ranks of reputability if not respectability, and had proven itself to be a rationalized and nationalized medium able to circulate important messages quickly. If outdoor advertisers had any question about the significance of their trade association or about the benefits it could confer upon the individual firm, wartime activities put those to rest, as government and business linked arms in a wedding of private industry with public good. It was a marriage that lasted another decade, if not a century. With this as the backdrop, we can turn to the specific developments of the outdoor advertising industry, beginning with the establishment of the mobile market as America became a nation on wheels.

PART I

PRODUCING A LANDSCAPE OF SIGNS

A NATION ON WHEELS

In the densely populated cities of the late nineteenth century, outdoor advertisers had found ample audiences of pedestrians, carriages, and trolleys for
their painted walls and posted billboards. Yet each decade of the twentieth
century was increasingly characterized by rising automobile use, urban traffic
congestion, and the suburbanization of both the upper and middle classes.
Especially in the decades following World War I, huge increases in automobile
ownership, nationally distributed goods, and highway construction reshaped
American travel, settlement, and shopping patterns as well as the perception
of the urban landscape. The automobile had turned America into a "nation on
wheels." At an annual conference of the Outdoor Advertising Association of
America in 1929, one billboard operator characterized the changes. "People
have become physically and mentally restless," he said. "They have developed
the habit of being on the go from place to place. To-day one room in most
American families is outdoors. It is the family car. In it the members of the
family go hurrying up and down the country"[1]

Almost immediately, the outdoor advertising industry set out to package
and sell these new automobile travelers by turning ordinary drivers into a mass
mobile audience. Henry Ford's assembly line had rationalized the production
of automobiles, allowing wage earners and middle-class white-collar workers
alike the luxury of automotive independence. Likewise, the outdoor advertising industry strove to produce and package the heterogeneous mass of people
as a commodity for sale to interested advertisers. That is to say, the commodity sold by outdoor advertisers was the attention of a great new audience, the
motoring public. The decades around the turn of the century are often viewed
with respect to America's shift from a production-oriented ethos to a con-

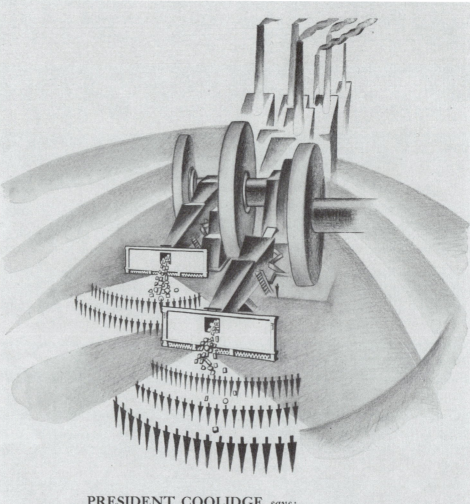

PRESIDENT COOLIDGE *says:*

"Mass production is only possible where there is mass demand. Mass demand has been created almost entirely through the development of advertising.

Outdoor advertising is essentially mass advertising.

FOSTER & KLEISER COMPANY
General Offices, San Francisco

9. Advertisement for Foster and Kleiser Company, 1928.

sumer culture and from fears of scarcity to an embrace of plenty.[2] But critical emphasis on consumerism and mass consumption too frequently skates over this fact: consumers are produced commodities.[3]

With every coming year, automobiles could be found in more and more places, thus expanding the marketing frontier and potential location of billboard spaces to areas heretofore untouched. Yet for outdoor advertisers this growth was not enough. The industry looked not merely to follow automobility trends but to augment and propagate them. After all, the more mobile the motorist, the more advertisements he would pass, often repeatedly and sometimes daily. If outdoor advertisers could actually encourage the practices of automobility, the value of the industry would soar.[4] One 1928 Foster and Kleiser Company advertisement for the billboard industry illustrated this point (fig. 9). Using an authoritative quote from President Calvin Coolidge, it depicts the engines of industry churning out masses of identical packages. Yet left ambiguous in the image is whether the billboards are producing the goods or if they are producing the hordes of stick-figure audiences lined up and standing at rapt attention, mass consumers who are the commodities ready for distribution and sale.[5]

In either case, the advertisement depicts the central preoccupation of the industry in mass producing mass-consuming audiences: where to find audiences, how to make their mass grow, and by what means to communicate with them. These were issues that each advertising medium addressed differently in the 1920s and 1930s. As for the outdoor advertising industry, since their billboards were located on the road and since their target audiences were mobile, it is not surprising that fostering a culture of mobility should have become central to its two inextricable goals: (1) to package and sell motorist attention to big business, and (2) to commodify spaces for motorists to traverse and consume.

CHAPTER 2

THE CULTURE OF MOBILITY

In the early 1920s it was still unclear how automobiles would affect the country and the city. Though prescient commentators such as regional planners Benton Mackaye and Lewis Mumford warned that sprawl would take over the country-side as well as the cityscape, generally their comments were muted by the chorus of support for the expansion of business enterprises made possible by the automobile.[1] When the outdoor advertising industry envisioned the happy future, it saw country turning into city, and the congested city turning into a freely circulating one—lined, of course, with advertising billboards.[2] Automobile-oriented streets, boulevards, and highways that facilitated development in fringe areas outside of city centers and streetcar suburbs represented an ideal commercial world. The vision was summarized in numerous advertisements by billboard companies and commentaries by industry pundits, including one that explained: "Cities expand. Towns grow larger. Other towns spring up along the way. Little by little the countryside becomes to many motorists merely the territory to be covered in hurrying from one city or town to another. The connecting highways become primarily commercial highways, taking on more and more the appearance of business streets—streets crowded by streams of cars in each direction."[3] This image of "Prosperity Avenue" beckoned outdoor advertisers as well as real estate developers, automobile manufacturers, and petroleum distributors. All profited by turning open countryside into commercial byways and business streets. Growing municipalities offered little resistance since these, too, sought to boost local commerce by satisfying an automobile public.

The newly expanding highways were the logical place for outdoor advertising to develop since, as one industry commentator put it, the job of outdoor advertising was to go "'where the people are,' which used to be assumed to be at home. But now we are out of doors." Audiences went outdoors not just for weekend expeditions, movies, golf, and football. The outdoors also included larger patterns of migration, such as "during the World War," as one industry commentator explained, when "there was a vast movement of Negroes from the south to the industrial plants of the cities of the north."[4] Another industry booster agreed that "We do not have to go far to find the underlying causes of . . . this national sense of transience. The World War had much to do with it." Soldiers with an enhanced taste for travel lost their provincialism and experienced "a new sense of personal independence." Their wives also experienced new independence that granted them modern mobility. "They too went everywhere and lost their age-old repressions and limitations and now take part in all these movements and excursions into the outdoor world."[5]

Independence through automobility sometimes came in rather abstract forms, as the car altered the geographical imagination of travelers formerly accustomed to measuring physical distances according to train schedules and routes. Railroads of the nineteenth century had similarly altered spatial sensibilities, as people covered greater distances at greater speeds than before. But while the railroad opened up new spaces, it also dissolved the spaces between the railway stations and off established routes. The automobile promised to open up those spaces between and beyond even while it promoted a new perceptual paradigm based on individual and private mobility. With the car, speed and distance were no longer bound to iron tracks. While the railroad stuck to the same route with the same view as every other passenger and train, the automobile allowed travelers their own way, their own view, and their own opportunities to interact with tourists and "locals." It meant freedom from railroad timetables, certainly, and perhaps from the stranglehold of corporate monopolies on time, whether in the form of the factory punch clock or the station schedule.[6] Being able to travel at one's own speed, even when dictated by machinery and road conditions, gave a motorist the impression of slowing down or speeding up time and of extending or shrinking space at will.[7] And even though both the train and the car were products of industrial technology, motorists could claim a closer connection to nature, and a more palpable sense of place: they were nearer to the ground, and could feel the wind blowing in their hair or the change in terrain and climate of driving from "pines to palms," deserts to mountains.[8] The experiential dictates of train and stagecoach travel had been loosened.

"Time and space are at your beck and call," auto tourist Elon Jessup rejoiced. With the time clock miles away, he followed his "nomadic instinct for a free life in the outdoors world."[9] For Winfield A. Kimball and Maurice H. Decker, who wrote of their family camping experiences, cars afforded access to "a liberal dose of outdoor recreation" much needed especially by "sick, overcivilized man" and other city folk overtaken by worries about material life, from the stock market to parking-space problems. Like many, their yearly jaunt into nature—under their own power (or that of their cars)—was a means of escape from urban anxieties, a journey back in time, even, to more "primitive" lifestyles that promised to restore a sense of self-control diminished by modern corporate life.[10]

The automobile was also lauded for providing independent access to the great outdoors. Viewing the outdoors as a place of self-renewal and self-realization had intensified with mass industrialization and the rise of an increasingly specialized and bureaucratized middle-class work force. Seeking personal renewal and empowerment in the natural world, the middle class flocked to the great outdoors, where they could exercise their physical faculties while they regained a sense of self considered lost in the industrial city. In the twentieth century, auto tourism offered a similar means of rejuvenation and self-empowerment, as the individual traveled freely to wherever his car could take him.[11]

Though impassable roads frequently hindered desired mobility in the early years of the automobile, such challenges enhanced the physical exertion of driving, making the very journey to the outdoors a sport as well as an adventure. Many compared this favorably to the passivity of train travel, which divorced one from the physical experiences and choices of auto travel. Although motorists certainly engaged in passive spectatorship as they gazed through goggles or windshields at the view beyond the car and the road, it was in fact difficult to navigate ruts in the road, change tires, and ride over unpaved, rocky paths. As James Montgomery Flagg wrote of his cross-country automobile journey, "There is freedom about motoring . . . that is lacking in the train ride. . . . There is adventure, uncertainty, and freedom in motoring that compensates for hardships."[12] The main character of Sinclair Lewis's novel *Free Air* (1919), Claire Boltwood, also experienced the exhaustion of such physical exertions and triumphed in the satisfaction of having conquered both the natural elements and the machine. Successfully repairing her motorcar, making it through muddy ravines, and climbing a slippery slope all involved hands-on physical labor missing from her urban bourgeois life. Automobile travel thus offered her an otherwise unknown feeling of power, an experience and a strengthening of self that did not require anyone else's consent or validation—a marked contrast to the reigning ideals of feminine domesticity.[13]

A Brahmin Brooklynite, Claire Boltwood also believed that her muddy, laborious travels allowed her to take the pulse of America, to participate in its spirited social movement, and to experience a perspective different from her own. For Boltwood, like many motorists, auto touring was a "voyage into democracy," and the roadside environment a "democratic" space.[14] Mingling between the privileged and the lower-income "flivverist" classes (named after the car of the masses, the Ford Model T, whose bumpy ride was said to be good "fer-the-liver") had a romantic appeal, as people from different places and social strata were joined together by the mud on their boots, dust on their clothes, and the less traveled roads they had conquered.

Travelers, journalists, and promoters commented frequently on the fraternity of auto-touring strangers as proof of how the experience of the road could renew one's faith in America. Mixing with other auto tourists, even the "provincial-minded man" was transformed, as *Motor Camper and Tourist* reported in 1924, "into a national-minded one." Tourism thus "must aid Americanization and the nationalization of the people at large."[15] The motorcar was the "most potent antidote to ignorance," claimed A. L. Westgard in his 1920 *Tales of a Pathfinder*. There was no better way, he said, "to cultivate toleration and sympathy." Frederic F. Van de Water agreed: "The motor camper," he explained, "is helping to drive out sectionalism and to knit the American people into a more cohesive, more sympathetic union."[16]

Yet despite his newfound tolerance, Van de Water was discomfited by the pestilent presence of auto tramps, itinerant laborers, and migrant families that "swarmed" the auto camps. They "choked" the free camps, invaded communities with their "rattle trap" cars, and bored everyone with their "hard luck stories."[17] Other travelogues mention flivverists with disdain as well. "We had met Fords and yet more Fords, in the usual unwashed state of dilapidation, piled high with paraphernalia . . . numerous progeny," wrote Caroline Poole in 1919. Flivverists and their "Hand to Mouth disease" also perturbed Flagg.[18] Did such contempt for their fellow travelers mitigate the belief of these authors in the democracy of the American road? Not necessarily. For Lewis Gannett, writing in 1934, the rickety Model T's ridden by the "hundreds of people who live in mud-floored log cabins" suggested, in particular, the "decent democracy of the West."[19] The road, particularly the road leading west, was a new frontier where mobility spelled democracy, in the imagination if not in fact.

Nonwhites were rarely mentioned in the scores of self- and commercially published automobile travel narratives of the 1910s to the 1930s. Nor were people of color generally featured in mainstream (white) newspaper accounts and published photographs of auto traffic and travel. When they were mentioned, it was as background, quite literally. African Americans seen working cotton fields in the south, Indians in the pueblos of the Southwest, and even Chinese and Mexican migrant field workers passed on the way west were described as part of the picturesque scenery, as objects for visual consumption rather than participants in the experience of the open road.[20] In reality, the road was a segregated space in which different classes and races were separated first by their access to vehicular transportation and then by their self-enclosed journey within the automobile itself.

Yet whites were not alone in believing that the car offered social independence. Nor were they the only people on the road. It is true that in 1921 the *Automotive Manufacturer* reported its belief that automobile ownership was limited to white, native-born middle- and upper-class whites, while *Motor* magazine asserted that "illiterate, immigrant, Negro and other families" were unlikely to join the fray anytime soon.[21] This did not stop African Americans in Augusta, Georgia, in that same year to rally their peers to "buy a car of your own and escape jim-crowism from street car service." Nor did the report seem to represent African Americans in Southern California, who regularly contributed information on their auto travels to the "Exhaust" column of the weekly black newspaper, the *California Eagle*.[22]

By the middle of the 1920s, as automobile prices dropped, a secondhand market flourished, and installment buying became more common, automobile owners represented a wider cross-section of the urban and rural population. In comparison to 1920, when 1 in 10 Americans owned automobiles (on average), in 1929, 1 in 4.5 owned a car.[23] One in 3 rural families owned a car, well below the urban average. The car made economic sense on the farm, as a tool of labor and as a way to access more marketplaces. Socially, it relieved the isolation of rural life. By the 1920s, then, the automobile had become an esteemed part of rural life as well as urban, helping to bring country folks the benefits of the city and helping city people escape to the country.[24]

Even in the years of deepest depression, the automobile remained a priority for many, including the unemployed. "People give up everything in the world but their car," Robert and Helen Lynd reported in their community studies of *Middletown*.[25] African American southern farm tenants and urban families with hardly enough to cover basic emergencies did the same.[26] This was the case, too, for Dust Bowl refugees, those displaced farm families, who, as documented by New Deal photographers such as Dorothea Lange and writers such as John Steinbeck, made "the highway their home," according to the *Grapes of Wrath*, and "movement their means of expression."[27]

More money went into highway construction during the Depression than ever before, and, until wartime prohibitions and gas rationing, vehicular travel was relatively unhampered. But for two years of the Depression (1932 and 1933), gasoline consumption and miles driven by Americans persistently grew. In those same years filling station sales fell less than 5 percent, in contrast to all other retail trade, in which there were sales declines ranging from 38 percent to 85 percent. The rise of mass tourism during the 1930s also suggests that automobile use and travel were unhampered by the depression, relative to other industries.[28]

Though it is difficult to ascertain the race and class of those owning and registering cars, there is evidence to suggest that both ethnic white and African American middle-class people—as well as smaller numbers of the working class—were purchasing cars, even if the kinds of cars and the ways they were used differed dramatically from those of the white upper classes. For instance, the interracial and interclass appeal of car ownership comes through even cursory surveys of portraits and family snapshots in public collections, which show people of different colors, backgrounds, and regions posing proudly with their automobiles in the 1920s and 1930s.[29] Photos and other commentaries suggest the ways in which the automobile had become a symbol of both physical and social mobility. As proof of the prosperity enjoyed by African Americans, Robert Russa Moton wrote in his 1929 *What the Negro Thinks* that "in every city of any considerable size Negroes are to be found in possession of some of the finest cars made in America—and they are the original purchasers, too." For sharecropper Nate Shaw, buying a car served another important function: it proudly defied racial and class assumptions about who should have a car.[30]

The appeal of the car was undoubtedly aided by growing public distaste for the railroad and traction companies, upon whom many people were dependent for daily travel and trade. Many urban and suburban dwellers rebelled against what they saw as the dictatorial and monopolistic power of the railroad and streetcar companies. Traction companies, in particular, were accused of raising fares without improving the service and schedules of the crowded, slow-moving, and uncomfortable trolley cars.[31] African Americans had even more cause for complaint, particularly in southern cities in the 1920s, where segregated street cars and poor service to black neighborhoods by white-owned companies created greater animosity still.[32] For those of all races, the automobile became a means of distancing oneself from the corporate menace and asserting independence. Similarly, independence was the issue for rural populations, whose interests had little to do with avoiding the streetcar. Tenant farmers in rural Georgia, for instance, also made independence and the "democratizing" potential of the automobile an issue, noting, "Scarcely ever before have rich and poor, educated and ignorant, self-styled superiors and acknowledged inferiors, landlords and landless, white folks and black, ridden in the same type of vehicle; and never before have they ridden so fast that they could not see who was approaching."[33]

The car had come to symbolize an autonomy otherwise lacking in many people's daily lives. The ability to separate oneself from the huddled masses of other travelers offered the potential for self-exploration and a mobility that went beyond the mere need to get from one place to another. Even the full knowledge that one was part of the automobile masses did not squelch the sense of independence. Automobility allowed one to imagine being part of a collective, yet still offered social atomism.[34]

Sorely limiting this mythology of the open road was what nonwhites experienced once they had to stop their cars. Traveling in the Shenandoah National Park in 1940, keen-eyed African American motorists might spot a small sign pointing the way to "Lewis Mountain Picnic Grounds for Negroes," or might consult the *Negro Motorist Green Guide*, published by New York travel agent Victor Green beginning in 1936, to find accommodations. Both documents suggest the racial hostility African American tourists might encounter on the road. The experiences of the black auto tourist were lessons in Jim Crowism, Lillian Rhoades wrote in a 1933 article, "One of the Groups Middletown Left Out"; she echoed the sentiments of George Schuyler, who had written the same thing several years earlier. Schuyler, however, still urged African Americans who could do so to "purchase an automobile as soon as possible in order to be free of [the] discomfort, discrimination, segregation and insult" of the railroad cars.[35] If mobile spaces did offer a freedom to people of color that railroad cars could not provide, this sense of independence came to an abrupt end with the need for food, gas, and shelter. In many areas of the South, well into the late 1960s, stopping was not the only issue. Just driving down the "wrong" street could have dire consequences for African American motorists.

The kind of autonomy the car offered is best considered in terms of consumerism, or "mobile privatization," a term Raymond Williams coined to describe the tendencies of the modern era toward both mobility and a home-centered, self-sufficient way of life. This trend emerged in the 1920s with the rise of consumer durables such as electrical appliances, radio sets, bicycles, and motorcycles and escalated in the post–World War II period of increased television and single-family homeownership.[36] Like the automobile, such goods literally and metaphorically empowered, granting individuals autonomy and helping bridge geographical space, all from the privacy of one's own home or vehicle.

They were central to suburban life, too. Mass automobility emerged, then, as a central feature of consumer-oriented society and economy and had an attendant impact on notions of time, public and private space, and civic engagement.

While some motorists saw the open road as a place of freedom, democracy, and individuality, others saw it as a promise of profit. American wanderlust represented over $3.3 billion worth of business, as forty million tourists took to the road in 1927. General auto use (not just recreational travel) represented an even larger figure.[37] "This country is literally being remade by the automobile," reported *System* magazine in 1925; "[p]ractically every type and size of business will sooner or later be affected." The *Saturday Evening Post* acknowledged, "The amazing capacity of the American people for buying an ever-increasing output of automobiles is a favorite barometer of our national prosperity."[38] Others went a step further, claiming that automobility was more than simply a measure of well-being. It created wealth and promoted higher standards of living.[39] Even in the 1930s, the popular press consistently depicted automobility as an essential element in lifting the country from the Depression.[40]

Outdoor advertisers were among those for whom automobility spelled prosperity. "It has been said that no other one factor has been so largely responsible for the remarkable growth of poster advertising during the past decade as has the motor car," claimed D. G. Baird in a 1923 issue of the outdoor advertising trade magazine, the *Poster*.[41] The car had expanded the stock and trade of the outdoor advertising industry, the mobile market. Better still, the mobile market now consisted of a mass of wage earners and every other upwardly striving group. Or so outdoor advertisers claimed, repeating the popular phrase that billboards appealed to both the "masses" and the "classes," "a select clientele of everyone who passes." Ultimately, the democracy envisioned by outdoor advertisers was one of dollars and egalitarian audience attention. By locating their audience as any mobile population, billboard advertisers claimed they addressed everyone equally. Every person walking, riding, or driving down the street—any street—constituted its audience. Only the bedridden and the blind, one company proclaimed, were excluded.[42]

Advertisers noted the high rate of car ownership, auto touring, and other outdoor recreational activities enjoyed by a broad cross-section of Americans in the 1920s. "The shortening of the hours of labor, the nearly universal eight-hour day," explained Philip Chandler in the *Poster*, "put everybody in the leisure class after the five o'clock whistle blows." Even a woman, he said, now had plenty of opportunity "to seek recreation outside her own front door," what with the adoption of "labor saving devices" in the home from vacuum cleaners to electric

10. "The Motorist as a Market," an outdoor advertising promotional pamphlet, c. 1936, explained that the more a man drove, the more ads and gasoline he consumed.

washing machines. Prohibition, too, contributed to Americans' "open air tendencies": "Men no longer spend hours in saloons. Instead of alcohol they buy gasoline and take their families out into the open."[43] Chandler and other commentators also correlated higher standards of living with the coming of the automobile, and saw the ways in which automobility ensured an endless chain of consumption. One article explained that "the more a man drives, the more gasoline he uses, the more outdoor advertising he sees" (fig. 10). This could be continued indefinitely, and the outdoor industry could only profit from what *Fortune* magazine also noted, that "the automobile became the opium of the American people," and as the motorist drives round and round, there are "ten thousand little ways you can cash in on him en route."[44] The task of outdoor advertising was to keep this mass moving and to produce and sell it efficiently as a commodity. Automobility seemed liberating and empowering to many for all of the reasons described, but it was up to outdoor advertisers to take this spirit of automotive independence and turn it to private profit, tapping into the wishful notions of even those audiences whose race and class limited their automotive access. The job of advertisers was to capitalize on the culture of mobility as well as its attendant national mythology of the democratic and open road.

CHAPTER 3

PRODUCING MOBILE AUDIENCES AND CORRIDORS OF CONSUMPTION

Billboard advertisers sold their services on the premise that, located outdoors, their advertising could reach all of the people all of the time. This, they asserted, was increasingly true as Americans became "a nation on wheels," "a People on the Go," an "outdoors population" who frequented sports stadiums, golf courses, and movies. The president of their representative trade organization, the Outdoor Advertising Association of America (OAAA), summarized developments of the previous decade in 1929, noting that "we have changed from essentially a 'home people' to an 'automobile and movie people.'"[1] Particularly in the face of competition from radio advertising, the outdoor advertising industry presented itself as unique in efficiently appealing to moving audiences.[2] But as the billboard industry depicted the nation as an outdoors population, the radio industry noted how the telephone, the radio, and colorful magazines really made Americans an indoor people. To survive the threat of new forms of indoor advertising, outdoor advertisers directed attention to the great—now automobile accessible—outdoors.

Although billboard companies benefited from the American tendencies toward outdoor life, they also believed that they "played no small part in creating the very conditions" of that outdoor life.[3] The task outdoor advertisers set themselves in the 1920s and 1930s was to maintain and build upon the outdoor "drive" of the postwar population, whether by selling goods related to "outdoor tendencies" or by simply urging, in all ways, the traditional American belief in mobility of all kinds—social, economic, and physical.

Many campaigns in the 1920s for unrelated products featured elements of an "outdoors life" as endorsements for the lifestyle and culture being sold. Kuppenheimer clothes and Chesterfield cigarettes showed almost identical scenes of audiences at a sporting event cheering for their favorite football teams and consuming the products advertised. Gasoline companies presented women engaged in sports in order to represent power and speed, as in campaigns by General Gasoline, which depicts a female water-skier, and Atlantic Gasoline, which shows a female archer, golfer, and swimmer (fig. 11).[4] They narrated the sporting lifestyle of the "new woman"—an ideal emblem of modernity—and plastered the landscape itself with her larger-than-life-sized nubile form of athleticism and good health. In all of these cases, leisure-oriented activities set the stage for the advertisements—emphasizing pleasure and consumption rather than work and production—and themes of youth, energy, and action denoted the outdoor spirit of the age. Each propagated the idea that independence and mobility were achieved through consumption, and promoted lifestyles that maintained high outdoor circulation.

Outdoor advertisers shared with print advertisers a quest to associate the products publicized with class ascension and modernity.[5] However, they defended their methods as literally moving people, driving them to the shop or to the next leisure activity before they hit the road again. Since the road, with all its connotations of independence and democracy, was the ideal site for imagining social mobility, wasn't the outdoor ad in the best position of all to inspire consumerism?

Salesmen for poster advertising explained that the appeal of the poster was its outdoors setting, where nature "puts people in a friendly, cheerful, optimistic frame of mind." The poster, "allied with air and sunshine," was "kith and kin to Nature herself." "When the buying public is a-walk," they noted, "motoring, on the street, in the hills, it is out from under the dead weight of much materialism, of worry, of self-analysis."[6] Out-of-doors, the consumer's mind "is most open to suggestions."[7]

The outdoors was more than just the setting for realizing oneself. It was another commodity for sale. Marketing a place as a commodity entailed selling a packaged identity to potential businesses, visitors, and residents, including the regional pleasures of nature, history, commerce, and climate.[8] Ironically, packaging places by advertising their characteristics also served to dissolve local boundaries and distinctiveness, as place images were frequently fictionalized and stereotyped in order to be easily understood by outsiders.

In the nineteenth century, tourists had sought the well-advertised natural and commercial attractions of places like the Hudson River Valley, Niagara Falls, and New England. Tourism helped create identities for these regions.[9] Elsewhere, too, steamship and railroad companies advertised excursions and the sights to be seen via their transport systems, as did streetcar companies. In

11. Series of posters designed by McClelland Barclay featuring sportswomen, 1927.

the twentieth century, those forms of advertising continued, along with other regional and national efforts, such as See America First, a booster campaign begun in 1906 by a group of businessmen, civic leaders, and politicians to promote both commercial development and tourism in the West. The slogan lived longer than the association, however, and became the rallying cry for various other groups publicizing national tourism as a patriotic act, particularly as the war in Europe restricted overseas travel.[10] After the war, and gaining momentum during the real-estate speculation boom of the 1920s, enterprising communities sought to attract business and tourist dollars or to develop their rural areas by forming groups devoted to publicity. One such group was the All-Year Club of Southern California, organized by a coalition of chambers of commerce, merchants, realtors, and other business leaders.[11] Starting in 1921 they underwrote a national advertising campaign "to tell people of the East about the climate of Southern California" in order to induce tourists as well as manufacturers to move to the area. They advertised throughout the Depression, claiming in 1938 that their efforts had yielded 150 percent increases in tourism.[12]

The 1920s was the heyday of civic boosterism, as novelist Sinclair Lewis illustrated in *Babbitt* (1922), where local businessmen wore Boosters' Club buttons, and in *Main Street* (1920), when Gopher Prairie's Commercial Club began a "campaign of boosting" on the heels of wartime economic prosperity. "The town sought that efficient and modern variety of fame which is known as 'publicity' . . . with banners lettered 'Watch Gopher Prairie Grow.'" In both books Lewis depicted advertising as part of the material culture of the cityscape. He described Babbitt's familiar route to the office in terms of its proud assets, which included "billboards with crimson goddesses nine feet tall. . . ."[13] Such advertisements helped transform the countryside into an arena neither totally rural nor totally urban, a place where moderately sized towns could envision themselves as budding metropolises and small towns could believe that their localities were as rich in offerings as the largest of cities. Boosters claimed that billboards gave "big-town flavor to small town stores."[14] They turned the road to market into the market itself, one that appeared more like the merchandise-crowded display cases of a big-city department store than the dusty shelves of the local general store. The advertisement of specific products served as an advertisement for the place, too. And though a town might have the signs of commercial success, they need not lose their regional identity, as the Foster and Kleiser Company hastened to say, claiming that "the small town is bending its energies to become as modernized as the larger cities. And it is doing all this without the loss of identity which it is making every effort to retain. These little worlds go to make up a big world."[15] In essence, the advertiser claimed that billboards served as a kind of web binding the nation together, retaining distinctions between places yet uniting people through consumer goods and the images and ideas that represented them.

Fictional Gopher Prairie was not alone in using outdoor ads to promote its prosperity. Boosters frequently used billboards to express community identity and pride.[16] Merrick, Long Island, used them in 1922, featuring historical events from its early days ("which in themselves were mileposts in the original development of America") for its civic advertising, and, in so doing, joined the national movement for historic roadside markers.[17] Many towns on the West and East Coasts boosted their natural environment on billboards. In the Midwest, community billboards commonly gave statistics on the rate of growth of the town, its businesses, hospitals, and entertainment facilities, as proof that they had as much to offer as a metropolis. Their ads were similar to those of real estate subdividers who made extensive use of highway billboards as well (fig. 12). Most often, billboards served both as local booster and directional sign, mapping the way to nearby scenic and industrial attractions.[18] It seems fitting, then, that Garnet Carter, a real-estate developer (and the inventor of miniature golf), would choose to use painted barns and billboards to both

12. Billboard for new homes in Silver Lake, northwest of downtown Los Angeles, c. 1928.

mark the miles until you could "See Rock City," on Lookout Mountain, Georgia, and to build a business in tourism. His success was but a mere harbinger of another: Wall Drug. On the dry, hot edge of the South Dakota Badlands, a young couple struggled to keep their dying drugstore alive. A few billboards and free glasses of advertised ice water later an American landmark was born.[19]

As more real-estate developers and tourist industries got into the promotional act, poster designers decided to take a more upscale approach, experimenting stylistically in their art by removing didactic information entirely and reducing text to but a few words, choosing instead to capitalize on exoticism and escapism. All along the West Coast, Foster and Kleiser Company billboards for the Los Angeles Steamship Company offered an exuberant flash of color and abstractly stylized tropical foliage to dramatize cruising west to Hawaii, while on the East Coast, George Merrick's new real-estate development of Coral Gables, Florida, was advertised as the "Miami Riviera" and "America's Only Tropics," through Mediterranean-hued scenes of the city's richly landscaped and ornamental Italianate and Spanish colonial architecture (plate 4).[20]

Tourism itself was a means by which drivers could be made into consumers and the landscape into consumable merchandise. Automobile travel, for instance, promised to provide a variety of experiences: a pastoral reprieve from industrial life, sensations of physical exertion and sport, a reawakened curiosity for exploration, and even a patriotic sentiment of democracy. Yet many tourists were just as likely to acknowledge, as did Charles Finger in his 1931 memoir of a cross-country motor trip, not just the "glory of northern clouds, and of orchards and elm trees, and of pastoral landscape" but also "the thrill of well-conducted filling stations, and the joy of riding on four good tires with two extras ready for service."[21] The dominant themes of auto tourism were contradictory, including both an embrace of technology and a quest for the preindustrial, pastoral, and noncommercial world of the "great outdoors." Even the sensate experience of open land was filtered through the material joys of commercial consumption. Finger's experience paralleled those of nineteenth-century travelers to Niagara Falls and Mammoth Caves whose excursions included feats of physical daring from which they would emerge unharmed but jubilant at their safe deliverance.[22] His description, however, puts the jubilation in consumerist terms.

Letitia Stockett, recording her experiences in a 1930 travelogue *America: First, Fast, and Furious*, compared the view of the open landscape from the window of her steadily moving car "as new and glistening as any on 5th Avenue in Manhattan."[23] The tourist's and the shopper's gaze were the same.[24] Whether landscape or consumer goods, the scene beyond the glass was part of the market that characterized both the natural and the built environment. The advertising industry understood this explicitly, and put the identification of landscape with commodity in dollar terms, as the *Magazine of Business* did in a 1927 article, "Nomadic America's $3,300,000,000 Market." "Motorists are annually buying scenery," it noted, some "taking it 'straight' by touring historic country and picturesque lanes from hotel to hotel and others buying theirs over the bargain counter of a tourist camp."[25]

For urban tourists, pastoral scenes were what they expected of rural or small-town life, and towns seeking the tourist trade were often happy to accommodate. Towns presented the expected imagery of agrarian life by advertising the quaint charms of their locale or by selling the agricultural souvenirs of the surrounding farmlands. Yet urbanites' expectations of rural hospitality could get out of hand. Conflicts between tourists who would stop along the road to pick fruit and flowers from the adjacent fields (which they saw as public property) and the farmers who owned the fields were notorious.[26] Many a farmer realized that a more profitable option to theft and conflict was to set up a roadside stand, a move that brought new clashes, as some motorists resented this commercial interruption of their scenic view.

The influx of tourist dollars along with service stations, hotels and "auto-cabins" (or motels), shops, and restaurants compromised the rural quality of the countryside that tourists wished to experience. These commercial developments could, however, become part of the auto tourist's experience of regionally distinct places. The purposeful packaging of nostalgic rusticity–through stylized architecture of log cabins, Tudor cottages, New England clapboards, or colonial Spanish missions as well as themed promotional items and souvenirs–aligned with the "premodern fantasies of automobile sightseers" and offered a seeming counterpoint to the forces of big business, incorporation, and loss of community that had accompanied modernizing America.[27] As an antidote, small towns produced idyllic images, products, and attractions thereby "packaging" their regional flavor for the passing motorist to taste for a price. Despite the fact that the automobile was one of the fruits of industrial technology, as were the best-laid roads, the automobile nevertheless represented the possibility of escape to a pastoral idyll. It did not seem to matter that reaching it was through the modern automotive industry, while experiencing it was through the modern mass tourism industry, which were far from unique or individualized affairs.

Billboards promoted the tourism experience and the commodification of the landscape by directing people to the goods they might require to continue their journeys, and by offering glimpses of regional life they might crave. The spectacle of nature thus became as much an object to be consumed as the souvenirs one might bring home from the journey. Tourism and billboards brought the natural landscape into "the world of market transactions."[28]

Goods unrelated to tourism or to automobility could profit from associations with the outdoors, while the goal of promoting mobility itself could be accomplished in the selling of just about any good. The author of "Posters and the Winter Tourist" commented on an advertisement for chewing gum that depicts a verdant California landscape, "It's a fine poster for chewing gum but it is superlatively better as an advertisement for California." Its benefits were that "two salable commodities are advertised in one motion."[29] A billboard campaign by Standard Oil Company of New York (SOCONY) depicted the natural wonders to be experienced if one traveled with Standard Oil (plate 5). Presumably, it was a guide to landscapes the traveler was already traversing. The visual cue became sort of a mise en scène, in which the picture at the side of the road encapsulated what could be seen if one looked past the billboard frame. By renaming the highway environs "Soconyland" and by marking the way to natural wonders such as Mt. Desert, Maine, Standard Oil both proclaimed its ownership of the landscape and of the view while it packaged nature for the tourist market. Standard Oil had turned a commodious scene into a commodity for sale.[30] Gasoline, the view, and Mt. Desert were all advertised on one billboard. Budweiser ran a similar series, with one campaign featuring the Natural Bridges of Virginia and Budweiser as the "two commodities for sale," and others depicting the Old Faithful geyser at Yellowstone Park and the Grand Canyon.[31]

More generic nature scenes, such as the "port of coffee contentment" (resembling the harbor at Catalina Island in Southern California) that Crescent Coffee advertised, or the western landscapes of painters Maurice Del Mue, Maynard Dixon, and N. C. Wyeth that were the backdrop to ads for all manner of consumables, served to connect nature with commerce, offering the authenticity of the outdoor scene to ground the truth and purity of the product. They were also beautiful images with which to pleasantly associate the products being sold. Moreover, they focused attention on the wondrous vistas opened up to mobile Americans.

Posters did more than sell the sights and the goods and services required to continue the touring experience. They also acted as educators in how to interpret the landscape. Posters often imitated the printed tourist guidebooks and magazines, which offered prescriptions for how to navigate both the roads and the alien situations one might encounter on the journey. In this, the poster silently participated in public discourse, guiding standards of public deportment to a growing mass of consumers and providing lessons in how to look at America's scenic wonders. Like road maps and guidebooks, the poster taught people to see the landscape as a pretty picture, yet another palatable product or commodity for their consumption.[32]

Gulf Oil exemplified such strategies in a series of posters that featured illustrations of gold-framed paintings of national parks and natural wonders, including Mount Rainier, Garden of the Gods, Roosevelt Dam, Harper's Ferry, and Stone Mountain Memorial.[33] In each, the painting occupies the majority of the poster's image area, subordinating the round, orange trademark of the company and a few words of copy to the side. These billboards, like the one featuring the Grand Canyon, depict the behavior Gulf Oil desired most from its automotive clients (plate 6). Having parked their large touring vehicle, the passengers stand cliff side to enjoy the view. By presenting the image in a gilded frame, as a work of art, Gulf associated motoring with good taste. And by picturing the touring car stopped to view the scenic wonders, poster viewers are taught to treat the scene—whether of the Grand Canyon or of the billboard itself—as a work of art, an object of upper-class consumption. As auto touring became a more middle-class activity, this association could work both to assure upper-class tourists they were the audience being cultivated, and to show the middle-class the status they could attain through their Gulf Oil purchases.

Along with SOCONY and Budweiser, Gulf's series of advertisements worked to promote consumption of both their product and the landscape. They became part of the machinery of tourism, both selling their specific product and lauding the trips motorists took to See America First. As attendance to national parks rose from 356,000 in 1916 to 1.5 million in 1925 and 2 million in 1927, these advertisers could claim that they were also providing a public service by galvanizing public interest in the nation's treasures.[34] Moreover, the artistically rendered posters and overt references to the realm of high art fortified their intentions not merely to sell products but to foster good will, to produce a receptive audience of mobile consumers. For gasoline companies and outdoor advertising firms this was especially important, as they came under increasing attack for their "defacement" of the natural landscape via the propagation of filling stations and billboards. By presenting scenes of beauty, artistically rendered, outdoor advertisers sought to evade this criticism.

Like other branches of the advertising industry, the billboard industry had well established its interest in public relations in the 1910s, galvanized by its successful collaboration with the federal government's Committee of Public Information during World War I. By the early 1920s, the OAAA had public relations committees that were dedicated to managing the distribution of information about the industry. It was standard for them to assert the aesthetic values of outdoor advertising and the important role of billboards as outdoor galleries of art for the masses.[35] Toward this end, the industry trade journal, the *Poster*, featured regular articles on the poster artists and art directors employed by billboard companies (both in-house employees and freelance artists, many of whom were also well-established magazine illustrators), highlighting both their professional training and their connections to the fine arts. Indeed, as commercial art became more established as a profession all its own, the outdoor advertising industry profited from the association and the implication that theirs was a specialized profession with similarly high aesthetic standards.

The efforts of outdoor advertisers to raise the reputation of poster art was surely fueled by the competitive threat posed by magazine advertising. Since the turn of the century, magazines had commanded the largest advertising expenditures. Advertising agents, who handled the majority of national advertising accounts, favored magazines, which granted them higher commissions than the outdoor advertising medium.[36] And, as printing technology improved, magazines began to focus on what had formerly been the claim to fame of the outdoor advertising industry: the ability to reproduce pictures and packages in full color.[37] Moreover, magazines gave their readers more than just advertisements. As one savvy advertising critic noted, the illustrated stories and news features were payment for the time and attention readers gave to the advertisements in the periodical.[38] What did billboards give their audiences?

His answer was that outdoor advertisers were also presenting entertainment and edification, the kind that most befit their motoring audience. While the stolid, uniformed serviceman in Hood Tire's billboard campaign warned motorists of impending curves in the road, street-level landscape paintings did what art in any museum might do: they elevated the senses and stirred the imagination. They inspired wanderlust, "an age-old lure, the universal longing to see what lies beyond the ranges, beyond the horizon's rim." Even if one was in their car for business rather than recreational travel, billboard scenes of natural wonders offered "the beholder a moment or two of escape from the too monotonous routine of modern business."[39] Such scenes were thus a way of "paying" audiences for their attention to the board, purporting to offer them a vacation from ordinary life by effacing the commercialism of the sign itself.

Billboards often capitalized on the fantasies of liberation that automobility inspired, that "out there at an appropriate distance a completely different life beckons."[40] The automobile and the highway offered an ideal liminal space in which travelers could play out desires far from the workaday realities of their own lives, identities, histories, or current political and economic situations.[41] As a transitional space outside of the fixed boundaries of home and work, the road symbolically suggested that one's own identity might also be in flux, open to reinvention or at least the possibility of refashioning. The act of driving–the sensations of movement and the knowledge that one could keep moving on, if necessary–and the relative anonymity of the road, where neighbors were bound to change in rapid succession, surely contributed to such perceptions of the road as a place of possibility. By allowing travelers to choose their own views, change direction at will, and probe distant areas, the automobile also "broke the rigid perspective of the train" and changed perspectives of landscapes, which were now "accessible from all angles, a fixed perspective dissolved into an abundance of views, a multitude of vantage points." This put nature, landscape, and recreation, as well as the traveler's relationship to these things, in a new light.[42]

Indeed, naturalistic landscape scenes paired with the highway that takes people there recur with great frequency in billboard posters, as do themes of social and economic mobility. Though drivers were already on the road, billboard posters frequently depicted a road and a roadside, and positioned the spectators as the travelers through the fictive space of the billboard, making them subjects of the advertisement as well as subjected to it. One mid-1920s Lincoln Motor Company poster (fig. 13) suggests the status of Lincoln drivers through its arrangement of forms, the elements of which are reminiscent of nineteenth-century landscape painting. The figures on the left look off to the right, at the distant settlement beyond. Those in the car stand in for the mobile and noble aristocrats, surveying the landscape as if all that lies beyond them (including the smokestack signs of capitalist industry) is under their control.[43] Lincoln owners do not simply drive cars, they drive the industry of the whole countryside. They look upon the scene with "imperial eyes," which colonize the view beyond, taking ownership of all that falls within their magisterial gaze.[44] The commanding gaze over all that is surveyed is similar to the tourist's consuming vision of the scenic wonders beyond the car windshield, transforming the built and natural environment into spectacle, commodifying the landscape, and endowing viewers with a sense of prowess and control, as if, on the road–in contrast to the disorder of the modern metropolis and the white-collar world of corporate bureaucracy–they were masters of their own destiny.[45] Located at the side of the road, the Lincoln billboard helps viewers in their driver's seats to imagine themselves in the fictive space of the poster, simultaneously participating in tourism and nation building.

Just as the poster served as a didactic tool of tourism, so did it narrate con-

13. The small L marking the coast-to-coast Lincoln Highway (above the car hood on pole) offered a clever note of realism tying into Lincoln Motor Company's theme of auto tourism, 1924.

14. United States Tires' "Book Board," c. 1921.

temporary notions regarding the relationship of city and country, work and leisure. Notably, the figures in the Lincoln ad are at a remove from the industrial scene of work they look at. Their pastoral setting is far more befitting the upwardly mobile motorist, for whom the quest for arcadia—as exemplified by the rush to the suburbs as well as escape to nature—served as antidote or at least palliative to modern corporate life.[46]

In the car, one could even go back in time. History became as important as scenery as a subject for billboards.[47] One example was O. J. Gude's coast-to-coast "Book Boards," a campaign that ran from 1917 through the 1930s by the United States Tires company (fig. 14). The campaign featured unique "free-form" billboards in the shape of an open book with a pen and quill beside it. The book usually featured text on one side announcing an upcoming site, town, or city, accompanied by a brief bit of colonial history. "Toledo, five miles from here," announced one board. Another told motorists, "You are now entering Long Branch, New Jersey. Long Branch was originally purchased from the Indians in 1670 for $20 by Eliakim Wardell." The other side of the book showed the brand name and tire. Sometimes framed illustrations of regional scenes augmented the advertisement.[48] As if the landscape was not enough of an open book, the advertisement told the traveler the history of the spot, offering a corporate sponsorship of Concord, Massachusetts; Fort Lee, New Jersey; or whatever other place might be historicized. Though promoting mobility, the campaign emphasized the particularities of place, pointing to the historical significance of the locale as if to suggest the roots of all Americans in the land and in their national heritage. Both consumption and tourism are thus presented as part of an edifying and patriotic journey into American history, acknowledging that forward momentum did not require the obliteration of the past, nor did it indicate selfish hedonism.[49]

Some campaigns used events of local history to sell a product nationwide. Piedmont, "the Virginia Cigarette," whose campaign was designed by the noted poster illustrator Walter Whitehead, used three different posters representing historical scenes of colonial Virginia. Circulated in different regions of the United States were posters Piedmont titled "Bartering with the Indians," "The Bride's Passage," and "Paying His Fines." Is it a coincidence that each happens to teach a historical lesson in market exchange? Each also employs the visual technique of clustering people at one side of the composition with a panorama of open landscape as a backdrop for their activities. The middle of the image area invariably functions as a clearing in the composition through which viewers can enter the scene, drawn into the panorama depicted. By putting you right into "Olde Virginia," the ad uses the geographical location and a depoliticized, sanitized, rendition of the history of the tobacco industry as a marketing tool to authenticate the product, to give it "pedigree."[50] The scroll bearing the legend at the bottom of the poster casts the advertisement as a history painting, a status symbol of high culture with the benefits of a civic lesson, while the regional specificity of its depiction promised individuality and authenticity.

If one is to believe their advertising campaigns, Associated Gasoline provided enough fuel to transcend historical space and time completely. The ascension is suprahistorical in their series of ads, "Follow Roads to Romance," that depict scenes from the Spanish colonization of California Indians. In one ad we see missions and in others missionaries, such as Father Juniper Serra, shown with the California Indians he seeks to convert. As the advertiser explained, incidents in the history of the West were "diligently studied in order to find events combining romance with dramatic action," to sell "interest in the history and romance of the Pacific Coast." The goal was not just to sell gasoline but "rather the things that gasoline gives the purchaser." But could gasoline really be so empowering? By erecting over twelve hundred posters along the Pacific Coast from Canada to Mexico that show Seattle being "saved" from hostile Indians by the sloop-of-war *Decatur* in 1856 and other such scenes of natives being subdued by European and Anglo-American settlers, Associated Gasoline claimed to be "selling travel through romance."[51] *Whose* romance is obvious, as the narrative subordinates racial conflict in favor of a progressive view of history as evolution from savagery to civilization.

Romanticizing history was also a way of reinventing America as a new frontier for exploration and travel. It aggrandized the touring activity as a pioneering event, one that was both virile and history making. Hearkening to an earlier era of westward expansion, advertising campaigns employing such artists as Maynard Dixon and N. C. Wyeth featured cowboys, Indians, buttes, and canyons paired with automobiles and tires. This was automotive manifest destiny. Famed illustrator and painter Wyeth produced Fisk Tire advertisements as one of a series of artistic poster campaigns (to which Maxfield Parrish also contributed), choosing to render the automobile as a bucking bronco driving into the wild blue yonder, watched by Indians on horseback in traditional dress (one complete with papoose) who gaped after the touring car from behind the clouds of dust left in its wake (fig. 15).[52]

The southwestern backdrop and the contrast between the modern touring machine and traditionally garbed Indians in these advertisements were, in part, aimed to inspire imagination for sights one would see on a western excursion. The iconography of the ad also would have been familiar to art aficiona-

15. N. C. Wyeth's poster was one in a series by American artists commissioned by the Fisk Tire Company, 1919.

dos and tourists alike, as such scenes were part of the revival of regionalist art, especially in the American West, and because Indians had been used for decades to personify the regional identity of the Southwest and to emblematize tourism itself.[53] The Indians included in the images serve another purpose. They authenticate the touring experience as one that will bring viewers back to "primitive" nature, to a preindustrial connection with the land, though through spectatorship rather than physical interaction. The image of the automobile in the ads, on the other hand, promises power—power to conquer and colonize, to burn up the road, to leave behind that which one has already consumed in order to proceed to the next experience.

Or, one might choose to settle down. One 1924 article, "The Automobile and the Pioneer," claims to offer the motorist the tools of frontier settlement: "Today there are thousands of square miles of territory that await . . . transformation. . . . [T]he automobile and motor truck will be the prime implements in the *empire builder's* hands." The author described the automobile as "the foremost agency, first in the pioneering, and then in the filling up of the interstices that shall knit communities together and bring new areas into production to meet the needs of an ever-expanding race."[54]

The connections among automobility, tourism, and commercial development thus came full circle. Entire regions first experienced on tour became reconceptualized as open terrain, ready for homes, shops, and recreation.

Ultimately, the automobile promised its owner not just an escape route from city to country, from east to west, from banality to character, from present to past, and from conquered to conqueror, but also from one's own socioeconomic level to another. Indeed, billboard images of the open road and the panoramic landscape depicted both vertical and horizontal motion and mobility. Though the wealthy appearance of the figures in the Lincoln Motor Company ad or the fancy automobile of the Fisk Tire ad seemed to present upper-class activity as a promise of social mobility, such images were hardly necessary for the promise to be made. Merely envisioning travel through space suggested social mobility, especially when rendered through vast panoramas and attention to luminist techniques of color and "vaunted light."[55]

Similarly, when we "Follow Roads to Romance" with Associated Gasoline, our mobility is not limited to the road we take somewhere over the horizon. Transcendence is assured, as the road represented in the poster leads heavenward. It is as if, fueled by Associated Gasoline, endless mobility and ascension are attained. This is achieved as much through the path curved like a rainbow taking motorists to their pot of gold as it is through the snow-covered mountains, valleys, waterfall, and denuded trees, all of which verge on parody of the nineteenth-century sublime of the landscape painter (fig. 16).

Panoramic natural scenes that mimic landscape painting and the luminist tradition imply transcendence. Historically, romantic depictions of nature and open spaces have been used to represent passage, purification, and deliverance, all of which are crucial elements of American frontier mythology. They suggest physical travails leading to moral regeneration.[56] Perhaps naturalistic imagery in posters even functioned to cleanse the advertisement of its sullying commercial properties, offering pure spiritual uplift and endless ascendance. Such depictions suggest the role played by outdoor advertising in developing the twentieth-century American culture of mobility, which was about not merely representing movement or sharing a delight in travel but also promoting and commercializing a traditional theme in American mythology: the promise of social, geographical, physical, economic, and even spiritual mobility. Mobility is a rich metaphor, the cornerstone concept of the frontier, manifest destiny, westward expansion, and even the American Dream, all of which depend upon the pairing of freedom and movement, and all of which were exploited by outdoor advertisers in their endless quest to sell, and thereby improve their own mobility as well.

Advertising has commonly been thought to play an important role in representing an urban life to rural communities, teaching country folks and immigrants how to consume with the spirit of urbanites who had long availed themselves of

16. This 1929 illustration by Fred Ludekens also advertised the radio program hosted by Associated Gasoline in which motor-mates Jack and Ethyl marry and go on a honeymoon tour of the Pacific Coast.

the metropolis's wealth of department stores and other consumables. But far more was happening in terms of shifting conceptual categories of city and country, nature and commerce. This was, after all, a time when urban industrialists, white-collar professionals, and other members of a widening middle class strove for the purity and uplift of the country excursion and suburban lifestyle; when small town dwellers began to envision their villages as glittering metropolises; and when rural denizens were both visiting faraway places and were being introduced to distant peoples and goods. Outdoor advertisers strode a middle line in appealing to all categories of consumers, a necessity whether they wanted their products to have a national appeal, an urban attraction, or a rural fascination.

In their striving to reach the "masses" and the "classes"—the entirety of the "outdoors" population of "a nation on wheels"—outdoor advertisers were training people to discard their class and regional distinctions in favor of the mobility, domesticated privacy, and individualism promised by mass consumption. This was basic to the cultural ideology of mobility and the successful sale of the ideas related to travel, class ascension, and higher standards of living. It was in the interest of advertisers to uproot people, not only to keep them moving (to the store, to their new home, to the office) but to allow them a sense of unfixed identity, a sense that through goods they could be anything and everything—a country spirit with urban sophistication, a simple pastoral soul with city wit, an upper-class debutante able to survive in America's uncharted wilderness.

CHAPTER 4

THE AESTHETICS OF SPEED AND THE POWERS OF "PICTURIZATION"

Reduced amounts of text and ornate images in outdoor advertisements of the 1920s suggest that advertisers struggled to make ads quickly legible to motorist passersby. As motoring speeds increased, from thirty-five miles per hour in the mid 1920s, to forty-five miles per hour and fifty-five miles per hour in the 1930s, just how to communicate with moving audiences—now more accustomed to a faster pace of life in general—became a pressing question. The challenge was how to consolidate the message, to speak silently yet read loudly, without losing the point or the attention of moving audiences.

Just as the text-heavy billboard of the nineteenth century had slowly given way to pictorially based posters in the twentieth century, so did the complicated and ornate scenes that featured panoramic landscapes, history, and pastoralism progressively give way to more simplified, abstract, and streamlined means of representing and selling the lessons of mobility. Although multiple stylistic approaches flourished in the interwar years and beyond, there was an increasing focus on achieving singularity, simplicity, and speed of communication. The overlapping stylistic approaches to this are illustrated through a comparison of two of the images previously discussed (see plates 5–6). Though both the Gulf Oil advertisement of the Grand Canyon and the SOCONY advertisement of Mt. Desert feature place-specific panoramic views, they differ dramatically in their approaches. The former employs great detail in rendering the figures and the view, enhancing its realism with variations of color, hue, and tone. In contrast, the landscape of Mt. Desert is boldly delineated through flat expanses of solid color, and includes few details and no chiaroscuro (or shadowing). Easier to reproduce, and more legible from a distance and to fast-moving viewers, the style of the "Soconyland" advertisement represented new methods of poster illustration shared by a vanguard of designers. These contrasting approaches emblematize the questions those in the industry addressed at the time, of the relative value of realistic versus modernistic approaches.

Whether the poster should properly be treated as a handmaiden to art or to commerce, and whether it was possible to serve both, was also part of the professional discourse of the period that played a role in the articulation of a billboard aesthetic appropriate to the automobile age. At a time when print advertisements still used a great deal of text and highlighted the role of the copywriter as primary in importance, poster advertisers focused on the powers of "picturization" and introduced a different question: could consumers read text at all?[1] Critical to the debates between poster artists, industry leaders, and industrial psychologists was whether mass, moving audiences could read and understand associative, metaphorical, and narrative advertisements—much less overly abstract art—without explanatory text.[2]

Their conflict tapped into larger questions that emerged with the rise of mass communications during World War I. Can people communicate effectively to one another without face-to-face contact? Can communication be individualized when speaking to masses? Can people with different lifestyles, professions, and classes be reached through the same vehicles of communication? And, as a recurring question, can they be reached efficiently and economically? The need and ability to communicate to the masses as a critical part of distributing mass-produced goods made these pressing questions for all advertisers. Outdoor advertisers answered the questions in part through an articulation of an *aesthetics of speed*.[3] It is yet another cultural ramification of the displacement of the market to the open road.

The speed and movement integral to notions and sensations of mobility have come to characterize not just an "outdoors" people but also the "nervous" generation of the 1920s and, indeed, much of post–World War I modernity.[4] The sensations were represented by modernist writers such as John Dos Passos, Gertrude Stein, and William Carlos Williams, artists such as Marcel Duchamp and Pablo Picasso, and futurists such as Giacomo Balla and Filippo Tommaso Marinetti, who sought to express the dramatic changes that characterized their era and their understanding of the world around them, from the impact of mechanized modern warfare to Albert Einstein's theory of relativity to the role of psychology in altering notions of objectivity and subjectivity.

There are two ways to consider the role of advertising in fostering an expression of modernity. One is by looking at formal change: the incorporation of the cubistic forms, zig-zag lines, sans-serif typefaces, and curvilinear "teardrop" shapes that have come to be known variously as modernistic, art deco, skyscraper style, streamline moderne, or some variation thereof.[5] The other is by looking beyond such formal signatures of modern communication to the type of quick looking and reading that simplified advertisements, plastered in bulk across the landscape, helped to foster and that the poster industry depended upon for its growth. The speed and mobility of the highway traveler, and the corresponding "new American tempo" of life in the age of airplanes, radio, movies, and all sorts of labor-saving devices, demanded corresponding changes in visual communication.[6]

As part of this new aesthetic, advertisers refined their use of the trademark, the slogan, and the massed image that allowed for a quick impression. They also replaced the more text-heavy and readerly devices employed by advertisers in previous periods and in other media. More than merely streamlining or reducing the quantity of text in favor of images, this involved creating messages through pictures that appealed quickly and without reading, understandable to mobile masses who remained, ideally, part of a continuous stream of flowing traffic. To accomplish this, an aesthetics of speed was required that could deliver messages yielding unblinking recognition.

This set of aesthetic practices, which incorporated what we today consider logos (then referred to as trademarks), was not thought by advertisers to be a means of training audiences in visual literacy. That critical stance would imply the ability to read and interpret. Rather, advertisers wished to make superficial correspondences graspable without requiring focus, without calling upon the conscious reasoning powers of their audiences.[7] An image, a logo, and a few words, all barren of a wide range of possible expressions or interpretations, was the ideal form of communicating to mobile audiences in a state of distraction. This simple presentation provided a sensation of speed that did not disrupt the actual speed of travelers yet still delivered its message. Though usually the aim of advertisers is to attract attention, the strategies of an aesthetics of speed assumed *distraction*. Accordingly, it was a significant challenge to create an image that could not merely survive the inattentive gaze of viewers but rather *thrive* on the inattention of viewers, requiring no critical faculty whatsoever, and yet somehow remain indelible.

Poster advertisers sold their services in terms of the power of their images to quickly, silently, and universally communicate to the masses. They called it "picturization" and declared that "regardless of tongue or race, the poster was understandable to all." This was fortunate, since outdoor advertisers asserted that their audience was everyone who went outdoors, including those folks who "are probably not of the worthwhile families but who still wear shoes and clothing and eat ham and bacon and lard,"[8] namely, "workers, factory hands, a class of people who either did not read magazines or newspapers to any appreciable extent, or who, because of racial limitations, [could not]." Outdoor advertisers claimed that "the poster spoke a universal language, understandable to all, regardless of tongue. The poster could tell its entire story in pictures."[9] The implication was also that the poster would both Americanize "the many thousands of foreigners who do not read English" and educate "the huge army of illiterates to be found in enlightened America," whose ultimate worth to the nation as workers and consumers would, as a result, be raised by millions.[10]

The changes in daily life that made America an "outdoors" nation on wheels also created audiences who no longer had time, inclination, or even intelligence enough for reading. As more than one industry spokesman exclaimed, America was now "a nation of *headline readers*."[11] One study by a professor of advertising and marketing at New York University showed that the shorter the heading for newspapers, the better—five being the "maximum number of words in a line that can be grasped at a single glance," though "three words are best."[12] Pictorial, not print, copy was far more memorable, reported researchers at the University of Wisconsin, who went on to claim that even still, "the number of items that can successfully be introduced in an advertising picture" is three or fewer.[13] "The American public is picture-minded," they concluded. So did other experts in the field of commercial art, who advised that if print media was to compete in the fast-paced modern world, it too should "posterize," taking cues from the new innovations in billboard design. The outdoor advertising industry was pleased with the comparison and it publicized at every occasion the magazine and newspaper ads that used miniature posters or followed the strategies of minimal text with enlarged imagery.[14]

Professionals in the advertising industry looked to psychological studies and intelligence tests to affirm their notions regarding the limited capacity of their audience.[15] The popularization of basic principles of psychology egged them on. What was the point of publicizing the objective facts about a product if the average person was guided not by reason but by instinctive, unconscious desires, as Sigmund Freud had found? Through emotions—and not logic—was the way to reach people, explained Walter Dill Scott, then the foremost authority on psychology as applied to business purposes. More and more, he claimed, people made their decisions "as a result of imitation, habit, suggestion, or some related form of thinking."[16] Yet what was the fate of democracy if, as psychology had shown, people were irrational and easily impressed by external forces and were distanced from one another by virtue of new forms of transportation and communication? This question troubled intellectuals like Walter Lippmann, author of such books as *Public Opinion*, *The Phantom Public*, and *Propaganda*. The very foundations of our democracy, the Enlightenment faith in reason and the tradition of rational public discourse, had been undermined. As Lippmann and many of his contemporaries came to believe, the answer was to redefine democracy as a government for the people but by enlightened and responsible elites.[17]

Advertisers positioned themselves as among the enlightened elite capable of molding, or "crystallizing" public opinion, joining other experts in the social sciences (such as those who had discovered the ways that human nature worked), government, and journalism.[18] One adman asserted that people "are tremendously different in intelligence. While the body and the emotions of the average man are like those of the man of the professional class, his mind operates in an extremely different fashion. The mental development of the average adult is about equivalent to that found by school children in the seventh grade . . . ordinary words . . . are not understood by the average man. . . . The danger of exceeding [his] comprehension is exceedingly great."[19] A 1922 advertisement for the George Throop outdoor advertising company cites the "exhaustive investigations by Professor Walter Dill Scott . . . and other eminent psychologists," who show that "80% of the people of this country have a mental capacity equal to, or below that of a normal CHILD of thirteen or fourteen years." He extols the power of the poster to reach "not only the 80% [of the population] with the mental capacity of children, but also the 20% with superior mentality."[20]

Marketers frequently described the mass of consumers as either childlike or primitive in their intellectual and emotional development. Consumers had only instinctive and visceral reactions to stimuli. The masses, it was deemed, "live in the present. They are open to *impressions*. They take up the latest song, cast longing eyes toward the most recent automobile model, they crave the new thrill!"[21] The idea was that the "impression" made by the poster was immediate, superficial, lacking in depth, and that, as one poster artist put it, the mind was like "a sensitive piece of film" onto which images were imprinted with barely any time exposure.[22] It is a form of communication that does not require any critical attention span, as observed by professor of psychology Hugo Munsterberg, who noted that "a look or a glance from the eye does not necessarily involve any intellectual attention. In other words, it is purely an instinctive or automatic form of attention."[23] A good poster could "hit the mind through the eye, instantaneously."[24] Instincts and emotions could be appealed to through color, large size, and simple pictures. The goal was to avoid "clever verbal devices," analogy, or complex graphics that required subtle reasoning processes.[25]

Advertisers usually considered women, the illiterate, and immigrants to be childlike in mentality, and most susceptible to the emotional appeal of pictures. Outdoor advertisers claimed that women did not read newspapers so it was useless to advertise to women through them.[26] Testimonials by women seemingly supported this: "I do not buy things because of facts; I buy them because they appeal to an emotion. . . . Those pictorial ideas that appeal to me most are 'motherhood.'"[27] Campaigns such as Palmolive soap's "Gee, mother—but you're pretty," in which a young boy gazes adoringly at his doting and rosy-cheeked mother (fig. 17), suggests the investment of advertisers in both Freudian psychology and women's sentimental nature.[28] Women who worked in the advertising industry were called upon to contribute to trade journals with articles that explained their gender position. For instance, Augusta Leinard wrote in "Women and Color Appeal in Advertising," one of her many contributions to the *Poster*, "The feminine mind likes soft tints suggestive of delicacy and refinement; the male of the species . . . prefers strong colors. . . ," and the "advertiser needs to forget about himself and put himself in the position of the buyer."[29] Advertisers in all media during the 1920s tended to identify the consumer as female, regardless of class, and to employ female illustrators and copywriters (in small numbers) to better tap feminine sensibilities.[30] Some

17. Clarence Underwood became widely known as the creator of the "Palmolive girl" (here grown-up), 1926.

used statistics that showed women were the real shoppers of the family, while others showed that women were simply the most impressionable, their natural inferiority complex inciting them to spend more than men to make up for their seeming lack (Freud's influence yet again). In either case, the advertiser could plan his campaign to use color, pictures, and simplistic messages, all of which were sure to affect if not women, then at least immigrants and children!

Immigrants and children were considered suggestible, gullible, and easily attracted to the color and large scale of posters. Children—especially girls—were an important market, not only because they would grow up to be the majority of consumers but because they were bred to be good consumers, starting with school lessons in shopping, cooking, cleaning, and proper hygiene. Nationally advertised products, trademarks, and standardized sizes also helped to make shopping child's play.[31] Boys and girls from five to eighteen comprised one-quarter of the population and were part of a new generation "trained to take education through the eye." They had been trained by motion pictures, comic strips, mass-produced magazines and lithographs, and the changing forms of advertising imagery.[32]

The universal language of posters, understandable by people of all backgrounds, meant that billboards would work nationally and internationally without any losses in translation. Leonard Dreyfuss, vice president of the large company United Advertising, stressed that for national campaigns posters were most effective because they commonly appealed to those in Alabama, where there was a 20 percent illiteracy rate, and in New Jersey, where only 6 percent could not read.[33] But Dreyfuss also grappled with how to have local specificity in the face of national distribution. How could the advertiser communicate to the individual and to the masses? Or, as one psychologist asked, "Do all men respond the same?" He cautioned that one could not assume that the "emotional reactions of the average man are much like those of superior men, such as the men who write advertisements."[34] By making distinctions, advertisers asserted their own superiority and sought to soften the conformist danger of the universalist message. If they had the mental ability, individuals (such as admen) could form their own impressions, and properly influence others.

The outdoor industry credited the movies, in particular, for helping to stimulate audiences in the types of visual communication crucial to poster advertising. Movies had not only pioneered techniques such as the close-up, but were, like poster pictures, described as a visual language that could communicate to immigrants as well as a more varied cross-class population.[35] The "hieroglyphics" of the motion picture—as Vachel Lindsay, in his seminal *The*

Art of the Moving Picture (1915), called the language of motion pictures—could communicate without visual or any other kind of literacy demanded of the audience.[36] The poster was, similarly, described as an ideogram, because it used an abstract representation of the product or related concept rather than words. "Its message is short, quick, confronts one suddenly, is gone in a flash," wrote Frederick Kurtz, vice president in charge of outdoor advertising for N. W. Ayer and Son advertising agency. "It permits no argument, allows no reasoning."[37]

In both mediums, proponents lauded the universality of pictorial communication while critics worried about the immediacy of the expression as a threat to moral order. D. W. Griffith called film a "universal language—a power that can make men brothers and end wars forever." He believed that film communicated with a directness that came closer to pure ideas than any expression. His ideas about this had something to do with the proximity of the eye to the brain, not unlike what advertisers advanced regarding the direct eye-to-mind communication of poster pictures. Griffith, as well as many middle-class reformers of the period, saw the possibilities for film to uplift people, to allow people to "relax their active rational minds, let images penetrate into their subconscious, shed concerns of social lives, relinquish individuality to the image on screen."[38] But the idea that moving pictures could bypass interpretation, educated reasoning, and rational thought in favor of unmediated emotion posed frightening possibilities. The filmgoing experience, after all, made no demands on the audience, offered a standardized product, and did not invite active engagement or debate on any level.[39] It was a public discourse with a one-way transmission. Such a universal language as film, capable of uplifting the masses, could just as powerfully manipulate them to revolt, to cease active political engagement, to give up their powers of rational thought entirely. Moving images, or any "universal" language that could pass unmediated from "eye to brain" posed a potent risk to democracy and individualism even while promising benefits in terms of its power to train the masses in the lessons of consumption, work, or nationalism.

Film and billboards shared modes of pictorial communication that utilized size as well as speed. Whereas posters presented images at a large scale to moving audiences, film presented moving images at a large scale to static audiences. As one poster advertiser wrote, "This is the age of big things. . . . Motion pictures have enlarged the vision of this generation. . . . The poster is *big*. . . . It is a tremendous stage upon which to set an advertising appeal."[40] Film presented images at a scale that audiences had never had the opportunity to see before. Moreover, the idea of a mass of individuals coming together for the viewing suggested a scale of communication that was unprecedented. For early viewers, the gigantism of film, especially the disembodied view of the close-up, a technique developed by Griffith, was an awesome and sometimes frightening experience. The camera had enabled a concentration and magnification of the human face that was simply not possible in the realm of the real world of social interaction.[41] Poster artists were urged to "never forget the lesson and example of the motion picture 'close-up,'" for its dramatic communicative purposes. "Develop a natural mental focus," they were advised, "which will shut out all the many things which tend to destroy any poster's effectiveness, and concentrate on the salient essentials." Design critics and teachers discerned that effective posters conveyed a singleness of purpose, one idea whose main elements were enlarged as big as possible. This way, audiences would not have to work so hard to get the message, since "great size . . . takes less concentration to assimilate."[42] As approaching motorists zoomed in on the billboard from afar, the imagery would enlarge further, exaggerating the sense of it as a close-up and as a cinematic experience.

The billboard was also described as a screen frozen or paused on a single frame of the drama. The viewers' own movement activated the scene as the image flashed before them and then passed quickly out of view.[43] If the designers had done their job right, in that flash the audience would subconsciously register the image and quickly fill in the plot and scenario of the larger (unseen) narrative. Billboards were, as illustrator Howard Scott put it, "one-act plays to five-second audiences."[44]

Over and again poster designers, outdoor advertising company representatives, and art directors emphasized that "to get the meaning across in a glance," "human-interest pictorials" were unsurpassed.[45] "Big, broad, universal, underlying humanity," it was noted, "is . . . the same in Maine as it is in California." Appeal to human emotions, in other words, was the ideal way to avoid sectional differences in national campaigns.[46] A poster with "powerful story-telling value" would humanize even the most technical of products and convey meaning even to the common man (who "[couldn't] be expected to understand specialized information").[47] A diverse range of advertising campaigns followed this adage, from Fatima cigarettes to the Ford V-8. They were excerpted dramas of the idealized everyday lives of the white leisure class. For instance, in one Fatima billboard, two women linger over tea, perched on a plush divan that is part of a scarcely sketched background setting, to highlight the characteristics of their upper-crust lifestyles. Camel cigarettes, Kuppenheimer clothing, and Palmolive soap similarly portray scenes in midstream, with close-ups of

18. When they were included, African Americans were depicted in posters as smiling servants and "mammies," as in Marshall Reid's award-winning illustrations for Oxydol, 1930.

upturned faces captured as they seal a business deal, cheer their favorite sports teams, or read a story (see fig. 17).[48] When African Americans appeared in billboard advertisements, as in campaigns for Oxydol detergent (fig. 18), Armour ham, Sambo pancake mix, and the Ford V-8 ("They's mostly out since they got that new Ford"), they were depicted as smiling servants or "mammies," much as they were in print advertisements.[49] Though billboard industry leaders strenuously asserted that their audience included the broadest spectrum of consumers, including those of color and the laboring classes, and advised that their colleagues study the needs and habits of those classes, they rarely deviated from larger advertising norms, which had long employed gross racial and ethnic stereotypes in picturing people of color.[50]

Renowned poster illustrators including Gerrit A. Beneker, Jon O. Brubaker, Andrew Loomis, and Haddon Sundblom exhorted colleagues and students to study their audience, and to canvas them door-to-door if necessary, to find out what worked. "No amount of clever execution can make up for a poor understanding of human types nor for an inadequate concept of how different pictorial renditions normally affect the average observer," noted illustrator McClelland Barclay.[51] Brubaker agreed: Learn about human nature, he told his colleagues and students. Only then could the designer convey the personality or spirit of the ad, "the poster 'it,' if you will."[52] The goal was not sim-

19. Norman Rockwell's poster for Beech-Nut Gum exemplified the folksy tone of many ads of the period, 1937.

ply to make viewers *see* the ad, but to make them *feel*.[53] For most of these designers, wholesome, sincere characters—such as the dewy-eyed, rosy-cheeked young women and children who populated Sundblom's Coca-Cola ads, Loomis's Ivory soap ads, and Clarence Underwood's Palmolive ads—in ordinary domestic situations (though never working there) or engaged in leisure activities were the route to emotional engagement. They were the same kinds of all-American scenes and images that illustrator Norman Rockwell had become famous for through his advertisements (fig. 19) and *Saturday Evening Post* covers of the 1920s and 1930s.[54]

The colossal scale of the billboard lent itself well to such drama. Figures and scenes were writ larger than mortal life, transfiguring regular folk into heroes. And private, interior scenes and internal emotions starkly contrasted their outdoor context, boldly and colorfully enlivening the anonymous public arena and populating the built and natural environment of the roadside. Dominant in its size and impact, pundits claimed, the poster was more alluring, impressive, and powerful than print ads, many of which employed the same imagery and strategies.

Indeed, by the 1920s, many of the same artists were illustrating mass magazines as well as print and poster advertisements. The ads and the magazine illustrations were keen analogues to the formulaic but wildly popular melodramas of serial fiction in magazines. Similarly formulaic, the human interest stories of the ads became "little dramas of consumerism." As one commentator noted, *commercial art* was a misnomer; the real job to be done was to illustrate the advertisement.[55] Nevertheless, illustrators acknowledged the differences between outdoor and print advertisements, even, as Walter Whitehead claimed, finding that they had "better success applying posters to magazine work than vice versa."[56] Art directors and owners of outdoor advertising companies made the same exhortations: "No advertiser makes a mistake greater than that of amplifying the ordinary magazine or newspaper copy and placing it on an outdoor panel."[57]

There were other differences between the two mediums. Whereas a magazine advertisement remained framed by the borders of the publication, the billboard advertisements lined the road like a zoetrope, reel of film, or cartoon strip, awaiting viewers' movement through space to be activated. Just as we scan the comic strip to get to the punch line or sit still in a darkened theater to see a film, our movement on the road offers an unfolding of the advertisements and landscape beyond the highway's edge. No outdoor advertising campaign embodied this idea more literally or achieved greater fame than the serial roadside signs of Burma-Shave.

With two hundred dollars, a can of paint, and wood salvaged from a wrecking yard, Allen Odell (son of the Burma Vita Company owner Clinton Odell) set out in 1925 to save the family's ailing business and advertise a new product: the brushless shaving cream. Taking his inspiration from filling station signs that gave motorists advance notice of amenities available ahead (see fig. 10), he planted six ten-inch-by-thirty-six-inch red-painted wooden signs one-hundred feet from one another along Minnesota's Highways 61 and 65. With verses like "Does your husband—misbehave—grunt and grumble—rant and rave—shoot the brute some—Burma-Shave," the company illustrated the countryside with the frames of a picture-free comic strip whose jokes were always genial even if its poetry was less than transcendent.[58] By 1935, the company had 42,000 signs dotting the landscape, and had captured the public imagination. Burma-Shave copy was clean and wholesome, with a folksy tone that could appeal across regions, ages, and religions, yet it still had an edge: "He played—a sax—had no B-O—but his whiskers scratched—so she let him go—Burma-Shave" and "Are your whiskers—When you wake—Tougher than—A two-bit steak!—Use—Burma-Shave." Though selling a new product to a modern motoring audience, the Burma-Shave signs retained a small town, Old World charm that might have been refreshing, both to new era audiences of the 1920s and later to Depression audiences quick to blame big national corporations for the country's economic ills. It may have helped that many of the verses were publicly minded, as well: "Past a schoolhouse—take it slow—let the little—shavers—grow—Burma-Shave."[59]

Spanning decades of mass appreciation for the "funny papers" and slapstick movies, the Burma-Shave sign campaign provided a similar, though real-time, moving picture in which motorists could—and did—participate. In fact, the company's competitions for advertising verse were greeted one year with 65,000 responses. The novelty of the signs, their "clean and wholesome" copy, and the grassroots outreach employed by the company, which sent regular mailings of the chatty house organ, *Burma Shavings*, to the farmers from whom they leased roadside space, may have charmed people into supporting Burma-Shave.[60] Certainly this provided the sort of folksy, sentimental appeal that many outdoor advertising experts were touting.

The Burma-Shave signs were retired in 1963, when the Philip Morris Company purchased Burma-Shave and decided to put the $200,000 sign advertising budget into television instead. Perhaps Philip Morris had a point. The signs had done their job, training people in reading the simple message of moving ads. TV did this too, and you didn't have to worry about people moving too fast to get it. As one eulogy for the campaign put it, "Super highways—Super speed—People have—No time to read."[61]

Most in the outdoor advertising industry had agreed well before the advent of television that the super speed of travel (even if it was only forty-five miles per hour) and the competition between different forms of mass leisure had already, by the 1920s and 1930s, left people with little time to read. Indeed, reading was the last thing they expected from audiences. In fact, even the focus on human-interest stories and sentimental, illustrative advertisements—themes considered universal because they appealed to emotions—was subject to debate. One trade manual suggested that those illustrations were fine for pedestrian markets, but not the open road, where simpler ads were the only way to go. Others toyed with the idea that for an image truly to be universal in communication, pictures were less effective than color, line, and geometric forms. Still others imagined some combination of realism and abstraction as the best way to hedge their bets regarding the question of which was more effective. By the 1920s, even those poster illustrators and outdoor advertisers who had long resisted the affiliations between their practice and the realm of the fine arts began to look to modern approaches in art and design to justify their work.

CHAPTER 5

MODERN ART AND ADVERTISING

The question of effectiveness remained troublesome, even to an industry that embraced the social sciences and sought to apply its techniques to business. Advertisers might agree that psychology was important to their industry, but just how to tap into the mindset of mass America remained debatable. Starting in 1924, the Barney Link Poster Advertising Fellows at the University of Wisconsin began human response studies to determine the relative memory value of billboard advertisements. Although market research of consumer preferences had been conducted in the United States since the 1890s, systematic recollection surveys of billboard advertising had not been previously undertaken. By the 1930s, such studies became an important means by which the industry, like many others, sought to become more effective and efficient during lean economic times. By the 1950s, studies by professional market research companies such as Arthur Little, A. C. Nielson, and Daniel Starch were standard.[1]

The goal of the 1924 Link research was to determine the design elements that comprised effective advertisements. Audiences were asked to recollect advertisements, and were also shown series of posters that they were to rank based on their visceral reactions, "on feeling alone and not on reason and judgment." The results, surveyors wrote, were decisive. Pictures, not text, were best remembered. Moreover, even the most uncultured and uneducated viewer instinctively responded to posters that followed basic principles of art: unity, harmony, proportionality, and congruity. The better the artistic value of the poster, the longer the viewer remembered the ad. "People desire and appreciate good art values," the study concluded.[2]

The study thus supported the axiom that art is a universal mode of expression. It offered evidence that "good art is good business." This was a valuable message for several reasons. It could be used to convince skeptical outdoor advertising companies and their clients that professionally designed posters were worth the investment, that "liberal appropriations for art expense will be fully justified by returns on their sales sheets."[3] It also established a set of criteria or standards with objective value—derived from both scientific survey and the culturally authoritative realm of the fine arts—that the outdoor advertising industry could use to deflect criticism; if a poster was designed by renowned artists and professional illustrators or followed artistic principles, then complaints that it fouled the view or was unsightly could be more easily refuted.

A designer seeking to produce posters according to the guidelines the survey provided would be hard pressed to do so. This, however, was not the point. To assume the moniker (and status) of art was what really mattered, particularly as the outdoor advertising industry honed its machinery of publicity in the 1920s and began to deploy art as a strategy of public relations. The outdoor advertising industry had had some relationship to the fine arts since the 1890s, when an art poster craze seized Europe and then the United States, turning small posters by high-end publishers into collectibles (see plate 2). These were, however, a distant relative to the huge, multistoried painted and posted outdoor advertising signs that stretched for city blocks and towered over urban mansions and professional buildings (see figs. 6, 48). At the height of opposition to such billboards by civic groups and municipal art societies in the early 1900s, the trade association for the outdoor advertising industry began to highlight aesthetics by establishing standards of practice, creating a uniform poster size of twenty-four sheets (104 inches by 234 inches), calling upon members to create more artistic outdoor advertisements, and employing reproductions of old masters and commissioning paintings for public service campaigns.[4] Bearing witness to their enhanced aesthetic sensitivities, the trade association changed its name in 1912 from the Associated Billposters' Association to the Poster Advertising Association, in an effort to remove the taint of the unregulated and inartistic practices of the transient billposter (who had been part of the group's name since 1872) and to align themselves with the art poster.[5]

The greatest victory for outdoor advertisers hoping to ally their industry with art came during World War I, when illustrators of popular and professional success such as Howard Chandler Christy, James Montgomery Flagg, and J. C. Leyendecker created posters for the war effort (see plate 3). The fanfare surrounding their contributions cast the billboard industry in a positive light as well. So did the "Art in Posters" campaign initiated by Fisk Tire (see fig. 15), which was kicked off in 1916 by a commissioned illustration by muralist Maxfield Parrish, well known for his storybook fantasies of medieval times rendered in pastel washes of rich blues and hues of pink and gold.[6] These were all well-publicized precedents for the incursion of professionally trained artists into the world of outdoor advertising, a phenomenon that grew as advertisers spent more money on pictorials while publishing companies and elite magazines (the primary commercial patrons for artists and illustrators before the 1920s) spent less.[7] Regular profiles of poster artists in the *Poster* (the journal that served as the primary mouthpiece for the trade association) and other advertising industry journals, annual poster competitions beginning in 1925, and the publication of poster design manuals professed to the billboard industry's newfound devotion to aesthetics.[8]

The entry of professional illustrators into the arena of billboard design, many of whom had long vied for fine-arts status themselves, was not without its tensions. As billboard owners had acknowledged before the war, few painters and illustrators deigned to do commercial work: "To design a 24-sheet poster was to sell himself to the devil of greed indeed."[9] Then it wasn't an "artist" who made and even signed his advertisement, but whoever was in the employ of the engraving (or lithography) houses and the outdoor advertising company: "In those days the 'real' artists, the highbrows, would have none of it."[10] Still, billboard businessmen knew the advantage of having art on their side, and saw that "the stamp of approval of the best connoisseurs" could be registered in dollar signs, adding to the value of their product. The Foster and Kleiser Company, for instance, recognized that if "Commerce [would] cling to the hand of Art," the future of the poster advertising industry would be lifted beyond businessmen's dreams. Lest this interest seem materialistic, others hastened to explain that the artistic poster played a larger public role from an educational, and even a spiritual, standpoint.[11] Lillian Lilly, publicist for the outdoor advertising trade organization, clarified that the "art route to success is no doubt prompted by what Herbert Hoover commends as 'an intelligent self-interest.' But the net result will be a great influence on art appreciation in America."[12]

Others in the outdoor advertising industry resented the implication that "the standard of posters [was] being raised by painters who now condescend to consider a poster a 'real commission.'" Such men had in mind "only an artistic achievement which shall maintain and enhance their personal reputation." A painting and a poster were not the same thing, critics asserted. Simply enlarging a fine painting to the size of a poster would be "folly from the advertising point and a crime from the art point of view." One did not "stand in front of a poster and study it in an endeavor to find out what it advertises—not even if it were painted by Raphael, Rubens, or Maxfield Parrish."[13] And no matter how beautiful the poster, if it did not embody and put across a "selling idea," then it was a failure. From across the street, did Parrish's posters have "carrying power"? A vociferous contingent believed not, and suspected that his $3,000 commissions were ill-deserved. His "excessive elaboration of detail" and "minutely filled-in backgrounds" might make for picturesque beauty, critics said, but this was at the expense of "poster efficiency." "Artwork *must* sell the public—not *please* the advertiser," they declared.[14]

Members of the outdoor advertising industry may have liked the enhanced reputation they could achieve through an association with art, but as business boomed in the 1920s, they also wanted to claim their own professional niche and cultural significance, without kowtowing to "high" art. Now called the Outdoor Advertising Association of America (OAAA), and representing those with interest in both painted and printed billboards, the trade association's nomenclature paid homage neither to the sticker of bills of the early years nor to his high-art minded sibling. Rather, it signaled corporate modernity, a scientifically engineered enterprise whose art was apropos of the economic ascendancy of the new era. Business had produced a new, "virile" art form, promoters announced, representative of the "throb and color and romance" of American industry. It was the poster. "Decidedly characteristic of America," I. L. Fleming wrote, posters are "symbols of the forward striding American spirit."[15] Which was more representative of American culture, poster proponents asked, dusty museums filled with European art or the all-American billboard? "Art is aristocratic," they said, but the poster "is democratic and for the masses."[16] "Passed in rapid succession," poster boards offered visual scintillation and inspired all who passed by reminding them of "the magnitude and multiplicity of American business . . . [and] the complexity of human interests involved therein." Future historians seeking to understand the spirit of early twentieth-century America, wrote Dugald Shaw, would find more on poster panels "than in much of the art and architecture that we see today."[17]

Over and again, critics wrote of "a distinctly American poster art" that was developing. Americans might not have Europe's centuries of artistic traditions, but they had originality and a pioneering spirit, and soon enough "the native poster artist" would "outdistance his foreign rival."[18] For instance, W. G. Sesser, art director and artist for the Detroit-based outdoor advertising firm Walker and Company, was born in Vienna and trained in Munich, but his style was 100 percent American. He had the perfect blend of "Continental technique with American ideas"—a focus on art tempered by scientific analysis.[19] Indeed, many of the artists profiled in the *Poster* had some European training—this was part of their cultural panache, proof of their ability to uplift the field of advertising as a new art—but they had all escaped its "enervating" effects with "heartening demonstration of real American independency."[20]

On both sides of the Atlantic, artists and intellectuals flaunted the same message, seeing in American industry and engineering the basis for a new and distinctly modern art. Europeans proclaimed that America, unencumbered by Old World cultural and historical baggage, was the youthful progenitor of an aesthetic suitable to the modern technological age. This aesthetic was to be found not in the museum but on the streets. Genuine American culture was "outside the art world," Robert Coady declared in the inaugural issue of the *Soil*, one of the many short-lived "little magazines" that flourished in the United States in the mid-teens.[21] Advertisements, as Mathew Josephson wrote several years later in "The Great American Billposter," were among the elements of a native tradition, serving as "a faithful record of the national tastes, the changing philosophy, the hopes and fears of a people; they compose, in fact, the 'folklore' of modern times." Josephson, like others who contributed to the transatlantic magazine *Broom* (published from 1921 to 1924) claimed that "America will never enjoy an indigenous art, led by its Intellectuals, [if] it adopts approved European methods of living or painting or writing. . . . It is time to examine our home products sympathetically." For him, that "indigenous art" came from mass culture, the "cacophonous milieu . . . where the Billposters enunciate their wisdom, the Cinema transports us, the newspapers intone their gaudy jargon; where athletes play upon the frenetic passions of baseball crowds, and sky-scrapers rise lyrically to the exotic rhythms of jazz bands which upon waking up we find to be nothing but the drilling of pneumatic hammers on steel girders."[22]

Not everyone agreed that advertising and mass culture were suitable subjects for an art that would express the essence of the American character. Critics Van Wyck Brooks, Waldo Frank, and Paul Rosenfeld, along with Alfred Stieglitz and the circle of artists gathered around him, were among those cultural nationalists who believed art should be an antidote to, and not a celebrant of, the unremitting materialism, spiritual torpor, and political conservatism of the machine age. Art, it was felt, should transcend base material existence and restore a humanism eviscerated by soulless technocracy and the controlling hands of efficiency engineers and time clocks.[23]

It was in the face of industry's elevation as the new messiah that these contrarians stood their ground. Indeed, by the 1920s, America was commonly equated with the machine and business, which were, in turn, elevated beyond high art to a religion. "The man who builds a factory builds a temple," pronounced Calvin Coolidge, while advertising man Bruce Barton's parable of Jesus as a businessman topped the best-seller lists of the decade.[24] Joseph Stella devoted himself to painting the kaleidoscopic views of New York that one saw at night from the domes of its "temples devoted to commerce," where the colored lights of the billboards created a "new hymnal of praise." Paintings by Charles Demuth reverentially illustrated the new faith in commercial culture, using the factory, the billboard, and the grain elevator as central images, aestheticized by billowing smoke and exalted light. These works seem to proclaim that industrial culture is a heroic subject for American art.[25]

Demuth not only took commercial culture as his subject, but strove to create an aesthetic that sprang from it. Beginning in 1923, he began a series of eight paintings that he called "poster portraits" in reference to the flat, pareddown style and bold expression of the billboard advertisements he saw around him. Indeed, all of these posters were painted on board and all but one in poster paint to more closely resemble the style of the billboard.[26] Most famous of these posters is *The Figure 5 in Gold* (1928; fig. 20), an homage to his friend, poet William Carlos Williams, and a visual enactment of Williams's spare poem "The Great Figure," which records his impressions of a clanging, howling red fire truck emblazoned with a golden figure 5 that raced by him one rainy summer day. The painting is as much a memorial to the commercial sign painter (and to Demuth himself, painter of signs and creator of a new visual poetics) as it is to Williams. At the top of the image are cutoff letters spelling "Bill," in reference both to his friend William and the billposters craft, while hanging in midair most of the name Carlos is spelled out in lights, as if part of a rooftop illuminated spectacular. In fact, the entire painting, as art historian Wanda Corn explains, can be read as "a poster or billboard advertisement for William Carlos Williams, the Great Figure of American Poetry."[27]

Corn describes the style that Demuth used for his poster portraits as "billboard cubism," a self-conscious fusion of the high art of modernism (as seen in the streaming lines and abstractions of *The Figure 5*), and the lowbrow practices of "bluntness, scale, modern typography, and legibility of 1920s posters." American artists Stuart Davis and Gerald Murphy, she explains, also practiced versions of billboard cubism, as they too sought to create a distinctly American art form that would pay tribute to advertising as the "folklore of modern man."[28]

20. Charles Demuth, *The Figure 5 in Gold*, 1928. Oil on cardboard, 36 x 29 ¾ inches. The Metropolitan Museum of Art, New York, Alfred Stieglitz Collection, 1949 (49.59.1).

Murphy, who lived in Paris, and Davis, who lived in New York (after a year in Paris), both were influenced by their European colleagues' enthusiasm for things American and for formulating a machine-age aesthetic that would speak of the everyday world. In Europe, artists had used advertising to signify both modernity and the need for a new aesthetic. "Smash the museums, wake up to the present," Italian poet Filippo Tommaso Marinetti wrote in his 1910 *Manifesto of Futurism*, using the bold headline typography of advertisements, free floating on the page, to dramatize his point that modern machine technology was more expressive of contemporary life than that which could be found in the gallery, and that art, like advertising, was a form of propaganda. Pablo Picasso and Georges Braque also looked outside the museum and incorporated snippets of advertisements in their cubist collages (Picasso even made a painting referring to billboards, *Landscape with Posters*, 1912), while Guillaume Apollinaire declared poster advertising urban poetry, inspiring the later Dadaists, who used the typographic design and sloganeering of advertising to subvert expectations for both advertising and literature.[29]

The bright colors of the poster offered a plastic contrast to the bland neutrality of the natural landscape, painter Fernand Léger explained. He welcomed the presence of the billboard as a way of shattering sentimental bourgeois expectations of the picturesque in both nature and art. The sensations of speeding in an automobile had displaced the importance of scenery to the traveler, he suggested. "Now, trains and cars . . . take all the dynamism for themselves, and the landscape becomes secondary and decorative." "Posters on the walls, [and] illuminated signs," he continued, "are of the same order of ideas."[30]

Léger's work sought to express the visual sensations of the urban scene, complete with advertising imagery, but without offering particularities about the products or their time and place. The paintings of Léger's friend, American expatriate Murphy, reflected the dynamism of modern commercial culture by more forthrightly appropriating the specific features of the advertisements and product packaging that were his source of influence (and enjoyment). *Razor* (1924), for instance, showcases three consumer products: a Gillette safety razor, a Parker Duofold fountain pen, and a box of Three Star matches, all popular brand-name goods that would have been familiar and easily recognizable to his audiences. The painting is dramatic in its flat, posterlike quality, as each object is schematically rendered (albeit with exactitude), without shadowing or tonality, and enlarged to fill the three-foot-wide canvas.[31] The objects are painted as if to be read from a distance, fulfilling the billboard painters' dicta for simplicity and legibility. Murphy even seems to have learned the lessons provided by the movies, zooming in on his objects like a close-up (as Léger aptly observed).[32] Though the objects are set on a background of abstract shapes (in the palette of early cubism), the picture looks undeniably like an advertisement, and the artist seems to delight in its blatant commercial and materialist expression.

Also rendering the popular artifacts of everyday life with the graphic assertiveness of an advertiser, Davis sought to capture a sense of the American experience in paintings of such subjects as Odol disinfectant and Lucky Strike cigarettes. His was an irreverent and witty form of cultural nationalism, deeming even a common household cleaner worthy of art and expressive of Americanness. Davis's goal was not just to represent everyday life, in all its pedestrian incarnations, but also to do so in a manner immediately recognizable to the man on the street. As with Léger and those who wrote in *Broom*, Davis perceived advertising to be an American vernacular, as were jazz and other elements of mass culture.[33] In *Lucky Strike* (1924), one of a series of cigarette paintings he made, Davis illustrates this (fig. 21). The painting featured a

21. Stuart Davis, *Lucky Strike*, 1924. Oil on paperboard, 18 x 24 inches. Hirshhorn Museum and Sculpture Garden, Smithsonian Institution, Museum Purchase, 1974. © Estate of Stuart Davis/ Licensed by VAGA, New York.

billboard of the front page of a newspaper sports section, with a cartoon at center, along with packages of Lucky Strike tobacco and Zig-Zag rolling papers, and a pipe—all of which bear "garrulous, masculine, and populist association."[34] Like Murphy, Davis does not abstract his sources. They remain clearly recognizable, and are even selected and arranged in a manner not unlike the poster artist, with an economy and abbreviation of imagery aimed toward easy legibility. Davis's appropriation of the formal strategies of advertisers—flattened forms, unmodulating colors, simple logos—and his references to the subject matter of mass culture were part of his quest to create work that was distinctly expressive of the advertising world's popular picture making.[35]

At the same time as artists in the 1920s were celebrating advertising as art, and seeking to model its picture making, advertisers were considering the value of modern art to their work. The West Coast, in particular, became known within the outdoor advertising industry as the most forward thinking, with Foster and Kleiser Company being in the vanguard of the "new wave" of poster design. The biggest company in the west, Foster and Kleiser organized their first formal art department in 1917, offering complete art services to clients and advertising agencies and employing artists from the realm of the fine arts, such as Maurice Del Mue and Maynard Dixon, as well as those who favored stylized designs, such as Arnold Armitage, Jacob Asanger, Robert E. Lee, Fred Ludekens, and Otis Shepard. With art directors versed in modernism, the company produced the most progressive posters of any in the industry, including Del Mue's "Along Pacific Shores," Armitage's Los Angeles Steamship to Hawaii, and Asanger's "symbolic conception" of the "Evolution of Whole Wheat Bread." All employed cubofuturistic elements, using overlapping abstract forms and bright, contrasting colors (in a palette lighter than was the norm) to provoke attention and to evoke sensations or make symbolic associations with the products advertised.[36] Through such work, Foster and Kleiser became known as an incubator for modern design, a reputation they embraced, as exemplified by their ads throughout the 1920s in the *Poster*, which not only featured the work of the artists in their atelier, but employed innovative typefaces, geometric abstractions, cubist perspectives, and art deco motifs—zig-zag lines, starbursts, and skyscraper set-backs.[37]

For many of the commercial artists who embraced formal strategies drawn from contemporary art, these new techniques expanded the range of solutions to the problems of advertising to modern audiences. The "exaggeration of sizes and proportions, use of many planes and dimensions, new arrangements and relations of lettering and design, symbolism, the teachings of all other isms down to the newest movement: 'Die neue Sachlichkeit' (new objectivity), are media at the disposal of the designer today to express emotion, speed, our domination of space and time," Asanger wrote. The designer could "solve his problems in an abstract or purely intellectual way; . . . appeal to humor and the heart-strings of humanity without employing old, cheap, sob-sister stuff." In the quest for the new, modernism offered a seemingly universal vocabulary of forms that required less and delivered more. It marked the logical next step in the speed-up of modern visual communication, offering visceral stimuli to an audience moving faster and becoming increasingly inured to pictorial conventions.

Indeed, the West Coast style that Asanger represented marked a notable departure from the realistic, Rockwellian posters—those with "human-interest appeal"—that dominated outdoor advertising (see figs. 17–19), particularly in the Midwest and East Coast, where more conventional approaches prevailed.[38] Foster and Kleiser's billboard for Tacoma Gas Company, for instance, with its "sharp silhouette" of a cubist figure stoking a furnace set against rippling lines of glowing color, was said to create an "immediate sensation" (fig. 22). Its reliance on line, color, and form rather than sentiment or narrative, and its use of the formal qualities of modern art to represent industry defied expectation.[39] Other designers concurred that modern art techniques provided a "valuable force in memory value," and were capable of quickly attracting the eye.[40] For the Montmartre Café in Hollywood, modern stylization—including sans-serif lettering, repeated forms, and machinelike figures, all arranged in an angular pattern—was employed to emphasize the nightclub's French pretensions of cosmopolitanism. Food was never featured in their ads, the club boasted, and only the "highest type" of futurism was employed to suggest "Elegance, Luxury, Fashion" and to convey "sumptuous sophistication."[41] A modern appearance expressed their elitist predilections.

Not all poster ads used modern art just to seem sophisticated. Others sought to represent the accelerating pace of contemporary life, and an ethos of freewheeling enterprise. For instance, billboards along Los Angeles's Wilshire Boulevard (among other locations) for Joe Toplinsky Real Estate offered a futuristic transcription of car culture and the frenzied pace of real-estate speculation in Southern California of the 1920s (fig. 23). The letters sway in the motion of the all-over design, in which the nocturnal view of cars with shining headlights speed by towering skyscrapers in a blur of glimmering activity. The ad suggests the changed relationship of viewers in the automobile age to time and space, exalting speed and movement as if to fulfill the manifestos of the Italian futurists "to express our whirling life of steel, of price, of fever and of speed."[42]

22. **Modernistic poster for Tacoma Gas and Fuel Company, 1928.**

23. **Painting of "speed in night traffic," for Joe Toplinsky Real Estate Company, Los Angeles, by Foster and Kleiser Company, c. 1930.**

Unlike static representational imagery, modern art techniques were an embodied expression, as Leonard Stevenson put it, of the "pulse of the modern world." Its visual language bespoke "the kaleidoscopic changes of relationship between a social and industrial world." Stevenson's commentary suggests that the formal approach of the modern designer was guided by underlying, ideological reasons. Advertisers, he explained, used art that proceeded "step by step with the evolution of our now gigantic industrial system." "Is it not natural," he asked, "that the Outdoor Design which is closest of all to the life of the people should begin to sense the transition from a commercial world that was hand-made, self-willed, absolute and individual to one which is mass-produced, merger-managed, problematical and statistical?" Stevenson advised that advertisers employ "universal, impersonal, symbolic and colorful expressions," not merely to appear modern or sophisticated, but because this better expressed corporate society, in which the individual was sublimated to the mass.[43]

Poster artists regularly invoked symbolism as one of the hallmarks of modernity in poster design. Otis Shepard—a dyed-in-the-wool outdoor advertising man who had joined Foster and Kleiser in 1917 and was its art director from 1923 until he left in 1929 to design posters for Wrigley's—explained, "The artist who works in the modern style works in symbols of one kind or another, either intellectual, such as words and phrases; literalistic, representations of the photographic kind; or subconscious symbols, getting his effect through an appeal to certain mental reactions without the realization of the onlooker. The modern approach differs from the traditional method in that it makes greater use of the latter kind of symbols." Like modern artists, Shepard also believed that line, color, and form had aesthetic values unto themselves, whether they represented something or not, and that they were a means of universal communication, speaking "an almost primitive language" and appealing to "intuitive emotions."[44] Thus, he advocated the use of abstract forms, even though his advertising campaigns in the 1920s never relied solely on abstraction. Rather, as in one of his series of ads for General Gasoline, Shepard uses the representational figure of a baseball player captured in the act of catching a ball to symbolize quick pick up (fig. 24). Streaming lines suggest the speed of the ball, and the sans-serif letters spelling General Gasoline run off the top of the poster to emphasize the action of the scene. In his 1929 Chesterfield cigarettes billboard, Shepard uses a backdrop of abstract geometric shapes and diagonal lines to highlight the schematized rendering of a fashionably vogue young woman in art deco attire to illustrate the message of the ad: "After all, it's taste." In later campaigns for Wrigley's Doublemint chewing gum, he abstracts the female visage further, multiplying them and cleverly using the negative space between each to incorporate Wrigley's trademark arrow (the "spear" in *spearmint*; plate 7). The flattened frontal view of the repeating faces, the overlapping planes of color in strong tones, and the machined surfaces and geometric forms are reminiscent of the abstractions of Léger, whose techniques were well known in advertising circles through their influence and application by another poster artist, A. M. Cassandre, whose work plastered the streets of Paris in the 1920s. A Russian-born designer who migrated to Paris as a youth, Cassandre's posters emphasized the two-dimensional, and clean, smooth-edged, machine-derived forms.[45] His work in the United States was dramatically stark, employing symbolic imagery in his 1920s campaign for the Star of the North railroad company, and an eye with "V-8" reflected in it for Ford's 1937 campaign "Watch the Fords Go By."[46]

Shepard was influenced by yet another European designer, Joseph Binder,

24. Otis Shepard's depiction of General Gasoline's quick "pick up," 1927.

25. Airbrushed poster by Vienna-born designer Joseph Binder, 1938.

whom he visited in the late 1920s in Vienna. Binder came to the United States to teach in 1933, then settled in New York with his wife in 1935. His airbrushed style, chiseled forms, and concrete graphic simplicity—as seen in his award-winning 1938 poster for Ballantine beer (fig. 25)—is paralleled in Shepard's work of the 1930s.[47] Binder, Cassandre, and other European designers such as Lucien Bernhard and Jean Carlu were generously mentioned in trade journals and, throughout the 1930s, received recognition in poster annuals. Bernhard won poster design awards regularly in the 1930s and was widely discussed, particularly for his belief in a comprehensive approach to design from the manufacture of the object to its merchandising, and his assertions that poster design should use "all the power and speed [that] line, form, mass, and color give you."[48] Several of these artists went on to contribute well-regarded posters to World War II publicity efforts (plate 8).

However, while poster designers liked to talk about modern approaches, their employment of them was quite uneven. Most were unwilling to engage completely the symbolic and abstract approaches of European modernists. Indeed, most outdoor advertising companies were conservative in their approaches to design, staying distant from the cubist and futurist modes of representation that were toyed with on the West Coast. However, even those illustrators and art directors whose work did not outwardly read as "modernistic" did oftentimes strive toward the modern through appliqués of streaming lines, slightly abstracted forms, overlapping planes, or fractured perspective. Inconsistently employed within even one poster, such devices read as mere overlay, lacking conviction. Still, the attempts to employ modernistic elements were relevant to the formulation of an aesthetics of speed. *Dynamic symmetry* was the oft-repeated term for the underlying structure that the poster artist was urged to follow. In the 1930s this was a catch phrase for more abstract approaches that were aimed to streamline the design of billboard advertisements as a means of metaphorically galvanizing or efficiently boosting the flow of the economy itself.[49] Most of all, designers were encouraged to capture a sense of motion in their work, to lure viewers into the scene and quickly back out of it again. Billboard campaigns such as McClelland Barclay's for Atlantic Gasoline (see fig. 11), Clarence Underwood's for Palmolive Soap (see fig. 17), and Shepard's for General Gasoline (see fig. 24) were all lauded for their expressions of dynamic movement, with elements arranged "to follow the natural course of the eye" in a sweep that arched from left to right.[50] Such work represented the persistent concerns for immediacy, speed, and simplicity.

In 1929, the *Poster* summarized questions members of the industry had been asking for several years: "Do you want modernism in advertising art?" Participants agreed that whatever imagery would work most immediately was what they wanted, since "people buy with their eyes." Proponents claimed that modernism expressed complex thoughts rapidly and simply, while opponents stressed that the public was not educated enough to "understand the expression of modernism." "Too highbrow" was a common criticism.[51] Several years earlier Andrew Loomis, well known for his tear-jerking Ivory Soap poster illustrations, simply said, "Understandable art is always better than the so-called modernistic art," while another designer said that the advertiser wants to reach his barber, not a cubist.[52] Interestingly, the participants in the 1929 discussion expressed a different view, one claiming that his experience was "that a clerk in a store frequently knows more about modernism than is generally known by a member of the so-called 'upper class.' Is it not a fact that the clerk is closer to everyday life than anyone else? Modernism itself expresses the present time in everyday life." Even a critic of modernism agreed, claiming that he did not believe "that all the culture is to be found in the upper classes."[53]

Despite their egalitarian reasoning, outdoor advertisers persisted in their use of realism. But this did not mean that they were any less committed to the idea of immediate and universal modes of aesthetic expression. On the contrary, the stereotypes they employed in Rockwellian posters were also a kind of flattened form, emptied of excess detail and void of the need for thoughtful concentration. Though perhaps overtly realistic, such billboards nevertheless abided by basic ideas of simplicity, limiting the number of elements in the advertisement, and seeking the most elementary themes to communicate as universally as possible. As historian James Fraser explains, stylized realism, as employed by Otis Shepard, rather than stylized symbolism, which was the domain of European-influenced modernist design, was as avant-garde as the outdoor advertising industry would get.[54]

The increasing reliance of advertisers on the simple picture, the slogan, and the trademark was part of the aesthetic of speed they developed to reach motorists. The methods they employed were frequently literal. They sought not just to be read quickly but to actually embody speed, movement, and power—instinctive forces, they believed, that would be naturally understood by the primitive, childlike mentalities of their audience. Whereas spectators pictured in the panoramic auto advertisements of the 1920s surveyed the landscape through which they motored (see fig. 13, plate 6), the brand name and the logo usurp the scene in other outdoor ads of the 1920s and 1930s (fig. 26).[55] The "magisterial gaze" was now corporate controlled. Yet the transition to logo devices did not alter the basic aims of outdoor advertisements, which still sought to instill in auto tourists the correct behavior of consuming landscapes. Representational signs of mobility and the landscape are still present, even though they begin to include the overshadowing presence of the logo. This may have been a way to "naturalize" the logo, accustoming audiences to the sign as stand-in for an otherwise difficult-to-visualize product, and placing it outdoors where it served as the literal signpost. Over the course of the 1930s this would give way to less descriptive and more embodied logo expressions, though many competing designs still persisted.

A survey of poster ads for Union 76 motor oil from the 1920s and 1930s shows how the landscape imagery became further reduced in each campaign, to the point where the logo *is* the landscape (fig. 27). The overblown numerals have a sway or swagger, the extent of which is one of the few changing variables in its design over the years. The *7* and the *6* have become the logo, a fact

26. Margaret Bourke-White's photograph for a 1928 Goodyear campaign offers a three-dimensional logo as landscape.

27. The 76 logo comprises the entire landscape in this 1935 poster.

that many designers might have missed. Indeed, numerous other campaigns used similar symbols for power and motion, but they misunderstand the technique regarding the repeated and dominant form as the element of greatest importance. Refiners gasoline company illustrated its 1933 assertions of power by presenting a brutish arm with sleeve rolled up, larger than life and ready to do the job. The poster takes human power in conjunction with mechanical power as its subject, conveying an important Depression-era subtext of optimism and the power of human ingenuity, strength, and willingness to work hard. Its image of power and mobility, as with many other posters from the period, offer hopeful suggestions for economic and national rejuvenation, bringing the nation back up to speed. Still missing, however, is the one singular, repeated, and easily graspable image of the logo.

Sinclair gasoline posters from 1934 and 1935 (fig. 28) show the transition

28. Sinclair's dinosaurs and "lifting power," 1934–35.

from the ornate panoramic scenes of the Lincoln Motor ad (see fig. 13) and the historical "Book Boards" (see fig. 14) to the logo. Unlike the 76 logo, Sinclair's whale, dinosaur, and tanker each have some relationship to oil (from which gas is refined), even if a bit farfetched. Sinclair's logo in these ads is the round seal with *HC* in the center. However, the dinosaur is what had staying power and is what in later years became Sinclair's primary symbol, attesting to the power of the image, the icon, over the name spelled out. Also, unlike the 76 logo, there is still some referential quality to the dinosaur as a symbol of the archaic, extracted resource of gasoline and the power that it provides. The dinosaur has a terrific power; though extinct, its remnants have persisted. These referential qualities distinguish the dinosaur as logo from abstract forms as logos, the latter requiring fewer imaginative leaps of interpretation. The dinosaur marks a transition to the modern logo.

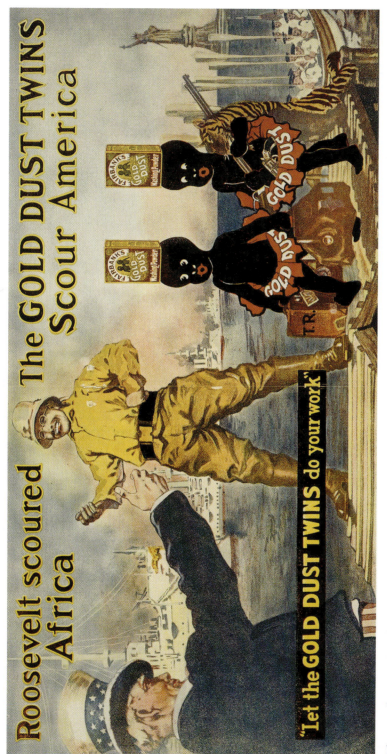

Plate 1. The American buyway on the heels of Theodore Roosevelt's African safari, 1910.

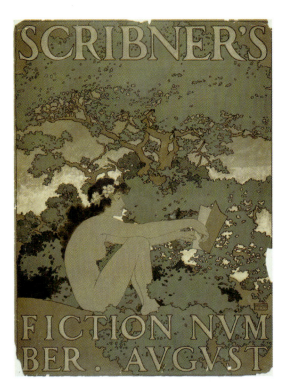

Plate 2. Maxfield Parrish, poster advertisement for *Scribner's*, August 1897.

Plate 3. Howard Chandler Christy, Third Liberty Loan poster, 1917.

Plate 4. George Merrick's real estate development of Coral Gables was advertised in New York City, among other places, 1926.

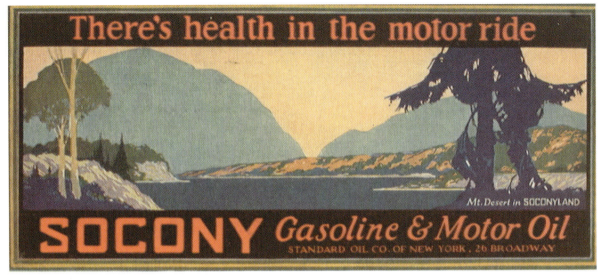

Plate 5. Mt. Desert, Maine, 1926, one of a series of posters for Standard Oil Company of New York featuring scenic destinations.

Plate 6. Grand Canyon was among the natural wonders presented in a gilt frame by the Gulf Refining Company, 1924.

Plate 7. The abstract stylization of Otis Shepard's 1932 Wrigley's poster granted him recognition as a European-influenced designer.

Plate 8. Jean Carlu, who came to the United States in 1937 from Paris, won acclaim for his wartime poster for the Division of Information, Office of Emergency Management, 1941.

Plate 9. Coca-Cola followed contemporary dictates for good poster design by employing silhouettes and Freudianisms, 1950.

Plate 10. Bursting out of the billboard frame, bright as Technicolor, 1950s.

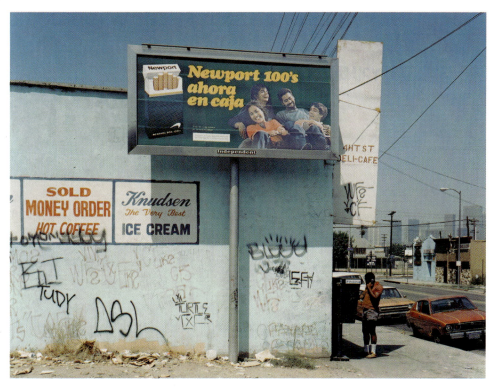

Plate 11. By the 1980s, it was common practice to target ethnic communities through billboards. Photograph by John Humble of Fourth Street at Pecan Street, Los Angeles, July 24, 1984. Courtesy Jan Kesner Gallery, Los Angeles.

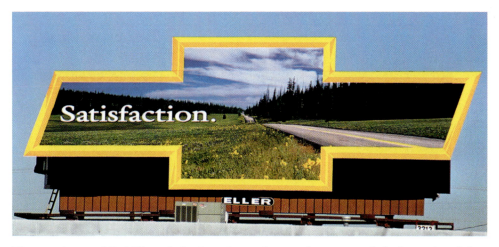

Plate 12. Automobile billboards in the 1980s and 1990s demonstrated the longevity of the myth of the open road and the design strategy in which the logo becomes the landscape.

Plate 13. For years, the Marlboro Man, flanked by Calvin Klein, loomed over the Sunset Strip in West Hollywood, 1995.

The power of the image to make quick identifications or associations remained central to mobile communication and the way it was discussed throughout the years between the two world wars and beyond. Ford ran an extremely popular and acclaimed series of posters for its V-8 that featured a sinewy greyhound and a barrel-chested terrier speaking of speed and power (fig. 29). This "talking dogs" campaign ran from 1931 through the 1950s. It won poster awards and was heralded by the general art director of the Foster and Kleiser outdoor advertising company, Walter Warde, in his 1947 publication *Poster Design.*[56] Warde shows the image silhouetted to illustrate his three most important goals for outdoor advertising: that it is "quick reading," has a "simple" message, and avoids "subtleties." This "three-element plan," he shows, is the way to good design (fig. 30). From the look of it, modernist artists of the day, from Davis, Demuth, and Léger to the constructivists and suprematists in Russia to the Bauhaus designers in Germany, would have agreed. The silhouette that Warde promotes here proves his point of simplicity without sacrifice to speed. Indeed, only the most basic of block images, nuance-free, without detail and without multiple dimensions, will work.

Warde's message has continued to define the approach of outdoor advertisers to the present day. In the 1940s and 1950s, bigger was better, but without forgetting the basic principles of the aesthetics of speed, as encapsulated in Warde's theory of the silhouette (plate 9).[57] The effectiveness of the silhouette is a result of the compression that takes place in producing the outlines and massed forms so that detail and shadowing become less important to legibility. The logo is similar to the silhouette in that it does not need to be viewed frontally or with the illusions of the three-dimensional to be recognized. Glimpsed from the corner of one's eye, through a windshield of a moving car, the image need only flicker for a moment to be perceived. Its outline is what forms an impression, and, advertisers would hope, a lasting one.

By flattening and reducing the number of forms employed in the advertisement, these techniques offered ways in which meaning might be left open, not for the sake of multiplicity but rather for transferability. A compressed and standard-enough image can be traded from one product to another, regardless of who or what is produced or sold. With the logo as the tool of communication, greater numbers of products and advertisements can be distributed without loss in legibility. Indeed, quite the opposite is the case. As time wears on, readership may recognize with greater speed the even slighter variations, especially notable when viewed with less time and attention. These aesthetics of speed and powers of picturization were strategies by which outdoor advertis-

29. Howard Scott's "talking dogs" campaign, c. 1931.

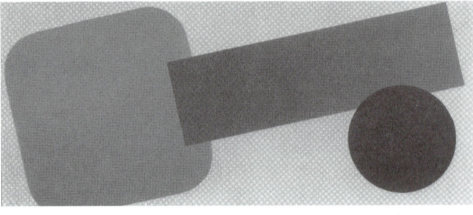

30. Illustration of Walter Warde's "three-element plan" integral to good poster design, 1947.

ers could both represent and induce mobility. They were intended to enhance the quantity and the quality of production–of both mobile audiences and of landscape of signs–without suffering loss to the transience of either.

To keep motorists moving right along, with a few stops for the goods and services that would keep them going, was envisioned by outdoor advertisers as the ultimate in assembly-line production of mobile consumers. In order to truly succeed, however, they needed to figure out not simply mass production but also mass distribution, of outdoor advertisements as well as the commodity that the billboard industry bought and sold, mobile audiences. The distribution of both was key to the industry and to understanding the shape and experience of the American landscape in the age of the automobile.

PART 2

DISTRIBUTING TRAFFIC AND TRADE

DECENTRALIZATION AND THE BIRTH OF THE STRIP

VISUALIZING DISTRIBUTION

In 1925, Secretary of Commerce Herbert Hoover announced with pride that since the end of the Great War America's ability to make quality goods had reached historic levels of efficiency and magnitude. America had become the most productive country in the world. Along with this boast, however, the secretary felt he needed to issue a warning. Massive production was worthwhile only if was matched by consumption. Otherwise, goods would pour off American assembly lines only to sit in warehouses. For production to match consumption business had to predict, and even promote, what the amount of consumption would be. That is to say, businesses required a clear picture of how to distribute to new markets all the things it produced. Hoover bemoaned that, for all its recent economic progress, America still lacked "the basic data of distribution." He called for "accurate and adequate knowledge of where and what the market is, and the means it can be reached most economically and effectively," and he delegated this task both to the U.S. Department of Commerce and to private industry in a shared, cooperative effort.[1] Later, as president, Hoover went so far as to advocate government help in "stimulating consumption."[2] He suggested that business and government together could promote product distribution and thereby secure a firm financial future for all classes of Americans. Advertisers welcomed Hoover's warning as confirmation of what they had claimed from long before the war and, moreover, claimed that their service was the best way to create these mass markets and solve the national problem of distribution.

Outdoor advertisers concurred with Hoover, but they also especially understood a further distribution dilemma: the market now *moved*. Compared with the compact urban market of yesteryear, audiences now expanded seemingly without boundaries. Outdoor advertisers had helped to put people on the road to consumption by promoting automotive products and tourism, while these same efforts created automotive audiences. But now that people steadily used the road they had to be reached there. With automobiles and the open road, *there* could be almost anywhere. To compete in the larger national advertising industry, outdoor advertisers had to quantify and qualify the mobile market in terms understandable to the advertising agent, retailer, and manufacturer alike. In short, advertisers had to learn where their mobile audiences were going and how to place outdoor advertisements to reach them efficiently and nationally. They began to recognize the "crying need for closer analyses" and "keen visualization" of "markets and methods of reaching them."[3]

By recognizing a mobile market, charting its patterns, inscribing those patterns onto the landscape through an architecture of mobility, and promoting the commercial strip—the ideal space for mobile consumption—outdoor advertisers would help to define the shape of the decentralizing environment. Outdoor advertising emerges as a significant missing element in the story of commercial growth and urban deconcentration. Beyond this, the question of how to court a mobile market now concerned far more business arenas than that of the roadside in which outdoor advertisers first raised the issue. How could business identify the parameters of a constantly shifting market? Was it possible to locate, predict, court, and sell to an audience on the go?

CHAPTER 6

THE CONSOLIDATION AND GROWTH
OF NATIONAL ADVERTISING

Though national advertising campaigns began in the nineteenth century, the advertising boom really came with the twentieth. It accompanied such phenomenon as developments in communications and transportation, the expansion of public leisure activities like movies and sporting events, the rise in mass-produced goods, and the concomitant decline in home-based production.

Of all these developments, perhaps the steady increase in the use of brands and trademarks was most critical in allowing advertising campaigns to go national. Before the 1870s, generic products, sold in bulk, were not branded. Once they were put into standardized consumer-sized packages, however, they could be named, and, as historian Richard Tedlow has noted, "What a manufacturer could name, he could advertise." While a national cracker campaign was inconceivable for most of the nineteenth century, Uneeda Biscuit was a recognizable product.[1] Similarly, Ivory could be distinguished from other soaps, Crisco from other fats, and Coca-Cola from other sugar waters. Branding also offered a sense of unchanging quality and accountability, and consumers learned to trust the name instead of their own abilities to discern product quality. When traveling through unfamiliar terrain, just seeing the name Gulf or Standard was enough to signify quality and nationally consistent values. The brand became its own endorsement.

Along with the use of branding, businessmen also became aware of the fiscal sense in advertising en masse. As the head of Aunt Jemima Mills put it, "National distribution demands national advertising with its attendant cost, which in the very nature of things would be less per unit of sale on a nationally distributed piece of goods than it would be on a locally distributed piece of goods."[2] In other words, though large advertising efforts had large price tags, the cost was small per unit. Outdoor advertisers agreed that their provision of masses of posted and painted ads were "an economic necessity to many of the large manufacturers."[3]

Prior to the 1880s, outdoor advertising enjoyed greater revenues than any other media, but by the end of the nineteenth century it lost its privileged place to print advertising with the growth of mass magazines.[4] Magazines exploited the economies of scale possible through their national circulation. In 1893, when Frank Munsey began pricing his monthly publication (called, modestly enough, *Munsey's* magazine) far below those of his competitors and even lower than his cost of production, his circulation rose considerably. With increased distribution, Munsey then sold volumes of advertising exceeding the money he had spent on production.[5] He had caused a media revolution, and other magazines were soon forced to follow suit, increasing their advertising and profiting not from sale of their publication to readers, but from the sale of their readers' attention to the advertisers featured therein.

Attention to circulation changed both the magazine and advertising industries. Prior to this time, advertising agents were space brokers, bartering with publishers for blocks of advertising space that the agent then sold off piecemeal to clients. By the 1890s, magazines and newspapers were beginning to standardize their advertising rates and to verify their readership. As competition between advertising agencies increased, they demanded more uniform and justified practices. Space began to be charged according to circulation, and attempts to verify circulation figures became points of contention. Publishers resisted efforts of outside agencies to determine circulation figures but were soon overcome. The Audit Bureau of Circulation (ABC) was established in 1914 as the nonpartisan adjudicator to verify circulation. Though publishers still did not like being surveyed, magazine membership in the ABC rose from 54 publishers in 1914 to 173 in 1924; 217 in 1944; and 267 in 1954.[6]

Outdoor advertisers watched the rationalization of periodical advertising space, with the accompanying rise in revenues, and sought to appropriate the new system. But print and outdoor advertising were quite different. Circulation figures for publications could be assessed by counting how many magazines were printed, purchased, and transported through the mail or by delivery. Initially, radio followed a similar procedure when it determined its circulation according to numbers of radio sets owned, where and by whom, and what broadcasting stations could reach them. In both print and radio, advertisements circulated to the audience. For outdoor advertisers the contrary was true. Their advertisement stood still while the audience moved. Though they could look to periodical circulation auditing procedures somewhat, they needed to determine how to reach an audience actually *in* circulation.

Despite the difficulties of tracking a mobile audience (a process described in the next chapter), outdoor advertisers recognized that to compete in increasingly nationalized mass markets with magazines, at the very least they needed to centralize the oversight of their industry and create their own functional Audit Bureau. They watched Henry Ford and Chevrolet refine the "scientific" methods of mass production and witnessed chain stores master methods of mass distribution.[7] Manufacturers and advertisers alike realized "the truth of Henry Ford's principle . . . that, 'The way for the little man to use the best methods is to get big.'"[8] It had also become obvious that the magazine had positioned itself as the best big medium with which to advertise nationally. If the outdoor advertising industry did not begin to better standardize and distribute its space, as well as begin to justify its prices with reasonable circulation figures, it would be driven out of the competitive market. The industry had to follow the "definite trend toward larger distributive units with increased centralization of control" in order to compete in the economies of mass distribution.[9] Otherwise it would face the same sense of doom felt by the independent baker who watched the Piggly Wiggly Supermarket chain move in next door to hawk Uneeda Biscuits, and the cobbler who found Tom McAn his new neighbor.

Consolidation was no small matter for an industry that, historically, had been composed of small "mom-and-pop" shops. Well into the 1920s, trade journals published nostalgic stories about how businesses passed from father to son, many of the elder generation having started in show business or as theater, opera, and town hall managers. Obituaries also told of fathers, husbands, and brothers whose outdoor companies were taken over by female relatives. Other articles highlighted women-owned companies, congratulating the women for their success in running the business when their husbands or brothers became incapacitated or died. The occasional photo illustrations indicated their authors' delight in the image of the women in painters' overalls carrying and climbing ladders all around town. These published accounts as well as sales advertisements for billboard businesses reveal the nature of the work and the capital it required: after the initial investment in billboard construction, the business had low overhead and expenses and could be managed by few employees (a frequent claim being that the "owner can do everything").[10]

The haphazard ways in which outdoor advertising space was bought and sold baffled advertisers who had become accustomed to the easily available circulation figures and standardized rates for space in periodicals. Thousands of different companies scattered across America owned outdoor poster boards and painted displays, the prices of which were equally diverse. Geographic regions had different population densities, and even the visibility of advertising structures differed. Prices seemed to be dictated more by whim than by market.[11]

By 1891, poster advertisers created their own regulating body, the Associated Billposters' Association, which underwent several name changes until the group joined forces with owners of painted bulletins in 1925 to create the Outdoor Advertising Association of America (OAAA), which still exists today. From less than 100 members in 1897, the association grew to 5,137 in 1918; 6,139 in 1920; and 9,297 in 1922; it quickly became the conduit for all national advertising.[12] It authorized representatives as solicitors and established consistent methods for tracking the locations and durations of national outdoor campaigns, calling them "showings." This step in the organization of the industry changed the billposter, as one trade journal put it, "from a wandering, irresponsible poster of paper to an important link in the chain of distribution. He became a 'plant' owner and a business man."[13] (A "plant" comprised all of the advertising structures owned by one billboard company within a city or town.) The transformation was also from itinerant (and sometimes illicit) billposter to real-estate broker, responsible for buying, leasing, and vigilantly searching for new properties. He was also responsible for maintaining the structures he erected according to standards supplied by the association.

The association thus created the modern outdoor advertising industry as it sought to capture the national advertising market by establishing national standards. From its inception, the trade association boldly advised its members not to work with general advertising agencies even though most print advertising was placed through these agencies. Beginning in 1911 it required members to take national work only from designated "direct-selling" companies; soon, only solicitors that handled outdoor advertising exclusively could be recognized as a direct selling company. This meant that even the N. W. Ayer and Son agency, which had handled outdoor advertising since 1898, was cut entirely out of the loop.[14] Direct-selling companies could be licensed as such only if they agreed to place national ad campaigns with association members exclusively. Members, in turn, were prohibited from accepting business from nonlicensed solicitors. The situation remained advantageous to members, since the association denied new applications for membership unless the applicant billboard company covered territory not represented currently, and only one billboard company from any one city or town was granted membership. The association also pressured lithography companies not to furnish posters for nonmembers. All of these activities resulted in reducing the number of nonmember billboard companies, and practically eliminated the role of advertising agencies in the outdoor advertising business.[15]

Unfortunately these arrangements were not entirely legal. In 1912, the association and several member companies were accused under the Sherman Antitrust Act of intent to conspire. Resolution came with the Landis Decree of 1916, which forbid the association and its members from continuing their exclusive relationship. The association was forced to allow advertising agencies and nonmembers to compete in the distribution of national outdoor advertising campaigns and was enjoined from restricting membership to one member for each city and town. In theory, at least, the association and its members complied. In practice, they continued to favor direct-selling companies, though without requiring this in writing.[16]

The 1912 antitrust case served as an important marker in the history of the industry, not so much marking its limitations but rather its unstoppable consolidation. Soon after the Landis Decree the large companies of Barney Frank and Kerwin Fulton joined to form the Poster Advertising Company, which, between 1916 and 1925, handled 75 percent of all national outdoor advertising campaigns. Meanwhile, a group of advertising agencies formed a nonprofit service organization, the National Outdoor Advertising Bureau (NOAB), to procure national campaigns, which in turn colluded with the Thomas Cusack Company, begun in 1875 and by 1924 the largest outdoor advertising company in the world, with assets of over $26 million, and transacting approximately 50 percent of all outdoor advertising in the United States.[17] The Poster Advertising Company and the Thomas Cusack Company battled for dominance of the East Coast and the Midwest until 1925, when they decided that it was better to join forces than to whittle themselves away through senseless competition. They formed the General Outdoor Advertising Company (a consolidation of approximately 140 companies), and continued to collude with the NOAB, which gave more than 90 percent of its business to General.[18]

Not wishing to be bereft of the benefits of conspiracy, the West Coast firm of Foster and Kleiser demonstrated its approval of the 1925 merger when George Kleiser agreed to sit on General's board of directors, and also accepted fifty thousand shares of General for the Foster and Kleiser Investment Company–owned by Kleiser, Walter Foster, and members of their families. The companies also agreed that Foster and Kleiser would limit its operations to the region west of the Rocky Mountains while General would remain in the east, thus further avoiding the irritations of competition. This division of the national market between two behemoths put them in control of "approximately 90 percent of all poster and paint plants in the United States located in cities, towns, and villages having a population of 10,000 people or more." Even in towns of less than ten thousand, the two companies exercised substantial control simply through their domination of national campaigns, which was becoming close to 75 percent of the outdoor advertising business.[19] Needless to say, these two utterly dominated the OAAA.

It surprised no one when in 1928 the OAAA was again accused of violating antitrust laws, this time with General, NOAB, and Foster and Kleiser as the accusation's focus. The case was dismissed when the OAAA volunteered to reorganize conditions of membership, but trade association papers of the time reflect no upheaval or discontinuity. Though the national association agreed to turn control of membership over to state associations, it continued to insist that only one membership per town, city, or market could be granted. The stubborn practice would lead to their third antitrust suit in 1950.

Meanwhile, advertisers were becoming more insistent that advertising agencies handle all aspects of their national campaigns. By 1928, outdoor advertisers were watching their national business drop even as radio advertising–which had used agencies from its inception–boomed. They were forced to admit that their longstanding contentious relationship with agencies benefited no one. This admission was probably abetted by the U.S. Department of Justice's investigation of General's monopoly, and a new consent decree in 1929 that forced the company to let NOAB and agencies place business where they wished.[20] With the onset of the Depression, however, few gains could be made. It was with this in mind that in 1931 Outdoor Advertising Incorporated (OAI) was formed, with Kerwin Fulton at its helm, for the purposes of publicizing outdoor advertising as nationally feasible and repairing the unpleasant relationship with national advertisers and agencies.[21]

Although the scale of operations at the big outdoor firms advantaged their securing national campaigns, they still depended on smaller OAAA members to fulfill promises of countrywide coverage. The fate of the giants was tied up with the industry at large. Indeed, as the volume of national advertising campaigns grew, so did the problems of providing adequate and consistent coverage. The OAAA scolded members not to promise coverage they could not deliver. "You are your brother's keeper," wrote one billboard owner, explaining that when one of them took on a national campaign their service reflected on all participating outdoor advertising companies.[22] Some advised that "care should be exercised that a new customer does not expect letter-perfect service from all posting plants. The ideal in this respect can never be fully realized as long as so many different individualities and changing physical conditions are so largely factors in the actual execution of our business."[23]

OAAA trade papers presented the perils of insubordination by small shops. In one article the Fisk Tire company agreed, stating frankly that "the individual plant owner has nothing to sell to national accounts; the national advertiser is looking for wide poster distribution and not for a local showing; in fact, we make it a specialty not to use posters in towns that are not association plant-owned. The advertiser does not want the mass of details that would come with dealing with hundreds of plant owners; he does want a standard and a uniform service. . . ."[24] Testimonials from advertisers as well as from fellow plant owners communicated the need and value of effective and cooperative national service. They also helped foster a corporate culture, uniting the geographically dispersed groups of big and small outdoor advertising companies.

The OAAA also viewed consolidation as a means to curtail increasing public opposition to billboards. The OAAA sought to permit multiple clients to use the national service, and repeatedly, but also wished to avoid saturation, over-building, and unwanted notice from billboard detractors. Even the character of the client became an issue: "Great care should be exercised that those commodities and businesses which use the medium are of such a character that their forceful presentation will be welcome to the public and will in no way detract from the prestige of the medium or its other customers." All of this meant that OAAA members had to recognize their common interests and their codependence.[25] They had to build a national front in order to grow into newly developing areas and to expand their businesses without covering the entire nation in billboards. Consolidation did reduce the total numbers of billboards overall. Numbers decreased further as the OAAA embarked upon programs such as their "five-year plan," announced in 1925 to standardize the sizes and structures of billboards, which were now to be 12 feet by 25 feet, with 2 feet of vertical lattice between each poster panel and a $3^1/_2$ foot lattice "apron" under each panel. To assure structural soundness, construction codes were specified. In addition, no one location was to hold more than four poster panels facing the same direction of traffic. The plan aimed to unite the billboard structures and to remove small, irregularly sized, and randomly placed boards.[26] It was part of a publicity program to sell the good character and self-regulation of the industry to OAAA members, the advertising profession, the government, and the general public.[27]

Numerous independent entrepreneurs—especially along the rural highways—who were not members of the OAAA and whose roadside signs and billboards did not comply with its standards persisted in erecting handmade, hand-lettered, and variously sized advertisements. Over them, the OAAA had little control. Even the folksy rhyming signs of the Burma-Shave Company were among those irregular postings that needed to go, according to the OAAA. Companies that used the services of OAAA members were sometimes a problem as well. For instance, Adohr Dairy used standardized (and often deluxe, illuminated) billboards in Los Angeles (fig. 31), but also erected distinctly nonconforming advertisements. The latter took the form of monumental advertising statues. One was an agrarian scene, featuring mother and child with grazing cow, set on a high solid base on which was inscribed the name and logo of the dairy (fig. 32). In mode with a genre of roadside sculptural advertising, the farm family shared highway crossings with the occasional oversized bull used to point the way to Ye Bull Pen Inn or molded bellboy to attract motorists to a hotel with free parking.[28] While OAAA might not have held much sway over the innkeeper who had no relationship with the standardized outdoor advertising industry, it could use its clout to convince Adohr to stick with the standards.

Companies such as Coca-Cola, which used outdoor advertising nationally but had never committed to using only the boards of OAAA members, became targeted as part of the industry's standardization program. Correspondence between OAAA leaders and Coca-Cola advertising executives reveals a spirit of friendly cooperation between the leaders of each group, but the letters and memos do highlight problems the OAAA sought to address. Coca-Cola (like Morton Salt and others) had been plastering the roadsides throughout the country with small tin, paper, and painted signs, using every available space on trees, fences, walls and buildings under construction, and covering over the layers of existing signs when space was not available. In many cases, the spaces were neither leased nor intended for advertisements, a detested practice called "chance-may-offer" posting or "sniping" (see fig. 53).[29] Though this had been common since the turn of the century, the OAAA knew that sniping hindered the professional standing and competitive advantage of their industry. Every campaign for which Coca-Cola hired a traveling billposter, leased its own spaces, or used a company that was not an OAAA member meant the deterioration of the OAAA's monopoly. The snipe signs also degraded the advertising value of the legally leased and posted spaces in adjacent areas. With the removal of the ad-hoc, nonstandard, and nonmember-owned signs, the remaining outdoor advertising boards would gain value, garner higher prices, and be more effective.

Companies like Coca-Cola came to recognize the public relations and legal hazards of their ad-hoc posting practices and soon put their outdoor campaigns in the hands of the OAAA.[30] Outdoor companies that wished to remain OAAA mem-

31. Adohr billboard, northeast corner of Wilshire Boulevard and Western Avenue, Los Angeles, 1934.

32. Adohr highway advertising sculpture, c. 1935.

bers in good standing were persuaded to remove signs on spaces that they had not rented and to construct boards according to OAAA guidelines. Civic groups also assisted in the clean up. Their attention to the sign-infested landscape led to greater enforcement of laws prohibiting signs on unleased property. In some states, civic groups removed illicit snipes themselves, by the thousands. They also advocated taxation of all signs, which was another means of monitoring snipes.[31]

Though the OAAA's programs helped to consolidate, standardize, and upgrade the value of the organized outdoor advertising industry, they also limited the space available to potential advertisers. The fundamental problem of how to grow the national outdoor advertising industry had been magnified rather than solved.

Even during economic slumps of the 1920s, the dilemma of where and how to expand the outdoor advertising industry while maintaining the quality of national coverage continued. Poster boards sold out, construction of new boards doubled, and contracts usually made one to three months in advance were booked up sometimes a year in advance.[32] Both small towns and the roads on the outskirts of cities emerged as targets for outdoor advertising expansion. Using the 1920 U.S. Census data for evidence, the OAAA claimed that though most advertising targeted cities of a quarter million people, smaller cities of less than twenty thousand, were responsible for the majority (52 percent) of all merchandise purchased in America. Ten years later, it was learned that 45 percent of all retailers were also located in these small towns. Figures like these convinced OAAA leaders that "The time has come to build poster plants . . . in every town . . . of 200 population or over."[33] "Growing," as one plant owner put it, "does not necessarily mean that we should overbuild the towns and cities we have. It should mean a uniform growth over a wider area. Build the unbuilt and trading areas and towns around us."[34] The markets outdoor advertisers needed to tap lay in areas made accessible by the automobile well beyond the urban arena.

All could see that highways and cars were transforming the circulation patterns of rural residents and town dwellers alike. Dirt roads became highways, which in turn became commercial arteries from which sprang new cities and towns. It was purely logical, one California legislator noted, that outdoor advertising would go where the people were going, and that other businesses would join them at the side of the road.[35] Formerly desolate South Florida was now noted for its "wonderful network of velvet highways extending in every direction but all leading to the shopping centers of the terrain served. These highways have played their important part in building the prosperous cities of today."[36]

The outdoor industry sold small and newly developing towns to advertisers by claiming these were the missing links in the riddle of national distribution. Though mass-produced and trademarked goods had become a part of contemporary life, truly nationalizing their presence and availability remained difficult. Of the 150,000 manufacturers in America in 1921, only 18,000 distributed products nationally, usually through retail stores and not direct mail or catalog sales.[37] The outdoor advertising industry claimed that 70 percent of its clients were these very retailers, and that manufacturers that wished to tap the same market would do well to join them.[38]

In the many remote but populated areas where other advertising media were not localized or available, marketing was best accomplished through outdoor advertising. As one strategist explained, "In 95% of the towns under 10,000 population . . . no daily newspaper is published, and no other media provide for more than a limited percentage of complete market penetration."[39] Outdoor advertising functioned as "a national business, locally applied."[40] Since plant owners were knowledgeable about their localities (often as long-term residents), the OAAA explained, they could best address the regional tastes and educational backgrounds of the population, something neither mass manufacturers nor national print advertisers could claim.[41] Local posting targeted specific audiences with local dialect. Painted wall signs could particularize an ad and list local retailers who carried the products. Stock posters that were printed in bulk (so that small shops could afford to buy them) also left space for the local retailers' information.[42]

If a manufacturer wished to increase distribution to wider arenas, the billboard industry maintained that the poster could also serve as a "stimulant" in developing demand for these goods locally.[43] Billboards would foster consumer desire, creating a clientele that local retailers would feel obliged to satisfy. "Planting the ideas" about a product and "cultivating" the market for local sale would go far toward "breaking down, to a great degree, dealer resistance and making the task of getting distribution the easier."[44] Thus, outdoor advertising would dissolve the role of the "jobber" or wholesaler who traditionally encouraged retailers to stock products.[45] Unlike the typical jobber, the outdoor advertisement served both manufacturer and retailer by developing public markets, not just wholesale ones: "The poster is a rugged way of saying to the man who sells your goods: 'We are trying in every conceivable way to move the product from your shelves, for we realize the importance of a quick turnover. We are coming right into your own town, your own territory, and helping you sell.'"[46] The poster acted as a spunky salesman for the retail merchant. It was the "salesman behind the salesman." It was "salesmanship on paper."[47]

Outdoor advertisers thus claimed that they could centralize and standardize mass distribution with less waste than radio and print media. Kerwin Fulton boasted, "Every panel is like an open book held up before the reader's eye, and the book is always open to your page. . . . It has no cover on it." "We have the best pure medium of advertising in existence," another commentator extolled. "It has no editorial policy, no particular type of religion, no politics; it is just product advertising."[48] Even when a poster might "editorialize" by hosting a public service announcement (e.g., safety awareness), advertising remained the poster's main purpose. By contrast, audiences went to the radio and magazines for information or entertainment, and ads were happenstance.[49] In its purity of function and inescapability, broadcasting to captive audiences unable to change their view, outdoor advertising claimed to be capable of selling anywhere and to anyone, nationwide.

In 1925 the poster and the painted outdoor advertising trade associations merged. Both paint (a more expensive and local medium) and poster services could now simultaneously be used in a single national campaign.[50] This further rationalized the industry. By association it also granted posters a greater sense of permanency. The expense and effort of painted displays meant that they were usually more carefully placed and presented, and for longer periods of time. Moreover, painted advertisements on the walls of buildings conveyed permanence in architectural terms, asserting the place of the two-dimensional advertisement as part of the cityscape and identifier of the marketplace. The poster branch of the industry sought this impression of architectural solidity and permanency as well, and hoped to make their posters as integral to the economy as any retail shop, office building, or manufacturing site. They imagined the billboard structure as a visible piece of the network of sales and distribution that defined the trading area, just as legitimate a business as any other. They believed that their association with paint added to that legitimacy.

As the outdoor advertising industry consolidated, standardized its national service, and blanketed the nation's small and large towns and thoroughfares in painted and printed advertisements, it faced the same issues as retailers and manufacturers: just what constituted the marketplace in the age of automobility? Though outdoor advertising companies could claim to reach a national audience, they still lacked the kinds of proof that advertisers demanded. How could the real estate and the purchasing power of a mobile marketplace be assessed on a consistent, national basis?

CHAPTER 7

TRAFFIC AND TRADE:
"BUYING POWER IN MOTION"

In 1924, traffic expert Miller McClintock began to wonder whether automobiles had changed markets permanently. "Stores that were once remote may now be close in the element of time," he wrote. "In a very real sense no merchant's plant stops at his property line. Rather, it extends out and along every street and artery of travel to the home of his most remote potential customer."[1] He articulated the central issues that the outdoor advertising industry had yet to master fully: if the audience defines the market, and if the audience is mobile, then the market is also mobile.

Until that time, outdoor advertisers still lauded their product by emphasizing the simple physical display space or region. To potential customers they presented information regarding the population, industry, and physical characteristics of the geographic arena in which their boards were located.[2] Essentially, they tried to sell outdoor advertising as if it were print advertising, and as if their audience stood still. Even in rhetoric they usually only thought to compare themselves to magazines. The poster was "the magazine, the newspaper of the Broad Highway."[3]

But soon the industry began to realize just how much it differed from circulating media. Unlike any other form of advertising, the benefits of billboards accrued with the mobility of the audience. The more these audiences traveled the more advertisements they passed. Though the industry began to register the special benefits of addressing an audience in motion, it still had not found ways to calibrate the meaning of circulation figures. Besides identifying the circulation patterns and figures of their mobile audiences, somehow the industry also had to package these audiences in a way useful to their clients.

Most basically, outdoor advertisers needed to determine where to place ads and how much to charge for them. Like real estate and retail developers, they had to locate optimal areas within which people would travel and shop.[4] Traditional means of establishing locations for retail were geographically rooted, relying on population density, existing buildings and rail lines, as well as proximity to homes and other businesses.[5] But as one adman noted, "Traffic flows over city, county, and state boundary lines without in the least being influenced by their existence."[6] Political boundaries did little to delimit self-propelled vehicular movement. Nor did they account for all different kinds and classes of people who traveled the same roads.

In the past, streetcars and railroads had mostly defined new retail and residential areas. Their routes were immobile and easy to locate. Though highways suggested such a fixed space, they offered individuals infinitely more options. The automobile granted Americans "freedom of movement. It has kept citizens from vegetating; it has changed the individual from a 30-miles-a-day to a 300-miles-a-day man."[7] Another outdoor advertiser remarked that the mileage people covered in their cars led to an expanded trading radius. Whereas people used to travel ten to fifteen miles to shop or trade, now they could cover seventy-five or one hundred miles. "[C]ertain roads have thousands of cars passing over them daily," he noted. "True to what we might expect, the passing of large numbers of cars past a given point gives that point business possibilities. . . . It is claimed that these wayside trade points did a hundred million dollar business last year, and these roads are fast taking on the appearance of business lanes."[8]

Outdoor advertisers were realizing that "the economic limits of urban communities often [lay] far beyond political boundaries" of downtown business districts. Whereas once one might have assessed a market by census data, the producer could "no longer . . . look to people as political groups; he must study them as markets; he must know their peculiar characteristics, as once knowing these he can more intelligently lay his promotional plans." Progressive companies such as Foster and Kleiser, on the West Coast, realized they needed to address a number of factors for "estimating markets and possible sales returns," including "population, buying power, buying inclinations, literacy, economic stability, the tourist, and future possibilities."[9]

Sometimes the industry could rely upon the standard data furnished by the U.S. Department of Commerce or Census Bureau, while sometimes it used popular business publications from various industries.[10] But these standards of business information indicated only "the size and extent of the fixed or resident population." However, it was noted, "population *movements* are at times even more important."[11] Poster-plant operators needed more than what these sources supplied: "What is your own trading area? What people come into your town to buy and why do they come there to buy and when they come what do they buy?"[12] Precise information on the fluid elements of a place and, even more important, verifiable circulation figures went beyond what was available. If the automobile opened the geographical arena and changed the relationship of the motorist to time and distance, as outdoor advocates claimed, then knowing the region was less helpful than *knowing the mobile audience itself*.

Traffic had emerged as the key to prosperity. It could serve outdoor advertisers as well as real-estate developers, automotive industries, and retailers. The power of traffic was often described biologically: "Traffic is the blood stream of the social and economic life of the community," claimed one writer. Another announced, "[t]he automobiles that roll along the traffic arteries are like the white corpuscles of the blood that carry health and strength to all parts of the body."[13] Necessary to maintaining the good health of the market were instruments for taking its pulse: "[L]et us not think of traffic statistics as dry figures but as something real, vital, and human."[14]

As traffic was recognized as the lifeblood of industry, doctors of engineering and economics were called in to prescribe both curative and preventative treatments for congestion and poor circulation.[15] With steadily increasing automobile ownership came street congestion, parking problems, and accidents. Smooth circulation and its relationship to trade became a primary concern to city, state, and federal agencies. From the 1920s on, it became a national issue, especially after Secretary of Commerce Herbert Hoover convened the First National Conference on Street and Highway Safety in Washington, D.C., in 1924.[16] The federal government's Bureau of Public Roads as well as local, state, and municipal planning divisions, established in the 1910s, set out to provide statistical data regarding road conditions and the numbers of cars using roads.[17]

Leading the nascent field of traffic engineering was Miller McClintock, director of the Erskine Bureau for Street Traffic Research at Harvard University. McClintock was granted the first Ph.D. in traffic engineering from Harvard in 1924. He then began his own consulting firm, Traffic and Transport Associates. From 1926 to 1938 he directed the Erskine Bureau, first funded by the Studebaker Corporation then by the Automobile Manufacturers Association. The Bureau then moved with him to Yale University, where

McClintock worked and taught for another four years. McClintock spent much of his career consulting with big and small cities alike, Chicago, Detroit, Kansas City, Los Angeles, Terre Haute, and Washington, D.C. among them.[18] For most of the 1930s he also worked with the OAAA.

McClintock had a theory about traffic: it was all about friction. Where a business had access to the road, there was the marginal friction of merging traffic and the internal-stream friction of cars passing one another (parked and moving). Where two streets met, intersectional friction would slow traffic. Medial friction was caused by the face-off between two opposing lanes of traffic. Traffic was an organic phenomenon. It was like the flow of a river—if dammed up, circulation would be stilled. If obstructions were removed, movement would be restored. Frictionless travel thus signaled good circulation. It was an unsticking of whatever was stuck, and a salient metaphor for dealing with problems of distribution. It was also an apt Depression-era metaphor. To keep the economy flowing—and society moving forward—unnecessary friction needed to be eliminated.[19]

McClintock's quest for frictionless traffic was reflected in the traffic codes he set in different cities. He removed obstructions like parked cars from downtowns by creating no parking zones. Pedestrians were kept out of the stream of traffic through jaywalking laws. Other solutions were more visionary, and unrealized until decades later, in the form of interstate limited-access highways (where entrances were widely spaced, meaning businesses did not have direct access to the highway) and grade separations (whereby overpasses or underpasses removed cross traffic and cloverleafs carried cars fluidly from one highway to another).[20]

In devising plans for "frictionless" traffic, McClintock collaborated with industrial designer Norman Bel Geddes, first as part of a promotional campaign in urban planning for Standard Oil, then for the Futurama display at the New York World's Fair of 1939–40, which envisioned ideal superhighway travel in the automobile future of 1960. Their model captured the imagination of thousands of visitors, not to mention President Franklin Delano Roosevelt himself. Though the ideas represented were not wholly new, having precedents in the limited-access parkways and throughways of the previous two decades, many were later represented in the 1944 Interregional Highway Plan that established the blueprint for the 1956 National System of Interstate and Defense Highways, a program lobbied for by many of the same automobile-related industries that had funded McClintock's work.[21]

Throughout his career McClintock worked on enhancing the beneficial relationship between circulation and marketing of all kinds. In 1941 he made a foray into another spatial arena that had always been of great interest to him. He was named the first paid president and chief executive of the Mutual Broadcasting System, which then operated 207 radio stations, "the largest number ever hooked up in a single network." He later began the Rural Radio Foundation. The ease with which he moved among traffic engineering, advertising, and radio suggests the complementary nature of highways and airwaves, both of which catered (and broadcast) to diffused markets of mobile consumers.[22]

Consultants like McClintock worked with the Domestic Commerce Division of the U.S. Department of Commerce as well as with individual chambers of commerce and urban planning divisions. With McClintock's help, many cities began conducting traffic surveys in order to develop comprehensive plans that made more efficient use of public streets in the late 1920s.[23] They followed precedents set by streetcar engineers, whose surveys of passengers went toward establishing new routes and verifying the cost efficiency of existing ones.[24] By the mid- to late 1930s, businesses and all levels of government, from the local to the federal, became committed to traffic surveying and the need for traffic engineers in urban planning and highway development.[25]

The first state highway surveys were conducted in the first two decades of the 1900s, to determine the numbers of different vehicles on the roads. They were more like spot checks of road use than scientific surveys of traffic congestion or investigations into any attendant economic impact. In 1920 and 1922 the Bureau of Public Roads and the California State Highway Commission worked together to record typical daily traffic and total annual movement of all traffic on state highways. But their purpose was to establish rates for gasoline and registration taxes and to measure the relationship between traffic and road conditions. They did not yet see the connections between traffic and trade. Harland Bartholomew and Frederick Law Olmsted did, but for their *Major Traffic Street Plan for Los Angeles* they hardly had the funds to prepare traffic counts in the all-important areas outside of the central business district. So, on February 14, 1924, from 7:00 in the morning to 6:30 at night, troops of Boy Scouts were given a day off from school (and service credit) to conduct traffic counts in outlying areas. Needless to say, their findings were uneven.[26] By the mid-1920s, however, as local, state, and federal agencies worked cooperatively to study traffic, they determined sampling methods for assessing the ebbs and flows of traffic at different times of day, in different seasons, and so on. Soon they became more sophisticated, employing origin-destination interviews and postcard questionnaires to determine how far vehicles had traveled, how many passengers they held, and the purpose of the trip. Such data was used to determine which roads should be improved first, and whether they were of primary or secondary importance as part of the state's highway system.[27] It was also used to predict future traffic, to show the highway commissioners where to spend funds to stay ahead of traffic demand. Starting in 1935, the Bureau of Public Roads funded comprehensive state-by-state traffic surveys; their traffic flow data was used, as before, to project future desires based on present road use. This time, however, the information became the foundation for the routes of the interstate highway system, and a quantitative means by which engineers could claim that highway locations were based not upon political motivations but upon unbiased study of consumer demand.[28]

The traffic survey quickly gained support as a most popular tool for the promotion of automotive- and business-friendly urban planning and traffic regulation schemes. Businessmen and politicians had come to "a full realization that the streets of a city are the most important element in its economic usefulness," and sought to record how it functioned, and how its traffic flowed or bottled up.[29] The resulting traffic surveys and reports confirmed what many had otherwise guessed—traffic delay caused economic loss. In Worcester, Massachusetts, the cost of congestion was $35,000 a day; in Cincinnati, $100,000 a day. One Detroit survey estimated their annual loss due to traffic congestion at $30,000,000. Though authors of the survey neglected to explain how they had reached this figure, they mostly wanted to assert that public streets and motor vehicles were not being used efficiently, and that planners and business leaders were not acting on the evidence provided by traffic engineers like McClintock that "streets are actually a part of every business house in the community."[30] Worse still, inattention was sure to badly affect the economic flow of the entire nation.

Traffic flow studies became a numerical, easily visualized means by which coalitions of engineers, planners, and business leaders in metropolitan areas could identify and communicate to the public the unfavorable effects of urban growth and congestion, and seek support for solutions that would accommodate the frictionless traffic of automobiles.[31] Their findings had use for others, too, including the outdoor advertising industry, which was more than happy to see just where traffic was flowing, and what roads were likely for expansion or improvement. Outdoor advertisers wished to utilize these existing surveys but they also felt the need to develop their own in order to better determine the relationship between trade and traffic. Each plant established its own version, incorporating elements from the Bureau of Public Roads and city traffic surveys, census reports, and other manufacturing and distribution data. This combination came closer to describing trading areas and the purchasing power of those moving within them. In the 1920s, some OAAA members took another approach, and divided their territories into different regions to match those of wholesalers, who had centralized distribution centers.[32] The Foster and Kleiser Company, for instance, divided their West Coast markets into the "basic unit of wholesale distribution" rather than binding themselves to city or municipal lines, and considered these areas in terms of their transportation corridors, car ownership statistics, agricultural production, tourism, national parks, and scenic beauty. They also recognized that low population (and low-income population) did not necessarily mean low marketing potential.[33] Traffic, not population, was what mattered.

That was a fine approach for big companies like Foster and Kleiser, but not as feasible an undertaking for smaller plants, which were an important part of the national scene but were resistant to investing in expensive studies. "Where is *Your* Population?" an OAAA trade bulletin asked, urging members to utilize existing traffic data to determine where to post billboards. "'Populated area' is NOT merely the population within *corporate limits* of a community," the article explained. The area also covered "the closely adjacent built up and populated area just outside the corporate limits."[34] Without surveys tailored to the industry, however, just how far to go outside those limits remained mysterious. The outdoor advertising industry still needed a "distribution director," and more scientific research, trade magazines asserted.[35]

In 1924, the OAAA decided it needed a national research clearinghouse with the expertise and legitimacy of an academic affiliation, and established the Barney Link Poster Advertising Fellowship at the University of Wisconsin. The fellowship sponsored research on "1. Development of a more attractive structure including landscaping and embellishments. 2. Poster readership. 3. Development of a method of easily and accurately determining traffic."[36] It soon established programs at Notre Dame University, setting up an Outdoor Advertising Library there, and offered the first business courses in outdoor advertising at both Notre Dame and Wisconsin. Through McClintock, Harvard and Yale also offered courses in traffic and marketing. Later such courses became a part of the curriculum of engineering, planning, and business schools nationwide.[37]

Among other things, the Barney Link Fellowship aimed to improve site selection of billboards and their landscaping. Advised were sites "with high advertising value and little or no beauty value, which with landscaping can be changed from unsightly spots to something which will please the eye." Such insights had been gained through surveys of four locations: a homeowners community, an industrial city, an industrial farming locality, and a rural community. Also subject to scrutiny were the survey techniques and sampling methods for traffic counts employed by the Bureau of Public Roads, advertising agencies, Foster and Kleiser, and other outdoor advertising companies. The studies aimed toward several goals: apprising the OAAA's own membership of proper plant placement; convincing potential customers of the billboard industry's professionalism, public spiritedness, and efficiency as a national medium; and establishing consistent methods for auditing circulation.

Despite the work of the Barney Link Fellowship to improve the services of outdoor advertisers, the industry after 1928 was suffering losses in national advertising accounts. The Depression slowed national business further. The problem was that it was still too hard for national advertisers to use billboards. Verifiable national circulation figures for the outdoor medium were simply not available, and no one seemed able to agree upon methods for getting them. The stormy relationship the industry had with advertising agencies hindered the cause further. By 1931, as part of its efforts at reconciliation and to boost business, the OAAA joined forces with the Association of National Advertisers (ANA) to study traffic on a national basis and to create one system, upon which advertisers and sellers could agree, to verify mobile circulation.[38] Confirming that their conflicts were now in the past, Turner Jones, vice president of Coca-Cola and chairman of the outdoor advertising committee of the ANA, explained that "buyer and seller have met on common grounds for a scientific evaluation of services in which they have a mutual interest." Their collaboration had even larger significance. He continued, "Though people may have known traffic flow was related to business, this is the first comprehensive study, and will be a contribution to business in general in the form of trading area definitions which will simplify the process of distribution and cut its costs."[39]

The OAAA/ANA hired Miller McClintock, assisted by John Paver, an Erskine Fellow at Harvard, to study the "relationship between daily population movements and trade activities."[40] Paver had previously worked for the OAAA, where he ran the Field Service Department, Division of Plants, in 1927. He had received a graduate degree in civil engineering in 1925 from Northwestern University with a thesis on traffic engineering. Prior to that he had worked in the Produce Research Department of Sunmaid Raisins and at Northwestern under advertising psychologist Walter Dill Scott. Later in his career he promoted what the OAAA called "the formation of a world clearing house for outdoor advertising information." Paver, like McClintock, was a life-long devotee of traffic and engineering sciences, especially as they pertained to advertising. While working for the OAAA, Paver developed a system of surveys for use in member towns and, with McClintock, formalized those methods for nationwide application. For this he and McClintock embarked on a huge marketing effort to convince OAAA members to follow their guidelines for surveying and assessing traffic in each plant region. Since the OAAA funded the studies, members had added incentive for doing so.[41]

McClintock explained his goal as a nationally recognized method to authenticate and systematize circulation and trade data.[42] For this he required an accurate definition of the trading area, one based on previously "wholly overlooked and fundamental facts"—"the distribution of populations, the travel habits or movement of people, and actual trading characteristics." After months of careful research, observation, and theoretical speculation about the real boundaries of a trading area, McClintock was forced to admit defeat: "We could not help but come to the conclusion that *markets do not have geographical boundaries that can be definitely fixed.*"[43]

So defeated, McClintock and Paver focused on the functional parameters of trading areas, and not political or even geographical boundaries.[44] They recognized that though geography might be essential to determining the circulation of a medium like radio, "traffic is the only medium which can be counted as the circulation of the outdoor advertising industry."[45] Following traffic now became their emphasis. They established guidelines whereby traffic surveyors used the registration addresses on car license plates parked in various trading centers to determine travel distances from home to shop. They also interviewed consumers about their driving habits and their shopping patterns—where did they go and what did they buy? They combined this information with other data pertaining to street use, from the location of schools, stores (chains and independents), gas mains, telephone wires, and trolley routes to the width and pavement type of streets and highways. (Their allies in this fieldwork included Coca-Cola, Gulf Refining, Kroger Grocery and Baking, and Standard Stations, Incorporated) By the end of the 1930s electronic eyes and mechanical "traficounters" were the preferred means of surveillance. By the 1950s electronic computation of millions of license plate numbers allowed compilation of extensive traffic data. True, by checking the home addresses of registered vehicles, traffic surveyors could determine where the cars were coming from. But more important was that they could determine the age, sex, race, and income level of the registered owners, as well as how many times each car had passed a given poster location.[46] They had not given up entirely on the concept of the trading area, but it became less useful than the concept of traffic. More precisely, trading area and traffic became one and the same.[47]

In 1933, the OAAA formalized its version of the Audit Bureau of Circulation with the Traffic Audit Bureau (TAB), under joint sponsorship with the Association of National Advertisers (ANA) and the American Association of Advertising Agencies (AAAA)—the National Outdoor Advertising Bureau joined them later—and within a few years was auditing most of the boards in service. The circulation of each panel was evaluated, as was its "space position value" or exposure value. With this, a price could be set for the billboard that took into account its effectiveness according to location, orientation to the street, distance of visibility, speed with which oncoming cars were expected to travel, and so on. This meant that the better the display, the higher its price tag—a simple yet novel idea. As a result of this revelation that fewer boards could be worth more, billboard owners finally had the incentive to reduce the total number of boards they erected on each site.[48]

In 1935, McClintock and Paver published their work on surveying and assessing outdoor advertising as *Traffic and Trade*. As the OAAA reported to its members, "Based on the fundamental and basic theorem that 'where traffic moves, trade flows,' the market studies proved that traffic counts plotted on a map produced a 'traffic flow map' [that] would disclose the extent of a market, or buying area, of an urban trading center."[49] Where the traffic flow decreased the trading area faded. This point marked the edge of the trading area. It was the frontier of trade, determined by mobile consumers rather than by population density, city limits, or any politically or geographically imposed boundary. The continued exploration of this frontier was part of the point in visualizing traffic and trade.

Or, as McClintock put it, "the traffic flow can be used as a thermometer or gauge of sales possibilities in the market," and as a solution to the "problems of market penetration," "outlet development and location." Indeed, this was the unanticipated outcome of the studies—not just to distribute billboards but also to place retail shops and to guide the future locations of both.[50] They charted traffic circulation to identify where people were traveling and how far they were willing to go. By monitoring the growth outward from traditional metropolitan centers, retail and advertising continued to push that edge further out.[51] McClintock made this point directly, noting, "This industry is represented by . . . outposts along the far-flung economic empire, covering all parts

. . . of the country, [and] no other agency is so advantageously situated to render such a service to American industry."[52] These impressive claims were corroborated in another study, *Sales Management*, which declared the *Traffic and Trade* study to be "so broad in its possibilities as to be of utmost importance to sales managers as well as advertising men. This operation has opened the way to an entirely new and apparently more accurate method of outlining trading areas by traffic flow, which will increase sales efficiency and lower distribution costs."[53]

For the outdoor advertising industry, at least, results were swift. In the years 1933 to 1937, the volume of their national business increased more than 100 percent, with 95 percent of poster business coming from national advertisers. In 1938 its decline in income "was less than half the rate of decline of newspapers and magazines."[54] Although fewer funds were available for advertising during the Depression, outdoor advertisers succeeded more than other advertisers in securing business. This may have been because outdoor advertising was less expensive as a national form of advertising than newspapers and magazines. Or perhaps the upturn in business was due to the improvement in national services, and, as one advertising agency considered, "new confidence in outdoor as a medium based on known values."[55]

The most notable change in the shift from center to circulation pertained to the small town. According to outdoor advertising representatives, it made "no difference how small a town may be if the outdoor plant that is located there receives a suitable volume of circulation. . . . Sometimes a town having a resident population of 250 persons has a daily circulation of 11,000 when the plant is located on a primary highway."[56] Smaller towns in Iowa, for instance, enjoyed considerable extra business soon after traffic flow maps were published showing their formidable circulation on through-traffic highways.[57] However, there were tens of thousands of towns where circulation was too minimal to be viable for business. As a result of its findings, the TAB advocated the removal and redistribution of over 100,000 billboards in these small towns that were not located on federal and state highways. The net result, engineers boasted, was that "[a]s advertisers and their representatives would ride across the country these individual units would fairly boom out the advertiser's message."[58]

Business leaders and other advertising industries realized the opportunities offered by visualizing traffic as trade through the TAB and McClintock and Paver's reports. The TAB's board of overseers represented both buyers and sellers, the cooperation of which made its circulation assessments seem nonpartisan. Both groups, however, benefited from the TAB's assessments. One board member, vice president of Bristol Meyers, explained that outdoor advertisers had laid out "a new workable and scientific national system of trading area delineation . . . a system that all of us can accept." The TAB could "scientifically evaluate the retail sales *potential* of any given location in a given trading area." "I need not tell you," the Bristol Meyers executive continued, "that such scientific information would go far in eliminating wastes in distribution."[59]

The outdoor advertising industry had answered Hoover's call to assess distribution. By finding that traffic was "buying power in motion" and charting its flow, it had managed to address present and future markets. It could advise concerning the distribution of both advertisements and consumers. The concept of traffic had become a cornerstone of efficient mass distribution and the ever-continuing growth of industry.

CHAPTER 8

AN ARCHITECTURE OF MOBILITY

The changed locations and relationships between buyers and sellers in the age of mass advertising and the automobile meant that advertisers, architects, merchants, and manufacturers had to develop techniques geared toward mobility. Trademarks and brand names had facilitated the job of advertisers in their project of "salesmanship in print" by providing simple and identifiable imagery with which to represent nationally distributed goods. The strategies of "picturization" that outdoor advertisers employed to advertise to mobile audiences without much use of text (described in a previous chapter as an aesthetics of speed) functioned to reorient viewers visually so that they could quickly recognize an abstract, massed, and iconic form as representing a product without much more than a side-window glance.[1]

Advertisers and retailers also had a vested interest in the *spatial* reorientation of mobile audiences. Outdoor advertisers therefore developed an *architecture of mobility* expressly suited to the decentralizing commercial arena. The structures, locations, and even animation of outdoor advertisements constituted a new physical organization of built forms aimed to acclimate motorists to mobile viewing and shopping. Utilizing elaborate and sometimes expensive devices of animation, an architecture of mobility called the attention of moving audiences to the advertising billboard. It also served a transitional purpose in marking the way to the new shopping emporia of the automobile age–the chain, department, and self-service stores cropping up outside the central business districts of cities across the country by the late 1920s. By developing architectural devices specifically suited to automobile audiences, the outdoor advertising industry helped to develop both the shape and the look of the roadside strip. Having charted traffic, they knew where to plant their signs of commercial development. They predicted, too, that where structures were built for traffic, trade would also ensue.

As retail shopping became increasingly dispersed and depersonalized (ads replacing salesmen, self-service markets replacing full-service shops) outdoor advertisers, perceiving themselves as conduits between consumers and merchants, needed more novel and eye-catching means of communicating to mobile audiences.[2] They often used visceral as well as visual cues to advertise new, unfamiliar, and difficult-to-represent goods and services. Not surprisingly, movement of all sorts was used to attract the mobile audience.

Electrical companies sponsored perhaps the most architecturally dynamic and spectacular of all outdoor advertisements in the 1920s and 1930s. With billboard plant owners in over 18,000 cities and towns, the outdoor advertising industry gave a great deal of business to utility companies. In 1932, they claimed to be "one of the largest consumers of electricity in the country."[3] Outdoor advertisers used a lot of electricity but they also saw the great potential for electricity to help them create new markets for their industry. As one advertising plant manager wrote, "only 30% of business established in cities have any sort of electrical advertisement," which suggested "a real opportunity for the outdoor companies to capitalize on this underdeveloped market."[4]

Electrical illumination had a long relationship with promotional enterprises of all sorts. As early as 1878, a traveling circus brought the "magic and mystery" of electric lighting to Kansas City, while myriad state and world's fairs similarly presented illuminated displays to sell people on the promising future and technological wizardry of the "theater of science" staged by electricity.[5] The first glimpses of this new and magical electrical "fire" drew huge crowds. Also of a promotional nature well beyond the products advertised were the electrical "spectaculars" that turned night into day along New York's "Great White Way," so named for its fantastic quantity and illumination of electric bulb-adorned signs along the Broadway and 42nd Street theater district. This was a form of institutional advertising, promoting entire industries rather than just products. The industries promoted by spectaculars along Broadway included tourism, the progressive city itself, electricity, and the outdoor advertising industry, not to mention the theaters and other great palaces of entertainment.

New York's electrical displays were unique in their nationwide reputation. At the turn of the twentieth century, the Hotel Cumberland (later the site of the Flatiron building) featured on its wall an incandescent-light-emblazoned Heinz pickle in "57" varieties. In 1917, Wrigley's gum erected what was then the largest electrical display in the world, featuring six of its trademark "spear-men" doing acrobatics amid the extravagant plumage of a colossal peacock. By the 1930s, Times Square visitors thrilled at the eight-story-high and one-block-long Wrigley gum advertisement of brilliantly colored tropical fish (made up of 18,000 electric bulbs) gliding through waves of sea-green lights (fig. 33). The electricity it consumed could have served a city of 10,000. All of these campaigns (and others) were commented on internationally.[6]

These displays demanded high capital investment and maintenance costs and depended on the high circulation of urban throngs. Yet many small towns, inspired by Broadway, believed that electric devices would *bring* the crowds. Civic boosters across the country embarked on "Great White Way" campaigns throughout the 1910s and 1920s to make their towns the next New York City.[7] Even fictional Gopher Prairie, the setting of Sinclair Lewis's *Main Street*, participated, when "glory of glories, the town put in a White Way. White Ways were in fashion in the Middlewest. They were composed of ornamented posts with clusters of high-powered electric lights along two or three blocks on Main Street."[8]

33. Dorothy Shepard designed the 75- by 188-foot, 110-ton electric spectacular that occupied an entire block on Broadway between 44th and 45th Streets, New York, 1936.

34. Northwest corner of Broadway and 46th Street, New York, c. 1923.

Soon it became an accepted architectural principle to include electrical and structural requirements for rooftop, facade, and wall advertising signs in commercial buildings (fig. 34). There were multiple advantages to laying such plans. H. H. Magdsick, president of the Illuminating Engineering Society, reiterated this in a 1930 address to the Society titled "Building Prosperity Avenue": "Light has always been a fundamental in the work of the architect. But its general use as an architectural element in itself is something of recent growth." He urged that modern life, which brought people outdoors far more than in the past, demanded the use of light as "one of the architectural elements," particularly in commercial and public buildings, and "especially in the after-dark hours, when we are most impressionable and receptive."[9] The provision of diversified types of electrical decorative displays, he explained, "should form a part of every building on *Prosperity Avenue*."[10] Electric advertisements promised the transformation of ordinary byways into buyways.

A crucial conceptual step in selling the American public on the new utility and the lifestyle it promised was to convert electric and gas power from a mysterious and showy science to an accessible and ordinary part of urban and domestic life. This was the job of a diverse group of architects, engineers, politicians, businessmen, retailers, and salespeople that historian Mark Rose calls "agents of diffusion."[11] They attempted to sell the idea of progress (granted through the science of electricity), pragmatically applied to the home and shop. Outdoor advertisers also served as agents of diffusion, since they showed the wonders of electricity and modeled its consumption through their electrical spectaculars. They powered their displays with electricity, and thereby displayed electric power. In doing so, they promoted not just private use of electricity, but public usage.[12]

Electricity also advanced the rearrangement of population centers.[13] Light and power utilities expanded into rural areas, towns, and cities in the 1920s. Industry of all sorts followed "the slender copper highways" leading from the nineteenth-century metropolises to outlying communities.[14] Electricity transformed trading areas, too, with street illumination and, in the largest department stores and supermarkets, air conditioning, all of which opened possibilities for longer hours and seasons of operation for leisure activities, shopping, and work. Department stores, the newly built "park and shop" suburban shopping centers, movie palaces, and other citadels of commerce helped convey the magic of electrical power and the technological progress it promised.[15] The diffusion of electricity, for which advertisers were agents, was not confined to the distribution of goods but also of people, homes, and trading areas. The physical and the experiential boundaries of the urban environment itself were being diffused.

Although cities were illuminated by electricity starting in the 1880s and almost half of urban America's homes were electrified by the early 1920s, in 1929 only one in four American homes sported more than two electrical appliances. For instance, not until refrigerators could be purchased with loans guaranteed by Title I of the 1934 National Housing Act were they consumed in mass. Other New Deal programs also developed markets for electrical goods, such as the Tennessee Valley Authority (TVA), which provided subsidized power to utility companies. The TVA sales program assisted manufacturers in building mass markets for electrical appliances.[16] Vigorous publicity campaigns in all media helped this process along. Gas companies, realizing their business would be overtaken by electrical utilities, also initiated national advertising campaigns.[17]

Newfangled products made consumption more complicated and the job of advertising more burdened with the long-term task of educating people. Indeed, gas and electric stoves and electric refrigerators remained the province of upper-income consumers until after World War II.[18] Still, the lengthy education of consumers was a burden that outdoor advertisers were happy to assume.

Outdoor advertisers promoted utility companies and appliances through the presentation of dramatic tableaux vivants that trained consumers in the use of new products and the habit of driving to purchase them. Electrified billboard displays in the 1920s and 1930s proved to be as lavish as the show windows of the palatial department stores of the late nineteenth century, which had also indoctrinated shoppers in the excesses of conspicuous consumption.[19] The novel and spectacular displays created by outdoor advertisers operated along the same principles but with a different goal. Rather than luring the consumer into the structure on its site, they aimed to inspire audiences to drive farther along the boulevard to fulfill their consumptive yearnings. Billboards thus became the showrooms of the new driving city. They defined the strip by offering a horizontal picture window of consumer delights to be enjoyed from the privacy of one's own vehicle and to be accessed through one's own power: power to drive to the shop, select the items, and carry them home with scarcely a jostle or a nudge from salesmen or fellow shoppers.

Billboards offered uniquely moving, visual displays and theatrical stagings of goods for sale and their domestic uses. While Maytag Aluminum Washer, Standard Plumbing Fixtures, and Remington Typewriter illuminated New York's Broadway district with their fifty-foot towers and waterfalls of flashing, moving lights (fig. 35), smaller versions lined Detroit's Michigan Avenue and Los Angeles's expanding shopping district on the edge of downtown.[20] But in these cities the show was also being presented at ground level. Horizontally stretching "special bulletins" as well as spotlighted and other illuminated billboards opened an entire nighttime market of advertising exclusively handled by outdoor companies. As one advocate put it, "After dark, a brilliantly illuminated poster, set against the blackness of the night, stands out like a diamond on black velvet."[21]

Regional "sign committees" of the electricity trade association worked with the OAAA to promote electrical advertisements all over the country. They started with places such as California, where, "on account of the favorable weather conditions and the many miles of highways close to power lines, illuminated billboards and painted signs . . . found almost unlimited use."[22] They also engineered new devices that helped outdoor ads to stand out more dramatically in areas already illuminated, and to bring the spectacle of light to

35. Nearly six thousand moving lights showed the operation of the Maytag washing machine, from the gyroscopic action of the washer to the lifting of the lid and wringing of clothing put out on the line, 1926.

those that were not. The electrical engineers also developed special equipment for different roadside uses. Reflective surfaces and lighting were designed to maximize their dramatic effect, but without blinding passing motorists.[23] Electric-sign manufacturers became fascinated with the "increased speed of vision" that they believed would be obtained through the use of "higher intensities" of light. The pairing of light and quickly moving viewers promised an exponential increase in perceptual cognition.[24]

Since lights needed to be both near power lines and within the private property lines of the area rented or owned by the outdoor company, illuminated billboards required a great deal of space. Consider, for instance, that the standard eleven-foot-high board required mounted lighting units approximately six feet out from the board; the higher the board, the greater the distance of the mounted lighting units.[25] These were electrified advertising spectacles that created not only a new temporal arena of fast nighttime commerce, but also a new spatial arena extending beyond the retail shop and boundaries of the cramped and congested business districts of years past. They fulfilled traffic engineer Miller McClintock's 1924 claim that the retail arena in the age of the automobile went beyond the edge of the shop, moving into and along the arteries of traffic along with the mobile consumer.

Outdoor advertising companies recognized the physical changes to the city and the corresponding changes taking place in "current thought and trends" of their modern mobile audience. For this, the outdoor industry was increasingly recommending three-dimensional advertisements. As a sales manager for Foster and Kleiser explained in 1934, "Today's scene insofar as public life and thoughts are concerned is, to say the least, kaleidoscopic. . . . To catch the public mind with an advertising message is doubly difficult under such conditions; to hold the public mind is even more than doubly difficult." While previously advertisers seeking "animated effects" were confined to roof spectaculars (such as along the Great White Way), three-dimensional painted and poster bulletins could better compete in the kaleidoscope as an architectural representative of speed, animated by lights, colors, and forms.[26]

As illumination became more available and important in "increasing attention-value and often bringing light to streets otherwise practically dark," the "third dimension" of the billboard frame took the form of a larger stage on which cutout figures or actual objects—not just their pictorial representation—were presented. These displays were sold based on their "additional attention-factor of *Action*." It was a well-accepted design principle among outdoor advertisers that "moving objects, light, and color always catch the eye."[27]

A popular architectural device that used animation was the oversized, electrically powered and illuminated clock. It joined the usual advertising copy on the billboard structure. National advertisers such as Sunkist, Coca-Cola, Anheuser-Busch, and Firestone used clocks, as did regional campaigns. Chevrolet became well known for theirs in Atlanta, Detroit, Los Angeles, and Minneapolis, among other places (fig. 36). Their billboard clocks measured between seven and twelve feet, were visible at great distances, and could be promoted in terms of the public service they provided. Practically speaking, these displays induced repeated and purposeful looks. They offered "a case where the outdoor display doesn't seek the public but the public seeks the outdoor display!"[28]

The clock supplied the requisite eye-catching elements of light and motion, and drew attention to the public and private uses of electricity and the products that would supply those services. A more abstract purpose is also possible: the clock on the billboard occupied an architectural place in the public arena along

36. Pico
Boulevard near
La Brea
Avenue, Los
Angeles, 1937.

with the railway station, bank, and post office whose clock towers were traditional cornerstones of the communal space of the market or square. These were
the timekeepers that calibrated activities of all strata of the population. The
bank, in particular, represented both public exchange and private industry; the
clock on its exterior literally embodied the principal that time is money. If outdoor advertising was to be established as an essential economic element and as
a respectable architectural feature of the urban fabric, the association with banks
and other public institutions, however negative the Depression might have made
those affiliations, were legitimating. By associating the clock with advertised
goods featured on the billboard, this form of display also communicated a sense
of standardization, reliability, and efficiency. Other electrical animation devices
of similar principles were the thermometer (which sometimes had a connection
to the product advertised, like General Electric air conditioning or "frosty cold"
Coca-Cola) and moving display lights that chased one another from one end of
the board to the next. All sorts of other illusions were electrically produced, too,

including burning houses, pouring bottles of beer, and moving locomotives.[29] These could be said to invert the usual architectural function of another downtown institution: the theater. Rather than housing the entertainment, the moving imagery on the billboard screen brought the show to the street.

Animated effects more theatrically conceived than these were also staged in what were called "shadow-box" or "third-dimensional" presentations. One, used by the Los Angeles department store J. W. Robinson, included a platform extending from the painted billboard of two cutout figures at the eighteenth hole of a golf course. Bullock's, also in Los Angeles, similarly oriented their third-dimensional bulletin toward selling men's apparel through a thematic lesson in style. The cutout figures extended in front of the billboard and above it too, breaking the outline of the frame while still keeping the suited and overcoated men tied to the outdoor domestic scene, which included a large automobile, a bicycle delivery man (with a floral delivery of the long-stemmed variety), two boys being entertained with a newly purchased black-faced puppet, and a matronly nanny. In targeting the difficult-to-reach male consumer, Bullock's depicts a male-defined suburban vision of "masculine domesticity," calling forth imagery used as early as the turn of the twentieth century to illustrate the benefits of suburbia.[30] In the billboard tableau, the men have contact with their children, shop, have a home of their own removed from the signs of urban congestion, and are assisted in it by servants.

It was a scenario with which people might be familiar or for which they might long, especially during the Depression. The billboard also allowed them to gaze upon the private domestic scene from within the similarly private space of their cars. The store featured in the advertisement promised a similar experience, one in which they could remain independent and free from the urban crowds. The male consumer courted by these ads (most likely assumed to be less interested than his wife and daughters in shopping) could drive up to Robinson's or Bullock's, park his car in the provided spaces, and run into and out of the men's shop with nothing to hinder the speed and economy with which he carried out his tasks. Both Bullock's and the outdoor advertiser had pitched self-serving messages in the pleasures and conveniences of the mobile shopping enterprise.

The third-dimensional bulletins frequently offered a view into other private domains of suburbanized life. Sometimes the startling contrast of the private context of domesticity in the public realm of the street enhanced their theatrical attraction. Quite popular were displays of bedroom, kitchen, and living room furniture sets, aimed at replacing the "monstrosities of the Mid-Victorian period, with its continual change and waste in home decorations" with "harmonious arrangement and setting such as have gone far toward making home more homelike with less foolish buying of things which were soon thrown away." This was "the renaissance of good taste,"[31] modern living displayed not through two-dimensional representations but through the third dimension of the billboard as figurative display case and object lesson.

Lachman Brothers, self-proclaimed to be "one of America's largest home furnishers," used cutouts and a shadow box to create a realistic display of model bedrooms. "The room is recessed several feet from the face of the structure and is lighted from within at night." There was even a cutout figure of a woman "seated at a dressing table." Its realism was enhanced by the antics of a regular passerby who snuck into the box every morning. He was described by Herb Caen in the San Francisco *Chronicle*: "Gaily, he sits on the bed. Then he tiptoes over to the lady and tweaks her ear. Following this, he puts his arm around her waist and sits beside her, carrying on an exhibitionistic conversation."[32] Lachman continued to feature third-dimensionals in the 1940s, and passersby continued to step into the ad, as is documented in a photograph of another display featuring a cutout figure of a Marine carrying his bride over the threshold of their new house, cheered on by four real soldiers (fig. 37).[37] Again, like the Bullock's ad, this scene affirmed a masculine domestic bliss.

The presentation of entire rooms and lines of goods—the actual goods for sale, with price tags included—"taught consumers better buying habits" and, as one advertiser claimed, helped introduce the "Better Homes idea" to a national audience.[34] Better Homes in America was an organization founded by Secretary of Commerce Herbert Hoover in 1922 to stimulate consumption through home ownership after the postwar recession. In 1931, during the Depression, as president, Hoover went further, establishing the Commission on Home Building and Home Ownership, essentially subsidizing the single-family private home as an economic means of growth and recovery.[35] Hoover's program offered reduced interest for different credit and loan programs. This is advertised as part of the Lachman billboard display, which advised "Two Years to Pay." In essence, then, the advertisers could claim a civic role, as government publicists, and as agents of diffusion for home-ownership (and suburbanization) itself.

In Atlanta, Los Angeles, Milwaukee, and St. Louis, avenues and boulevards displayed electric-powered model kitchens, modern bathrooms, and gas appliances. The Georgia Power Company could tell Atlanta viewers, "You're right, it's a real model kitchen behind the plate glass window of this display" (fig. 38).[38] Laclede Gas Light Company did this in St. Louis with a fourteen-by-forty-eight-foot billboard with two display windows, each eight feet deep and

37. Four soldiers in the model living room of the "third-dimensional" billboard constructed for Lachman Brothers, 1942.

nine feet high. Behind one glass display window was "the beautiful new aristocrat of the kitchen, the Magic Chef range. In the other window is a gas radiant heater." A 1929 article that described this advertisement claimed that viewing the ad only required a few moments of attention from passing motorists. If so, then why was there a stone bench placed in front of the board? Its presence suggests that onlookers were encouraged to stay awhile. Though the display required some attention—these were not schematically silhouetted images for easy glimpsing—advertisers had contradictory expectations with the display. Aimed toward audiences in moving automobiles, these were spectacles demanding a closer look. Along a driving route to popular entertainment sites, the Laclede Gas billboard was meant for the motorists' gaze, but the board was also across the street from a popular restaurant. Even more perfect for the training of automobile window shopping, the restaurant was a "drive-in," which "enjoys a huge curb service, and patrons who sit in automobiles partaking of refreshments are confronted with the [billboard] displays."[37]

Billboard owners and designers frequently likened their jobs to those of stage and film producers, but with traffic arteries as their theater. The designer "must break through the clamor and haste of traffic," one billboard artist wrote. "He must, figuratively speaking, grasp the head of his prospect in both hands, compel him to look in the right direction and read, understand, remember." Billboard advertisers were well positioned to do this given their historical background in theater, circus, and movie picture houses.[38]

38. Demonstrations of the electric kitchen appliances were held behind the glass plate of the Georgia Power Company display, 1936.

Outdoor advertising maintained a close connection to the theatrical trade, with companies like Foster and Kleiser even locating their Los Angeles headquarters adjacent to the Paramount Studio lot. Film studios, of course, did not need advertisers to tell them the value of spectacle. As one advertiser put it in 1926, "The motion picture interests today would no more think of merchandising a picture without suitable posters than they would think of running a theater without electric lights and signs."[39] According to a 1928 interview with Adolph Zukor, president of Paramount, his company distributed 195,000 posters in an average month. In the golden years of Hollywood in the late 1920s and 1930s, it was not unusual for 50 percent of the business of many outdoor advertising plants to come from the motion picture industry.[40] This is not surprising, especially if MGM's record in August 1936 is any indication: the film company spent $800,000 to $900,000 to post 9,500 locations for six months.[41]

Zukor worked with Foster and Kleiser to develop educational materials that would help Paramount's sales staff to understand how to best use outdoor advertising. These included a "key book" that listed population for different advertising regions, the best amount of time to show posters, the sizes for different markets, and tests to measure the effectiveness of the poster campaign.[42]

In cultivating the glamour (and business) of Hollywood, the movie studios and the outdoor advertising industry shared a common interest. Colorful, dramatic, and boldly designed movie posters offered starstruck fans the faces of their beloved film idols at a size more closely matching their larger-than-life celluloid projection than magazines could achieve. These were slathered upon the posterboards on the exteriors of movie theaters and in other locations across America. Advertising campaigns in Los Angeles incorporated even more theatrical and elaborate displays. Three-dimensional billboards set up as huge stages for live performances were one dramatic device. These utilized open lots and the passing traffic of the growing boulevards and arterial highways of the expanding city. They also directed people to the movie theaters far beyond downtown, where they were accustomed to going. Motorists might not have needed much incentive to drive to the Carthay Circle movie showcase, halfway between downtown and the beach (south of Beverly Hills), where they were bound to find ample parking, but they did need advertising notices to point the way.[43] Foster and Kleiser provided them. For Paramount's 1932 season, they posed live actresses on a stage that extended out from the front of the billboard, whose poster space with promotional information served as the backdrop for "a most unusual form of animation." Two costumed, trumpet-blowing actresses would appear on the "stage" to turn the four pages of a booklike display advertising "four season film hits of the Paramount Studio" with Harold Lloyd, Maurice Chevalier and Jeanette MacDonald, the Marx Brothers, and Marlene Dietrich (fig. 39). The billboard was even given a "premiere" at which "over 5,000 persons congregated around the bulletin, in addition to the steady stream of passing automobiles and busses, many of whose passengers stopped and added their presence to the throng. . . . Harpo Marx and Frances Dee entertained the audience in front of the display."[44] Luckily, the billboard property and the lots around it offered ample space for the congregation and their parking needs.

Outdoor advertisers tapped the success of the movie studios, not just by seeking them as clients or using starlets in their celebrations, but also by appro-

39. At the "world premiere" for the billboard, live models turn the pages of the giant book advertising Paramount Studio's new releases, Wilshire and Windsor Boulevards, Los Angeles, 1932.

priating their tactics.[45] During the Depression, when audiences sought escape from the dreariness of daily life in the darkened movie theater, outdoor advertisers invented new theatrical events of their own. In Pittsburgh, the General Outdoor Advertising Company hired members of the Pittsburgh Pirates to mark the opening of a new billboard display for Kellogg's Corn Flakes. "During construction, the site was hidden by a huge canvas shield upon which was a question mark. . . . [P]receding the unveiling two smaller signs announcing the ceremonies . . . were tacked to the canvas." The tactic compared to the way department stores galvanized interest in their changing displays by curtaining their work in progress. At the specified day and time, "star twirler 'Cy' Blanton sent a baseball through a glass target to light the new semi spectacular."[46]

In 1936, Ideal Dog Food used a billboard display case to serve as a kennel, and presented dog shows behind the three-paneled glass window (fig. 40). General Electric provided the air conditioning and presented two breeds of blue-ribbon dogs in weekly showings.[47] A canvas awning fringed the top of the display case. The fringe had a practical function, certainly, to shield the case from the hot sun, but it also had a referential meaning, suggesting that the board was not just a showcase but also the neighborhood shop. The nationally advertised dog food was theatrically announcing its presence in the neighborhood and suggesting that people drive to their chain grocers or supermarket to

40. Dog shows were held weekly in the air-conditioned spaces of the Ideal Dog Food display case, 1936.

get themselves some. If they did so around Los Angeles, they might visit Ralph's, where they could even shop in the cool comfort of air-conditioning.[48]

Though these sorts of advertising spectacles seem contrary to the common sense of the outdoors medium, which sought to convey a message quickly to moving passersby—*not* to force them to stop and linger—they served a transitional purpose. They helped to decentralize shopping by presenting audiences with an opportunity for automotive window shopping. Even if the car needed to stop and let out its passengers to see the sights within the billboard display, the ads did entertain and sometimes even train their consumers in the use of the products featured as well as the benefits of taking and parking the car for a shopping excursion.

Billboards that combined the real and the illusionary, the actual object for sale and the imagery that advertised it, acted out the steps consumers would need to take on their path from viewing to shopping. For instance, on multiple sites around Los Angeles, Pierce Arrow dealers featured actual automobiles—their 1926 model—behind the glass of an elaborately sculpted ornamental frame (fig. 41). Immediately adjacent was an even larger billboard poster whose bold colors, modern lettering, and futurist design advertised the car and the car dealership where one could take a test drive. Lest the print ad serve too abstract a purpose in signaling modernity and high culture, the brand-new framed car embodied the message in three dimensions. Collapsing the lines between advertiser and seller entirely, an outdoor advertisement for Ford dealers in Indianapolis featured their 1935 model as part of an "outdoor salon," with additional cars displayed on the lawn around the billboard showroom. In six days, fourteen cars were sold right off the billboard lot. The property was hardly small and modest, and the next year it was used again for a Ford ad, this one including a reflecting pool and landscaped grounds. The car was presented in an actual show window (complete with curtains), flanked by a procession of receding, curvilinear walls in the newly popular "streamline" fashion.[49] It was as elaborate as the swanky dealer showrooms of the 1920s that had created "automobile rows"—a new genre of the commercial strip—along main roads on the outside of towns.[50]

Even this was demure in comparison to the "super-spectacular" animated outdoor advertising structure built in Cleveland by the Central Outdoor Advertising Company. The tripartite structure was 36 feet in height and 106 feet in length. The chandeliered central tower showroom featured the car on a revolving platform, flooded with intermittently changing colored lights.

41. Pierce Arrow car behind glass, Los Angeles, 1926.

Flanking the tower were two wings with painted display messages reporting the "center-poise ride" and the "comfort zone" of the new Ford V-8, with the name spelled out in neon.[51] Taking its visual cues from Ford's pavilion at the 1934 Century of Progress exhibition (the world's fair where the first stream-lined trains of the Burlington and Union Pacific railroads were on view), the deluxe display set off a flurry of talk among advertisers about the need to keep pace with their "modern-minded clients." "If outdoor advertising is to keep its foremost place among advertising mediums it must keep its foremost place in design, too," *Signs of the Times* reported. "It must have a physical appearance devoid of the old-fashioned." Lessons could be learned from the railroads, which had been "forced by streamlined competition to do something to save themselves, so they went streamlined, too." Just as many manufacturers and retailers had sought to open stagnant markets by revamping their products through modernized design and color, billboards needed to make that leap into the future, "to 'sell' a modern product in a modern way."[52]

Around Indianapolis, St. Louis, Atlanta, Kalamazoo, Portland, and Wheeling, Ohio, billboard companies felt the new streamline urge. It was an impulse tempered by many in the industry, as heated discussions ensued regarding the propriety of such modernistic devices. Conservative critics declared that such devices defied the standardized sizes and shapes that the OAAA was seeking to maintain. More progressive plant owners retorted that there was no better way to suit the modern automobile than to streamline. Even George Kleiser, president of Foster and Kleiser on the West Coast, whose artists had revolutionized modernistic poster design, demurred to the middle liners, claiming that he could see no real demand for such structures. (The journalist reporting this reminded readers "of the famous statement of a big-time advertiser–Wm. Wrigley, wasn't it?–who said: 'Demand? I create demand!'"[53]) Quickly proven wrong, Kleiser was, by 1938, selling space on the new model of billboard beauty adopted by the OAAA and its members: the Streamliner (fig. 42).[54]

In its most basic form, the Streamliner was white porcelain-enameled steel with stainless-steel trim and had rounded corners, streamlining stripes, and beveled edges. Its wide molded base rooted the structure to the ground (replac-ing the wooden latticed aprons of previous years). Variations included abstract and geometric forms bursting out from the borders of the frame or set askew, as if a cubist collage of elements aggressively dislodged the formal unity, jar-ring the otherwise stolid, oblong picture frame into visual action. It was an architectural framework that suggested speed and modernity, its rounded edges and streaming lines suggesting fluidity of movement, yet low-slung and with a weighty presence or stance that conveyed stability. In its gleaming, virile bulk, this was no flimsy fly-by-night construction; it had pure and solid architectural girth. In the midst of the social and economic dislocations of the Depression, such streamlined forms, as historian Jeffrey Meikle has written, served as a comforting expression of both security and fast, smooth progress, reflecting "the ease with which most people wished they could slide through the Depression."[55] It was the architectural embodiment of "frictionlessness" that Miller McClintock had wished for traffic. The Streamliner was modern but assuring enough so that the Fisk Tire Company used it to inaugurate a national campaign reintroducing its famous yawning boy and slogan "Time to Re-Tire" from thirteen years prior.[56]

Though OAAA members had initially raised a ruckus over the introduction of this new modernist design, it represented well what the industry had been doing for years: streamlining their operation and their billboard displays. Studies sponsored by the Barney Link Fellowship and then by Miller McClintock and John Paver had shown that less was more. They evaluated the exposure or "space position" value of billboards (as well as window displays

42. "Streamliner" billboard frame, c. 1938.

and retail building locations), and came up with "scientific" formulas for locating billboards with maximum viewing potential in relation to the street and highway. In Hugh Agnew's 1938 history, *Outdoor Advertising*, "before-and-after" photographs of the same billboard location made the point. Vertically reaching tiers of billboard structures holding numerous ads were consolidated into individual, larger, horizontally stretching boards. Orientation shifted also. Rather than paralleling the streetcar passengers' view, billboards catered to the motorists' forward-looking view.[57] The boards now imitated the lateral expansion of the city itself, from vertically oriented metropolis to horizontally sprawling strip and suburban developments. Simplified and modernized, the boards signaled efficiency, aiding the fluid movement of passersby and smoothing the road between production and consumption.

Each of these dramatically stylized billboards, from the shadow boxes to the Streamliner, transformed the two dimensions of the poster into three-dimensional architectural space. They were not just signs, they were structures that housed goods for sale; they also served as stand-ins or models for the stores and shops that might eventually occupy the site, or accompany it on an adjacent lot. In some photographs, it is difficult to discern if the image is of a store or a billboard show-window display.[58] As both billboards and store fronts increasingly relied upon the use of neon embellishments in the 1930s to spell out the brand or store name and to activate the front of their structures, their visual similarities increased. The front of the store was a "living billboard," one journalist wrote of a Los Angeles drive-in market. This same concept was embodied by retail shops, supermarkets, and gasoline stations whose one-story, horizontally stretching buildings included a high-reaching facade of stucco or porcelain-enameled sheet metal on which the cutout or painted letters were arranged, poster like. An A&P supermarket, for instance, had a one-hundred-foot-long facade of light-colored stucco that sported little more than a sign.[59] Industrial designer Walter Teague arranged all of the architectural features of one of his storefronts–from the doorway to windows to signage–as if they were visual elements of a "two-dimensional poster design," according to Meikle, creating a streamlined, unified facade that would read easily in one swift glance.[60] Teague's approach, integrating all elements of architecture and advertisement within one harmonious yet dramatically simple design, was advocated by many architects, industrial designers, and signmakers whose work was in great demand given that between 1924 and 1938, according to a survey by the *Architectural Record*, "three-quarters of the nation's commercial establishments conducted face-lifting operations."[61] Teague's design for Standard Oil gasoline stations in 1934 also filled these prescriptions. It read as one unified plane of visual activity, the white oblong box mimicking the overall dimensions of a billboard; reproduced ten thousand times across the countryside, it served as an exemplary marketing campaign, the building as both billboard face and package design for the branded product.[62] As an extra assurance of visibility, the station was often bounded/skirted on one or more sides by billboards bearing the same posters that marked the highway drive to the station.

As retailers sought to accommodate themselves better to the automobile, to locate outside of downtown business districts, or to distinguish themselves from the other signs and structures of the commercial strip, their architectural challenges matched those of billboard advertising and they sought to do what billboards had historically done—to capture in a single moment, with a singular image or idea, the attention of passing motorists. Though many proprietors still followed the basic designs of downtown, with buildings fronting the street and signage scaled to the pedestrian rather than the motorist, others moved their buildings back to allow auto access and parking, and embellished the structures with more flamboyant decorations, pylons or towers, and illuminated signage.[63] A distinct form of roadside architecture emerged, from the hands of both professionally trained architects and individual entrepreneurs who created their own commercial vernacular designs. Strategies differed according to the financial means (or willingness) of the merchants and whether their operation was corporate or independent, local, regional, or national in scale. On the rural roads and on the boulevards and highways of metropolitan areas, their goal, however, matched that of the outdoor advertiser—to arrest the attention of the audience, whether it took the tactics of a still-life painter, a theatrical impresario, or a circus barker.

By the 1920s and 1930s, the growth in automobile ownership and the competition to cash in on motoring audiences led to a great range of roadside structures aimed to startle, amuse, or otherwise attract the attention—and cash—of the mobile consumer. In rural areas, where entrepreneurs were preying on mostly recreational drivers and truckers, and on the urban periphery, where businesses were banking mostly on the routine travels of area residents, an array of fantastic and fanciful designs joined the more commonplace restaurants, shops, wayside food and produce stands, "pumping" stations, auto cabin camps (mo-tels in California), and curiosity shops.

Thematic regionalism flourished in the designs of all varieties of roadside architecture. At auto camps, motorists could pay a dollar or two a head for the privilege of driving right up to one of the ten or fifteen teepees, adobes, or log cabins arranged courtyard style off the side of the road—unless you were in Maine, where you might visit a Danish Village instead. Oil companies as well as markets and restaurants offered drive-up service in thematic splendor too, constructing mission-styled stations in California, Colonial clapboards in New England, and pagodas in the most improbable of places. While at times the themes were related to the locale—serving as a kind of place marker—escapism was the point, providing travelers with a sense of the extraordinary, that they really had left home for a faraway place, and ensuring the memorability of the stop.[64]

No piece of highway architecture loomed larger on the landscape and in the public imagination than the roadside giants that sold what they pictured. Who could resist stopping at the Jumbo Lemon, Giant Orange, or The Big Cone for a refreshment? Need a cup of tea? Sip it while sitting in a huge copper kettle. Wondering where to get gas in Winston-Salem, North Carolina? Look for the Shell trademark, blown up into three-dimensional concrete with just enough room inside for the station attendant to sell some oil and make change.[65] This was architecture as advertisement. Sometimes the giant statuaries of men, women, and animals at the side of the road were not selling any one item at all, but, like the fifteen-foot sculpture of Paul Bunyan and Babe the Blue Ox at Bemidji, Minnesota, built in 1937, acted as place markers of huge proportion, pointing the way to local attractions and paying homage to folk heroes and regional lore.[66]

All were part of "The Great American Roadside," the glorious marketplace unveiled by James Agee in an article for *Fortune* in 1934. The lesson he learned from the homegrown entrepreneurs he met on the road was that "The Eye is Quicker than the Brain . . . and therefore Freda Farms, near Hartford, Connecticut [in the shape of an open container of ice cream] does very nicely." So did papier-mâché owls lettered "I-Scream" (yes, selling ice cream; fig. 43), a smiling pig with orange neon teeth with tamales inside, and the Big Duck where eggs were sold.[67] Agee had it right—this was not about deep thinking or pondering the meaning of the architectural symbolism. One glance revealed all: it was advertising, straight from P. T. Barnum's handbook. And it was perfect for the roadside strip, where land was cheap, parking was ample, and a flamboyant idea was the biggest investment required to catch the attention of passing motorists.

The heyday of these thematic and colossal works of vernacular commercial architecture was from the late 1920s through the mid-1930s, with Southern California as one locus, hosting an estimated ninety such structures.[68] As that number suggests, these roadside fantasies were not omnipresent. They were memorable as part of a larger roadside scene that included a panoply of way-

43. Hoot Owl Café had a rotating head and blinking eyes made from Buick headlamps, Long Beach, California, c. 1926.

side stands and other structures, many of which were covered in a riot of hand-lettered signs and tacked-up tin or poster product advertisements.

Not all roadside businesses embraced these carnivalesque tactics. For instance, the billboard industry, which had spent decades polishing its tarnished heritage in Barnumesque ballyhoo, struggled to distance itself from the hot-dog stand owner and his jumble of handmade, irregularly sized signs. Others also sought more standardized approaches. By the late 1930s, streamlined and modernist designs were favored for gas station chains, supermarkets, and roadside restaurants. The flat-roofed rectangular boxes of glazed glass and steel or stucco lacked the literalism of thematic and fantastic roadside architecture but nevertheless served as its own advertisement. Like Teague's designs for Standard Oil stations, the aesthetic was a stripped down, functionalist packaging of the product, its transparent wrapper offering clarity of volumetric expression and allowing the interior goods, brand name, or other services to be read from the facade.[69] The Gulf, Shell, and Standard oil companies distributed thousands of these prefabricated structures along the nation's highways, planting them and national billboard campaigns as branded packages to distinguish what was otherwise a visibly undifferentiated product. While the Jumbo Lemons and Big Kones were oversized replicas of independently produced items for sale, the streamlined boxes were their mass-produced and packaged successors.

As gargantuan products and packages, the buildings and billboards lining the highways helped turn the landscape itself into a giant shopping emporium. Arterial roads were the aisles, cars the shopping carts.[70] One Victor Gruen design for an Inglewood, California, furniture store called forth this analogy as well, its critic declaring it a "roadside display case," an example of "pure and simple exhibitionism," as if the private, inner recesses of the store had been laid promiscuously bare to public view.[71] As arterial highways became the new Main Streets defining the linear expansion of the marketplace, *exhibitionism* was but a demure term to apply to the variety of ways in which many businesses unabashedly revealed their commercial purposes without a hint of modesty. They joined billboards in wearing their function on the outside, hiding nothing from view, blurring the lines between indoors and out, private and public space, center and periphery.

CHAPTER 9

THE STRIP

'

A constellation of factors, including the activities of the outdoor advertising industry, laid the groundwork for the commercial strip of the postwar period. By the mid-1920s, central business districts of small and large cities were overrun with automobiles, congesting streets designed to handle only a fraction of the demands put on them.[1] Real-estate developers and merchants recognized the growing frustration of shoppers and, with and without the benefit of extensive market and traffic studies, they went to the fringes of the central city, where land was less expensive, parking ample, and congestion not yet an issue. Businesses logically migrated toward arterial highways.

Since the nineteenth century, metropolitan areas had grown in this fashion, with trunk lines extending from the central city developing simple, inexpensive one-story structures that could be easily used for a variety of retail purposes. This provided the property owner with rental income while he waited for the land to appreciate in value. These lanes were called "taxpayers" and they stretched from several blocks to several miles, their range increasing with the growth of automobility.[2]

These linear corridors of commerce were not limited to the areas around downtowns or alongside streetcar routes. They extended far beyond the edge of the incorporated city, persistently following the improving highways and widened boulevards. In rural areas, "ribbon" and "shoe-string slums" of commerce developed too.[3] One realtor was amazed that even the most arbitrary and deserted areas sprouted successful businesses if they were on the path between two destinations and accommodated the car. What mattered to businesses, he added, was not the number of pedestrians and automobiles passing a location, but their ability to stop. After all, traffic might be key to trade, but parking was the only way to get those dollars in the door.⁴

In metropolitan areas, other factors—such as zoning—contributed to the formation of the strings of businesses along boulevards and thoroughfares. Following the passage of the first comprehensive zoning codes in New York in 1916, many cities established separate zones for residential, commercial, and industrial property use (with a smattering of mixed residential-commercial and commercial-industrial zones). Zoning prohibited billboards, filling stations, and hot-dog stands from being planted next to homes.⁵ Although business was restricted from residential areas, planners tended to over accommodate it elsewhere, automatically allocating the property fronting main roads for commercial use. Often, they dedicated far more land than could ever be realistically used for that purpose, particularly since commercial property tended to be more expensive than residential lots. The error of this approach was encapsulated by this example: "if every boulevard frontage in Los Angeles County were to be zoned for business there would be more business frontage than could be reasonably expected from all the population of the United States." In Milwaukee, surveys revealed that due to this "shoe-string zoning," "only 39.88 percent of all the area zoned for business was actually in business use."⁶ Often this meant there were long stretches of vacant lots lining streets and boulevards. Moreover, acknowledged Harland Bartholomew, responsible for over sixty comprehensive city plans during the period of 1912 to 1940, the surplus of business property stimulated unreasonable speculation, created problems of taxation, and oftentimes invited "blighting of large stretches of property along our main thoroughfares."⁷

To the speculator-developer of these taxpayer blocks, the billboard provided revenue by using the walls and roofs of the generic commercial buildings for income. Inexpensive by comparison to other structures one might erect on the land, billboards also became a popular use of otherwise vacant lots. First, landowners completely covered their real-estate taxes with the profits from renting to billboard owners. This benefited both themselves and the municipal agencies to which they paid taxes. Billboard owners who leased from landowners could depreciate the posterboards on their taxes (until 1934 they did not even need to supply supporting evidence), and billboard owners who also owned the land could write off both. Considering that billboards occupied otherwise neglected space, it was a good deal all around.⁸

Billboards activated these areas both economically and visually. Photographs of commercial strips in many metropolitan areas reveal the omnipresence of billboards as accouterments to single- and double-story commercial taxpayers,

adding vivid color, height, illumination, and multiplicity to the repetition of similar storefronts. Images of Los Angeles in the 1920s and 1930s also show how billboards served as physical and conceptual markers of the evolving commercial
strip (figs. 44–45). On boulevards that were originally planned as residential areas,
but were arrested in their development and were now semicommercial, billboards
occupied vacant lots next to Victorian houses, presumably until other more lucrative uses arose. Along the east-west boulevards of Wilshire and Sunset and the
north-south avenues of Vermont and Western, scattered rows of commercial
development were interspersed with lots containing ornately columned billboards
arranged in a broad V shape, one facing each direction of traffic, whose individual proportions mimicked those of the shops nearby.[9]

Marking the site for later commercial development, billboards, as one
industry spokesman said, put "vacant lots to work carrying the pictorial messages that stimulate the traffic of the economic merchandising of goods. They
spread and stabilize distribution," and cultivated the "spirit of growth, of development, [and] of economic progress" that "every city desires."[10] Despite the
overblown language, the statement is plausible, especially given the large
amounts of property that billboards occupied when they were properly positioned for long-range viewing and illuminated with high-powered floodlights
to optimize nighttime broadcasting. Done up according to Outdoor
Advertising Association of America (OAAA) guidelines—with well-maintained
landscaping and freshly painted columns, frames, and lattice fringe—the structures surely activated the site, transforming otherwise desolate stretches into
zones of commercial occupation.

Though large plots of land used for displays helped motorists see the ad
before they actually arrived at the spot, their size also served the common
practice of billboard owners to purchase or lease more land than they intended
to actually use. They did this to avoid being displaced by their landlords'
desires to use the land for other, more profitable uses, such as "parking
grounds, used car markets, and purposes other than for building." With bigger
parcels of land at their disposal, owners had the option of "subrenting the
space in the rear of our panels for parking purposes." Many companies also
crafted vacant property leases that would protect them "against competition
and unscrupulous property owners."[11]

Companies like Foster and Kleiser tried to procure ten-year leases of land
and to purchase outright any property with actual or potential advertising value.
Walter Foster explained: "If we can buy any property that will be paid for in ten
years, we buy it."[12] Like Foster and Kleiser, the Detroit-based Walker and

44.–45. Billboards occupy the
vacant lots along Wilshire
Boulevard, Los Angeles, 1928
(right) and 1938 (below).

Company had ten-year leases. Their leases strictly regulated the terms by which the billboard operator would be asked by the property owner to vacate the premises. Though the landowner had the right to terminate the lease "in the event of the erection of a permanent building on said premises," Walker had another stipulation: "As a measure of protection against the unfair lessor who has no intention of building but only wishes to make use of this clause to evict us, we have added 'in the event that the proposed building is not erected as planned, the privilege herein given shall continue in force for the full term herein specified.'"[13]

Many outdoor companies were aggressive in their land acquisition, like Foster and Kleiser, which sent teams of trained men to travel the entire Pacific Coast to make "an actual count of all important cities, roads, and places" with vacant lots of potential advertising value. The task of the engineering assistant, armed with lists of ideal locations in and around every town, was to strike up relationships with local businessmen, the mayor, members of the chamber of commerce, and the leading clubs with political or social influence, including "women's clubs which may have influence." He kept track of locations and, every thirty days, he or another company man checked with landowners previously unwilling to lease or sell to see if they had changed their minds.[14] The company leased and purchased at least one-third more land than it needed. Industry leaders advised companies to safeguard themselves from space shortages by planning for 50 percent more sites than what they currently used at any one time, and to establish a "fund for protection" that enabled them to purchase extra land. These practices granted companies the advantage of both a real-estate investment and the prevention of competitors from moving in. It also helped companies to expand into fringe areas at a low cost and to hold onto the land until it garnered a higher price. In short, it was a form of real-estate speculation. Foster and Kleiser even purchased land along scenic highways in California as a means, they said, of preserving it from excess commercialism; the federal government saw this differently, as an attempt to hinder fair trade and competition.[15]

The serious concern outdoor advertisers paid to their real estate suggests that billboards provided much more than a mere symbolic tool for building automobile-oriented commercial strips. The purchase and lease of land and other display space was an economic force that contributed to the diffusion of the roadside strip. In this, billboards joined a host of other pioneers of the roadside strip, from department stores that eased their way out from central business districts in the 1920s, to chain stores, filling stations, drive-in markets, and food stands. They served as catalysts for further commercial development, whether on the urban fringe or more distant and rural thoroughfares.

Chain stores, for example, could afford to build on sites on the outskirts of commercial centers. They had numbers on their side, from research information on traffic compiled through their many branch offices, to bulk sales that could make up for other branches that might lose money. Other local and regional roadside businesses could afford to go even farther afield, since they required lower investment. For instance, there were twenty Big Freezes—boldly painted white and red shops shaped like old-fashioned ice cream makers—erected on vacant lots around Los Angeles in the late 1920s, from Laguna Beach to the San Fernando Valley. Simple, inexpensive structures, easy to put up and take down, the stores could be packed up and moved down the road when the landlord decided to erect a more permanent building on the lot.[16] Indeed, such food stands served as good taxpayers, occupying vacant lots in urban areas, as well as marking the rural stretches where gas stations, motels, and other services aimed to recreational drivers tended to aggregate.[17]

The most numerous of roadside businesses to "colonize" the commercial strip were gasoline stations. They invaded the countryside in the 1920s, when oil companies vastly overdeveloped their fields, resulting in an immense glut of gasoline; flagging sales due to economic hard times in the Depression years led to the same result. The response of oil companies was to build filling stations devoted to their brand, to develop their market more intensively. As zoning restricted them from residential areas, companies like Standard Oil of New York established real-estate departments devoted to acquiring sites in the exurban arena and on rural roads. While in 1920 there were 15,000 stations in the United States, by 1930 that number was 124,000. To put that in perspective, and to suggest that the 1920s were, in fact, the initial moment of the automobility and decentralization explosions, consider that in 1990 there were 111,657 stations.[18] Notably, where filling and service stations went, other businesses followed, inciting more development still.[19]

The outdoor advertising industry allied itself with roadside businesses, emphasizing its "local service, nationally applied" in order to appeal to both chains and independents. Oil companies, needless to say, were among the biggest users of outdoor advertising. As oil companies consolidated and standardized their stations and national advertising campaigns, billboards became an especially important component of their marketing, since it put the brand name in front of the public where they had reason to look for it (see fig. 10).

The outdoor advertising industry claimed it could do the same for a form of automobile-oriented commerce new to the 1930s—the supermarket. Growing out of drive-in markets and chain stores of the 1920s, supermarkets were a creation of the age of distribution.[20] They were huge warehouses (compared to contemporary markets) that stocked a wide variety of goods and counted on profits that would come through bulk sales at low prices. They saved money by being wholly self-service, and carried nationally branded items that people would know to look for and want to buy without a clerk's assistance. Supermarkets required a lot of space and demanded parking, since customers would be driving to do their buying in bulk, so they were located on cheaper land, far from established nodes of commercial activity (or even residential areas), and drew upon a larger trading area of mobile consumers. National branding strategies, which put the burden of advertising on manufacturers rather than on the supermarket (in contrast to the chains, which were establishing their own private brands), the availability of the refrigerator (which allowed people to stock up on goods), and of course the automobile, helped bring the supermarket into being.[21]

Food and beverage manufacturers were second only to gasoline companies and automotive goods as clients for outdoor advertisers until the 1950s, when the astronomical growth in supermarkets put food products to the top of the list. As much as outdoor advertising serviced the supermarket, the relationship was reciprocal. For one, the supermarket represented an additional source of circulation of mobile consumers. As independent and chain supermarkets grew nationally in the 1940s and 1950s, they began to affect the traffic patterns upon which outdoor advertisers based their trade. Starting in 1938, Outdoor Advertising Incorporated (OAI) called upon OAAA members ("a veritable research army") and the Traffic Audit Bureau (TAB) to study supermarket sales volume and circulation in each of their regions, and to come up with a map of those locations and figures. OAI recognized that the travels of motorists to supermarkets represented a built-in, easy-to-locate secondary market for outdoor advertisers, one that would also be easy to sell to supermarkets and national manufacturers in addition to the usual coverage promised by outdoor advertisers. This, they thought, would give outdoor advertising an edge over other media, all of whom (especially radio) were being employed by big food manufacturers for their national branding campaigns.[22]

Able to target mobile consumers precisely, OAI could thus claim: "Outdoor Advertising is Made-to-Measure for the demands of Self-Service." Why worry about "inferior shelf position" when one could reach "*all* of America's food market" through billboards? Customer selection in the age of self-service is entirely visual, one publicist wrote, giving outdoor advertising the extra advantage of "appetite appeal," picturing the product larger than life, in four colors, with packaging and trademark intact. He added that billboards offered the extra ingredient of "recency," providing the "last word," as a "point

46. Cutouts of Tenderay Beef (painted by Lyman Simpson) used "appetite appeal" to mark the way to Kroger supermarkets, Cincinnati, 1959.

of purchase" display before the shopper entered the store (fig. 46).[46]

With the benefit of the TAB studies, supermarkets were thus able to target audiences at just the right places, to the extent that Oscar Meyer could claim that their ads were within $3\frac{1}{2}$ minutes of most metropolitan shopping centers. The national and local coverage of outdoor advertising by the 1950s was indeed a science, tailored to reach not only specific retail areas or shopping centers but also specific occupational, language, and social groups.[24] In this sense, outdoor advertising was not only targeting audiences, but inscribing the landscape itself with social, cultural, and class distinctions.

In the post–World War II years, the streets and highways of the decentralizing urban landscape became more crowded showrooms for a consumer culture of renewed vigor, where not one but two cars in the ranch-house garage were the best way to keep up with the Joneses. During the war, rationing of gasoline and tires and restrictions on unnecessary building construction and travel had slowed roadside development. Highway construction halted, too, and did not resume again until the mid-1950s. Car production, on the other hand, started right up again after the war, and by 1955 reached an all-time peak.[25] As a result, the arterial highways formerly seen as the endless, frictionless frontier for auto-friendly commercial expansion became a congested morass.

The cacophony of the commercial strip escalated in proportion to the growth in automobility and lack of adequate roads to handle the flow. The more businesses and signs there were, the greater the competition to gain the attention of mobile consumers. Shop signs, often standing separate from the building, became bigger and more glaring. Billboards increased in size (a 30–sheet poster of 115 inches by 259 inches becoming an alternative to the twenty-four-sheet standard of 104 inches by 234 inches), height, and level of animation. Objects and cutouts made from molded plastics and acrylics as well as borderless Fiberglass board allowed the advertising content to explode off of the billboard surface (plate 10), while new reflective paints and superreal painting techniques gave two-dimensional art an enhanced sense of verisimilitude.[26] Efforts to compete with the new advertising medium of television also led to the innovation of rotating tripanels, which offered three changing scenes on one billboard. OAAA members continued to follow the trends in industrial design, and hired Raymond Loewy, one of the innovators of streamlining to create an aerodynamic billboard frame that became the new industry standard (barely changed for decades thereafter) with its slender beveled nineteen-inch molding, border of pearl gray, angled gold stripe, and white enameled surface.[27] By the 1950s, the frame was lifted high in the sky on aircraft-grade alloy legs. New "boom" trucks, which held racked-up sections of billboards and a crane to lift them up to the frame, allowed signs to be placed at greater heights where they could be more visible to the strip-driving public.[28] As the strip increased in density and length, it also rose in height, a concrete jungle forested by signs.

For many, the fanfare of signs, shops, and billboards stretching out in linear fashion was an uncoordinated mess of crass, tacky grotesqueries, a honky-tonk. To regional planners like Clarence Stein and Catherine Bauer, and to Wilderness Society founder Benton Mackaye, this unplanned arterial growth forecasted nothing less than an endless "roadtown" based on the prioritization of the automobile and commerce over social and communal facilities. The public arena was being forsaken by such dispersion. For Stein and Bauer, the shopping center emerged as the somewhat improbable solution to the problem. They thought that planned centers, where all retail could be gathered in one place and all the signs clustered onto one standardized unit, would reduce the proliferation of linear commercialism.[29] Unfortunately, though, the shopping centers merely became another form of roadside architecture contributing to the automotive way of life. Other urban planners and highway officials thought that building bypass roads would free up highways that had become cluttered with commerce. Of course, those bypasses eventually faced the same plight as the trafficked ones they were built to alleviate. For Mackaye, planned towns that were separate from highways, and highways that were clear of the residences and commerce of towns, were the answer. Decentralization, Mackaye, Lewis Mumford, and others believed, held great potential for humanizing urban life and bringing people in contact with nature. Unchecked and uncoordinated commercial growth along the highways did little to achieve this. As metropolitan regions grew into the countryside and highways connecting rural settlements developed into linear corridors of consumption, the distinctions between city and country seemed lost. Commerce was colonizing the natural environment. And the strip was paving the way. Though strip growth reached a frenzy in the decades after the Second World War, its roots—and a good deal of its trunk—grew in the 1920s and 1930s.

The influence of outdoor advertising thus resonates on several levels, but allow me here to conclude with just one—the fostering of our present sense of placelessness and the meandering of the market beyond geographic boundaries. The nationally standardized billboard structures, advertisements, and featured goods created a web of recognizable material similarities that served to visibly connect different people and places while it marked and encouraged highway lanes as commercial strips. This diffused and spread the market, leveled regionally specific place characteristics, and standardized spaces dedicated to advertising and selling. As national chains and franchises revolutionized retail, restaurant, and hotel industries by the 1960s and 1970s, their signs, structures, and billboard advertisements served as another means by which local distinctions became leveled. As a regional and local medium, increasingly adept at targeting mobile audiences, with greater and greater specificity from the 1950s onward, outdoor advertising did offer local variations on the national themes. Mostly, however, the specificity they provided was not regional. Ironically, the successful charting of diffuse markets had led right back to a kind of fixing of market boundaries, not by geography but according to social delineations related to presumed patterns of travel and buying. Traffic had acquired distinguishing contours, while places lost theirs. It had been this realization of the outdoor advertising industry—that traffic itself, wherever it went, now comprised the market—that had helped make places as diverse as Houston, Minneapolis, Oklahoma City, Atlanta, and Los Angeles come to resemble one another as the same sprawling commercial buyway.

PART 3

"THE BILLBOARD WAR"
SCENIC SISTERS AND THE BUSINESS OF HIGHWAY BEAUTIFICATION

"THE BILLBOARD WAR"

Outdoor advertisers envisioned the crisscrossing country roads and newly paved highways as a commercial utopia of endless "buyways" wrapping the nation in what one company in 1955 called "ribbons of gold." But to other observers, the nation's beauteous bounties were being wrapped in "shoe-string slums" of billboard alleys.[1] In their dystopic vision, the byways were becoming buyways, but they were buyways of blight, less representative of the opening of opportunity than of the closing of its corridors (fig. 47).

Opposition to outdoor advertising began in the late-nineteenth-century urban arena and then stretched into the countryside along with cars, highways, and national advertising campaigns. By the 1920s and 1930s, resistance to outdoor advertising became a national battle over aesthetic rights to the roadside environment, a battle that lasted more than forty years. The soldiers of the "billboard war" pitted the beauty of nature against the beast of commerce, and usually women against men. Roadside reformers, drawn from the ranks of women's clubs, garden clubs, and other civic associations, set out to rid the public highway of the signs of commerce. Outdoor advertisers comprised their foe, men who asserted their private commercial right to broadcast across public space.

Each side fought from behind traditional gender lines that had been articulated in the previous century according to an ideology of separate spheres and a "cult of true womanhood" in which women were unpaid domestic caretakers while men were breadwinners operating in the public arena.[2] By focusing on aesthetic and social concerns, women involved in roadside reform remained faithful to their traditional gender roles. Cleaning the face of the country was women's work. They justified their presence in the public arena by describing roadside reform as domestic housekeeping writ large. Or, as Rheta Childe Dorr

Highways, or

Buy-ways?

Nature Magazine, Washington, D. C.

47. Anti-billboard cartoon, 1929.

put it in 1919, "Woman's place is Home, but Home is not contained within the four walls of an individual house. Home is the community."³ Contentions over the appearance of the roadside environment expanded the arena of domestic housekeeping, from the home front to the road front, from the (ideally) stable and rooted private realm to the public spaces of transience. The billboard war thus emerged as a struggle as much over the public roles of women and men as it was over the shape and appearance of the road and the roadside.

However useful it may be to note certain dynamics of gender in the billboard war, as well as other dichotomies such as private interests versus public rights, and even commercial versus domestic concerns, these pairings fall short and dissolve. The two seemingly opposed groups were less divergent in their views and backgrounds than we might first imagine. Their similarities in the face of purported difference exemplified a common core of belief in corporate liberalism, or the hope that benevolent business, aided by the timely nudging of government, would eventually take the best path for the good of the nation. This, in short, is what was meant by the American Way. Both sides in the billboard war shared the belief (although to varying extents) that the confluence of government and compassionate corporations could best manage the roadside environment. This alliance of government and business was accepted, even assumed, by roadside reformers at a pivotal moment in the history of media conglomeration, as fewer companies began to control more outlets of public expression.[4] The result of this fundamental agreement is what we experience when we drive the highways and buyways of America today.

Both the warring women, named "scenic sisters" by scornful outdoor advertisers, and their billboard "brethren" (also called "boys" and oftentimes "barons") were cultural producers and arbiters of the road and the roadside environment.[5] Both sides sought to define the proper use and appearance of the public space of the road and roadside and both factions asserted their rights as private citizens to profit from the public highways. They also agreed to their respective gender roles, and exploited these fully. They did disagree concerning which legal (and extralegal) means could maintain their priorities constitutionally.[6] They also differed, in essence, on what comprised the real value of the roadside. To outdoor advertisers that value was simple to gauge. Outdoor advertisers had to produce potential consumers wherever automobiles might take them, which by the 1920s was already quite far out. To the billboard industry, the value of the roadside was no different from the value of any space or place; it was determined entirely by its ability to reach these consumers. The roadside reformers, however, had a much more subtle and indeed prescient vision of where automobiles, roads, and urban decentralization were headed—directly toward sprawl. If the automobile helped one escape the city, what was the point of having the urban signs of commerce, work, and markets leading the way? To the reformers, the very value of the automobile and the road would be deflated if signs of commerce were to be found everywhere the car could go. Some spaces had to be saved as bucolic and scenic, or else people would have no sane reason to get into their cars in the first place. That is to say, while outdoor advertisers had an utterly commercial ideal of the roadside's value, reformers thought the roadside might have an aesthetic value as well, indeed one worth preserving.

Yet as much as the values of the two groups could sometimes differ, and as much as their worldviews seemed to share, they shared nothing quite as strongly as their common promotion of the myth of the open road and the different sorts of mobility it promised. Both sides idealized and promoted a pastoral view through the windshield of the automobile, saw the landscape and the road as commodities with value, and used the rhetoric of democracy, national identity, individual rights, and civic pride to express their visions.

CHAPTER 10

WHEN SEPARATE SPHERES COLLIDE

Women of the middle and upper classes had been vocal opponents of bill-boards for some time before the proliferation of the automobile. Around the turn of the century they participated in a wide variety of municipal art societies, civic clubs, and village improvement associations. They also helped found national organizations such as the American League for Civic Improvement (ALCI) and were auxiliary members of the American Park and Outdoor Art Association (APOAA), both of which joined to form the American Civic Association (ACA) in 1904.[1] Members of groups like these were determined to create cities that were "an education in beauty" and that bred "moral order" in children and new Americans. For them, leaving commercial enterprises such as billboard advertising unchecked was tantamount to condoning moral decline and urban disorder.[2]

Reformers considered civic virtue, morality, and the environment to be causally related. Whereas mid-nineteenth-century reformers asserted that immorality created slums, by the turn of the century most believed that the contrary was true: crowded, unsanitary conditions bred social disorder, unrest, and, as a consequence, immorality. Both theories allowed middle-class citizens to understand the transformation of the city from a relatively homogenous, cohesive community to an increasingly industrial, anonymous place hosting a diversity of people, factories, and leisure activities.[3] One idea was clear to both early and later urban reformers: social and environmental disorders were related, so control over one would restore stability in the other.

Reformers measured both commerce and manufacturing by a moral yard-stick, with some industries faring poorly in their estimation. Among the less savory commercial activities were theatrical enterprises, drinking establish-

48. "The Usual Class of Advertisements," Fifth Avenue and 108th Street, New York, 1913.

ments, and outdoor advertising.[4] Indeed, reformers deemed turn-of-the-century advertisements for burlesque shows, circus acts, patent medicines, and other personal-care products (from corsets to laxatives) to be especially egregious. Scantily clad performers and bodily functions depicted in ads were better left behind closed doors.[5]

Yet the content of ads was not the only problem. Their size and form were equally troublesome. Frequently large, brightly colored, multitiered, and multilayered (fig. 48), this "unsightly" and "undignified" form of marketing was a travesty to good taste; worse still, it robbed citizens of the benevolent effects of civic beauty. Reformers derided "gaudy" ads for supplying the wrong aesthetic training. They also believed the poor to be particularly susceptible to hullabaloo because of their inability to reason. Reformers thought that the spectacle of the ads would overwhelm the already guileless masses, convincing them to spend money on things they did not need and could not afford. The view of reformers, then, was based on both class-derived prejudice and discomfort with the rapid transition from a circumstance of urban scarcity and thrift to a mass culture of abundance and consumption.[6] But problems extended even beyond this. Billboards also seemed to symbolize to reformers what they perceived as the increasing disorder of the modern city, whose throngs of different classes, colors, and kinds of people impinged upon both middle-class mores and the reform ideal of a socially and technologically engineered environment. By articulating a collective vision for the proper appearance of the city—one without unruly signs of both mass marketing and masses—reformers asserted their status and their power.[7]

Urban reform efforts tried to improve physical infrastructure, including sanitation, housing, and transportation, and tried also to create an appropriate moral, aesthetic, and civic training ground for inhabitants. Or, as ALCI President Charles Zueblin claimed in a 1902 meeting, "The movement for civic improvement may be said to have a threefold expression, first, the new civic spirit; second, the training of the citizen; and third, the making of the city."[8] Accordingly, both the ALCI and the ACA participated in what became known as the City Beautiful movement. It complemented other urban reforms, including municipally sponsored amusements, tenement reform, park and playground development, civic pageantry, municipal art, and city planning.[9] Epitomized by the White City built for the 1893 World's Columbian Exposition in Chicago, the City Beautiful movement emerged during economic depression, worker unrest, overcrowding, and unsanitary conditions in many urban centers. With its model municipal center labeled the Court of Honor, the White City became emblematic of the hopeful promise of all that scientific (i.e., professional) urban planning could provide: order, cleanliness, edifying aesthetic beauty, community cohesion, civic responsibility.[10]

Planners of the White City, including architects Daniel Burnham and Louis Sullivan and landscape architect Frederick Law Olmsted, asserted that civic beauty and order could be achieved with wide, landscaped boulevards, public statuary, plazas, parks, monumental classical architecture, and neoclassical stucco buildings, as well as advanced systems of transportation and sanitation. Burnham and other architects, as well as Charles Mulford Robinson, whose 1903 *Modern Civic Art, or The City Made Beautiful* became the bible of the movement, believed these elements would foster a unified and corporate community and breed the civic responsibility necessary for its survival. These intentions were reasserted frequently in subsequent events such as the First National Conference on City Planning and the Problems of Congestion in 1909.[11]

Usually the leading businessmen and property owners of a town or city, whose interests supposedly stood for those of the community-at-large, brought in the planners to beautify their city. These leading citizens, men and women both, included active anti-billboard crusaders (fig. 49). In the 1890s, Robinson

Courtesy of **Mr. Donnell**

49. Those searching for the City Beautiful found their way blocked by overbearing advertising signs, as this 1910 anti-billboard cartoon suggests.

had led billboard reform and became a vocal City Beautiful publicist. Frederick Law Olmsted Jr., son of the landscape architect for both New York's Central Park and Chicago's Columbian Exposition, also campaigned against billboards. They were joined by J. Horace McFarland, a Harrisburg, Pennsylvania, printer and horticulturist who made City Beautiful his life's work. These reform voices continued long after city planning had become standard practice for towns and cities coast to coast. They crusaded with religious zeal for a landscape, if not free of commercial clutter, then at least organized with home, commerce, and nature each in its correct place. They wished not simply to create a more beautiful environment, but to impose upon others their moral and aesthetic ideals of what was proper.

Women formed their own phalanx in this movement for city beautification and urban reform. In his early articles, Robinson credited women's roles in shaping the movement. In 1912, women's efforts in urban affairs comprised an entire issue of the magazine *American City*.[12] This was no small matter, as the magazine catered to architects, planners, engineers, and other male professionals and laypeople who were as likely to be threatened as they were to be inspired by women's active role in the urban-public domain. The progressive historian Mary Beard, in her book *Women's Work in Municipal Reform* (1915), offers further evidence of women's visible role in the movement, claiming that women actually initiated the organized municipal reform movement. She writes, "Whoever labors for the city or town or village beautiful in the United States may find intelligent and hearty support on the part of women's associations, even though they are, in many places, merely organized for literary or 'cultural' purposes. Thousands of men may loaf around clubs without ever showing the slightest concern about the great battle for decent living conditions that is now going on in our cities; but it is a rare woman's club that long remains indifferent."[13] McFarland also traced the beginning of the movement to women, noting, "It was the women . . . who dinned and dinned into our ears until at last we men got ashamed of our laziness and selfishness as citizens." He claimed that in his planning work with over four hundred American towns, women had most forcefully promoted the "civic betterment movement." In Chicago, the vice president of the ACA concurred, reporting that while men had joined the civic improvement associations, "it was women who had started them . . . every one of the fifty-seven clubs."[14] Even the seminal 1909 Conference on National Planning, a benchmark in planning history, came from women's agitation, and women were vocal participants in its sessions.[15]

Women undertook the removal of billboard advertising as part of larger city beautification projects. They cast their objections to advertising outdoors in terms of moral aesthetics. This wed domains in which women's "superior" sensibilities held sway to a public culture otherwise dominated by men. Indeed, civic beautification projects played an important part in the history of women's voluntary associations. The latter grew in the late nineteenth century from art and literary clubs to civic reform groups. These considered not just culture and aesthetics but also social problems.[16] Municipal housekeeping groups sprang from the culture clubs, comprised of educated middle-class women who had limited acceptable work options open to them. Settlement houses such as Jane Addams's Hull House in Chicago served as a training ground for middle-class women in social reform, nurturing notable figures such as Florence Kelley and Mary Simkhovitch. The efforts of these women, among others, promoted the creation of an urban infrastructure to handle better housing, sanitation, and other civic concerns related to the problems of the industrial city.[17] Both the aesthetic and the social reformers maintained a fidelity to each other and to a domestic ideology positing that women should serve others; they undertook their efforts in the name of citizen participation and community self-determination that was aimed to promote "a higher public spirit and a better social order."[18]

Starting from urban arenas, the activities of civic reformers soon stretched into smaller towns. Here planners applied their modern forms to entirely new regions that had not yet accumulated layers of urban congestion, pollution, and disorder.[19] College-educated Carol Kennicott of Sinclair Lewis's *Main Street* (1920) failed to find her calling in the desert of professions from which a woman could choose, but suddenly solved her dilemma: "That's what I'll do after college! I'll get my hands on one of these prairie towns and make it beautiful. . . . Why should they have all the garden suburbs on Long Island? Nobody has done anything with the ugly towns here in the Northwest except hold revivals and build libraries. . . . I'll make 'em put in a village green, and darling cottages, and a quaint Main Street!"[20]

Lewis's fictional character had countless real incarnations who belonged to municipal improvement leagues, civic associations, and women's clubs in towns across the country. Like Kennicott and her clubwomen friends in fictional Gopher Prairie, these women were often married to the business leaders and professional men of their towns. In their urban reform activities, many sought City Beautiful ideals: broad avenues, grand civic structures, and gardened plazas like those of Kennicott's dreams. These ideals could be realized most fully not in big and established cities like Chicago and New York, but in the newer suburbs and small cities dotting the nation. Women became boosters, promoting the growth and prosperity of their towns as much through aesthetic as through economic and political strategies. Typically, the rhetoric of domesticity enabled their entrance into the public realm, and soon it allowed them to take their interest beyond the town and on to the road.

In the 1920s, as civic reform and planning disseminated outward from cities along with large numbers and classes of automobilized Americans, women's civic and political interests followed. Opposition to roadside advertising became a counterpart to the aestheticizing of the City Beautiful. Many women's civic groups, including art and garden clubs, banded together in defense of the roadside, rural, and natural environments.[21] Later, when the Depression halted urban development and construction everywhere *except* along the highways, the women followed with broom and dustpan—not to clean up behind the Civilian Conservation Corps building the rural roads, but to sweep aside the advertisers, merchants, farmers, and others who wished to follow the paved paths to profit. Women took their urban reform on the road.

The General Federation of Women's Clubs (GFWC) had been involved in conservation programs since it was founded in 1890. With a formalized network of female associations in towns and cities across the nation, it offered a framework for efficiently addressing issues of common interest. By 1909, the GFWC numbered over 800,000 members in nearly 500 affiliate clubs. It had also established state "protective committees" aimed at saving the nation's beauty spots from "despoliation" by lobbying for forest preserves, water reclamation projects, and national parks. Generally they believed that "the national parks belong to the people. Every citizen of the United States has a certain right of personal ownership. That right will be taken away, wholly or in part, if Congress permits the natural resources of the parks to be used for commercial purposes."[22] Accordingly, the GFWC participated in President Theodore Roosevelt's conference on conservation in 1908, and led early debates about conservation versus preservation. They also endorsed the Good Roads movement of the early 1900s and applied its protective policies to the landscapes that highway construction was increasingly opening up to public view.

A woman emerged from this club scene of activism who would come to dominate the arena of roadside reform for forty years until her death in 1952. A graduate of Vassar College, Elizabeth Boyd Lawton dedicated her life to obliterating "billboard blight." Her epiphany was as sudden as it was visceral. One summer, while driving upstate to escape New York City's heat and disarray, Lawton became appalled by the signs that marred her view. Billboards had ruined the journey to her Lake George retreat. With the help of the Woman's Civic Club of Glens Falls, in 1920 she surveyed the highways in her area, noted who the advertisers were, and conducted a letter-writing campaign to convince them to remove their signs. She also petitioned for restrictive legislation.[23]

After some success, Lawton proposed to the New York State Federation of Women's Clubs that her local strategies be applied on the state and national levels. The GFWC promptly condemned billboards "as preventing the full enjoyment of outdoor beauty," and dedicated its national art committee to the issue.[24] By 1924, the GFWC, representing more than three million members, voted to support a coalition of forty organizations called the National Committee for Restriction of Outdoor Advertising and later renamed the National Roadside Council (NRC) in 1934. The NRC was to serve as a clearinghouse for anti-billboard organizations, including the various state members of the GFWC (and the

3,500 women's clubs they represented), the Garden Club of America (organized in 1912 and committed to conservation), the American Scenic and Historic Preservation Society (founded in 1895), and even groups with membership dominated by men, including the National Highway Association, the American Society of Landscape Architects, the ACA, and the American Nature Association. Initially the NRC claimed forty such affiliates. Five years later they had one hundred. With a membership representing over forty states, from rural areas and small towns to big cities, the NRC was well positioned to have a national impact.[25] Naturally, it was presided over by Lawton, as was the Billboard Restrictions Committee of the GFWC's department of fine arts.[26]

Lawton wrote for a great variety of planning and general interest magazines, lectured nationally, and lobbied widely for roadside regulations and nature conservation. She also conducted extensive state-by-state surveys documenting roadside conditions and then published the results in the journal *Roadside Bulletin*, for which she served as both editor and primary author. She recognized the new strength that lay in women's voting rights. She also saw that women's clubs had an "old-girl network" with access to the "old-boy network," which could be harnessed to persuade the men with whom they were affiliated. The outdoor advertising industry recognized these strengths and also understood the threat that the NRC posed when it inspired both women's and men's organizations devoted to nature conservation, urban planning, and architecture.[27] Rightly, they tended to see Lawton as the primary troublemaker. Her campaigns were so effective that when she died, leaders of the Outdoor Advertising Association of America circulated her obituary with a handwritten eulogy, "File: Nuisances Abated."[28] Within several years of her death, the NRC dissolved.[29]

With the slogan "Save the Beauty of America: The Landscape is No Place for Advertising," Lawton claimed that the NRC wished simply "to arouse and express public opinions" that the billboard "desecrates scenic and civic beauty."[30] While explaining the NRC's purpose to the federation, she benignly averred that "it consists solely in telling the advertiser how we feel about these rural boards; calling his attention to the fact that the scenic beauty of our country will soon be ruined if the rapid increase of signboards goes unchecked."[31] But politically savvy plans lay beneath her gracious words. While she established a base of grassroots consumer activism and welded "a chain of community interest," as one colleague said, the real core of her activity was aimed toward the men's realm—the legislature. Her true purpose was to induce zoning restrictions, taxation, and other regulations that limited outdoor advertising.[32]

For decades, however, the courts had ruled that aesthetic concerns were an inappropriate application of the police power's regulation of private property, which could only restrict land use to serve the public safety and welfare. "Aesthetic considerations are a matter of luxury and indulgence rather than of necessity," a New Jersey court ruled in 1905, "and it is necessity alone which justifies the exercise of the police power to take private property without compensation."[33] Similarly, a prohibition of all billboards in San Jose, based on the fact that they were "offensive to persons of refined taste," was invalidated by the California Supreme Court in 1909. Even when courts upheld billboard regulations, as one did in St. Louis in 1911, the judicial decision veiled all aesthetic concerns by making linkages to the ways that billboards jeopardized public safety and welfare. Billboards were fire hazards; they blew over in high winds; they obstructed light, air, and sun. The grounds behind them were used as privies, places of prostitution, trash receptacles, and retreats for "criminals and all classes of miscreants." A Chicago court in 1917 also ruled that billboards could be forbidden in residential areas, and for similar reasons: they were flammable, unsanitary, a public nuisance, and a cover for "dissolute and immoral practices" that were carried on behind them. These last two cases provided important precedents for restricting billboards, but courts did not utilize aesthetics to justify restrictions, nor would they until the 1950s and 1960s.[34]

Lawton and her organization thus faced a serious obstacle. One of her main arguments for the limitation of billboards was aesthetic. It was also the argument that most inspired the women who joined her organization, since many roadside reform groups grew out of art clubs. Yet the courts would not recognize aesthetics as legally significant. Her campaign, therefore, could not be waged strictly in the legal arena. Fortunately for Lawton, there was arising in the 1920s the recognition of an equally important arena, that of public opinion. "We believe that a public opinion campaign will pave the way for successful legislation later," Lawton decided, "and also will, of itself, produce a very real check on this nuisance. . . . That, club women, is our job."[35] By appealing to the public she could affect more than just the legislature. Business, too, was bound to see attitudinal shifts among its clientele in favor of beauty and the preservation of the natural environment, and against billboards.

There were also reasons of gender that pushed Lawton to make her case to the public rather than directly to the courts or the legislature. In the public arena, Lawton could stage the battle in terms of the sphere of interest with which women were most commonly affiliated–beauty and culture–when neither the courts nor the legislature seemed at all interested in these. Moreover, by limiting herself to a sphere suitable to her gender, Lawton did not overstep dangerous bounds and was able to attract men to her cause who would provide the masculine work that needed to be done, such as regional planning and design. This relationship was reflected even in Lawton's relationship to the NRC's attorney, Albert Bard. Both unpaid employees of the NRC, these two took complementary roles that aligned with gender expectations. Lawton emotionally rallied the all-important ground troops of clubwomen and got the public talking about beauty. Bard played the strategist behind the scenes who mapped the legal terrain, patiently advised, and tamed Lawton's heartfelt but sometimes unfeasible proclamations.[36] Between the two of them, Lawton and Bard efficiently covered publicity and policy, matters of the heart and the head. Within those roles, they managed to put America's billboard industry on the defensive.

Still, with so many women involved in civic improvement, interested men ran the risk of being feminized by the cause of beauty. In *Main Street*, Will Kennicott justifies not joining his wife Carol in her city beautification activities rather aggressively: "Would you like to have me go with you to Paris and study art, maybe, and wear velveteen pants and a woman's bonnet and live on spaghetti?"[37] Similar sentiments had been expressed in 1913, when reformers pushed for zoning to regulate outdoor advertising and real estate interests in New York City. Billposters, merchants, and laborers in such groups as the Lithographers Apprentice Union, representing a host of different ethnic groups, took to name-calling. The mostly Anglo-Saxon lawyers and businessmen of the Municipal Art Society and City Club were taunted as being "Art Leaguers" and the "aesthetic, lily white boys." Efforts at civic beauty called masculinity into question. Aesthetics and effete dilettantism were joined in feminine opposition to the masculine and muscular forces of free enterprise.[38]

Despite the slighting expectations of gender, the clubwomen often organized their publicity campaigns with the precision of a pyramid scheme. They learned to multiply the effects of concentrated efforts through the able use of club organization. A case in point was Philadelphia's Congress of Art, an active member of the NRC and supporter of Lawton's publicity campaign. The congress represented forty-five civic associations, including the City Parks Association, the Civic Club, and the Pennsylvania Academy of the Fine Arts. Each of those forty-five groups appointed four members to write weekly letters to advertisers who were contributing to "Billboard Boulevards" such as South Broad Street and Roosevelt Boulevard. Then, each month, all congress members targeted four national advertisers for additional canvassing.[39] The congress was just one sup-

**50. Anti-bill-
board bill-
board, c. 1933.**

porter of the NRC's platform, and it was a local, not a statewide, representative. Multiplied nationally, the NRC became more than just an annoyance.

Lawton and her scenic sisters used the mass media carefully. The NRC published its own quarterly magazine, and also used newsletters, pamphlets, circulars, and the publications of affiliated groups, to espouse their views. Members regularly wrote articles, editorials, and letters for daily newspapers and national magazines such as *Readers' Digest, Ladies' Home Journal*, and the *Saturday Evening Post*. The NRC hosted beautification contests "for campaign slogans, for roadside planting, for photographs of the worst and the best of roadside conditions, for the best essay on the right of the public to rural highway beauty."[40] They distributed postcards featuring winning slogans and billboard "blots of the month" through affiliated clubs, and didn't seem to notice when these slogans were represented within a picture of a billboard. Some even used billboards to advertise against billboard advertising (fig. 50), while others supported the erection of roadside screens to block the view of the billboards beyond.[41] Also popular among the clubwomen's publicity schemes were contests for schoolchildren, accompanied by game books and other publications. One book, titled *Growing Beauty*, featured boys and girls working in communities "turning ugliness into beauty" and depicting "the importance of appreciation, preservation and creation of outdoor beauty in our surroundings."[42] Such devices were not novel to the women. They were lifted from corporate strategies honed by professional practitioners of the nascent field of public relations.

Even while embracing modern methods of publicity, the women reformers continued to justify their activities with highly gendered ideologies. The

NRC began a campaign for road reform based on the role of woman as consumer. "Women are the buyers," Lawton explained. "It is claimed that 85 per cent of products sold in America are sold to women. When our merchants, local and national, realize that the women are determined to wipe out the rural billboard, the boards will fall."[43] She urged women to write to advertisers, manufacturers, retailers, and billboard companies to let them know that womanly sentiment was starting "to resent" outdoor advertising. Yet in this campaign the NRC had to learn to distinguish a fine line between expressing women's rights as consumers and the rightful place of women *away* from manly business. The scenic sisters discovered, slowly, never to challenge free enterprise, both in the probusiness climate of the Roaring Twenties and during the hard times of the Depression. Though in 1910 members of the GFWC had tried to pass resolutions to boycott manufacturers who used outdoor advertising, they did not garner support. Lawton was more successful in the 1920s, when she avoided the unseemliness of a boycott by urging clubwomen to exercise their commercial "rights of selection" (ably combining social Darwinism and consumerism).[44] "I favor products *not* advertised along the roads!" was the slogan of a national campaign, imprinted on stamps and stickers available at a dollar for a book of a thousand.[45] Throughout the 1930s, the NRC distributed a White List of manufacturers that clubwomen (and men) were urged to patronize (fig. 51). They published this "Honor Roll," as it was sometimes called, in the *Roadside Bulletin* and publicized it through garden clubs, the ACA, the American Federation of Arts, the American Institute of Architects, and the American Nature Association, along with other affiliated GFWC groups.[46] With this approach, clubwomen deflected arguments claiming they sought "to injure business generally and the advertising industry in particular." As one garden club speaker explained, "women are asserting their rights to rural beauty by supporting those merchants who do not use rural billboards," which, she thought, was quite different from purposefully interrupting business.[47]

Those reporting on Lawton's campaigns also described the movement in gendered terms. The women's appeals to national advertisers were usually described as attempts at "moral suasion." "Public Opinion" was their weapon, not "boycott, blacklisting, or intimidation of any sort," said the ACA.[48] The *Philadelphia Record* explained that the NRC's "purpose is to conduct a campaign in dignified, courteous and kindly manner." Seeing them as charmingly impotent rather than politically challenging, another paper called the clubwomen "priestesses of hospitality," "hostesses" of their towns, and "debutantes in public affairs." They were not meddlers in business, but rather keepers of

THE PICTURESQUE BEND IN THE ROAD

51. Although this motorist vowed to "make a list of advertisers I'm never going to patronize," club-women in the 1920s and 1930s generally chose instead to "favor" companies that did not use bill-boards.

public morality and aesthetic guardians, helping to nourish the corporate soul and to preserve public rights. They were doing their womanly civic duty. In turn, the men they affected, far from being traitors to the commercial cause, could claim a chivalrous responsibility, each becoming, as the *Brooklyn Eagle* claimed for Standard Oil president Herbert Pratt, "A Veritable Knight of Old" coming to the ladies' defense.[49]

Indeed, Standard Oil was the greatest public relations victory of the NRC, particularly after the company announced, in six hundred paid newspaper advertisements in 1924, that they would stop erecting signs on Pacific Coast highways and would remove those in scenic areas on both the West and East Coasts.[50] Standard Oil was also the only gasoline company to make the NRC's White List of environment-friendly companies.[51] At times Standard seemed not only to acquiesce to the NRC, but to outpace it. In 1929 Standard Oil of California sponsored "Scenic or Sign-ic?" contests for the best essays on how to eliminate objectionable signs, for "slogans which would best arouse public sentiment," and "for the best photographs depicting actual defacement" of the landscape. Over 300,000 submissions competed for sixteen cash prizes, from $25 to $1,000. Standard kicked off the campaign by distributing through their service stations a booklet by the popular, regionalist writer Kathleen Norris titled "What do you want to see?" It was a reprint of a syndicated article, in response to which Norris claimed to have received thousands of letters of support. This booklet, along with pamphlets from the "Scenic or Sign-ic?" contests, was sent to major California papers. As a result, the San Francisco *Call*, the *Examiner*, and other California papers regularly mentioned Standard Oil in the fall and spring of that year, while the company augmented their good public relations with paid advertisements for their contests. Forced to respond, California's outdoor advertisers began to circulate their own plans for "The Preservation of the Scenic Highways."[52]

Standard Oil's "Scenic or Sign-ic?" campaign was no mere publicity stunt. It reinforced Standard's relationship not only with the NRC, but also with others who favored roadside regulations, including groups of nature seekers and auto tourists, in which the company had a commercial interest. The activities of the Save-the-Redwoods League and the Redwood Empire Association to protect the scenic Redwood Highway from commercialism also broadened interest in roadside beauty.[53] Of course, the "old-girl network" was partially responsible for the NRC's success with Standard Oil, for roadside betterment was a pet project of Mrs. John D. Rockefeller, the wife of Standard Oil's president, whose donations funded the ACA's roadside improvement campaigns.[54]

Other national advertisers soon fell into line, including Pillsbury Flour, Kelly Springfield Tire Company, and Gulf Oil, which all agreed to limit their advertising to commercial areas only. Though the outdoor advertising association publicly smirked at these results, claiming that restricting signs to commercial areas was also their policy, their members hastily checked and repaired relations with national manufacturers. When national manufacturers even just appeared to heed the NRC it was cause for concern. Frequent alarmed reactions by the advertising industry suggest that the NRC made a large impact even if, quantitatively, we cannot assess their results, since the effects of public opinion are impossible to gauge precisely.[55]

Though Standard Oil's campaign, as well as the formation of the California Committee for the Restriction of Outdoor Advertising, intentionally coincided with meetings of the California state legislature and the California State Chamber of Commerce regarding highway regulations and establishing scenic reserves, their efforts were heeded by few. The chamber of commerce pledged a few owners of property abutting highways to keep their land free of ads, following the advice of the outdoor advertising industry in their publication "The Preservation of Scenic Highways." The state legislature appointed a joint assembly and senate committee to investigate the highway situation. Two years later, the report declared that the purpose of highways is to *open* commerce, not restrict it, and that outdoor advertising is a force that adds to the prosperity and employment of California. Elizabeth Lawton fumed when she realized that these findings parroted the very words of the industry-prepared documents, titled "Analysis and Review of the Highway Advertising Situation." The report saw no need for legislation beyond the existing law that forbid the placement of signs without the property owner's permission. It merely repeated the recommendation of the chamber of commerce (and the outdoor advertising industry) to seek voluntary compliance of property owners in scenic areas, and further recommended to establish county planning commissions to consider zoning frontages along scenic highways.[56] Building on that report, several years later California passed an Outdoor Advertising Act, which called for the removal of signs that were near intersections, curves, or blocked the view of approaching vehicles from five hundred feet.[57] "Lobbied through the legislation by the 'billboard boys,'" as one state highway official later recounted, it hardly marked a victory for Lawton.[58] It also did little to change the court's record on the application of police power, as the restrictions were based on safety and public welfare rather than aesthetics.[59]

There were successes, however, that involved voluntary compliance and did not rely on legislation. Honolulu's Outdoor Circle was one, and was held up as a model. Started in 1912 as an outgrowth of the Kilohana Art League, the woman's club was inspired by the City Beautiful ideas of Charles Mulford Robinson, who had prepared civic plans for Hawaii in 1906. Soap ads at the Punchbowl, Bull Durham billboards on Diamond Head volcano, and an immense pickle sign on the road to Waikiki did not figure into their ideas of panoramic vistas. The women had the editor of a major Honolulu paper, the *Pacific Commercial Advertiser*, on their side, and in 1914 the paper ran an incredible spread of condemnatory pictures and essays written by school-children and other residents. By 1923, the club was purchasing ad space and using the unusual tactic of boycotting stores and products that used billboards. They began a second boycott, refusing to frequent stores merely *carrying* products advertised on billboards. Four years later they hit the streets, tearing out the last billboards of the sole remaining local billboard firm in Honolulu. Each clubwoman paid $150 for the honor, and for partial ownership of the Pioneer Advertising Company, which the Outdoor Circle purchased (and then dissolved) at a much-negotiated price of $4,000. (A dozen years earlier the asking price had been $18,000.) The Hawaii State Legislature even came to pass restrictions in 1927, limiting outdoor advertising to commercial areas and imposing a high licensing fee.[60] Still, it was the vigilance of the women that kept their landscape free of advertising. In the 1950s, when airplanes trailing advertisements for whiskey cast unsavory shadows on Hawaiian beaches, the Outdoor Circle again sprang into action, using boycotts to convince businesses to refrain voluntarily from outdoor advertising. Today the Outdoor Circle still works on environmental issues and has branches on four islands. Hawaii is one of four states that ban outdoor advertising entirely.[61]

The Outdoor Circle contradicts the experiences of other women's groups in the United States, none of which were nearly as militant or willing to boycott businesses outright. Its personal approach of visiting each shopkeeper, its very defined and local geographical focus, and its persistent willingness to exert economic pressure comprised the Outdoor Circle's winning combination. Perhaps the Honolulu women were also better able to defend their activities given the dependence of the Hawaiian economy on natural resources and the tourist trade. As the Outdoor Circle claimed, "we are [just] a tiny Paradise in the Pacific."[62] But Hawaii could not serve as a useful example for the rest of the United States since, unlike elsewhere, it had no problems determining what qualified as scenic beauty (all of Hawaii) and in demonstrating why beauty was deserving of preservation (tourism). Elsewhere, things were not as obvious.

CHAPTER 11

THE PASTORAL VIEW

Could one justify protecting areas in Illinois, Nebraska, and Oklahoma as easily as California's redwood forests or Hawaii's tropical foliage and beachfronts? What about the myriad other landscapes that comprised the American terrain that highways were making accessible? What sorts of environments were the reformers aiming to conserve? Whose nature counted? And, since aesthetic arguments alone seemed to get nowhere, what were the expected benefits that these scenes would provide? In other words, how did one justify protecting landscapes opened to view by the automobile?

The first step Elizabeth Boyd Lawton took toward answering questions like these was to obtain data. Over fifteen years, Lawton and her husband Walter conducted at least twenty-two state and four regional surveys to document the advertisements, junkyards, filling stations, hot-dog stands, and other roadside businesses that defaced the natural landscape.[1] Photographs showed billboard alleys that had been tunneled through the countryside (fig. 52) and barns, trees, and posts slathered with tin, paint, and paper signs (fig. 53). Lawton published these along with charts, mileage counts, and narratives in *Roadside Bulletin*, *Nature Magazine*, and *Reader's Digest*. She distributed them as booklets and prepackaged slide lectures as well. Stories about the surveys often made the local newspaper.[2] The surveys thus offered quantitative, scientific documentation of the roadside environment, proof positive that rural roads were being overcome by commercialism. These surveys also proved that the desires of clubwomen were rational and clearheaded, and not, as they were often accused, "guided by purely emotional appeals."[3]

Lawton's surveys were not barren of qualitative assessments of course. Quite the contrary, they bespoke cultural values regarding nature and its

52. "Approaching the State Capital City, Illinois, Where There Are Twenty Billboards to the Mile for Every Five Miles," photograph by William Lawton, for a survey by Elizabeth B. Lawton, 1932.

53. "Snipe" signs covering trees on the west side of Los Angeles, c. 1930.

meaning for modern society. Packed into Lawton's surveys, as well as the other documents of the roadside reform movement, was an amalgam of several centuries of American and European ideas about nature. The reformers also employed long-held literary and artistic traditions concerning the landscape. They did not, however, merely mimic the visions of their predecessors. They fastened gender to these visions, and thereby transformed the roadside into a domestic enclave where one learned, through nature and beauty, moral rectitude and civility. They asserted that "outdoor beauty . . . is one of the greatest character-molding influences of the nation," a "public heritage" and a "spiritual resource," thereby assigning good republican motherhood to nature itself.[4] Extending the idea of the sanctity of the home to the landscape at large, women reformers claimed "a landscape free from unnecessary commercialism; a landscape where, escaping from the ugliness, the rush and the turmoil of our cities, we may find for both body and soul, the soothing calm and the re-creation which the beauty of nature brings."[5] The separation of spheres that had characterized the relationship between women and men, home and workplace, reformers now applied to the landscape at large, where nature became the domestic realm, necessarily separated from commerce and signs of the city, while women became upholders of its purity. As such, their ideal for the landscape was consistent with other domestic, middle-class, suburban, and arcadian, ideals.

To be scenic, reformers thought a landscape had to be picturesque and sublime. In the narratives accompanying her surveys, Lawton articulated her aesthetic standards, as well as how to meet them. She acknowledged that "some sections of our country have no beauty which can truly be called scenic"; for instance, Illinois, in Lawton's estimation, was not scenic, though it did have "a smiling landscape" of cornfields and green pastures. The same held true for Long Island, New York, which similarly lacked "the scenic beauty which comes with the grandeur of mountain majesty," but which did have vistas of "picturesque beauty" nevertheless. The state of Washington, however, had real scenic beauty. Lawton thought "no state has finer and more varied scenery, mountains, snow capped peaks, glaciers, clear streams, lakes and sea, and above all the forest. It is the forest which throws its mantle of beauty over all the rest. Snatch that mantle away and the beauty of the land is gone."[6] It could be no coincidence that her outline of the necessary aspects of a worthwhile landscape—mountains, waterfalls, cliffs, canyons, and forests—adhered to principles of landscape painting articulated in the eighteenth century by such theorists as Edmund Burke and William Gilpin, and were widely employed by such nineteenth-century American artists and writers as William Cullen Bryant, Thomas Cole, and Washington Irving.[7]

A 1928 calendar produced and distributed by the Billboard and Roadside Committee of the Garden Club of America expressed the same aesthetic criteria. The pictures are predictable country scenes and mountain vistas that follow landscape traditions of previous centuries and include little evidence of the industrial age. Serving as paeans to nature and to good taste, quotes adorn the pages from Bryant, Burke, John Greenleaf Whittier, and others who poeticize nature and the spiritual uplift it offers. Anti-billboard cartoons drew from the same pool of authors and images. Bryant and Burke were favorites, as were two categories of landscape scenes, which, if not for billboards, should have been seen by passing motorists: ruggedly sublime images of untouched nature, and pastoral scenes of rural peace and beauty, usually displaying rolling hills, orchards, and patchwork plots of farmland (figs. 54–55).[8]

Lawton's surveys emphasized the same ideals, and even served as a didactic guide to the landscape essentials from which a touring motorist would most benefit. The surveys announced picturesque scenes unfolding before the eyes of motorists traveling through Michigan, where virgin forests could still be found and fertile orchards gave way to views of Lake Michigan peeking through verdant trees. She described each of these scenes as if in a sequence of cropped and framed snapshots or film frames, focused in order to highlight the most dramatic natural features, and oriented to best draw the attention of the armchair traveler or motorist. Like the descriptions of Michigan, Lawton's survey of Florida served as a guidebook for landscape viewing. Without "mountains to lift the eyes," Lawton said, one was more likely to find their "memories of a Florida trip dominated by tree pictures—the picturesque cabbage palms dotted against the horizon, the citrus groves with golden fruit half hidden by glossy foliage, the strangely twisted branches of the pines against a sunset sky." Rather than offer a mere taxonomy of trees to be seen from the Florida highways, Lawton described the trip as a series of carefully composed works of art (mountains "lift the eyes," trees frame and foreground the view) and as a cinematic experience of sequentially unfolding views in which natural elements are obscured then revealed. Lawton thus transformed nature into scenery and codified it as a way to help audiences appreciate and savor the experiences.[9]

Lawton's lessons can be put in the context of a larger culture of tourism in which travel narratives, booster club materials, guidebooks, and advertisements similarly "evoked literary and artistic conventions" to valorize nature as culture. As in those materials, the publications of roadside reformers aimed to

54. "Go Prepared If You Wish to Enjoy American Scenery," 1925.

55. Sublime views displaced by commerce in this cartoon lampooning Massachusetts highways, c. 1928.

make nature and the automobile touring experience both spectacular—objects of visual consumption—and refined. By using the categories of landscape painting, they turned a mere view from the road into an experience of refined gentility, elevating "their tourist experiences from superficial and commercialized amusement to the level of highbrow culture."[10]

Not merely through allusions to high art did reformers seek to elevate the touring experience and validate landscape preservation. The categories of sublime and picturesque also referred to established assumptions about nature and its importance to society. Associations ranged from the Garden of Eden in Genesis, to the yeomen farmer and Jeffersonian agrarianism, to James Fenimore Cooper and Theodore Roosevelt. The rhetoric of reformers implicitly referenced Frederick Jackson Turner's enumerations of the importance of the frontier, in which taming of the natural landscape molded the American national character of individualism and self-reliance.[11] They reiterated ideas about nature's powers to inspire, civilize, and rejuvenate, notions that gained popularity as America and Europe industrialized. Nature and country came to be seen as a resource where one could escape from industrial social constraints that thwarted individualism, and one might find sanctuary from the hollowness and excessive artificiality of urban society. These arcadian ideals underlay the development of suburbs, too, with respect to both their design and ideology. Thus, armed with such a readily understandable and unquestioned cache of tropes about nature, those who promoted motor tourism (including roadside reformers but also the American Automobile Association [AAA], the National Park Service, the Bureau of Public Roads, and local and regional planners) could laud the road in more than functional and pragmatic terms. The road brought people into contact with the natural world, and the pastoral view from its side offered an optimistic promise of prosperity in cultural and even nationalistic terms. As Grace Poole, president of the General Federation of Women's Clubs (GFWC), noted, "beauty is not simply a money value to the United States of America, but it is a real underlying factor in the progress of this great country of ours."[12] Lawton completed the thought, explaining that "more than a commercial asset, [landscape beauty] is a spiritual asset, a power for uplift." Moreover, it "is one of the great character-building forces of our nation."[13]

That the landscape offered lessons in national heritage, spiritual uplift, and civic virtue were also selling points in promoting tourism as a worthy leisure activity. Given the national statistics, as figured by Bureau of Public Roads chief Thomas McDonald and the AAA, that 60 to 64 percent of highway use was non-business or recreational travel (others put 78 percent of travel in scenic areas as recreational), roadside reformers urged the state highway departments of the country "to face the fact that it must build highways to serve not merely as transportation arteries but largely as the playgrounds of the people."[14] Lawton explained one take on this principle, using language that was widely employed by others. "The roads and roadsides have become the *show windows*, through which millions of travelers would like to enjoy the panorama of the countryside."[15] Rather than separating outdoor recreation from consumerism, and nature from the market, Lawton brought them together. Though unwittingly, she cast the highway, like the department store and picture palace, as another site of mass consumption, and the panorama of nature was the commodity for sale. Paradoxically, nature as a picture (or, to moving audiences, a series of moving pictures) was endowed with value for its surface qualities, its ability to provide a cinematic experience when traveled through. In this sense she valued it as image rather than reality, a human construct or cultural mediation rather than being solely, essentially "of nature." Instead of being a reprieve from the increasingly mechanized world of production, the jaunt into nature became yet another iteration of production. Though representing an agrarian idyll and suggesting timeless, primeval nature, the language of modernity (or, in its jumble of historical moments and memories, of postmodernity) and markets remained.

Thus construed, the recreation to be found at the roadside was no walk in the woods. It was the passive act of gazing at objects on view. Indeed, Lawton did not consider whether nature would be better experienced through physical engagement; nor did her cohorts. Nature was an object to behold, not necessarily a place of activity, interaction, or even depth. That which was beyond the view from the road was of less concern than what lay within the gaze of the motoring spectator.

With this in mind, Lawton and the clubwomen lobbied for highway landscaping and for greater attention from engineers to roadside beauty. Lawton explained that the aim was "to get away from the standardization already too prevalent in highway construction and to restore as far as possible the natural characteristic beauty of each road."[16] If nature could not accommodate the picturesque ideal, that ideal should be fabricated. For instance, flat states such as South Carolina (which Lawton thought were "like plain children; it takes twice the effort to make them attractive"), depended on generating their beauty "from the immediate vicinity of the highways." In such cases, where the unfortunate topography offered no dramatic vista or where vegetation had been stripped or plowed under by the highway engineer, composed views of trees and plants in natural groups rather than formal arrangements "should come out to the road in an irregular line." She advised that the monotonous horizontal expanses of flat terrain should be broken up by vertical lines of trees.[17] Again, she was describing nature by the side of the road strictly by its pictorial possibilities, and recommending ways in which the scenes could be fabricated to look as naturalistic—as picturesque—as possible. This was quite in keeping with Anglo-European romantic principles of both landscape painting and design. The goal, then, was not to preserve natural scenery, but to produce a good picture according to very specific cultural and aesthetic principles.

The roadside aesthetic that Lawton idealized had both a precedent and a contemporary application in the parkway, whose undulating curves and scenic rural vistas had transported carriage-riding pleasure seekers of the nineteenth century from park to park. Parkways were intended to offer the "carriage class" a rural sojourn without venturing far from the city. They arose along with the urban industrial city, aiming to provide a taste of nature at a time when the city had become crowded and polluted, and even the countryside was losing its rural charms to the traffic and industry that grew out to meet it.[18] Twentieth-century motor parkways were construed as antidotes to the same problems. Frederick Law Olmsted and Calvert Vaux, designers of New York's Central Park, Brooklyn's Prospect Park, and the early suburb of Riverside, Illinois, coined the term *parkway* in the late 1860s. They were influenced by the writings of Andrew Jackson Downing, who had taken his lessons from English romanticists, and they applied these lessons to domestic architecture, gardens, and park design. Olmsted and Vaux also greatly admired Georges Eugène Haussmann's designs of Parisian boulevards, which separated pedestrian and vehicular traffic, used a central median to divide traffic, limited access from intersecting and adjacent streets, and allowed higher speeds. For their parkways, Olmsted and Vaux drew upon Paris but added a twist—literally. Applying their romantic ideas about parks as a series of sequential vistas of picturesque landscapes, their paved carriageways were artfully designed to wend their way along the natural contours of scenic but otherwise useless land such as a ravine or river valley.[19]

By 1923, the first parkway intended for automobile use was finished, the Bronx River Parkway, and a modest frenzy of urban and regional parkway planning ensued.[20] The basic characteristics of the motor parkway matched those of Olmsted and Vaux's earlier intentions. Only recreational traffic was allowed, while trucks and other commercial vehicles were restricted. Pleasingly designed bridges and overpasses helped to avoid cross traffic. "Widely spaced and carefully controlled entrance and exit points" limited access, and strips of parkland flanking the roads "provided ample scope for designers to screen out objectionable sights, plant tens of thousands of trees and shrubs, and masterfully integrate the roadway with the surrounding landscape."[21]

Lawton saw that the "true parkway, with limited abutters' rights and with sufficient rights of way to prevent unsightly or inappropriate roadside development, is, of course, the ideal solution of all our roadside problems."[22] She and her clubwomen friends were supporters of the parkway movement, even though its ranks of professional landscape architects, engineers, and highway officials were not always friendly to their cause. Gilmore Clarke, chief designer of the Bronx River Parkway and the Mt. Vernon Memorial Highway, dismissed the roadside beautification attempts of the clubwomen as "mere palliative," the trifling hobby of amateur gardeners who should have left the real work to the professionals. While the women's concerns were "sentimental aesthetic fancies," the men were obliged to function, utility, and efficiency. So while the "professionals" welcomed the women's donations of plantings and lobbying for community support and state funding, they shrugged off the significance of those activities and resisted deeper engagement. Other officials indicated that once the women had drawn public attention to the conditions of the roadsides, their work must be left to the hands of the trained men.[23]

Many local women's groups battled to remain involved in parkway planning efforts. Lawton and the NRC, however, recognized the serious restrictions of the parkway model. "The use of them is limited to certain sections of the country, more or less scenic, and to undeveloped and comparatively cheap land. Otherwise their expense is prohibitive," Lawton admitted.[24] Besides, civic groups consisting mostly of women were only to engage in "spade work," said one Maryland Garden Club member. Lawton continued the thought, explaining that their limited purpose was "to develop public sentiment so that the real work of roadside control can be done by the official agencies."[25] Again, gender clearly circumscribed the activities of the NRC. Moreover, the parkway did not come to fulfill its promise, though it did establish precedents for the acquisition of generous easements that prohibited roadside commerce and advertising. Roads that were intended to provide easy access to parks ended up serving as commuter arteries. Like other roads, parkways came to link the urban workplace with suburban residences, thereby greatly increasing the value of nearby land for residential development, rather than protecting it from development.[26]

Roadside reformers often extolled the potential democratizing power of highway travel for its ability to bring the masses of motorists in contact with America's natural resources and beauty. They went so far as to imagine not just the road, but the roadside too as public space. They claimed a public right to the view. Their conjuring of nineteenth-century painterly images, and their desire to landscape that which was not naturally picturesque, indicates that this view from the road was not of the simple roadside as it existed. Rather, the public had a right to an imagined panorama, a landscape of the mind's eye that allowed viewers to ignore the brutal facts of commercial and industrial development and property division. In his 1836 essay "Nature," Ralph Waldo Emerson described this ideal view: "The charming landscape which I saw this morning, is indubitably made up of some twenty or thirty farms. Miller owns this field, Locke that, and Manning the woodland beyond. But none of them owns the landscape. There is a property in the horizon which no man has but he whose eye can integrate all the parts, that is, the poet."[27] Conceptual ownership of the landscape fell to the eye of the beholder. Roadside reformers wished the same, and on those grounds argued that when farmers Miller, Locke, and Manning erected signs on their property, they were invading that which should belong to "no man" and to all: the view.

In the twentieth century, the roadside reformers repeated Emerson's assertions, asking, "Who Owns the Scenery?" "The real estate developer or the farmer owns the land," explained Charlotte Rumbold from Cleveland; but "does he own the landscape?"[28] The road itself was public since taxpayers paid for it. Reformers desired more, however, and claimed that the roadside was also public because it was within the surveying, or scopic, field of spectatorial vision of the taxpayer. The act of viewing was acquisitive, appropriative, itself an act of consumption. Reformers considered the public part of the roadside to be all that one could gaze upon magisterially. The imperial eye of individuals determined its ownership by *conceiving* it, much as Emerson's poetic eye had conceived his landscape and thereby come to own it.[29]

As a commonly held property, and a democratic right, the NRC believed that access to the American landscape should be an everyday event. In a 1926 address to the eighteenth National Conference on City Planning, Lawton asserted her support for the national parks movement, but claimed that "it is not enough to save the great scenic spots, because the masses of the people will never see Yosemite and Yellowstone. The masses of the people, if they feel this power of beauty, must feel it in their every-day lives, on the streets of their towns and on the highways of their localities, and you find the demand expressed for the conservation also of this every-day beauty."[30] Several years later she argued against wilderness as the sole domain of natural preservation. She disagreed with the assumptions of the California's Scenic Reserve Plan, that "beauty can be protected only along . . . the roads which lead 'into the wilderness,'" and claimed instead that "the public clamors for beauty along the everyday highways, beauty which may be enjoyed as we pass to and fro in our daily affairs!"[31] J. Horace McFarland, director of the American Civic Association, agreed, expressing a similar belief that all highways, and not just those in particular areas, should be preserved for the enjoyment of the common man. "It is one of the ironies of billboard locations," he wrote in 1924, "that they are never permitted to exist near the usually palatial homes of the men who have grown wealthy through exploiting them. The 'Coca Cola' man has kept them entirely away from a great residential section he has promoted near Atlanta! It is the poorer citizen who must endure them."[32]

If the roadside vista was public space and thereby open to democratic access, then billboards comprised both a physical and a conceptual blight. They blocked the view from the road, that was obvious enough, but they also blocked the notion that the American landscape was held commonly, without property borders and free to all. By placing images of commodities in the midst of this landscape, advertising interrupted the ideal conception of the imperial eye that this landscape was somehow owned by all, and reminded motorists that not they, the people, but rather the market was in possession of even the most remote American vista. Billboard alleys lining the highways endlessly repeated that commercial fact. Billboards were "a palpable offense against society," "an invasion of common rights," an abominable "expression of private gain and public loss."[33] As Lawton put it, natural beauty "belongs to the people, and no individual, no corporation has a right to commercialize it for their own private gain."[34] She made this statement in 1924, in a decade drunk with commercialism and mere months after Calvin Coolidge won a landslide presidential election by equating America with commerce in his slogan: "This is a business country, it wants a business government."[35] But the reformers contended, rather boldly, that unlimited signs of business in the form of billboards that impeded the spectacle of the landscape foreclosed another foundation of the American way, namely democratic access, not just to the view, but to all it represented—the very notions of individualism, independence, freedom, and self realization.

Fittingly, Theodore Roosevelt became an exemplar for the roadside reform movement, and his words became its motto: "Here is your country. Do not let anyone take it or its glory away from you. Do not let selfish men or greedy interests skin your country of its beauty." During the Depression, as people criticized corporations for having failed in their promises of perpetual prosperity, the NRC became more strident.[36] The ravaging of the countryside marked an "age of barbarism." Reformers enjoined Americans not to be "submissive in the face of aggressions by blatant destroyers."[37] They put the conflict in terms of power and violence, and warned that pecuniary interest would not protect the public heritage of the landscape. In contrast, Anna Steese Richardson wrote in the *Woman's Home Companion* that women reformers were members of civic and art groups and were "working without compensation" for the public good. Those "certain commercial interests" against whom they battled were greedy, selfish, and parasitical. The billboard industry was "preying upon the economic welfare of the State," and, in an often repeated refrain, "a curse to the countryside,"[38] as if advertising was responsible for the rural depression and the dustbowl.

Outdoor advertisers claimed quite the contrary, that the rent they paid to farmers was often their only source of income and means of survival.[39] To these claims reformers explained that this kind of business was not a productive one. "Active" forms of commerce, such as roadside businesses that sold gasoline, oil, and food, were distinct from the "passive" industry of outdoor advertising.[40] Reformers claimed that the billboard on the rural highway "does *not* perform a necessary function," since it neither produced nor distributed anything. In seeking to distinguish between the different forms of roadside commercialism, and to use those distinctions to fashion roadside regulations that would permit only "productive" businesses, reformers once again betrayed their nostalgia, this time preferring a sentimental nineteenth-century "producerist ideology" that "counterpoised the virtuous folk—who created wealth through their own labor—with the conniving merchants and middlemen—who merely preyed on the labor of others."[41] By recognizing "active" businesses only as those that produced or delivered goods and services, they ignored the ways in which business developed and created markets for those goods. They also resented the ways in which outdoor advertising produced consumers as a commodity for sale. "'It sells the eyes of the public' without the consent of the public," one critic protested.[42] The bottom line, however, was still the old argument that although they paid for the land they occupied, billboard companies broadcast rent-free across public space, an exploitation of public facilities for private gain.[43]

Exploitation by advertisers was often cast in the most dire medical terms. Threatening to deform and disfigure the entire countryside, the "landscape leprosy" or "billboard rash" was "rapidly becoming virulent and infectious."[44] The commercial contagion had spread out of control and threatened to overtake a civic body whose good health and spiritual rejuvenation relied upon a natural order now corrupted. And what corrupted the civic body would also affect the civic mind. A letter to the *Boston Herald* decried outdoor advertising's untoward psychological powers. Ads were "seizing the eye against one's will," as the fleeting images impressed themselves upon their unwitting hosts, infiltrating their very subjectivity. Advertisements were an "affront to delicate nerves of eyes" and an "insult of jarring colors," declared Struthers Burt, a novelist and rancher who supported the National Roadside Council. It was downright "obscene," he exhorted in an article for the *Saturday Evening Post* titled "Obscenic Scenery."[45] Others agreed that such commercialism was "sordid," "vulgar," "promiscuous," "a cheapening influence," with "disastrous effects upon the sensibilities of the people." They conflated aesthetics and morality, envisioning the multiplicity of advertisements, hot-dog stands, and gas stations that had sullied the natural environment as lessons in disharmony and disorder, and breeding grounds for both bad taste and that to which bad taste led, social degeneracy. Beneath the effort to remove blight, then, was the implication that cleaning the face of the nation was tantamount to setting it aright, socially and morally. The restoration or preservation of the natural environment would instill "a greater sense of order on the part of the people."[46]

Such notions bespoke the environmental determinism of the urban reform arena of the nineteenth century in which a fearful middle-class sought to reinforce social order in the face of rapid industrialization and immigration. Indeed, anti-billboard pundits used the same language to describe the commercialization of the countryside. The signs of commerce "unfold in offensive, *jazzy* patterns along countless miles of our American highways," parkway engineer Jay Downer said. Instead of the "soothing calm that nature would bring," the commercialized landscape blared, screeched, and shrieked, jangling nerves and jarring sensibilities.[47] It created that state of "nervousness" and neurasthenia that city observers had noted from at least the 1880s, from Henry James to George Beard. And it brought the crowded, polluted, machine-age city into the country, replacing the purity and stability of nature with the artifice and flux of urban culture. While modernist poets and artists worshipped the energy and dynamism of metropolitan life, roadside reformers followed the impulses of several generations of antiurbanites and antimodernists, from transcendentalists to Arts and Crafts practitioners to "back to the land" homesteaders, who longed for the simplicity and permanence of values they believed could be found in preindustrial rural nature. Nostalgia helped cope with modernization, offering reassuring reminders of a familiar, well-ordered world. During the Depression, the impulse to preserve older values and basic institutions was surely related to social and economic upheaval, problems easily blamed on technology and corporate capitalism.[48]

For some, like photographer Walker Evans, the appearance of roadside stands, with handwritten signs announcing the local wares for sale, marked a pleasing vernacular folk culture of the industrial age (fig. 56). Photographer Ralph Steiner also luxuriated in the formal beauty of billboards hawking their wares, wryly marking the way these signs of industrial life became part of the social arenas of cities and the natural realm of the open landscapes where they were planted. But roadside reformers still saw these as pollution, and would not acknowledge another possibility. The image of the colonial New England village with hanging, painted, or carved wood signs, and rural highways with

56. Walker Evans, "Roadside stand near Birmingham, Alabama," 1936.

old milestones dating "back to the days of the post rider and the stagecoach" were about as much commerce as the reformers would tolerate.[49] Yet by privileging this ideal, reformers excluded from the expression of "public" opinion the ad hoc appeals for attention displayed by hopeful entrepreneurs of small towns and rural areas that Evans photographically preserved. Though they employed a rhetoric of public ownership presumably by a diverse public, reformer's guidelines to what was valid public display was personal, staked firmly to their middle- and upper-class arcadian aesthetic, and consistent with a nineteenth- and twentieth-century suburban ideology of escape from the city to the country, and division between commerce and nature.

CHAPTER 12

"BILLBOARD BARONS"

While roadside reformers favored beauty over business and usually skirted the financial implications of their choice, the organized outdoor advertising industry fought back. It did not, however, simply assert the opposite, that business should be privileged over beauty. Rather it claimed that both could be had, and that billboards were the ideal way to combine them. To the reformer's amazement, the outdoor advertising industry began to suggest that it, too, was guardian of the landscape, and moreover that billboards comprised the business of beauty. In printed materials circulated to clients and through efforts of specially organized groups of industry representatives, advertisers conducted a comprehensive public relations campaign. Typically, the industry appropriated select elements of the rhetoric of aesthetics expressed by the roadside reformers and civic beautifiers and used these to its own advantage. Why concede to detractors when one could potentially win them over? The serious investment of time, effort, and money in these campaigns suggest that the industry's gestures were not superficial. As is so often the case with public relations campaigns, in time the outdoor advertising industry engaged and propagated the very same idealized view of the landscape as its detractors.

Billboard businessmen most apparently engaged the arguments of their detractors in their common construction of a national myth of the American road. Advertisers utilized this myth to promote automobility and consumption on, alongside, and beyond the road. Advertisements, particularly for automobile-related goods and services, stressed the same ideals of pastoralism and scenic beauty accessed through auto tourism that clubwomen promoted. Both women reformers and admen stressed history, national heritage, and civic identity as part of America's uniquely pastoral landscape, and both commonly depicted this landscape as a rural idyll. This ideal view differed, of course, from the actual one seen from the road, even when billboards were absent. The commodious scenes of which the women dreamed were the very commodities that admen wished to sell.

Outdoor advertisers understood the advantage of a rural pastoral ideal. In fact, the Madison Avenue advertising executives were a mobile audience themselves, with ample means to enjoy both the suburban enclave and the rural retreat. Every day they saw the virtues of nature, but through eyes spinning with dollar signs. One billboard salesman explained that the benefit of his medium was that it stood outdoors, where nature "puts people in a friendly, cheerful, optimistic frame of mind. The poster is kith and kin to Nature herself. When the buying public is motoring, in the hills, it is out from under the dead weight of much materialism, of worry, of self-analysis."[1] His language compares with that of clubwomen who described "smiling landscapes" in Illinois and the "mantle of beauty" of Washington. Outdoor admen also agreed about the appeal of tourism, and recognized their own role in creating the desire for it. When a weekend jaunt or a "gypsy" camping vacation brought a motorist to nature, these trips also commercialized the roadside environment.

When outdoor admen engaged criticisms of female foes, they carefully addressed gender dynamics. Advertisers focused on their manly responsibility to distinguish the use of nature and art for the sake of the economy from their detractors' less useful desires for scenic pleasures. They used masculine obligations, as providers and protectors, to justify the hard monetary benefits of outdoor advertising for full employment and a healthy economy. When admen defined their role in rationalizing the distribution of both goods and consumers they addressed long-standing economic fears of having overproduction accentuated by underconsumption.[2] Their rational, even scientific, self-justifications criticized their female foes for soft emotionalism and idyllic delusion. While outdoor advertisers might sympathize with clubwomen and even share their ideals, as corporate facilitators of the flow of commerce essential to the nation, their duty was to the economy first.

Besides, said the admen, billboards did not blight, they built. They were usually put on semicommercial "marginal lands no longer desirable or saleable for residential purposes." They provided revenue to pay the taxes on that land, and sowed the ground for additional commercial development: "After a time, permanent stores are built, and property becomes increasingly valuable." This, they claimed, was the way new towns rose between cities. Billboards aided the proper use of highways as commercial arteries that contributed to the well being of the country.[3] The question posed in a 1924 issue of *Printers' Ink* summed up the position: "Are private property rights, effective marketing of goods, and the rights of industry to be sacrificed to a question of good taste? Good taste is relative."[4]

In the Depression, rhetoric sometimes grew ungentlemanly. The booklet "100 Reformers v. 25,000 Wage Earners," which, according to its own title page, had been "approved by every labor group to which it has been submitted," attacked the "professional reformers" and uncharitably described them as "wealthy 'leisurables' who with nothing else to occupy themselves must espouse a 'cause.'"[5] A similar debate occurred in 1931 when the Maryland House of Delegates sought to pass a bill to restrict billboards. One side, represented by garden clubs, the League of Women Voters, and chambers of commerce, argued to "save the beauty of the Maryland countryside" while the billboard faction argued to "save the wives and children of working men from being starved to satisfy a group of idle women."[6] The billboard defenders wrote that "esthetics have a time and a place but not when business is trying to recover from a depression. . . . Blighted areas may be rehabilitated but blighted hopes and homes cannot. Restoration and preservation of business will take care of the first and prevent the second."[7]

Outdoor advertisers also shared the clubwomen's rhetoric of municipal housekeeping. Billboards, they said, could provide a tremendous educational medium with civic welfare at heart. They donated space to such causes as highway safety and cleanliness. One adman asserted the value of the billboard in teaching thousands of people "a knowledge of letters," for which it "should win the blessing of every kind-hearted lady in this crusade for beauty."[8] It could even serve as a good example for those other "dirty" forms of advertising making their way into magazines and tabloids. Outdoor advertising "has one really peculiar characteristic," claimed F. T. Hopkins, president of the National Outdoor Advertising Bureau: "It is clean. It doesn't intrude itself into the bosom of your family with horror stories for the children, with nudity in pictures, with sex appeal, with dirty stories or dirty illustrations and it has no doubtful editorial policy."[9] Rather, the messages of billboards were wholesome, including lessons in Americanization, literacy, and hygiene. In case the posters themselves were not sufficient proof, the industry published books for grade-school students, such as the "Ad Andy" series of coloring books (fig. 57). In this series, youngsters met the comic-book figure of Andy, a billposter who was the main character in moralizing stories in civics. They could follow Andy's escapades in the books and then see him on billboards too. The Outdoor Advertising Association of America (OAAA) also published a manual for

57. Outdoor advertisers often promoted the same causes as their adversaries. Ad Andy's civic lessons made their way onto billboards and into children's comic books sponsored by Foster and Kleiser Company, 1947.

teachers who wished to use advertisements as part of their curriculum. They offered reprints of wartime posters to teach lessons in patriotism and provided other props to use in lesson plans.[10]

The organized outdoor advertising industry also sought to redefine the billboard as tasteful and even a work of art, in both its architectural structure and poster imagery. Just as reformers sought to provide access to the arts through their clubs and exhibitions, advertisers claimed a role for the poster in democratizing art, reaching "the great masses of people, the illiterate, the uneducated, the foreigners, those who are not yet Americanized." In contrast to "art for art's sake," this was "art for life's sake."[11] Another publication argued, "We have our beautiful museums and Art Galleries, but the people will not go to them—at least, not in great numbers. The attendance at the Metropolitan Museum of Art is small when compared to the ten million souls who live in greater New York. . . . Posters and Bulletins . . . provide a means of bringing Art to the people. . . . Most of the '80%' who read little and derive their amusement and recreation from the radio and 'movies' obtain more joy and satisfaction from a first rate poster than they do from an old masterpiece."[12] Another writer said, "This is an unpleasant but inescapable proof that art must be brought to the people. They will not go to it."[13] There was no better medium than the billboard, which could "talk the vernacular . . . the language of the common people," to mediate between high and low.[14]

The industry presented the billboard as an art gallery to the masses, such as when it exhibited five thousand posters, complete with gilded frame, of

58. Billboard reproductions of Thomas Gainsborough's *The Blue Boy* (1770) were said to bring art to the masses, 1938.

Thomas Gainsborough's *The Blue Boy* (1770; fig. 58). It included a caption crediting the original in the Henry E. Huntington Library and Art Gallery and explained that this was "A Masterpiece Presented for the Benefit of the Public by the Outdoor Advertising Industry."[15] In another bold act of charity, and with the hope of diffusing the "love and appreciation of beauty among the mass of people of America," the billboard barons (as contemptuous reformers took to calling them) decided to lend their assistance to the General Federation of Women's Clubs' (GFWC) effort to support the creation of a National Gallery of Art in 1924. The act seems a touch less charitable when one realizes that at their biennial convention, the resolutions made by the GFWC to support Congressional legislation for a national art museum were immediately preceded by the women's proclamations to renew their war on billboards with a committee devoted to its restriction.[16]

Even in its appreciation of art, the industry was careful to distinguish between that which was effete and unnecessary, and that which was practical. The poster artist provided for them an example of a useful artist, one who was down to earth, of the people, a regular working stiff. The industry ran articles highlighting the practical nature of the artists in the business. The articles began by contrasting the reality of the poster artist's studio, attire, and lifestyle with what the writers had expected. Instead of garrets they found offices; smocks and berets were replaced by shirts and ties; a flighty temperament was overridden by a sincerity of purpose and healthy desire for a steady income.[17] Such a description supported both the economic value of advertising as well as its aesthetic worth. By providing artists with commercial work, the advertising industry supported artists and the creation of a uniquely American genre that combined artistry and industry. Outdoor advertising, as one writer claimed, was "The Meal Ticket of American Art." In advertising one would see the real American landscape painting: a "livewire" of artistic expression. Outdoors companies like Thomas Cusack claimed that through their posters, they gave "more patronage to art than all the highbrow critics in the entire country." Furthermore, "If the market for commercial art were suddenly withdrawn, the support which makes for the growth and development of American art would go with it."[18]

The outdoor advertising trade magazines also highlighted the large number of women illustrators who worked in outdoor and other advertising firms. Practically minded women could triumph in the nascent field of commercial art, where their "natural" sensibilities toward beauty and service matched the poster's function. Of course the industry also took this opportunity to tout its employment of women, claiming this to be an egalitarian gesture.[19]

Sometimes the industry was so successful in presenting the aesthetic value of advertising that it had to convince skeptics of its value for business. To assure "the average business man" who questioned "the value of Beauty in the practical world," the outdoor advertising industry embarked on a program of research and surveys to test what classes of people best responded to various aesthetic approaches. In 1924 the University of Wisconsin established the Barney Link Research Fellowship for this purpose. It was founded by the OAAA and funded by the Carnegie Corporation. Some of its findings were published in 1932, in a report "dedicated to that great educational force called ADVERTISING and to that universal language of all races called BEAUTY." It found that the advertisements that instinctively pleased people followed artistic principles; those artistic principles were harmony, unity, color, and distinctiveness. Ads using the artistic principles set out by the Barney Link report would "make a deep and favorable impression . . . which drives home the selling message with a positive finality."[20] Such findings seem less than shocking. Nevertheless, the vast efforts made to investigate the psychological effects of design and to quantify the value of art to advertising suggests that the industry did not merely mouth words that "Art Leaguers" might wish to hear. Theirs was a "scientific" investigation aimed both toward enhancing the legitimacy of their profession and toward elevating the status of the commercial artists with whom they worked. In so doing, the advertising industry helped to create a new stratum of professionals and an incontrovertibly scientific means of proving their value.

The industry also professed to aid the roadside setting. For this they called upon the developing fields of industrial design and landscape architecture. More scientific studies regarding placement and orientation of posterboards led to the "gallery" style treatment or "exhibition" of billboards, in which multitiered poster structures had their heights reduced and their widths lengthened. The quantity of posters also diminished as the individual poster size increased. These changes had the effect of creating mural displays. Since the nineteenth century, many companies had added "Mural Advertising" to the name of their firm, to emphasize their prowess at painting wall-sized images. Now, everyone in the industry could claim to be a mural artist, in paint or on paper.[21] A standardized billboard frame with lattice dividers and aprons (to hide legs and joinery and to unify the individual elements of the structure) was developed in 1925 and described by its manufacturer as "a deep olive green that blends well with the surrounding landscape. This is an important factor because it helps turn any Garden Club feeling of antagonism into acceptance."[22] Landscape architect Franz A. Aust wrote "How Outdoor Advertising Can Be Part of the Natural Landscape" in 1924, describing that "with plantings of vines and shrubs, a structure of the right size and proportions can become as artistically at home in the world of nature as any other piece of well-planned architecture." Standardized billboards had "the opportunity to render themselves a part of the landscape, to seem to 'belong' in the very spot in which they are set."[23] To the outrage of the scenic sisters, Mac-Mar All-Metal Panel advertised their product as actually improving the landscape, adding "character . . . without being obtrusive."[24]

The West Coast company Foster and Kleiser wished not to blend in, but to make a neoclassical statement in civic reform with architectural innovations and the creation of "sign parks" complete with drinking fountains and benches (figs. 59–60). With a staff of over forty professional horticulturalists, Foster and Kleiser landscaped their billboard parks with manicured lawns edged with beds of roses and begonias. "Nature's gorgeous colors are used to supplement the work of America's foremost poster artists," the company boasted, citing

59. Foster and Kleiser advertised their radio show and offered gardening lessons on the sites of their "sign parks," c. 1930.

60. Sign parks were also spruced up by white columned "lizzies," 1930.

their maintenance costs as evidence that outdoor advertisers were essentially in the business of "good housekeeping" and could sympathize with women. It was a "real housekeeping job on a big scale . . . a never-ending fight against dirt, papers and all sorts of rubbish." Foster and Kleiser was exemplary, and other companies, from St. Paul, Minnesota, to Ponca City, Oklahoma, followed suit with parks of their own.[25]

Examples of Foster and Kleiser billboards from Los Angeles, Seattle, Portland, and San Francisco in the 1920s also show illuminated, white pilaster, and latticed billboards sporting neoclassical nymphs they called "lizzies." A sarcastic rendering of the garden club gal? Perhaps. But even more explicit was Foster and Kleiser Company's nod to the clubwomen with their weekly radio program *Garden Clubs of the Air*, which provided tips on gardening as well as free cuttings from the plants on the billboard lots.[26] It was a clever strategy for diffusing the criticism of the clubwomen. It was even more clever in its use of the very advertising medium that had recently emerged as their prime competitor, the radio.

Dumps, vacant lots, parking lots, and garages were cleaned up and hidden by walls of white or green latticed, landscaped, and adorned billboards. Shrubs and flowers were planted along the roadways, surrounding the billboard structure. Children's sandboxes and educational flower and vegetable gardens utilized the grounds behind the billboard structures, and during World War II that space was turned over to communities for victory gardens, with outdoor advertising companies distributing manuals for raising crops.[27] In California, Foster and Kleiser even bought up "special sites of land" that "have rare scenic beauty."[28] In this case the purpose was not so innocent, since the strategy kept valuable advertising space from their competition. These strategies aimed to beautify business and to defuse, if not outright co-opt, the scenic sisters' opposition: "Good business and community betterment can go hand in hand anywhere."[29]

The industry did not just plant shrubs, flowers, and crops. It also planted spies. In 1920, the industry undertook special public relations efforts in response both to the passage of the Nineteenth Amendment, granting women the vote, and the formation of special art and billboard committees of the GFWC.[30] Women previously perceived as merely annoying were now an organized, political threat to the billboard industry. In response, poster association leaders delegated "the best women plant owners in our Association" and any other "capable" women staff members (usually secretaries and typists) to attend the GFWC conventions and to speak on the industry's behalf. Their mission was "to learn first hand what's going on and how it is being 'cooked up.'"[31]

Orchestrating these industry women's activities and keeping an educated eye on Elizabeth Boyd Lawton and her roadside reformers was a special public relations committee headed by Lillian Lilly. With her Fifth Avenue, New York, address and her experience doing public relations work on censorship issues for the Motion Picture Association of America, Lilly managed an infiltration of the women's clubs with industry-friendly plants. She herself was a prominent figure on the club scene, an active leader in the GFWC, and frequent speaker, tea hostess, and slide presenter. She kept her influential club comrades friendly to the industry. Lilly also recruited the rich and idle female relatives of industry members to join clubs, to attend meetings, and to put a "pretty face" on the outdoor advertising industry.[32] Lilly's activities lasted for decades as she continued to shepherd the industry in its development of a comprehensive public relations division. In 1940, Lilly helped organize a group of female "infiltrators" that went by the name of the Woman's Fact-Finding Roadside Association. Its slogan was "Progress through Truth." Comprised of women directly related to the outdoor advertising industry, the group was indirectly funded by the OAAA.[33] (A variant of this group was formed in the early 1960s as the Women's Division of the OAAA, called the Outdoor Advertising Women of America.[34])

Lilly and members of her fact-finding association arranged teas and lectures to promote outdoor advertising to clubwomen. As both club members themselves and as industry representatives they acted as double agents, circulating back and forth across the battle lines, representing each side to the other, able to speak both the language of business and that of reform. Their circulation in both worlds neutralized the threat posed by the clubwomen to the billboard brethren in the political arena, and perhaps also neutralized the clubwomen's distaste for billboard blight.[35] What stands out about the formation of such an association are the similarity of interests and class positions held by both clubwomen and billboard men. These activities also suggest that the industry recognized women were part of their public, had political clout, and could potentially turn the buyway back into just a highway. The industry also viewed women as the primary market of consumers whose attention and good will they needed to court.

Perhaps unwittingly, clubwomen even joined the organized Outdoor Advertising Association in finding a common enemy in the small-time itinerant billposter who painted or tacked "sniper" signs to trees, rocks, and buildings (see fig. 53), and who generally was not a member of the organized trade association.[36] When reformers agitated for laws that kept advertisers off public land such as parks and highway easements, the OAAA stood at their side. When the women pushed for enforcement of those laws, advertisers were again with them. And when the women struggled to assure that ads posted on private property had permission, were properly leased, or paid requisite license and permit fees, they actually provided a free service for the standardized outdoor advertising industry.[37] They helped the companies consolidate nationally by removing the small, independent, and ad hoc competition that was otherwise difficult for the industry to combat. It is no surprise that Foster and Kleiser offered its services to help California women remove unlawfully placed advertising signs. They sent out their billposting crews to remove their competitors' sniper signs, at the behest of the clubwomen. Pennsylvania billboard operators did the same, removing 25,000 such "wild cat signs" in one summer.[38] By doing so, they enhanced the value of their own billboard spaces and their reputation among the women.

The outdoor advertising industry consolidated its services throughout the 1920s and 1930s with and without the women. They standardized their prices and the quality of their services nationwide during these decades. They offered national distribution through one service, which doled out advertising campaigns to only those billboard companies who were members. The industry effectively closed out the small, family-run shops characteristic of the industry in the nineteenth century. By the mid-1920s, many of the smaller billposting firms were already subsumed by larger companies. As that happened, more territory came under the control of fewer companies. In 1924 Foster and Kleiser was forced to fight an antitrust suit. Such suits were also brought against General Outdoor Advertising for "coercive activities" that included "controlling the national outdoor advertising market by acquisition of rival companies through stock market deals and mergers and by means of its majority vote" in the industry's national association and marketing arm.[39]

What emerges, then, is that the issues separating the scenic sisters and the billboard brethren were ultimately rather limited. The billboard war was neither specifically urban nor rural, neither specifically male- nor female-dominated in character or interest. Though at times reform groups seemed aimed against big business corporations, a closer look shows the contrary. Often the strategies of the outdoor advertising industry's public relations worked. Reformers did temper their attacks in order to safeguard business. By campaigning to remove small signs, for instance, they helped liquidate the smallest roadside businesses and billposting services and thereby belied their rhetoric promoting the rights of the individual citizen over the corporate conglomerate. Reformers were far from anti-commercial in their sentiments, while the billboard brethren were far from being against the enjoyment of aesthetics, or even of the open road. It was the myth of an open American road, promising all kinds of utopian mobility—either commercial or idyllic, but always bourgeois—that locked the contenders together in the first place.

Perhaps a better criticism would focus less on mere billboards, and more on the myth of the road itself. Some typical themes of this were present in a 1936–38 billboard campaign for the National Association of Manufacturers (NAM; in association with the U.S. Chamber of Commerce), which depicted a well-clad, rosy-cheeked all-American family enjoying various aspects of their middle-class suburban life, accompanied by such slogans as "There's no way like the American Way" (fig. 61) and "What's Good for Industry Is Good for You." In one "American Way" billboard with the tag line "WORLD'S HIGHEST STANDARD OF LIVING," the family cheerily drives through the rural countryside; in another they've stopped the car for a picnic in a picturesque spot; in a third—"WORLD'S HIGHEST WAGES"—Dad triumphantly returns home from work. This family seems to be weathering the Depression well. Or so was the message of the NAM's huge publicity campaign, which included billboards as well as radio shows, documentary films, syndicated cartoon strips, and newsweeklies, all aimed to foster optimistic faith in the ability of free enterprise and industry to meet the needs and expectations of Americans' during the Depression. Business, not the social welfare of New Deal policies, represented the interests of America. The outdoor advertising industry did its fair share to spread the word, contributing $1.2 million and $180,000 worth of free advertising space to the campaign, which featured 65,000 billboards placed in towns with a population of over 2,500.[40]

Yet for others, these probusiness clichés of consumer satisfaction were a heartless dismissal of Depression-era realities. Billboards and posters, in particular, became fodder for the corps of New Deal photographers who traveled the country at the behest of the Farm Security Administration (FSA) to document a different life in America than that promised by the advertisers. FSA photographers Dorothea Lange, Edwin Locke, Arthur Rothstein, and John Vachon all made deliberately ironic pictures, some featuring NAM billboards. Locke, for instance, contrasted an NAM billboard, with its image of the giddy family on their pastoral drive, to its actual and far less bucolic setting next to stunted leafless trees at the base of an otherwise desolate hillside.[41]

Most famous of all New Deal-era images is "After the Louisville Flood," by non-FSA photographer Margaret Bourke-White, which features black flood victims on line at a relief agency being virtually run down by the looming white family of the "American Way" billboard beside them (fig. 62). Bourke-White contrasts black and white, carefree and serious, mobility and immobilized. Her

61. Campaign by the National Association of Manufacturers, 1936-38.

62. Margaret Bourke-White's photograph shows flood victims lined up outside a Red Cross relief station, 1937.

juxtapositions were akin to those of the FSA photographers. Lange, in particular, focused on the theme of mobility to show that all was not right in America. Against Southern Pacific's billboard "Next Time Try the Train—Relax," with its image of a reclining, suited businessman, Lange juxtaposes two migrant workers in jeans and jackets, laden with suitcases, walking the dusty road (fig. 63). Underneath another railway ad, "Travel while you sleep," she shows a migrant family setting up their impromptu housing, their swatch of canvas tenting strung to the billboard, barefoot children huddled together behind it for protection from the wind (fig. 64). In these photographs, the migrants are on the road but their mobility marks the antithesis of the mobile freedom represented in the advertisement, their poverty a rejoinder to the ad's illusory promises.

Not surprisingly, neither the billboard industry nor their rivals, the scenic sisters, saw fit to utilize these photographs in their publicity materials. The OAAA focused on the productive role outdoor advertising played, helping farmers by paying them rent, and giving employment to more than thirty thousand men and women.[42] The scenic sisters made nary a comment in their materials about the plight of the Depression's hardest hit casualties, the poor. Nevertheless, what these factions, including the NAM and New Deal photographers, held in common were expectations of mobility and pastoralism. For all of them, hindrance to these ideals marked the failure of the American Way.

63. Dorothea Lange,
"Toward Los Angeles,
California," 1937.

64. Dorothea Lange,
"Billboard along U.S. 99,
behind which three desti-
tute families of migrants
are camped, Kern County,
California," 1938.

CHAPTER 13

ZONING AND THE ROAD TO
FEDERAL LEGISLATION

From the time she founded the National Roadside Council, Elizabeth Boyd Lawton asked the fundamental question, "Why commercialize the entire countryside?" "Why not keep business where business belongs?"[1] As Struthers Burt explained, "Nobody objects to anyone taking a bath in a bathroom, but there would be a great deal of objection if our highways were lined with people taking baths."[2] Legally, the means of keeping everything in its proper place was zoning. By the mid-1920s, Lawton realized that while the law might not be willing to regulate based on aesthetics, the growing application of zoning to cities and towns could serve just as well. Zoning divided building and land use into separate residential, commercial, and industrial districts. It aimed to protect public health, safety, morals, and welfare, and presumably property values. Towns that passed zoning ordinances might bar outdoor advertising from residential neighborhoods, since these areas excluded commercial and industrial uses. Though this worked for cities and towns that employed zoning, could the vast expanses of state and interstate highways that passed through rural areas also be regulated?

Throughout the 1930s, and originally in the face of strong opposition from professional planners and highway officials, the National Roadside Council (NRC) supported highway zoning as a promising approach for controlling the encroachment of billboards, junkyards, roadside businesses, and other signs of commerce along rural roadways. At a series of meetings in 1931 held at the U.S. Chamber of Commerce in Washington, D.C., and jointly sponsored by the Outdoor Advertising Association of America (OAAA) and the National Association of Real Estate Boards (NAREB), various factions with cultural and commercial interests in the roadside, including members of the sponsoring groups along with the National Roadside Council, General Federation of Women's Clubs (GFWC), the Garden Club of America, the American Federation of the Arts, and American Federation of Labor and Congress of Industrial Organizations (AFL-CIO), came together to discuss solutions to the conflict between roadside beauty and rural business. After the first day, the NRC and the Garden Club of America refused to return, claiming intractable differences with the other participants. They proceeded, on their own, to define and publicize a program for regulation that took its cues from zoning, and sought to separate natural and commercial uses of the highways by consolidating commercial development into regularly spaced intervals along the highways. By making business areas compact and centrally located, they hoped to maximize trading value yet minimize sprawl. Such an organization and separation of purposes, Lawton wrote, "would build up better towns, preserve the rural character of our arterial highways, and protect the beauty of the countryside."[3]

Zoning would also assure fluid travel and prevent "the choking of traffic by the constant cutting in and out induced by roadside business." Lawton warned that the old mistakes of the city could be avoided, specifically, "zoning too much area for business."[4] She also refined her initial assertion that billboards belonged in commercial areas, and resorted to the distinction between "active" and "passive" (i.e., necessary and unnecessary) businesses, each to be put in its proper place. Serving no active purpose, the billboard did not belong along rural highways, she then proclaimed. Only those businesses "demanded by the immediate convenience and necessity of the people—filling stations, food-stands, and the like" should be permitted in designated areas along rural roads.[5] The billboard industry did not agree that its business was "passive" (i.e., unnecessary), and they carefully fashioned proposals that did not distinguish in this way. They did, however, support voluntary designations of scenic highways to be kept free of commerce, if 75 percent of property owners agreed.

Many advocates of zoning for cities were against highway zoning. The road and roadside were neither political units, such as a city, town, or county, nor were they regional units that could be socially, commercially, or even geographically defined. Besides, they argued, zoning should not be employed as a restrictive tool but as "a constructive design." Instead, they suggested comprehensive and coordinated state and county planning, with roadsides included in the territory covered by each political entity.[6] Lawton and Albert Bard instantly recognized the perils of this approach. It was a form of spot zoning that could achieve only limited and piecemeal results, necessarily interrupting the integrity of the rural road as a freely flowing, distinct realm of picturesque possibility. If reformers followed the suggestions of orthodox planners and agreed to zone a commercial area after every four or so miles of highway, wouldn't travelers see a billboard every five minutes? This was no way to "save the rural and open character of our roads" and it was no way to enjoy a recreational jaunt.[7] Clogged with the traffic of incoming cars from roadside businesses, and then suddenly free of commercial distractions, always moving in fits and starts, the rural roadside would become a patchwork of conflicting uses that exactly replicated the jostle of urban life. Lawton and Bard insisted that legislators "give the State control over the full transportation corridor, including the right-of-way and a wide marginal strip on either side."[8]

In the 1910s and 1920s, zoning plans were usually promoted by residents, property owners, merchants, and real estate interests. In contrast, roadside reform groups advocated zoning as a national solution to national needs. They claimed to represent the interests of all mobile audiences, a traveling public from widespread parts of the country whose interests in the roads stemmed from their investment in them as taxpayers, citizens, and consumers. This mobile audience constituted the "public" that roadside reformers sought to represent. Though they may have been property owners while at home, their national political power derived from their mobility.

Like urban planners, roadside reformers sought to regulate the environment in which their constituents—the traveling public—had vested interests. They advocated for them based on their fundamental beliefs in mobility, moral aesthetics, and environmental purity as a national heritage. Under dispute, though, were the interests of the mobile public versus those of the property holders who actually owned the roadside. Reformers recognized that not everyone felt as kindly toward zoning as they did, acknowledging, "The communities and the rural sections that most need it are slowest to use it, and it is not rare to see, even in a zoned community, the entire length of the through road given up to business."[9] The rural and agricultural regions that roadside reformers were most intent to protect generally were the most resistant to controls. A pro-billboard group that represented the interests of farmers and landowners speculated that if reformers started by controlling billboards and roadside stands, eventually "unpainted houses and pig pens" would upset the reformers' "delicate sense of beauty." To this group, zoning had a single purpose, to appease these aesthetic "zealots," an idea that "may be consistent with the philosophy of countries under dictatorship, but it is not compatible with the American farmer's inborn sense of liberty and freedom."[10] Farmers usually saw the land as a site of work, and not simply a pretty landscape picture to behold. Frequently this meant that farmers and other rural proprietors were pitted against roadside reformers, who they saw as effete leisure seekers for whom nature was recreation, not work.

More than the farmer, roadside reformers found themselves pitted against the desecration of the landscape by the hand of "the ignorant vendor of hot dogs" and "the vandalism of the rich corporations that sell gasoline"—namely, the corporation and other organized big businesses such as those represented by the organized OAAA.[11] As such examples suggest, this was not merely a fight between urban middle-class visions pitted against those of the rural poor; it was a struggle between conflicting middle-class values and their relative emphasis on beauty or on business. Sometimes even the lines dividing the scenic sisters and the billboard brethren, between beauty and business, were imperceptible. One West Virginia outdoor adman, who had believed that he and his wife shared most middle-class values, was embarrassed to learn that she was chairwoman of the state federation group to restrict billboards.[12] Many clubwomen did share their husband's values and simply would not support the promotion of beauty at the expense of business. Even the New York City Federation of Women's Clubs, many of whose members were represented in NRC publications and in discussions of roadside reform, voted against supporting an NRC proposal for legislation limiting billboards to commercial areas. They claimed that further study was needed "of roadside beauty as a matter of both pride and good business." They found the NRC's proposals were unjust to the individual landowner, and maintained that the NRC had not adequately considered all interests involved, including the commercial and economic interests behind the advertising industry.[13] Perhaps the location of this group, in the advertising capital of the nation, meant they were more closely connected to the industry. Indeed, Lawton distrusted the leadership of the New York Federation, believing it to be a pawn of the outdoor advertising industry.[14] But their views cannot be so easily discounted as kowtowing or compliant. Though the heart of the message sent by the New York women was the defense of private interests, they justified their activity on behalf of the collective rights of those private entities. They stressed that the public was not just mobile; it was comprised of property owners and business interests as well. Accordingly, they decided that private property rights came first, and beauty came second. This, too, was a bourgeois value, perhaps equal to that of the landscape.

As the outdoor advertising industry consolidated and grew throughout the 1930s and 1940s, the issue of roadside reform began to interest groups well beyond the NRC. For instance, Herbert Nelson, the president of the NAREB, participated in the 1931 Conference on Roadside Business and Rural Beauty, which brought together both sides of the billboard war. He took the side of the billboard interests (with which the NAREB had worked since 1925) and sponsored a model legislative bill that the OAAA endorsed and widely publicized. The "Nelson Bill" was one of a series of model acts that the OAAA sponsored in the 1930s that included the same two basic elements: (1) voluntary restrictions, whereby owners of 75 percent of the property abutting any rural highway could agree to exclude billboards, gas stations, hot dog stands, and places of public entertainment; (2) acquisition, by condemnation or gift, of "an easement of control over property abutting the highway." This was far from the legally defined highway zoning that Lawton, Bard, and the NRC advocated. As a plan for voluntary agreements to restrict usage, it was untenable in any comprehensive way. Yet, for the OAAA and the NAREB it was inconceivable to support any regulation—voluntary or legally mandated—that did not compensate billboard and property owners for lost revenues and expenses. The NAREB's support of the OAAA was, after all, about increased revenues. The NAREB claimed that billboards helped to develop and increase the value of property in "new and uncharted areas," along rural and other exurban roads. Moreover, in the Depression years, outdoor advertising became a way of retarding real estate depreciation and "carrying the burden of unimproved property."[15] That real estate brokers often used billboards themselves may also have been an incentive to support them.

The scenic sisters did not support these bills, nor did they agree with the presumption that billboards played a necessary economic role. Less than a decade later, even Nelson was questioning his affiliation with the outdoor advertising industry. In 1940, both Nelson and the NAREB emerged as vocal opponents of outdoor advertising, mostly because they recognized that decentralization and the development of exurban areas had devalued urban real estate. At its convention that year, the NAREB unanimously resolved that billboards "tend to destroy public enjoyment of the vast investment of rural highways," and Nelson personally added that "the destruction of values caused by billboards is many times greater than the gross annual revenue of all outdoor advertising." The NAREB, dealing the outdoor industry a "body blow," joined forces with the NRC at this point.[16] Farmers also were beginning to defect to the women's camp. Outdoor advertisers had persistently claimed farmers to be beneficiaries of their munificence, so rural legislators had been loathe to support billboard regulations. Now, various state farm bureau federations, some under duress brought on by the active lobbying of clubwomen like Hilda Fox, president of the Pennsylvania Roadside Council, crossed over to support bill-board restrictions.[17]

The women had gained powerful allies. The Automobile Association of America (AAA) also entered the fray. In 1940, it supported comprehensive statewide zoning plans and drafted a model roadside zoning bill that borrowed greatly from the 1931 proposals of the NRC. According to AAA guidelines, "the greatest single contribution" of roadside zoning in unincorporated areas would be "to limit commercial uses to designated districts rather than allowing them to scatter at random along the highway." As had been advised by the NRC years before, the AAA designated "two types of roadside business districts, the 'roadside service' type and the 'general commercial' type." The former provided services essential to the traveler (gasoline stations, restaurants, motels); the lat-ter, to which billboards would be restricted, was to serve both traffic and the adjacent community. These two districts were the only commercial designa-tions for roadways that would otherwise be considered "scenic." According to the AAA guidelines, "the term 'scenic' is not confined to the spectacularly sce-nic: 'scenery' is correctly defined as a combination of natural views, or the nat-ural aspect of the landscape. According to this definition, all roadsides are sce-nic except those in built-up urban areas." The guidelines did not specify that "scenic" roads were primarily recreational, for the distinction was considered moot. "A highway carrying a heavy volume of commercial traffic might pass through a highly scenic area, but that fact should not justify the despoliation of the natural beauty of the landscape by billboards." Conversely, a commer-cial district might carry tourists through to a resort area, without having its designation changed.[18]

Highway zoning plans presented by the NRC ten years earlier (and duly mocked) now found support from powerful allies in their new incarnation as an AAA model highway zoning bill. The Federal Public Roads Administration, the American Society of Planning Officials, the American Association of State Highway Officials, the Highway Research Board, and the NAREB all sup-ported the bill.[19] Though frequently defeated by the billboard lobby, dozens of state legislatures throughout the 1940s debated versions of the model act. Counties in California seemed most successful in passing legislation, but other states had towns and counties that also followed suit.[20]

Though the billboard lobby usually succeeded in halting the passage of state and county bills, many localities successfully regulated through zoning, and some counties protected highways through the purchase of easements that restricted the use of abutting land. Even with small victories, the reform move-ment significantly threatened the billboard barons. Indeed, as the AAA gath-ered votes in favor of its model zoning bill, the OAAA tallied the ballots of its membership in favor of its first resolution favoring zoning in rural areas, as long as billboards were allowed in all areas zoned for business, commerce, or industry, without further restriction. The OAAA also began to bolster their troops, forming coalitions with trade associations representing highway sign manufacturers, hotels, restaurants, petroleum industries, automobile dealers, and other highway users.[21]

It seemed that the scenic sisters had become legitimate. Or had they? Addressing an assembly of New York State Garden Clubs in 1941, state sena-tor Thomas Desmond stated what many of those assembled already knew: the women of America had been "the shock troops and now, belatedly but very effectively, powerful male allies are swinging into line." Why, Desmond asked, had women been the vanguard of this regulatory movement, which was so clearly in the male arena of zoning politics? "It was the fiercely protective maternal pride of America's women, scrubbing the face of the country until it becomes shiny, clean and beautiful, as it was meant to be." "At heart," he claimed, "the women resented the billboards because they offended their sense of neatness." And, at heart, zoning was merely a "legalistic expression of the ancient adage of the tidy housewife: 'Everything in its place, and a place for everything.'"[22] Instead of dignifying women reformers by lauding the political power they wielded, Desmond, like others who supported roadside reform, chose instead to repeat tired clichés about women's proper place, granting them only the status of good housekeepers. Yet even after men had seized the reins of legislative activity, women continued in roles that were undeniably political, despite the belittlingly gendered terms with which they were described. Gender divisions persisted, as women were cast as the educators, civic conscience, and maternal protectors of a nation in need of tidying. Hilda Fox was a "spirited" reformer who took Elizabeth Lawton's lead in the move-ment, yet even she seemed to soften her vehement call for zoning, feminizing it as merely "good civic housekeeping," as "*protection* rather than *regulation*," and as a community's moral response to exploitation by the "selfish few."[23] Though women of the Associated Clubs of Virginia provided detailed expla-nations of zoning and how it worked, they stressed that women's role was to find men sympathetic to their cause to put on the planning commissions. Women were the grassroots activists, the soldiers rather than the officers; as they did twenty years earlier, they took their task to be the "arousing of public sentiment in a community," which meant the pedestrian chores of gathering names on petitions and writing letters.[24] In point of fact, their letter-writing and public education was essential, as many communities learned when their attempts at zoning ordinances failed because support had been gained only from county commissioners and no one else in the populace. It was the work of women to gain neighborhood support, house by house.[25]

As the reform movement increasingly focused on state and county zoning as its priority, the issue of aesthetics became displaced by arguments about speed and safety.[26] The female prerogative on behalf of beauty was now superceded by maternal instincts for safety, or so the outdoor advertising industry hoped, as they sought to diffuse attention to billboards as a source of highway danger by offering state women's clubs billboard space by which to advertise safety campaigns. Though the GFWC and Parent-Teacher Associations in sixteen states took up the offer in 1947, others cried treason, repeating Struthers Burt's blustery cry that "any man who puts signs along the highway today is unconsciously aiding and abetting murder."[27] For every such claim, the billboard industry countered with research reports and testimonials from insurance companies to prove that there was no relationship between outdoor advertising and highway accidents.[28] Nevertheless, reformers used the issue of highway safety to support their increasing legislative efforts. Since aesthetics would not be a category of public welfare (on which zoning was based) until the mid-1950s, highway safety was the next best argument. Ribbon slums were a public blight, reformers in California stressed, since they destroyed scenic beauty and depreciated property values, but they were a public menace since they created traffic hazards. In New York and Connecticut, reformers favoring county zoning made the same claims of excessive roadside commercialism that hindered commerce and jeopardized safety.[29] Traveling along U.S. 1 in 1941, Elizabeth Lawton reported that billboards had increased 54 percent since 1934 in Maine and 20 percent in the last year in Florida. Each billboard and commercial stand was a "potential zone of friction and congestion: each unit of roadside development invites a possible interruption to the smoothly and swiftly moving flow of traffic on the main roadway."[30] Though her survey stressed the possibilities for picturesque views, aesthetics were secondary to "frictionless" traffic, safety, and the importance of freely flowing highways for military defense.

As the country mobilized for war, these became the pressing issues, but solutions could not be fully considered until after the war. National lobbying efforts in favor of roadside regulations calmed during World War II. The wartime role played by the advertising industry undoubtedly diffused national reform efforts and lessened criticism of billboards. As they had done during World War I, the outdoor advertising industry donated poster space and publicity to war bonds and other wartime efforts (see plate 8). This recast outdoor advertising in terms of national welfare and economic well being; the outdoor advertising of bonds, even if attached to advertisements for other products, could not possibly be critiqued as selfish profiteering when it served patriotic purposes. Furthermore, outdoor advertising supported more than just the war, but the economy at large. Healthy business, good citizenship, and social progress were all parts of a whole. By wrapping lessons of consumption in the language of patriotism, the industry sold more than war bonds. It also sold the attention and good will of its audience. Its provision of educational and economic service granted it both legitimacy and public support.[31]

After World War II, when highway construction and, notably, plans for a national system of interstate and defense highways resumed, reform efforts also returned. After a dozen years of wrangling over the form and funding for an interstate highway system, President Dwight D. Eisenhower signed the Federal-Aid Road Act of 1956, authorizing a 41,000-mile system of highways, 90 percent of which would be funded by the federal government, and 10 percent by the states, at an estimated cost of $25 billion.[32] Envisioned as a modern, safe, and efficient solution to roadways that had long been ill equipped to accommodate the swollen ranks of motoring Americans, the system was comprised of limited-access, high-speed expressways built according to uniform design standards. The designs aimed to keep traffic moving safely at a constant speed and included wide rights of way, broad shoulders and medians, the minimization of steep grades, the elimination of sharp curves, and cloverleaf interchanges. Gently curving country roads with unfolding picturesque views, which clubwomen and parkway architects so esteemed, were not part of the plan. Neither were there plans for controlling the billboard blight that had disfigured the roads of yore.

Was the largest, most costly public works program ever undertaken in the United States to be the "greatest giveaway of all time," "a huge theft from the public," and "a subsidy to the billboard industry," critics asked, as they envisioned thousands of miles of open highways converted into billboard alleys?[33] While the U.S. Congress drafted legislation to create the interstate system, first-year Oregon senator Richard Neuberger, an ardent conservationist, suggested an ambitious plan to "encourage" states to acquire land and easements along highways and to keep all but essential signs at least five hundred feet from new highways. It was a short-lived amendment, squelched by bipartisan opposition that claimed it was antilabor, antienterprise, and a federal interference of state's rights. Instead, Congress adopted a weaker measure, the "Bonus" Act of 1958, that left billboard control in state hands: states that regulated billboards within established federal standards would receive a "bonus" of 0.5 percent more than the 90 percent federal subsidy of the interstate system. Two additional amendments compromised the act further, permitting signs on those parts of the interstate highway that "incorporate previously used rights of way and others that pass through zoned business and commercial areas of incorporated municipalities." Engineered by Oklahoma senator Robert Kerr, who led the opposition to banning billboards, the amendments were supported by Texas senator Lyndon B. Johnson.[34]

The battles of the 1950s and 1960s continued along the lines established in the previous half century of activity. The weapons each used also remained consistent. It was the billboard barons against the scenic sisters, dollars versus aesthetic sense, professional lobbyists and lawyers versus letter-writing, flower-sniffing crusaders. Though roadside reform had become a national cause and the subject of congressional debate and extensive coverage in the popular press, when the issues and sides boiled down to essentials the old stereotypes still reigned. Now, instead of Elizabeth Lawton being pilloried by her opponents, there was Hilda Fox of the Pennsylvania Roadside Council, Mrs. Vance Hood of the New Jersey Roadside Council, and Helen Reynolds of the California Roadside Council, and state chapters that continued strongly on even after the NRC dissolved, in an untimely way, just at the start of the postwar round of the billboard war. The roadside reform movement suffered greatly without the NRC as a clearinghouse. It needed not only the vision and vigilance of Lawton's leadership and the legal acumen of Albert Bard as counsel, but also the communications infrastructure and national reach of their organization. Still carrying on were the Garden Club of America, the American Planning and Civic Association, and the American Automobile Association, but without the NRC or some other group orchestrating the activities, the movement lacked a center.[35]

As state after state sought to enact standards and controls on billboards (usually failing), clubwomen used their decades of experience to garner public and legislative support. Maryland's Garden Club set up a "telephone chain," so that as "legislation started through committees, action signals flashed over the lines," alerting four thousand members in an hour. In the next days, the women flooded the state capitol, visiting legislators' homes and pouring letters into the legislature. After two years of trying, Maryland passed a law keeping billboards 660 feet from interstate highways and restricting them from property adjacent to all state expressways. After years of frustration while trying to get outdoor advertisers in Pennsylvania to abide by agreements they had made with the Roadside Council to stay off scenic roads, Hilda Fox masterminded a plot whereby she and one hundred Pennsylvania clubwomen bought stock in General Outdoor Advertising Company. They diligently attended stockholders' meetings, badgering officers about the twenty billboards on an eighty-five-mile scenic stretch of the Pennsylvania Turnpike that the company had promised to leave untouched.[36] California clubwomen continued their legacy of writing to advertisers to complain about billboard use. Finally, in 1957, after twenty-seven years of using outdoor advertising, the Union Oil Company simply discontinued the practice.[37] Reformers from across the country pressed on, writing letters and calling representatives to extend the time frame of the "Bonus" Act and to set billboard controls.[38] Despite these efforts, by the time the extended "Bonus" Act expired on June 30, 1965, only twenty-three states were signed up, relatively few miles of the interstate had been affected, and only seven states had fulfilled the requirements and received bonuses.[39]

If the outdoor advertising industry had consolidated itself in the 1920s and 1930s, by the 1950s and 1960s it had become a devastatingly effective lobbying machine. A reform sympathizer explained that "this lobby shrewdly puts many legislators in its debt by giving them free sign space during election time, and it is savage against the legislator who dares oppose it. It subsidizes his opposition, foments political trouble in his home district, donates sign space to his opponents and sends agents to spread rumors among his constituents."[40] It also claimed to represent labor interests such as the Brotherhood of Painters, Decorators, and Paperhangers of America and the AFL-CIO, as well as the general economic interests of the country. Against this immense industry and all of its supporters, Hilda Fox could only bemoan her reformers as "just a group of starry-eyed billboard fighters."[41]

But at this moment the roadside reform movement was given new life from an unlikely corner, the White House, and from the very man who had opposed stringent billboard restrictions in 1958, and had used billboards for his own campaigning in 1960 and again in 1964 (fig. 65). For Lyndon Johnson, the decision to fight for highway beautification was not sympathy for the cause, but love for his wife, Lady Bird. Her influence led him to call U.S. Secretary of Commerce Luther Hodges one day late in 1964 to tell him to do something to clean up the roadside, to form the Task Force on Natural Beauty, and to thrust

65. Campaign for Lyndon B. Johnson, 1964.

himself into the quagmire of the Highway Beautification Act. Even as he hit brick walls in Congress, Johnson persisted, telling his staff, "You know I love that woman and she wants that Highway Beautification Act. . . . By god, we're going to get it for her."[42]

Though the most powerful man in the nation led this new round in the billboard war, because it retained the old rhetoric of nature and beauty, and because his wife served as its catalyst and promoter, the struggle was again cast in gendered terms. "Many will have been disconcerted," one journalist wrote, "by hearing the President of the United States express himself before the Congress in the language of a guest speaker at a Garden Club lunch—'the national heritage of beauty,' 'beauty-destroying junkyards,' 'improving the natural beauty of urban open spaces,' etc."[43] Ada Louise Huxtable commented that the White House Conference on Natural Beauty, at which the president publicly launched the beautification program, sounded like a "top-level tea party for little old ladies devoted to the cause of simple pastoral pleasures." And though she did admit that "the roster of panelists and delegates reads like a who's who of the conservation and urban planning fields," her initial characterization remained potent.[44] Attention to beauty, no matter what the burly Texan in the White House said, was woman's work and the highway beautification act was "Lady Bird's Bill," "a frivolous frill, and a woman's whim," as some senators took to calling it.[45]

The commentators were right. Lyndon Johnson had used the same rhetoric as generations of clubwomen, associating natural beauty with moral order, spiritual uplift, and national heritage. When he called for a "new conservation" focused not just on national parks or wilderness areas but the streets and highways of daily life, accessible to all social classes with highways as "routes to pleasure and recreation," Johnson invoked the spirit of Elizabeth Lawton and echoed her early automobile age fears that unchecked commercial development encroached upon the natural beauty and open space of the countryside.[46] At the end of his remarks to the delegates of the White House Conference on Natural Beauty, Johnson reminded the women in the audience that while the men in attendance would "go back home and talk big" about what they did, it was really up to the women to force them into action, and to do the same with their congressmen and the rest of the public.[47] He was saying that this job was for women and that their tasks were essentially the same as they had always been, to "arouse public sentiment."

Journalists loved to report—often sarcastically—on Lady Bird's affection for flowers and her belief in the power of beauty to uplift even the economically depressed, as if she was the leader of the garden club armies that were championing beautification.[48] However, the women of the roadside councils and garden clubs, despite their field experience, were offered no role in helping to shape legislation and had scant contact with members of the administration. They had some correspondence with Senator Maurine Neuberger, who had taken her husband's seat in the U.S. Senate after he died, and they exchanged polite letters with Lady Bird Johnson and her staff, but little else.[49] The roadside reformers were never invited into the inner sanctum of the White House, and for good reason. The seats there were already filled by their competition, the lawyers and lobbyists of the billboard industry.

The outdoor advertising industry had been working its political connections behind the scenes. Early on it supported the Highway Beautification Act, knowing well from meetings with White House officials that the bill included the provisions it desired. As the bill was being drafted, members of the industry wrote letters to congressmen and ran newspaper ads zealously supporting "President Johnson's legislative program to improve the beauty of our country."[50]

The U.S. Department of Commerce, which had jurisdiction over the highway systems, had been consorting with the billboard lobby since 1963 to revise the billboard law. Once President Johnson decided to beautify the highways of the "Great Society," he charged White House staff member Bill Moyers to the task of working on legislation with Texas attorney and president of the OAAA, Philip Tocker. What they and the Bureau of Public Roads agreed upon—not what the clubwomen and conservationists had recommended at the conference—became the heart of the Highway Beautification Act. So it happened that as Helen Reynolds and Hilda Fox sat in their folding chairs on the White House lawn, shocked by President Johnson's concluding comments at the Conference on Natural Beauty, Philip Tocker peered out upon the scene from Bill Moyers's office, quite comfortable with what was being said below.[51]

What finally passed as the Highway Beautification Act of 1965 could hardly be called a victory for the roadside beautifiers. The act called for controls on federally funded primary and interstate highways, restricting billboards within 660 feet of highways but permitting them in areas zoned commercial and industrial and in unzoned areas used for commerce or industry.[52] The billboard brethren achieved, essentially, what they had been proposing for forty years. They even succeeded in having an amendment passed that assured "just compensation" to be paid to all billboard or property owners whose billboards were removed as a result of the Highway Beautification Act. For roadside reformers this was humiliating, as it meant the defilers of the landscape were now paid to keep from polluting, rather than being fined for having done so all these years.

The act was a giant step backward for legal reasons also. Since the late 1920s and 1930s reformers had "battled for and won court decisions upholding the rights of states" to use police power to control billboards as nuisances and that the placement of a sign to be viewed from a public highway was a "privilege granted and not a right inherent in the ownership of land adjacent to the highway." The just compensation clause of the Highway Beautification Act implied the opposite and offered federal support of that position. Moreover, it prohibited amortization, the most common way in which states with regulations compensated legal, nonconforming land use by allowing property owners to leave their billboards up for a grace period in order to recoup their investments through rentals.[53] The Highway Beautification Act, in effect, penalized those states that had already passed stringent billboard regulations, for even those states with constitutional powers to exert effective controls under the police power were now forced to pay just compensation for signs removed along primary roads covered by the federal act.[54] Needless to say, procuring adequate funds for the financial compensation of billboard removal was yet another fiasco of the act.

Support of the Highway Beautification Act by roadside reformers was half hearted, to say the least. As Helen Reynolds explained, "[T]he roadside beauty lovers—Roadside Councils, Garden Clubs, conservationists, etc.—were split into various segments. Some groups gave vent to their disappointment by cold-shouldering the bill entirely; some supported it but with so many reservations that their support appeared closer to opposition; others recognized in the bill a basic step in advance and set to work to give it what backing they could."[55] However, even those most loyal to the Johnsons and to the idea of the Highway Beautification Act as an important federal recognition of roadside beauty (despite its flawed content) found it difficult to stomach the just-compensation clause, and later recanted their support. Reynolds, for one, was appalled by "the shocking unbalance favoring concessions to the billboard lobby." Even federal standards for the size and height of billboards had been left to the billboard industry to decide, Reynolds complained, as the law left it to federal and state officials to decide upon limits based on "common practice."[56] Sure enough, the maximum size finally specified was twelve hundred square feet; no height restrictions were included. The absence of height restrictions left open to the industry a huge new species of billboard, the monopole. Monster billboards resting atop a single galvanized steel pole whose height "was limited only by the law of physics (the tallest is 15 stories)," had begun popping up across the countryside after the Bonus Act of 1958 was passed. Peering over tree tops and legible a half-mile away, they solved the problem of being located 660 feet from the edge of the road. And, since the pole occupied little ground space, it was economical even in high-rent urban areas (see fig. 71).[57]

As a result of the zoning allowances, many people besides roadside reformers declared the Highway Beautification Act to be a failure.[58] Since much of the land around rural highways was not zoned, and therefore in the domain of local government, detractors contended that outdoor advertising companies that had infiltrated local planning and zoning boards (as the billboard-industry spies had infiltrated the GFWC[59]) could easily sway matters in their favor. In an unzoned area, any property with a business function could designate the road around it as an unzoned commercial area and thereby eligible for billboard use, though these rules did differ between localities. This left the door wide open to shams and phonies, as one Department of Transportation report illustrated, showing "a deserted shed . . . labeled 'Mike's Welding Shop,' a private home billed as 'Carter's Drafting Service,' a solitary, old gas pump masquerading as a filling station next to a billboard set in the middle of a field."[60]

Several states that recognized these problems with the Highway Beautification Act continued to work for stronger state regulations. In 1968, Vermonters succeeded where all previous reformers had not, passing a law that rid the entire state of billboards, using a "historic conservation principle identifying billboards as a source of scenery pollution." Although the OAAA claimed that the law was unfair to the tourist industry, the major tourist associations and chambers of commerce backed the law. Maine followed Vermont's example, establishing similar laws in 1977, to join Hawaii and Alaska as the only four states banning billboards.[61]

Neither the actions of these states nor the Highway Beautification Act crippled the billboard industry. Far from it, the act actually recognized the outdoor advertising industry as "a legitimate business use of land."[62] It also helped put the outdoor advertising industry in the hands of fewer and bigger companies, sounding a death knell for the small-scale, rural billposting businesses and sign companies. More regulated spaces increased the value of properties already held, while compensation from the federal government made up for any losses due to the new regulation. Roadside entrepreneurs with fewer holdings could less easily balance their losses than those whose properties or leases extended farther and wider, or were primarily urban. As John Primrose, the owner of a western Kentucky outdoor advertising business bluntly interpreted the act, "it will work very little hardship on the big Metropolitan plants but it will practically put the small rural plants, like mine, out of business."[63] In this sense, the Highway Beautification Act actually smoothed the process of incorporation and consolidation that the outdoor industry had begun three quarters of a century earlier.

LOSERS AND WINNERS

Though through the years the battle lines in the billboard war tended to be drawn between aesthetics and business, the billboard advocates were not without their share of aesthetes, some of whom were quite illustrious. One journalist recounted a story of art critic Seldon Rodman: "Riding along Connecticut's Merritt Parkway one day . . . [Rodman] told architect Philip Johnson about New Jersey's Routes 4 and 17: 'Not a tree, not a blade of grass; nothing but billboards and gas pumps.' Replied Johnson: 'I'd prefer that to this green tunnel! . . . It's a nightmare of monotony. A nurseryman's bonanza.'"[1] Far from the realm of high art, Ruth Knight, of the *Kiwanis* magazine (and "a farmer's school-teachin' daughter" and amateur naturalist), shared Johnson's taste, looking for billboards to spice up not just the repeating green parkway tunnels but also the "monotonous super-highway treks where there's nothing to see but scenery." Surely there existed "a big contented majority who believe that the billboard is a satisfying and colorful illustration of the American way of life," she exclaimed. For her the "young gods and goddesses" that "wave from billboards . . . with laughter in their eyes, toasting me in magic Coca-Cola," were reminders of a "lusty" life beyond the driver's seat, where people "trade and advertise and buy things." "They dress up the plain old world," Knight wrote, and become memory markers of place and time, starting in the days of Mail Pouch tobacco through to Burma-Shave.[2] A writer for *Life* had a less lofty explanation for his billboard preferences, calling them "a kind of Benzedrine pick-up to keep the drivers from dozing."[3] Even the *New York Times* jumped into the fray, pairing Ogden Nash's 1932 rephrasing of a Joyce Kilmer poem (and a favorite quotation of roadside reformers); "I think that I shall never see / A billboard lovely as a tree. / Perhaps unless the billboards fall / I'll never see a tree at all" with the rejoinder, "You cannot unleash our liberty / Unless you do it locally. / And if you want to stay alive / Read 'poster panels' as you drive."[4]

These are reminders of taste distinctions that the popular press mostly ignored, or sidestepped, as they issued their wake-up calls to what they saw to be the "uglification" of America the beautiful. Thirty-year veteran of the billboard war, yet still not at a loss for words, New York's commissioner of parks and parkways, Robert Moses, wrote walloping editorials and speeches reviling the "horrors" "put up by devilishly ingenious promoters" with "selfish, contemptible" objectives. Moses just barely saved his New York Thruway and area parkways from billboard exploiters, but still lamented that federal action had failed so miserably. Social critic Vance Packard, author of best-selling exposés of consumer culture such as *The Waste Makers*, *The Hidden Persuaders*, and *The Status Seekers*, presented his opinion succinctly in the title of his *Atlantic Monthly* article on the subject of blight, "America the Beautiful—and Its Desecrators."[5] The loudest voice of all was architect Peter Blake's in *God's Own Junkyard*, an excoriating attack on the greed and indifference of the "defilers" as well as the legislators and general public who had let the landscape go to ruin. The book gained so much attention and was so damning of the billboard industry that the Outdoor Advertising Association of America searched for libel grounds with which to sue Blake.[6] For Blake it was clear: Americans had forsaken both the natural and manmade landscapes. More debates about taste and its relativity, he thought, would merely lead to more commercial obfuscation of the fact that billboards were simply ugly.

Billboards, of course, have come to wrap themselves around us so thoroughly that it would seem the scenic sisters failed. Actually, they succeeded in many ways. The reformers of the 1920s and 1930s may not have preserved the entire roadside landscape, but they took the first and necessary steps in establishing zoning and planning outside of cities. Curiously, they have been left out of zoning and planning history, perhaps because they seem almost to lampoon the social causes of their predecessors, whose municipal housekeeping work on behalf of less-privileged urban dwellers has been the subject of scholarship since the 1970s. Perhaps their contributions to urban and planning history are also overlooked because they focused on in-between places and mobile populations and did so on a national basis. Roadside reformers may have been the antithesis of their municipal colleagues, but they had tremendous foresight in addressing the areas and issues that would ultimately draw resources, development, and people away from cities and lead to commercial and residential sprawl.

Could the reformers have done better for their cause? The counterhistorical question cannot really be answered, but some speculation may be instructive. Perhaps if the reformers had not so quickly conceded the point that their aesthetic vision of the landscape necessarily infringed upon business and progress, then the reformers may have been more successful in unraveling the ribbon developments they so aptly predicted. Though in the first part of the century reformers had done well to emphasize the social and moral problems resulting from urban crowding and poor sanitation, in later decades roadside reformers needed to change their arguments with the times. Rather than to repeat old arguments about moral and civic costs, some focus on the negative economic effects of advertising on the landscape (and there are negative effects, certainly) would have been useful. By addressing the bottom line, and by not conceding that their vision was incompatible with it, reformers might even have worked toward developing an economically feasible roadside landscape as well as the scenic towns and villages they imagined. Instead they simply decried billboards as ugly. Then again, when we ask the scenic sisters to step out of their gendered, middle-class worldview and to make economic arguments in a sphere not their own, perhaps we simply ask too much.

Sinclair Lewis, however, did not think so. When he created the character Carol Kennicott, champion of civic beauty, he hardly kept her in her "proper" place. When Kennicott imagined the Main Street of her town combining country charm and city flavor, she did not believe that the billboard on Main Street was her real obstacle. Rather, the city's short-sighted leaders who could understand nothing but business were what frustrated her. In *Main Street* (1920), Sinclair Lewis conveyed hilariously how local interests were growing singularly shallow and middle class, while the final adjudication of all cultural and urban issues rested with the short-term needs of business (to make a quick killing) aided by the short-term needs of government (to win the next election through the financial support of business). This pairing of government and business, supposedly in the name of the public welfare, is the very definition of corporate liberalism, an ideal founded at the turn of the twentieth century that entrusts the public good to the benevolent despotism of business with very little voice given to the public itself. It is a faulty ideal that quashed the scenic sisters and has affected eras well beyond that of the Kennicotts, Lawtons, and Lady Birds.

Like the scenic sisters before her, Lady Bird Johnson ultimately bowed to business and limited her political involvement to ladylike beauty. Though her acquiescence to the corporate liberal ideal restricted what she could hope to accomplish, she did grant herself a significant and lasting role in her husband's administration. She brought to federal attention the cause of aiding natural beauty in everyday places as the right of all people to enjoy. She also deflected attention from the Vietnam War and urban riots, the events that stained her husband's administration. She continued a legacy of women reformers and defused the political nature of her activities by using nature, beauty, and the women's realm as her shield. Like generations before her, Lady Bird's political activity came in the benign form of a program of domestic housekeeping writ large. From her prominent public role as first lady, the ultimate position in the old-girl network, she rearticulated the pastoral ideal of the scenic sisters and propagated their myth of the open road, placing the Great Society of the 1960s onto the pavement and into the landscape.

CONCLUSION

THE ROAD AHEAD

While Lady Bird Johnson waxed poetic about the power of the birds and the trees, James Rosenquist and Andy Warhol were taking lessons they had learned from their billboard and advertising work and making art of the masses that they called pop.[1] Surely this was not the aesthetic the ladies had in mind when they spoke of beauty. If pop art entered the purview of civic beautifiers at all, it stayed within the confines of the museum, fixed to art as an object even if its sources were drawn from the art of everyday life.

It is also doubtful that Lady Bird Johnson and the scenic sisters would have been sympathetic, several years later, to the insights of *Learning from Las Vegas*, a book in which a pop perspective was applied to the roadside environment.[2] In it, architects Robert Venturi, Denise Scott Brown, and Steven Izenour charted the forms and structures they and their Yale School of Architecture studio found on the Las Vegas Strip in 1968. They criticized the modernist design aesthetic emblematized by the work of Ludwig Mies van der Rohe, which shucked ornament and symbolism in favor of a bare essentialist geometry of glass and steel. They rebelled against mainstream urban criticism of the 1960s, such as that published by Peter Blake in *God's Own Junkyard*, which regarded the chaotic nature of the everyday built environment as a design problem that needed an architectural solution (fig. 66).[3] The same images that Blake employed to show the "flood of ugliness" and environmental degradation caused by the automobile, the Venturi group also used in *Learning from Las Vegas*, but for another reason: to embrace the industrial-consumer aesthetic.[4] The Yale studio praised the lessons of expressive symbolic communication taught by commercial roadside architecture, from billboards

66. Rondal Partridge, photograph of El Camino Real, Palo Alto, California, published in Peter Blake's *God's Own Junkyard*, 1964.

to the sign-laden structures that had to scream to get motorists' attention. They claimed that "Main Street is alright" without urban renewal, model planning schemes, and other means by which its ad hoc qualities would be tamed or standardized. And in embracing "the ugly and the ordinary," the Venturi group was creating pop architecture.

As Stuart Davis and Gerald Murphy had used their artwork in the 1920s to focus attention on American commercialism (see fig. 21), so pop artists and architects also reevaluated the role of advertising and mass media in everyday life and art. Pop artists did not always defend commercialism, but perhaps they sometimes saw its appropriation as a way of transcending the "nausea of the replica" by making "no distinction between the unique object and the mass-produced object," as Susan Sontag once suggested.[5] Pop artists also created venues for presenting that which was commonly overlooked. They used billboards and brand names, soup cans and comic strips, to suggest the difficulty of disentangling commerce from aesthetics, popular culture from high art, reality from representation. Their art reminded us that the images, ads, and slogans that comprise consumer culture have infused not just our physical environments, but the very ways in which we see, understand, and picture the world around us. This insight has not always been disapproving. In *America*, Andy Warhol's black-and-white photographic odyssey of 1985, he censured nothing and made no appeal except for an open-eyed, guileless reception of the multitude of people, images, and structures that comprised the campy, messy pop landscape. Main Street was more than alright for him—it was capitalism's picture book, where America's ironies and inequalities were reflected in odd, funny, and ordinary hearts and lives.[6]

There were many who still found American commercialism to be a form of social and environmental degradation, and many who saw mass media as the standardizing machinery of a corporate bureaucracy that suppressed individualism. There were those who followed the model of the scenic sisters rather carefully, such as Scenic America, a national anti-billboard organization (dominated by women) devoted to preserving the scenic character of the American countryside, while others were less interested than their forerunners had been in supporting the middle-class establishment.[7] Since the 1970s, a new generation of activists determined to rid the landscape of "litter on a stick," and impatient with a system that favored corporate over grassroots interests, took up their own "extralegal" means of policing billboards. Their activities ranged from that of the "Billboard Bandit," who used a chainsaw to cut down billboards along Michigan highways in 1971, to feminist groups who staged demonstrations at the foot of billboards and spraypainted or pasted over sexist ads, labeling them demeaning to women.[8] Meanwhile, the radio blared the catchy refrain from the Five Man Electrical Band: "Sign, sign, everywhere a sign / Blocking out the scenery, breaking my mind / Do this, don't do that / can't you read the sign?"

Similar strategies were revived in the 1980s and 1990s, when urban residents noticed that while wealthy residential areas were billboard free, poor minority neighborhoods were under siege from liquor and cigarette advertisements. Beer and liquor brands have always been leading advertisers in the outdoor medium, with cigarette companies joining them after a forced withdrawal from television and radio advertising in the 1970s. For some time, the two products generated at least 40 percent of all outdoor advertising revenue.[9] Outdoor advertising has also been an important way to target ethnic markets for these products (plate 11).[10] Frustrated by his fruitless attempts to have such billboards banned in his impoverished African American parish on the south side of Chicago, Reverend Michael Pfleger took matters into his own hands in

1990, with a bucket of red paint and 118 billboards as his target.[11] Soon after, Reverend Calvin Butts, of the Abyssinian Church of Harlem, also took up battle with a paintbrush, whitewashing the boards in his neighborhood. With forty members of his congregation, Butts also staged a demonstration at Philip Morris headquarters, calling for the company to "stop selling drugs and stop selling death." Protests in other metropolitan areas followed (fig. 67). As a result, Metropolitan Outdoor Advertising in Harlem began to reposition or remove liquor and tobacco ads that were within five hundred feet of schools, churches, and hospitals. Philip Morris replaced its cigarette billboards with product advertisements from a subsidiary, Kraft Foods. This policy–prohibiting "adult product advertisements" in certain areas and encouraging "greater diversity of advertised goods and services in all markets"–also became important components of the Outdoor Advertising Association of America's (OAAA's) "Code of Advertising Practices," still in effect today.[12]

In the end, community protest played only a small role in limiting tobacco advertisements in minority areas. At most, it galvanized attempts already being made by the industry to diversify their advertising. By the late 1980s, tobacco and liquor sales were flagging, and outdoor advertising for both products dipped, sending billboard firms scurrying to drum up other business.[13] Still, tobacco remained important for the industry, representing 10 percent of outdoor revenues, until the 1998 Master Settlement Agreement between forty-six states and five territories and the tobacco industry, which banned tobacco advertisements outright on all forms of outdoor advertising.[14] At this time, Reverend Pfleger's fourteen-year battle to rid his neighborhood of tobacco and liquor billboards also came to an end, as the Chicago City Council approved a residential ban.[15] By then, however, residents of places like the South Side of Chicago, and Harlem, had a new set of concerns: the concentration of billboards showing weapons and using expletives.[16]

Extralegal efforts that challenge the messages and the placement of corporate advertising in public space have not always had specific goals as they did in Chicago and New York. They have included broader attempts to "improve," revise, or otherwise alter billboards, to sabotage the advertisers' message of consumption with a critique of the consumable item and how it is being pitched to audiences.[17] Pioneers in these billboard-busting efforts are Jack Napier and San Francisco's Billboard Liberation Front (active since 1977), Ron English, and other, anonymous "culture jammers" whose activities are often documented at Web sites and in magazines such as *Stay Free!* and *Adbusters*. Their projects have included such "interventions" as the transformation of Joe

67. Activist
Henry Brown
(a.k.a.
Mandrake)
paints over an
Olde English
"800" beer bill-
board, Chicago,
1992.

Camel into Joe Chemo (complete with an intravenous drip); the replacement of Albert Einstein's and the Dalai Lamai's photographs in Apple Computer's "Think Different" campaign with those of Charles Manson and Joseph Stalin; the scrawling of "feed me" on waifish woman models in ads by Calvin Klein; and the revision of Coor's Silver Bullet to "Liver Bullet," Absolut Vodka to "Absolut Hangover," and Ultra Kool cigarettes to "Utter Fool," among others (fig. 68).[18] Like the photographic social commentaries of the 1930s by Dorothea Lange and Margaret Bourke-White, these critics use sarcasm and irony, but with a heavier hand, commensurate with the increasingly media-saturated environment within which they work.

Proponents say that these subversions of intended corporate messages can turn the "one-way information flow" of advertising into a public discourse that gives airtime to a silent majority who cannot afford privately controlled public spaces. They describe these activities as reappropriating corporate-dominated channels of communication.[19] In many cases, culture jammers try to use the strategies of Madison Avenue against it, but the effect of this activity is hard to gauge. In some instances, altering an ad, a brand name, or a slogan draws even more attention to the product and simply reinforces the currency of the brand.

68. Photograph by Quackser Fortune of an "improved" Apple Computer "Think Different" billboard, c. 1998. Courtesy Billboard Liberation Front.

69. More than 150 outdoor advertising companies in 48 states participated in this ironic public service campaign, 1967.

In others, adbusters have succeeded too well in taking on the glossy look of Madison Avenue, and their manipulated ads become indiscernible from the originals, especially when both are fabricated using the same technology.

Moreover, since the time of the "creative revolution" in the 1960s, advertisers have absorbed the critiques of the counterculture and co-opted its messages of nonconformity, rebellion, and individualism (fig. 69). Starting with Bill Bernbach's classic ads for Volkswagen, in which irony and humor were used to mock the shallowness of consumerism and the techniques of persuasion used in the sales process, hip values have been used to sell all sorts of products that promise to let you be you. Even advertisers themselves have refashioned their own image to follow suit. In contrast to previous decades in which advertising was perceived as a science practiced by men in grey flannel suits, by the late 1960s, advertisers had become artists, or "creatives," as attuned to youth culture as to the vanguard in art and music.[20]

Irony, humor, and parody are now the standard tools of advertising, so that social critiques and commodity messages are often confounded, as when Diesel clothing ran a campaign depicting angry young demonstrators, and another juxtaposing frail "third world" workers with glamorous models.[21] Some audiences were confused: were these adbusting campaigns directed at Diesel or were they serious advertisements? In fact, they were serious. A similar question arose concerning billboards for British Petroleum (BP), one of which read, "We believe in alternative energy. Like solar and cappuccino." The tag line said "Beyond Petroleum," and the diminutive BP logo rested within a small green sun. Was this a parody, an oil giant claiming to be green? The $20 million invested in the campaign would indicate that it was no joke. BP needed to detach the image of the company from its real business, of oil production. Incidentally, this was the same amount that it spent on its total six-year investment in renewable energy technologies, such as solar power.[22]

Art has also been appropriated. Companies collect cultural capital along with their usual financial revenues when, like Absolut, they commission artists to create ads; or, like Calvin Klein, they employ risqué photographs in the tradition of Robert Mapplethorpe; or like Benetton clothing company, they depict scenes of social and political unrest. As advertisers have declared themselves to be artists, so artists have turned to advertising, both for paying work and for the powerful strategies of graphic communication it employs. As art broke free of the four walls of the museum and into commercial settings, the street and the sites and structures of outdoor advertising became a new location for a range of artistic practices, from conceptual and performance art to feminist and postmodern productions. By the 1980s, public arts funding had peaked and museums had discovered that they could tap the public service offerings of billboard companies. Art was on the boards, buses, and street furniture of major metropolitan areas, supplanting consumerist messages with social and aesthetic ones. These included Barbara Kruger's blown-up photographs and tersely worded slogans that questioned gender stereotypes and power relations (fig. 70). These also included Felix Gonzalez-Torres's 1992 billboards of an unmade, rumpled bed, wistfully memorializing occupants since departed. While some artwork—like those by Gonzalez-Torres—offered a visual reprieve within the commercial cacophony of the street, as if to grant a moment for personal reflection within the public realm, others, such as the artists' collective Gran Fury, used billboards for direct social purposes, to build public awareness of AIDS, homelessness, and racial discrimination.[23]

Finally, after one hundred years, the outdoor advertising industry could rightfully declare that billboards were the art galleries of the masses. The

70. Barbara Kruger, *Untitled (We Don't Need Another Hero)*, 1988. Billboard installation on 39th Street, north of Queens Boulevard, Queens, NY, 1988–89, part of a Public Art Fund, Incorporated, program. Courtesy of the artist and Mary Boone Gallery, New York.

prominent ad agency TBWA/Chiat/Day reinforced the point with their campaign for The Museum of Contemporary Art, in which billboards featuring museum-styled object labels identified various parts of Los Angeles as art. One billboard above the 405 Freeway read, "'A Study in Air Color,' 2001, nitrogen, oxygen, particulate matter and light, on loan from The Museum of Contemporary Art, Los Angeles." Cultural institutions were not the only ones investing millions in the medium once considered the "working-class grunt in the glittering media universe." By the 1990s there was a new cultural panache to the billboard, and Calvin Klein, Gap, Absolut, Apple, Disney, luxury car makers, and Internet trendsetters paid upward of $100,000 a month for coveted locations along West Hollywood's Sunset Strip, New York's Times

71. Billboard on the Sunset Strip in tony West Hollywood, 2003.

Square, and the highly trafficked route between San Francisco and Silicon Valley (fig. 71, plate 13).[24] Whereas nearly a century earlier New Yorkers had rebelled against the first illuminated sign, hawking homes on Long Island "swept by ocean breezes," and were positively appalled by the second, H. J. Heinz Company's thirty-foot green electrical cucumber, by 1986 even the Municipal Art Society (the group that had spearheaded billboard regulation efforts in the early 1900s) was arguing for zoning laws to ensure that new buildings would be covered by the eye-popping spectaculars that had become the identity of Times Square.[25] As West Hollywood masterminded its renaissance, it also zoned in the "tall wall" advertisements that previous generations had battled to keep out. The chamber of commerce began sponsoring the Sunset Strip Billboard Awards to fete the agencies and companies that brought so much income into the area and that made driving the Strip like turning the pages of *Vanity Fair*, as one councilman claimed.[26] What was once known as the "beer, butts, and babes medium," was now driven by "the big budgets of big-name marketers."[27]

In the 1960s, industry leaders such as John Kluge and Karl Eller diversified media operations. They realized that outdoor advertising could be seen as an adjunct to newspapers, radio, television, and entertainment rather than as their competitor. These leaders orchestrated several waves of consolidation in the next few decades that swept up many smaller, mom-and-pop shops (though many family-run outdoor companies persist today).[28] But even these mergers paled by comparison to the banner year of 1996–97, in which Clear Channel Communications bought Eller Media for a whopping $1.15 billion; three billboard companies—Outdoor Systems, Lamar Advertising, and Universal Outdoor—went public, making their CEOs multimillionaires; and in a case of "the minnow swallowing the whale," Outdoor Systems rose from seventh largest outdoor company to number one by purchasing the outdoor division of media megalith Gannett, itself four times larger than the original Outdoor.[29] Outdoor Systems stock quickly rose 1,460 percent, putting it among the top public offerings of the late 1990s—in the ranks of Yahoo! and Amazon.com. In 1999, Outdoor Systems was bought by Viacom. Together the "Big Three" outdoor companies—Viacom, Clear Channel, and Lamar—came to control 40 percent of the revenues generated by the approximately 400,000 billboards across America.[30] No longer recognizable as the successor to the rough-and-tumble world of the itinerant billsticker, the outdoor industry was now a multimedia, global operation.

The consolidations of outdoor advertising had been helped by the fragmentation of television markets, which had become too numerous and too market-specific for national advertisers to achieve mass coverage through them. New computer-painted vinyl bulletins that "make products look as good in 672 square feet as they would in a glossy magazine" (the first big change in printing technology since the advent of color lithography in the nineteenth century) also appealed to big-name brand marketers, since it meant the vinyl bulletins could be duplicated nationwide with very little lag time between advertising campaigns.[31] The consolidations also simplified the buying of national and international outdoor space, and convinced large companies definitively that billboards were not simply a local medium. Advertisers such as Coca-Cola, Gap, and AT&T now had the convenience of one-stop shopping for all their media needs. With tobacco vacating the outdoors, more space became available to higher paying clients with better reputations. Demand was high and supply low. As investors in outdoor companies realized long ago, the costs of their industry are fixed at the price of billboards and the price of leases. Since most of the legal sites have already been built and strict regulations make it difficult to build more, existing billboard sites gain in value along with demand.[32] In good times, when business is booming, billboard leases in urban markets soar; when the economy slows, the core of the outdoor business remains. Local and rural markets pick up the slack in the industry.[33]

In recent years, the outdoor advertising industry has weathered the difficult economic climate well. It has fared better than most other media even as it lost lucrative contracts with the dot.com bomb and the cutbacks in national advertising in the post-9/11 recession. It has proven the wisdom of the hundred-year push to diversify outdoor advertising and to promote the benefits of national coverage, locally applied.[34] While it would seem that the plethora of cable television channels and the rise in Internet use would threaten an outdoor medium that has always feared people going indoors, it is amazing how the old adages about Americans being a mobile population continue to serve industry pundits so well. At the 2003 OAAA national convention, founder and CEO of Clear Channel Communications, Lowry Mays, used the same language as outdoor advertising leader George Kleiser had in the 1920s and 1930s, noting that Americans are an outdoors population who drive farther and more often than ever before. Along with the personal, professional, and social realms of American society, he said, mobility now constitutes the fourth dimension of daily life.[35]

Mobility has been the cornerstone of both the outdoor advertising industry and the dispersal of markets along the asphalt highways that came to crisscross the nation over the course of the twentieth century. Now mobility is the underpinning of the new borderless marketplace, the Internet, our virtual buyway. The corridors of consumption that automobility and advertising promoted in the 1920s and 1930s, enabled by huge investments of the federal government in highway and interstate development, now spread out into cyberspace, thanks again to massive federal investment in global positioning systems (GPS) and other media-related infrastructures. Today the moniker *electronic superhighway* sounds almost "retro," a dinosaur of 1990s wonderment at the possibilities of new telecommunications media that superceded the grid-locked asphalt highways of the three-dimensional world. Yet the metaphor of the highway continues to be used to visualize patterns of circulation that are otherwise beyond ken. Like the metaphor of mobility, that of the highway still underlies the ideology of commerce. Microsoft's Bill Gates saw no better metaphor for cyberspace than that of the highway when he titled his 1996 book *The Road Ahead.* Still, he admitted that the road was too limited a descriptor of the nonlinear options of the Internet, which he felt could be most accurately described simply as the *market*, the "ultimate market."[36] But perhaps the road *is* the right metaphor, for as we casually cruise the Web with its pop-up ads, whose shape, speed, and animation represent the ultimate in billboard aesthetics, our every move helps to chart new corridors of consumption. Just as "trafficounters" were employed in the 1930s to track motorists' circulation patterns, now our site visits are noted, and our routes are marked by "cookies" and other marketing-inspired devices. Though today we favor the more organic phrase "networks" to highways, these basic facts remain: the distinction between private and public realms is still being eviscerated, and the commercial spaces we traverse while online are continuous with those we have long traveled in our automobiles.[37]

While it remains difficult to cover national and even targeted audiences through Web advertising, the diffusion of the marketplace is now axiomatic. Even in the real world, that diffusion continues apace, though the makers of TiVo, Replay, and other personal recording devices hope to free homes of television advertisements, and legal regulations continue to stem the tide of big billboards along public roads. But few are the places, public or private, that do not bear the literal and conceptual signs of the market. Advertising and marketing now follow us, the consumer, wherever we go. In the public bathroom we meet Flush Media, which has estimated that the fifteen minutes per day we all spend staring at toilet stall walls are worth attending to.[38] Where suburban regulations keep streets clear of advertisements, our post–World War II pedestrian spaces of malls and entertainment centers provide them aplenty. There has been an explosion of smaller boards in those heavily traveled spots as well as in airports, supermarkets, train and bus stations, and on taxicabs, buses, trucks, shopping carts, garbage cans, public benches, and even the nozzles at gas pumps. Whereas nineteenth-century audiences gaped in disbelief at the latest marketing device of painting messages on the heads of bald men, today another generation of those men will soon be paid with five-year leases for the product ads they tattoo on their scalps.[39] The wide variety of outdoor novelties, called "ambient" advertising by some and "guerrilla" or "stealth" marketing by others—including stickers on apples promoting the website Ask Jeeves, projections on the sides of buildings, and slogans or logos stenciled on college campuses and city sidewalks—all offer additional ways to surround audiences on the move with advertising messages.[40]

Size still reigns supreme, however, when it comes to garnering attention. A fruit sticker simply does not compare to a vinyl bulletin wrapped around an entire building or covering a tall wall (even when these irk residents by covering over their windows; fig. 72). Nor can a chalked sidewalk logo have the impact of buses or taxicabs shrink-wrapped in advertisements, in which audiences in motion are targeted by ads that also move.[41] Big new billboards are hard to pass through city councils, but there is a bright future in municipal partnerships for building outdoor structures to line the facades and interior spaces of arenas, coliseums, and other total entertainment complexes. The Oakland Coliseum sports a total of twenty-five outdoor structures, including ten-story-high vertical billboards, kiosks, and gateways with rotating signs. The city shares some of the advertising revenue. Drawing 3.6 million people annually, and visible to the 180,000 drivers who pass it daily on the 880 Freeway, the coliseum is a lucrative venue indeed.[42] Yet it is no longer necessary for the sports stadium to remain limited by the physical advertising structures within its boundaries. Today when games are televised, virtual billboards are inserted behind home plate or adjacent to goal posts (using digital mapping systems first developed for "smart-bomb" technology), exponentially increasing the ways to cash in on indoor and outdoor audiences.[43]

Over the past fifty years, we ourselves have become walking billboards, carrying the logo or the look wherever we go. When we serve the dual function of both consumer and brand messenger, who we are and where we travel matters deeply to advertisers and marketers. Since the automobile revolutionized daily patterns of mobility, outdoor advertisers have puzzled over how to track and assess audiences in motion. The Traffic Audit Bureau, formed over seventy years ago, can count who goes by, but it cannot determine the age, color, economic background, or spending habits of traffic. (One can only hope that privacy laws have impeded the wholesale use of license and registration records to procure detailed personal information about motorists.) Now the industry is working on a mobile version of the cookies that attach themselves to our Web browsers when we go online. Nielson Media Research International has come up with one such plan. For the purposes of Nielson's surveys, people are asked to carry with them at all times a small tracking device—a portable GPS monitor—that relays information on exactly where they are traveling and at what speed, regardless of their location, whether they go through mountain passes, skyscraper canyons, or just their homes on the

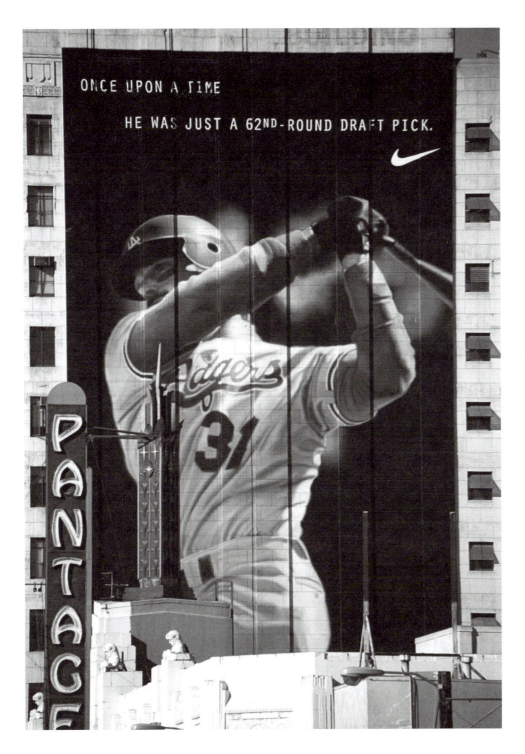

72. Tall-wall bulletin featuring Los Angeles Dodger Mike Piazza on Hollywood Boulevard, Los Angeles, 1995.

way to the refrigerator. No matter where you are, they'll know about it, Bob McCann, chairman and CEO of Nielson has recently explained. When McCann says that most people have nothing to hide and are quite willing to be monitored, he does little to quell the reasonable fear that a corporate Big Brother watches.[44] Today, outdoor advertisements are already equipped with the technology to talk back to you (via short-wave radio links and MP3s), to change as you pass them (through motion detectors, digital ink, and electronic modems), and even to follow you around town (thanks to taxi-top ads endowed with GPS and wireless Internet). It does indeed seem that advertising is not just omnipresent but that it is also omniscient.[45]

It has been more than three-quarters of a century since the young F. Scott Fitzgerald drove through the "valley of ashes" in the New York borough of Queens and, upon passing a billboard for the services of an optometrist, imagined that he had seen the eyes of God. Today, Fitzgerald's insight has renewed saliency, as the market and the marketer are everywhere present, attuned to our every move, sometimes more aware of our next step than we are. Fitzgerald's Gatsby represented the American fascination with mobility of all sorts, and so it seems fitting that the grey fog clouding the road he traveled from suburb to metropolis was pierced through by omniscient eyes staring down from an ad on a billboard. The signs of commerce have proliferated in the decades since Fitzgerald wrote, so that now they all but engulf us as they line the greatest expanses of our communities and landscapes. Still, in our landscapes and roads Americans have always found hope. So long as we remain aware of how we shape our surroundings, and of how our surroundings affect us, I will continue to hold out for a good view.

ACKNOWLEDGMENTS

We folk who have to do more constantly with reading and writing are apt to think that the other folk who have more to do with making and marketing have not so much mind, but I fancy we make a mistake in that now and then.

–William Dean Howells, *The Whole Family:*
A Novel by Twelve Authors (1908)

The quote above aptly summarizes the great variety of "folk" who have helped me with this project. I am grateful for the intellectual support provided by those who "have to do more constantly with reading and writing," including the friends, colleagues, and professors who, over the years, have helped and inspired me. This book started as a dissertation, the seeds of which were planted by Eric Monkkonen at the University of California, Los Angeles, more years ago than I care to admit. Thanks are due to him and to my committee at Yale University, including Jean-Christophe Agnew, for introducing me to the market; Nancy Cott, for redefining my conception of the political; and, most of all, to Dolores Hayden, for overseeing my dissertation from start to finish and for having faith in me even when my own faith was lacking.

For their camaraderie and abundant intellectual support, I am grateful to my friends in the American Studies program at Yale and to the other fellows at the Smithsonian Institution's National Museum of American History (NMAH), including Angela Blake, Elspeth Brown, Timothy Davis, Julia Ehrhardt, Kathleen Franz, Alicia Gamez, Jeff Hardwick, Janet Hutchison, Marina Moskowitz, Lori Rotskoff, and Rebecca Schreiber. Charles McGovern, curator in the Division of Cultural History at the NMAH, provided good humor and moral support as well as incisive comments on the manuscript. Other readers of the manuscript whose suggestions have contributed greatly to my understanding of automobility, consumer culture, and the outdoor advertising industry include Stuart Ewen, Mark Rose, Philip Scranton, and Marguerite S. Shaffer. I would also like to express my appreciation to Kathleen Hulser, for generously sharing her insights into and enthusiasm for the subject of outdoor advertising; to Dona Brown, Robert Goldman, Paul Groth, and Mark Rose, for their constructive comments on conference papers I presented at different stages in the genesis of this project; and to my colleagues and the staff of the Honors College at the University of Oklahoma, for making the going easy in finishing this book.

I have been extremely fortunate to be assisted in my research by those "other folk who have more to do with making and marketing." These include the many individuals and companies with the forethought to save their business records. James Fraser, former director of Special Collections at Fairleigh Dickinson University (FDU) in Madison, New Jersey, performed heroically in saving and actively collecting materials related to outdoor advertising. Without the warmth, generosity, and knowledgeable assistance of Dr. Fraser, I would have missed the good company of numerous historical figures from the advertising industry. As I went through the boxes of outdoor advertising materials at FDU, the collection was being transferred to its present home at Duke University, where it has grown greatly due to the boundless energy of Ellen Gartrell, director of the John W. Hartman Center for Sales, Advertising, and Marketing History. I am grateful to Ellen and to the many talented staff members at Duke who helped me with my research and acquisition of visual materials, including Lisa Chandek-Stark, Rick Collier, Lynn Eaton, Eleanor Mills, and Jacqueline Reid.

I especially wish to thank Nancy Fraser, president and CEO, and Stephen Freitas, chief marketing officer, of the Outdoor Advertising Association of America (OAAA), for taking the time to talk to me about the outdoor industry and for the opportunity to speak at the 2003 OAAA convention. Their recognition of the value of history to business, and the support of the OAAA in preserving archival collections, are exemplary.

I was lucky to know the late Joe Blackstock, and gained immeasurably from my conversations with him at Eller Media in Los Angeles (now Clear Channel Outdoor), the repository for the archives of Foster and Kleiser Company. At Clear Channel, Russ Mason, corporate director of digital services, and Jennie Seo, archivist, granted me liberal access to the library and were munificent in their assistance and provision of photographs. They also introduced me to a great group of sign painters and other crew, whose insights have enriched this study.

A good number of other people also aided me in my research, including Peter J. Blodgett, curator, Western Historical Manuscripts, and staff members at the Huntington Library, Art Collections, and Botanical Gardens; Milissa Burkart, Special Collections, University of Tulsa; Carolyn Kozo Cole, senior librarian, Photograph Collection, Los Angeles Public Library; John R. Lovett, assistant curator, Western History Collections, University of Oklahoma; Barbara Pederson, manager of employee communications, Unocal Corporation; Matthew Roth, manager of archives and historical programs, and Morgan P. Yates, corporate archivist, Automobile Club of Southern California; Dace Taube, curator, Regional History Collection, University of Southern California; Marca L. Woodhams, Archives of American Gardens, Smithsonian Institution; and Roger White, Transportation Collections, NMAH. Thanks are due as well to staff members at the Beinecke Library, Yale University; the Manuscripts and Archives Division, New York Public Library; the New-York Historical Society Print, Photograph, Architecture, and Ephemera Collections; and the Seaver Center for Western History Research, Natural History Museum of Los Angeles.

I have been very fortunate to receive material assistance in the form of grants and fellowships from the Graham Foundation for Advanced Studies in the Fine Arts; the National Museum of American History, Smithsonian Institution; the Schlesinger Library, Radcliffe College; the John W. Hartman Center for Sales, Advertising, and Marketing History, Duke University; the Lyndon Baines Johnson Library and Museum; and Yale University's Henry McNeil Fellowship in American Decorative Arts and Enders Grants. The University of Oklahoma also provided support for research and travel through the Honors College, the Junior Faculty Research Program, and the Research Council. I am grateful to my sponsors and evaluators at all of these institutions.

On cross-country research jaunts, many friends and relatives opened their homes to me. For providing good cheer and good company, my heartfelt thanks go to Paul and Ellen Alexander; Priscilla Alfandre; Cynthia Campoy and Brian Brophy; Julia Carnahan and Kevin Higa; Julia Ehrhardt and her family; Ellen Gartrell; Helen and Mark Hardwick; Marina Moskowitz; Michelle Plochere and David Dalzell; Beka Schreiber and Yosha Goldstein; Jessica and Eleanor Smith; the Steadman family; and Barbara, Dorian, Christine, and Andrew Tergis.

At Routledge, my series editor Sharon Zukin and sponsoring editor David McBride provided much-needed encouragement and valuable suggestions. I appreciate their support, and the efforts of Nicole Ellis, Donna Capato, and Angela Chnapko for shepherding the book through production.

For most people, their research and writing is related to some other event in their history. Mine surely relates to the small wholesale business my father ran on the Lower East Side of New York when I was growing up. It was called Wearever Novelty House Incorporated, a name that any marketer would be proud of, and a conflation of permanence and obsolescence that captures my own views about advertising. Thanks Mom and Dad.

This book is dedicated to my husband, Michael Alexander, for more reasons than can be listed here but first and foremost for always staying cool.

NOTES

Introduction

1. Scholarly works that specifically address commercial strip and ribbon developments include Brian Berry and Yehoshua Cohen, "Decentralization of Commerce and Industry: The Restructuring of Metropolitan America," in *The Urbanization of the Suburbs*, ed. Louis Masotti and Jeffrey Hadden (Beverly Hills: Sage, 1973), 431–55; John A. Jakle and Richard L. Mattson, "The Evolution of a Commercial Strip," *Journal of Cultural Geography* 2 (spring–summer 1981): 12–25; Brian J. L. Berry, "Ribbon Developments in the Urban Business Pattern," *Annals, Association of American Geographers* 49 (March 1959): 145–55; F. N. Boal and D. B. Johnson, "The Functions of Retail and Service Establishments on Commercial Ribbons," in *International Structure of the City*, ed. Larry S. Bourne (New York: Oxford University Press, 1971), 368–79. See also Michael Ebner, "Re-reading Suburban America: Urban Population Deconcentration, 1810–1980," in *American Urbanism*, ed. Howard Gillete Jr. and Zane L. Miller (New York: Greenwood, 1987), 227–242. Though suburbanization is popularly viewed as a post–World War II phenomena (and, indeed, that is its period of great growth), scholars have taken a broader view, attributing it to various nineteenth- and twentieth-century developments, emphasizing transportation technologies, home building, federal subsidies, tax codes, cultural ideals, or locations of industry, manufacturing, and retail. See, for instance, Robert Fishman, *Bourgeois Utopias: The Rise and Fall of Suburbia* (New York: Basic, 1987); Owen D. Gutfreund, "Twentieth Century Sprawl: Accommodating the Automobile and the Decentralization of the United States" (Ph.D. diss., Columbia University, 1998); Dolores Hayden, *Building Suburbia: Green Fields and Urban Growth, 1820–2000*) (New York: Pantheon, 2003); Greg Hise, *Magnetic Los Angeles: Planning the Twentieth-Century Metropolis* (Baltimore: Johns Hopkins University Press, 1997); Kenneth Jackson, *Crabgrass Frontier: The Suburbanization of the United States* (New York: Oxford University Press, 1985); Richard Longstreth, *City Center to Regional Mall: Architecture, the Automobile, and Retailing in Los Angeles, 1920–1950* (Cambridge, Mass.: MIT Press, 1997); Rob Kling, Spencer Olin, and Mark Poster, eds., *Postsuburban California: The Transformation of Orange Country since World War II* (Berkeley and Los Angeles: University of California Press, 1991); Margaret Marsh, *Suburban Lives* (New Brunswick, N.J.: Rutgers University Press, 1990); Mark Rose, *Cities of Light and Heat: Domesticating Gas and Electricity in Urban America* (University Park, Pa.: Pennsylvania State University Press, 1995); Mary Corbin Sies, "'God's Very Kingdom on the Earth': The Design Program for the American Suburban Home, 1877–1917," in *Modern Architecture in America: Visions and Revisions*, ed. Richard Guy Wilson and Sidney K. Robinson (Ames: Iowa State University Press, 1991); Fred W. Viehe, "Black Gold Suburbs: The Influence of the Extractive Industry on the Suburbanization of Los Angeles, 1890–1930," *Journal of Urban History* 8, no. 1 (1981): 3–26; and Sam Bass Warner Jr., *Streetcar Suburbs: The Process of Growth in Boston, 1876–1900* (Cambridge, Mass.: Harvard University Press, 1978).

Chapter 1

1. Frank Presbrey, *The History and Development of Advertising* (Garden City, N.Y.: Doubleday, Doran, 1929), 498–99, 506; Hugh E. Agnew, *Outdoor Advertising* (New York: McGraw-Hill, 1938), 27; David M. Henkin, *City Reading: Written Words and Public Spaces in Antebellum New York* (New York: Columbia University Press, 1998), 11, 15, 76, 82–83; engravings in John A. Kouwenhoven, *The Columbia Historical Portrait of New York: An Essay in Graphic History* (New York: Harper and Row, 1972), 298–300; James Harvey Young, *The Toadstool Millionaires: A Social History of Patent Medicines in America before Federal Regulation* (Princeton, N.J.: Princeton University Press, 1961), 112–13; "Defacing Natural Scenery," *New York Times*, 28 May 1877, 4. Engravings from the mid 1850s and 1860s show advertising wagons and men carrying signs along with many on-site advertisements for shops and businesses. See engravings reproduced in Kouwenhoven, *Columbia Historical Portrait*, 321; Clarence P. Hornung, *The Way It Was: New York, 1850–1890* (New York: Schocken, 1977), 8–9, 27, 29. By the 1870s there was something of a vogue for "perambulatory advertising." "You could not go down Broadway, or any of the busy arteries of trade, without meeting a moving sign. . . . A familiar sight in those days was the shirt man, who carried a nicely laundried shirt bosom in a glass-covered frame, which was suspended by straps"; see L. F. Vance, "Perambulatory Advertising," *Printers' Ink*, 28 September 1892, 374.

2. George Wakeman, "Advertising," *Galaxy* 3 (1867): 203–4; Young, *Toadstool Millionaires*, 118.

3. Henkin, *City Reading*, 69–70.

4. George G. Foster, *New York by Gas-light* (Berkeley and Los Angeles: University of California Press, 1990), 152. The jumbled message of the multilayered posters was a popular subject for engravings in the period. See, for instance, "The Bill-Poster's Dream," 1862, Eno Collection, Miriam and Ira D. Wallach Division of Art, Prints, and Photographs, New York Public Library (discussed in Henkin, *City Reading*, 69–72); an 1864 version, reproduced as plate 58 in Harry T. Peters, *America on Stone* (Garden City, N.Y.: Doubleday, Doran, 1931); and another of 1871 in the Prints and Photographs Division, Library of Congress (mentioned in Young, *Toadstool Millionaires*, 119).

5. "Special Notice," *Brooklyn Eagle*, 7 December 1869, 1.

6. "Thomas Jefferson Murphy, Esq.," *Billposter–Display Advertising* 7, no. 2 (1902): 24; "Bill Posting: How Various Showmen Advertise," *Brooklyn Eagle*, 6 January 1878, 2.

7. "Bill Posters at Variance," *Brooklyn Eagle*, 24 September 1878, 4; "Bill Posters," *Brooklyn Eagle*, 17 September 1879, 4; "The Rival Bill Posters," *Brooklyn Eagle*, 1 October 1879, 14; "The Bill Posters' Fight Renewed," *Brooklyn Eagle*, 24 June 1880, 4.

8. "Bill Stickers," *Brooklyn Eagle*, 25 January 1881, 4.

9. See, for instance, P. T. Barnum, *Struggles and Triumphs, Or, Forty Years' Recollections of P. T. Barnum* (New York: Penguin, 1981), 85–86.

10. "Rival Bill Posters," 14.

11. "Two Prize Fighters' Easy Job," *Brooklyn Eagle*, 6 September 1893, 10.

12. *Harper's Weekly* article reprinted as part of "In Gotham," *Billboard Advertising* 1, no. 1 (1894): 6.

13. Presbrey, *History and Development of Advertising*, 500; James Fraser, *The American Billboard: One Hundred Years* (New York: Harry N. Abrams, 1991), 12.

14. "How Street Car Advertising Is Done," *Printers' Ink*, 9 November 1898, 20; "Obstructing the View," *Brooklyn Eagle*, 11 January 1897, 9; E. S. Martin, "This Busy World," *Harper's Weekly*, 18 March 1899, 257. See also "The History of Transit Advertising," n.d., File: Transit Advertising, Box 1: Transportation, Warshaw Collection, National Museum of American History, Smithsonian Institution, Washington, D.C.; Steve Strauss, *Moving Images: The Transportation Poster in America* (New York: Fullcourt Press, 1984).

15. "A Horsey Tale," *Billboard Advertising* 1, no. 1 (1894): 6. A similar story was run in the *Boston Herald* in 1878, according to the typescript written on the one-hundred-year anniversary of John Donnelly and Sons, "Advertising in Public," 1950, 3, OAAA Collection, Fairleigh Dickinson University, Madison, N.J.. After I completed my original research, this collection was transferred to the John W. Hartman Center for Sales, Advertising, and Marketing History, Rare Book, Manuscript, and Special Collections Library, Duke University, Durham, N.C., where it is organized under the general title of

Outdoor Advertising Archives. Hereafter, materials from Fairleigh Dickinson as well as those subsequently acquired by Duke University will be referred to as OAA/Duke.

16. "The Question Nowadays Is One of Ways and Means," *Brooklyn Eagle*, 31 July 1902, 7.

17. "Prevention of Cruelty to Landscapes," *Printers' Ink*, 23 November 1898, 51.

18. "Defacing Natural Scenery," *New York Times*, 28 May 1877, 4; Young, *Toadstool Millionaires*, 114, 120–23; Pamela Walker Laird, *Advertising Progress: American Business and the Rise of Consumer Marketing* (Baltimore: Johns Hopkins University Press, 1998), 188, 190; Presbrey, *History and Development of Advertising*, 500–501; "He Would Protect the Rocks," *New York Times*, 22 May 1896, 11; Fraser, *American Billboard*, 39. Sign painter J. G. Asbury was hired by Mail Pouch Tobacco to cover the railroad lines of ten states, an order that "required two years in its execution"; see "J. G. Asbury," *Billboard Advertising* 4, no. 8 (1896): 1.

19. William Dean Howells, *The Rise of Silas Lapham* (New York: Vintage Books/ Library of America, 1992), 14.

20. Young, *Toadstool Millionaires*, 122–23; Victor Margolin, Ira Brichta, and Vivian Brichta, *The Promise and the Product* (New York: Macmillan, 1979), 36; "A Reminiscence of 'Hote,'" *Billposter–Display Advertising* 3, no. 8 (1898): 9 (this article includes extensive quotations from the 1880 *Scribner's* piece, "The Curiosities of Advertising"); "'Hote'–King of 'Kon,'" *Billposter–Display Advertising* 6, no. 12 (1902): 1. By 1896, Hote had in his employ "fourteen gangs of painters touring the country; see "Personal Mention," *Billposter–Display Advertising* 6, no. 9 (1896): 6.

21. Sign painters and billposters were frequently described as attracting enraptured boys wherever they went. Sigmund Krausz, *Street Types of Great American Cities* (Chicago: Werner, 1896), 154; H. C. Bunner, "American Posters, Past and Present," in Arsène Alexandre et al., *The Modern Poster* (New York: Charles Scribner's Sons, 1895), 74; Chalmers Lowell Pancoast, *Trail Blazers of Advertising* (New York: Grafton Press, 1926), 181–83. "Paint Galore," *Billposter–Display Advertising* 6, no. 9 (1896): 6; C. S. Houghtaling, "Poster Wisdom," *Billposter–Display Advertising* 7, no. 7 (1902): 1; Barton Wood Currie, "Painting-up a Continent," *Everybody's Magazine* 21 (October 1909): 541.

22. Currie, "Painting-up a Continent," 542; William Stage, "Wall Dogs," *Signs of the Times* 88, no. 3 (1938): 31; Agnew, *Outdoor Advertising*, 29.

23. "John Mishler," *Billboard Advertising* 5, no. 2 (1896): 4; Albert Lee, "The Moving of a Modern Caravan," *Harper's Weekly*, 25 May 1895, 494; "Miscellaneous Items," *Brooklyn Eagle*, 25 May 1870, 1; "How Theater 'Props' Are Borrowed," *Brooklyn Eagle*, 3 October 1886, 15; "Business Competition," *Billboard Advertising* 2, no. 3 (1895): 5; W. G. Millard, Letter to the Editor, *Brooklyn Eagle*, 27 September 1885, 7; "Life in New York City," *Brooklyn Eagle*, 14 December 1885, 2; "Theater and Music: Proposition for a Union of Managers," *Brooklyn Eagle*, 27 December 1891, 9.

24. Charles Philip Fox and Tom Parkinson, *Billers, Banners and Bombast: The Story of Circus Advertising* (Boulder, Colo.: Pruett, 1985), 14.

25. Fox and Parkinson, *Billers, Banners and Bombast*, 12–16; Richard W. Flint, "The Circus," *Quarterly Journal of the Library of Congress* 40, no. 3 (1983): 204–224; Margolin, *The Promise and the Product*, 1979, 15; Charles Goodrum and Helen Dalrymple, *Advertising in America: The First Two Hundred Years* (New York: Harry N. Abrams, 1990), 16–19; Earl Chapin May, *The Circus from Rome to Ringling* (New York: Duffield and Green, 1932), 189.

26. John W. Merton, "Stone by Stone along a Hundred Years with the House of Strobridge," *Bulletin of the Historical and Philosophical Society of Ohio* 8, no. 1 (1950): 28; Pancoast, *Trail Blazers of Advertising*, 56.

27. Manuel Rosenberg, "Billing 'The Greatest Show on Earth,'" *Artist and Advertiser*, February 1931, 6; Merton, "Stone by Stone," 30; Fox and Parkinson, *Billers, Banners and Bombast*, 12, 75; *Brooklyn Eagle*, 20 July 1890, 9; *Billboard Advertiser* 3, no. 9 (1895): 6. Cultural historian Neil Harris describes a visual reorientation in respect to the "iconographic revolution" of half-tone printing in magazines, books, and newspapers between roughly 1885 to 1915; the expansion of color and imagery in commercial poster advertising surely resulted in a similar visual reorientation. Neil Harris, "Iconography and Intellectual History: The Halftone Effect," *Cultural Excursions: Marketing Appetites and Cultural Tastes in Modern America* (Chicago: University of Chicago Press, 1990), 304–317.

28. Fox and Parkinson, *Billers, Banners and Bombast*, 211–18. Flaming posters were used for other purposes than to fight circus competition. For instance, Kenny and Murphy liberally distributed a "flaming" poster libeling the character of a misguided official who failed to grant them the privilege of posting on county property. See "Bill Stickers," *Brooklyn Eagle*, 25 January 1881, 4. Other billposters pasted incendiary bills ("this product is not safe") to avenge a canceled contract or to direct theatergoers to their employers' establishment ("Go to the Columbia Theater" pasted on posters for the Orpheum Theater, for instance). See "Bill Posters," *Brooklyn Eagle*, 1 June 1878, 4; "Whole Town Free to Look On," *Brooklyn Eagle*, 19 November 1901, 1.

29. Charles Philip Fox, *American Circus Posters in Full Color* (New York: Dover, 1978), 2; Alden N. Monroe, "Big Top to Bijou: The Golden Age of the Show Poster," *Queen City Heritage* (Cincinnati), Summer 1984, 4; Flint, "The Circus," 215; "An Extraordinary Feat," *Billboard Advertiser* 2, no. 3 (1895): 7.

30. "Bill Posting," *Brooklyn Eagle*, 6 January 1878, 2; "Whole Town Free to Look On," *Brooklyn Eagle*, 19 November 1901, 1.

31. *Billboard Advertising* 1, no. 1 (1894): 5.

32. "Brooklyn Bill Posting," *Brooklyn Eagle*, 11 July 1886, 7.

33. Agnew, *Outdoor Advertising*, 29; "Now is the Time," *Billboard Advertising* 5, no. 5 (1896): 1; Frank Fitzgerald, "I Remember," *Outdoor Advertising Association News* 35, no. 12 (1941): 15 (hereafter, *OAA News*).

34. "George W. Rife," *Billboard Advertising* 4, no. 4 (1895): 11.

35. The first issue was published in November 1894 under the full title: *Billboard Advertising: A Monthly Resume of All That Is New, Bright and Interesting on the Boards* 1, no. 1 (1894). In July 1897 the name was changed to *Billboard*.

36. C. S. Houghtaling, "Poster Wisdom," *Billposter–Display Advertising* 7, no. 7 (1902): 1.

37. George Presbury Rowell, *Forty Years an Advertising Agent, 1865–1905* (New York: Franklin, 1926), 436.

38. Agnew, *Outdoor Advertising*, 27, 29; Rowell, *Forty Years*, 501.

39. "Walker and Co. Celebrates Its Golden Anniversary," *OAA News* 25, no. 5 (1935): 6; "H. W. Walker," *OAA News* 31, no. 12 (1941): 16 (reprint of article from *Billposter*, April 1897).

40. Van Beuren and Company boasted the highest rental, for its triple-decker board on the corner of 37th Street and Broadway in New York, which ran 104 feet on the Broadway side and 175 feet on 37th and cost $5,200 per year. "The Highest Rental," *Billboard Advertising* 3, no. 9 (1895): 8; "An Expensive Bill Board," *Billboard Advertising* 4, no. 2 (1895): 6.

41. *Billboard Advertising* 2, no. 3 (1895): 7; Ad Shark, "Confessions of an Advertising Man," *Printers' Ink*, 4 January 1893, 23; A. Cressy Morrison, "Posters and Pamphlets," *Billboard Advertising* 5, no. 3 (1896): 4.

42. Fox and Parkinson, *Billers, Banners and Bombast*, 60; "A Word to Circus Posters," *Billboard Advertising* 2, no. 5 (1895): 5.

43. In addition to previously cited articles, coverage on Kenny, all in the *Brooklyn Eagle*, includes: "The Election Frauds," 19 December 1871, 4; "Court News," 13 November 1882, 4; regular articles from 16 January through 24 January 1883; "Doomed for Life," 28 January 1883, 6; "After Death," 11 February 1883, 6; and "That Pistol," 16 February 1883, 2. On Murphy's success, see "The Associated Billposters Protective Company," *Billposter–Display Advertising* 5, no. 2 (1900): 11. J. Ballard Carroll also spoke of the early years of his billposting business as "most prominent through police reports in daily papers," *Billboard Advertising* 1, no. 2 (1894): 5.

44. "A Glance at Association History," *OAA News* 31, no. 12 (1941): 18 (reprinted from *Poster*, July 1911); E. Allen Frost, *Outdoor Advertising . . . Its Genesis, Development and Place in American Life* (Chicago: Outdoor Advertising Association of America [OAAA], 1940), 14.

45. "The Official Journal," *Billposter–Display Advertising* 7, no. 11 (1903): 71; Frost, *Outdoor Advertising*, 14; Charles R. Taylor and Weih Chang, "The History of Outdoor Advertising Regulation in the United States," *Journal of Macromarketing* 15 (spring 1995): 49.

46. Agnew, *Outdoor Advertising*, 31–32; Fraser, *American Billboard*, 12, 14; "Lines of Communication," *Printers' Ink: Fifty Years, 1888–1938*, 28 July 1938, 44; Ralph M. Hower, *The History*

of an Advertising Agency: N. W. Ayer and Son at Work, 1869–1939 (Cambridge, Mass.: Harvard University Press, 1939), 426.

47. "Against Unauthorized Solicitors," *Billposter–Display Advertising* 3, no. 2 (1898): 14; "The Sapolio Proposition," *Billposter–Display Advertising* 3, no. 2 (1898): 19. The O. J. Gude Company sued Edward Stahlbrodt, president of the Billposters' Association, for libel because of the postcard the association sent suggesting Gude was undercutting standard rates. Sam Hoke, O. J. Gude, and even Sam Houghtaling were all refused membership in the Billposters Association, presumably because they were thought to be more favorable to paint than to posting services. This was the subject of great conflict within the industry and led to the formation of other, competing associations. "The Fight Is On," *Billboard Advertising* 3, no. 7 (1895): 5–6; "Anent Opposition," *Billboard Advertising* 4, no. 4 (1895): 20; "Hote Interviewed," *Billboard Advertising* 5, no. 3 (1896): 1, 10.

48. *Billboard Advertising* 2, no. 3 (1895): 8; "Are Paste Brush Artists . . .," *Billboard Advertising* 4, no. 4 (1895): 11; "Association Resolution," *Billposter–Display Advertising* 3, no. 7 (1898): 17.

49. See for instance, "The Situation in Chicago," *Billposter* 3, no. 7 (1898): 9; "The Chicago Situation," *Billposter* 4, no. 7 (1899): 7; Fraser, *American Billboard*, 14; "Big Combine in New York City," *Billboard* 12, no. 2 (1899): 4.

50. "Wilshire's Project," *Billposter* 3, no. 7 (1898): 15.

51. Agnew, *Outdoor Advertising*, 34–35; Phillip Tocker, "Standardized Outdoor Advertising: History, Economics, and Self-Regulation," in *Outdoor Advertising: History and Regulation*, ed. John W. Houck (Notre Dame, Ind.: University of Notre Dame Press, 1969), 31–34.

52. "Robert L. Anderson," *Billboard Advertising* 4, no. 3 (1895): 4; "Shall the Theatres Control the Bill Boards?" *Billboard Advertising* 4, no. 3 (1895): 6.

53. Nym Crinkle, "Theatrical Advertising," *Printers' Ink*, 20 April 1892, 1; "Shall the Theatres Control the Bill Boards?" *Billboard Advertising* 4, no. 3 (1895): 6; "Posters," *Billboard* 12, no. 1 (1899): 3.

54. "From the O. J. Gude Co.," *Billboard Advertising* 3, no. 8 (1895): 5; editorial, *Billboard* 7, no. 8 (1897): 4; "Lines of Communication," 45.

55. Merton, "Stone by Stone," 42.

56. *Billboard Advertising* 4, no. 4 (1895): 20; "Evening Session [of the Associated Billposters' Association Meeting]," *Billboard Advertising* 5, no. 2 (1896): 4; "'The Bill Poster,'" *Billboard Advertising* 5, no. 3 (1896): 10; "'The Billboard' Abandons Billposting," *Billposter–Display Advertising* 4, no. 3 (1899): 15.

57. In 1906, William Donaldson also started four other publications, only one of which succeeded. *Signs of the Times* continues its reportage on the sign industry today. See Fox and Parkinson, *Billers, Banners and Bombast*, 30; Ken Schlager, "On the Boards, 1894–1920," *Billboard: One Hundredth Anniversary Issue 1894–1994* (New York: BPI, 1994), 20, 24.

58. William H. Wilson, "The Billboard: Bane of the City Beautiful," *Journal of Urban History* 13, no. 4 (1987): 396.

59. "The Success of Heinz," *Billposter and Distributor* 7, no. 2 (1902): 24; "The Advance Guard," *Printers' Ink: Fifty Years, 1888–1938*, 28 July 1938, 25; "Instruments of Conquest," *Printers' Ink: Fifty Years, 1888–1938*, 28 July 1938, 98.

60. Hower, *History of an Advertising Agency*, 99–100, 115, 426.

61. Michelle Bogart, *Artists, Advertising, and the Borders of Art* (Chicago: University of Chicago Press, 1995), 81–88; Philip B. Meggs, *A History of Graphic Design* (New York: John Wiley and Sons, 1998), 184–99; Edgar Breitenbach, *The American Poster* (Washington, D.C.: American Federation of Arts, 1969), 7. See also Alexandre et al., *The Modern Poster*; David W. Kiehl, ed., *American Art Posters of the 1890s* (New York: Metropolitan Museum of Art, and Harry N. Abrams, 1987); Victor Margolin, *American Poster Renaissance* (New York: Watson-Guptill, 1975); Mildred Constantine, ed., *Word and Image* (New York: Museum of Modern Art/Greenwich, Conn.: New York Graphic Society, 1968).

62. "Beardsley and Buttons," *Printers' Ink: Fifty Years, 1888–1938*, 28 July 1938, 122–23; *Billboard Advertising* 2, no. 5 (1895): 4–5; "The Beardsley Posters," *Billboard Advertising* 3, no. 6 (1895): 6.

63. See, for instance, "Will It Come to This?" *Billposter* 4, no. 2 (1899): 19.

64. "Trying to Draw the Line," *Brooklyn Eagle*, 3 April 1892, 20.

65. "Indecent Posters," *Billboard* 10, no. 5 (1898): 13.

66. "Macmonnies Is Hard Hit," *Brooklyn Eagle*, 28 September 1897, 3; "Sunday School Celebration," *Brooklyn Eagle*, 16 October 1900, 17; "1899," *Printers' Ink: Fifty Years, 1888–1938*, 28 July 1938, 132; "The Question Nowadays is One of Ways and Means," *Brooklyn Eagle*, 31 July 1902, 7; scrapbook of newspaper clippings, 1904–1905, Archive, Clear Channel Outdoor, Los Angeles (hereafter cited as Clear Channel Archive); Quentin J. Schultz, "Legislating Morality: The Progressive Response to American Outdoor Advertising, 1900–1917," *Journal of Popular Culture* 17, no. 4 (1984): 37–44.

67. "Bill Poster Murphy Found Guilty," *Brooklyn Eagle*, 30 April 1885, 1; "Prudes on the Prowl," *Billboard Advertising* 2, no. 3 (1895): 7.

68. "Trying to Draw the Line," *Brooklyn Eagle*, 3 April 1892, 20.

69. "Prowling Prudes," *Billboard* 10, no. 5 (1898): 13; "A Year's Work Reviewed," *Brooklyn Eagle*, 18 October 1892, 5; Schultz, "Legislating Morality," 41; Kristin Szylvian Bailey, "Fighting 'Civic Smallpox': The Civic Club of Allegheny County's Campaign for Billboard Regulation, 1896–1917," *Western Pennsylvania Historical Magazine* 70, no. 1 (1987): 11. In Hartford, Connecticut, an anti-billboard group comprised of church groups, civic clubs, and the Municipal Art Society considered just banning the pictures from billboards but leaving the text, as a way to "weaken the billboards' powers of temptation." Peter C. Baldwin, *Domesticating the Street: The Reform of Public Space in Hartford, 1850–1930* (Columbus: Ohio State University Press, 1999), 60–61.

70. Laird, *Advertising Progress*, 214–15; Nym Crinkle, "Theatrical Advertising," *Printers' Ink*, 20 April 1892, 1.

71. "Bill Posters' Gossip," *Billboard Advertising* 4, no. 4 (1895): 11.

72. Tocker, "Standardized Outdoor Advertising," 32; "Billposters Meet," *Printers' Ink*, 3 March 1911, 74.

73. "The Restriction of Billboards," *Outlook* 86 (6 July 1907): 493; "Regulation of Public Advertising," *Nation* 78 (3 March 1904): 163–64; Clinton Rogers Woodruff, ed., *The Billboard Nuisance* (Harrisburg, Pa.: J. Horace McFarland/Philadelphia: American Civic Association, 1908), 18–23; Bailey, "Fighting 'Civic Smallpox,'" 9. Although the association's ability to enforce its codes of ethics was limited, it did assess and rate the services provided by members so that the higher the billboard grade, the higher the price they were permitted to charge. On the rating of service, see, for instance, Frost, *Outdoor Advertising*, 14.

74. New York building codes, for instance, forbade wooden billboards over ten feet. The case of *St. Louis Gunning Co. v. St. Louis*, 235 Mo. 99 (1911), supported municipal ordinances limiting the size and structure of billboards. *Report of the Mayor's Billboard Advertising Commission of the City of New York, August 1, 1913* (New York: M. B. Brown, 1913), 28–29, 103; Wilson, "The Billboard," 401; Taylor and Chang, "History of Outdoor Advertising Regulation," 51–52; Agnew, *Outdoor Advertising*, 28; Tocker, "Standardized Outdoor Advertising," 32–35.

75. See Laird, *Advertising Progress*, 242, and, more generally, chapters 9 and 10, 304–361.

76. Daniel Pope, *The Making of Modern Advertising* (New York: Basic, 1983), 184–226; Stephen Fox, *The Mirror Makers* (New York: William Morrow, 1984), 68; Stuart Ewen, *Captains of Consciousness: Advertising and the Social Roots of the Consumer Culture* (New York: McGraw-Hill, 1976), 71; Laird, *Advertising Progress*, 351–52.

77. Filene, quoted in Stuart Ewen, "Advertising and the Development of Consumer Society," in *Cultural Politics in Contemporary America*, ed. Ian Angus and Sut Jhally (New York: Routledge, 1989), 89; also see Ewen, *Captains of Consciousness*. Earnest Elmo Calkins lays out the same point in *Business the Civilizer* (Boston: Little, Brown, 1928).

78. Laird, *Advertising Progress*, 354.

79. Fraser, *American Billboard*, 25; "Barney Link, Poster Advertising Power, Dead," *Printers' Ink*, 8 March 1917, 73.

80. "Nativity Poster," *Poster* 20, no. 12 (1929): 26; Frost, *Outdoor Advertising*, 15; Fraser, *American Billboard*, 16.

81. J. Horace McFarland, "'The Devil Has a Headache,'" *American Institute of Architects Journal* 2 (May 1914): 246.

82. J. Horace McFarland, "The U.S. Government and the Billboards," *American Institute of Architects Journal* 2 (April 1914): 183. On McFarland and his role in the anti-billboard movement, see

William H. Wilson, "J. Horace McFarland and the City Beautiful Movement," *Journal of Urban History* 7, no. 3 (1981): 315–34.

83. On the CPI and World War I publicity, see Stuart Ewen, *PR! A Social History of Spin* (New York: Basic, 1996), 104–27; Stephen Vaughn, *Holding Fast the Inner Lines: Democracy, Nationalism, and the Committee for Public Information* (Chapel Hill: University of North Carolina Press, 1980); Daniel Pope, "The Advertising Industry and World War I," *Public Historian* 2, no. 3 (1980): 5, 15–17; James R. Mock and Cedric Larson, *Words That Won the War: The Story of the CPI* (Princeton, N.J.: Princeton University Press, 1939).

84. Ewen, *PR!* 104, 112–13.

85. "Contributors to National Defense," *Printers' Ink*, 2 March 1916, 110; "War, Patriotism, and Free Space," *Printers' Ink*, 27 April 1916, 118; Vaughn, *Holding Fast*, 143–47; *Poster: War Souvenir Edition* (Chicago: Poster Advertising Association, 1919), 10.

86. Throughout *Poster: War Souvenir Edition* are letters of praise from dignitaries; see Pope, "The Advertising Industry and World War I," 20.

87. William D'Arcy, "The Achievements of Advertising in a Year," *Printers' Ink*, 11 July 1918, 17.

88. Bogart, *Artists, Advertising, and the Borders of Art*, 107–9.

89. "Quick Work in Distribution of National Service 'Stickers,'" *Printers' Ink*, 10 May 1917, 63–64; Anne Classen Knutson, "Breasts, Brawn and Selling a War: American World War I Propaganda Posters 1917–1918" (Ph.D. diss., University of Pittsburgh, 1997), 29–30.

90. *War Souvenir Edition*, 11, 15, 21, 69; Knutson, "Breasts, Brawn and Selling a War," 2.

91. Bogart, *Artists, Advertising, and the Borders of Art*, 64, 109; Eric van Schaack, "Artists and Art in the Service of War and Peace," *Journal of the Picker Art Gallery* 3, no. 2 (1990–91): 29; Fairfax Downey, "The War of the Fences," *American Legion Magazine*, April 1957, 48. See, for instance, photographs at the Still Picture Division, National Archives and Records Administration, College Park, Md., numbered 165-WW-232-B13 (Fatty Arbuckle), 165-WW-61-34 (James Montgomery Flagg), 165-WW-61-4 (Flagg), 165-WW-61-65 (Harry Rittenberg), 165-WW-61-7 (Henry Reuterdahl), and 165-WW-61-62 (Reuterdahl).

92. Bogart, *Artists, Advertising, and the Borders of Art*, 61.

93. George Creel, *How We Advertised America: The First Telling of the Amazing Story of the Committee for Public Information That Carried the Gospel of Americanism to Every Corner of the Globe* (New York: Arno Press, 1972), 136.

94. Matlack Price and Horace Brown, *How to Put in Patriotic Posters the Stuff That Makes People Stop–Look–Act!* (Washington, D.C.: National Committee of Patriotic Societies, n.d.), 2, 10; Gibson, quoted in Vaughn, *Holding Fast*, 150.

95. "Posters and Slogans," *Nation* 104 (21 June 1917): 728.

96. "Art: The War Poster," *Nation* 107 (14 September 1918): 303, 304; Lee Simonson, "Mobilizing the Billboard," *New Republic* 13 (10 November 1917): 41.

97. James Albert Wales, "Start Now to Offset War's End," *Printers' Ink*, 25 May 1916, 104; "War-time Business and Advertising," *Outlook* 118 (6 March 1918): 382; Presbrey, *History and Development of Advertising*, 567–68.

98. Presbrey, *History and Development of Advertising*, 567–68; Roland Marchand, *Creating the Corporate Soul: The Rise of Public Relations and Corporate Imagery in American Big Business* (Berkeley and Los Angeles: University of California Press, 1998), 89; Pope, "The Advertising Industry and World War I," 19. See also Ewen, *PR!*

A Nation on Wheels

1. Starting in 1925, the trade organization, begun in 1891 as the Associated Billposters' Association and renamed at intervals thereafter, began to represent both painted bulletin owners and billposters, eventually calling itself the Outdoor Advertising Association of America (OAAA). See "The History of Outdoor Advertising," *OAA News* 21, no. 6 (1931): 20; and "The Truth about Outdoor Advertising," *Press Bulletin*, no. 4 (1930): 2, OAA/Duke.

2. T. J. Jackson Lears, "From Salvation to Self Realization," in *The Culture of Consumption: Critical Essays in American History, 1880–1980*, ed. Richard Wightman Fox and T. J. Jackson Lears

(New York: Pantheon, 1983), 3–38; T. J. Jackson Lears, *No Place of Grace: Antimodernism and the Transformation of American Culture* (New York: Pantheon, 1981); Warren Susman, "'Personality' and the Making of Twentieth-Century Culture," in *Culture as History: The Transformation of American Society in the Twentieth Century* (New York: Pantheon, 1984), 271–85.

3. Dallas Smythe identifies the stock and trade of advertising and mass media in terms of the production, distribution, and sale of audiences as commodities. See Dallas Smythe, "Communications: Blindspot of Western Marxism," *Canadian Journal of Political and Social Theory* 1, no. 3 (1977): 4; Graham Murdock, "Blindspots about Western Marxism: A Reply to Dallas Smythe," *Canadian Journal of Political and Social Theory* 2, no. 2 (1978): 109–19; Dallas Smythe, *Dependency Road: Communications, Capitalism, Consciousness, and Canada* (Norwood, N.J.: Ablex 1981); Sut Jhally, *The Codes of Advertising: Fetishism and the Political Economy of Meaning in the Consumer Society* (New York: Routledge, 1990), 67–73; and Armand Mattelart, *Advertising International: The Privatization of Public Space* (London: Routledge, 1991), 203–4.

4. The term *automobility* refers not just to the automobile but also to the "emotional connotations of [its] impact for Americans"; James Flink, *The Car Culture* (Cambridge, Mass.: MIT Press, 1975), 1.

5. *Outdoor Advertising: A Primary Medium* (New York: Outdoor Advertising Incorporated, n.d.), 6, OAA/Duke; advertisement for Foster and Kleiser Company, *Poster* 19, no. 3 (1928): 4.

Chapter 2

1. Benton Mackaye and Lewis Mumford use the terms *metropolitanism* and *roadtowns* rather than *sprawl* to discuss the seepage of cities, roads, and cars into the countryside. See Lewis Mumford, "The Fourth Migration," *Survey Graphic* 7 (1925): 130–33 (this and other texts articulating the goals of the Regional Planning Association of America are reprinted in Carl Sussman, ed., *Planning the Fourth Migration: The Neglected Vision of the Regional Planning Association of America* [Cambridge, Mass.: MIT Press, 1976]); Lewis Mumford, "Introduction," in Clarence Stein, *Towards New Towns for America* (Cambridge, Mass.: MIT Press, 1989), 12–15; Benton Mackaye, *The New Exploration: A Philosophy of Regional Planning* (New York: Harcourt, Brace, 1928); Benton Mackaye, "The Townless Highway," *New Republic* 62 (12 March 1930): 93–95.

2. See, for instance, "Posting 'Main Street' 1300 Miles Long," *Poster* 14, no. 4 (1923): 3; "The Highway as Buyway," *Poster* 14, no. 12 (1923): 34; "San Francisco to New York on Concrete Highway," *Poster* 16, no. 5 (1925): 4.

3. "The Truth about Outdoor Advertising," 2. Other ads and announcements with the same message include: "Where Is Your Population?" *OAA News* 18, no. 7 (1928): 16; L. R. Bissell, "Key Towns and Business Lanes," *OAA News* 18, no. 9 (1928): 10–13; "Editorial Comment," *OAA News* 13, no. 1 (1923): 6.

4. Advertisements for outdoor advertising in *Poster* 18, no. 4 (1927): 4; *Poster* 18, no. 5 (1927): 3; *Poster* 18, no. 12 (1927): 4; *Poster* 18, no. 1 (1927): 3; D. G. Baird, "Outdoor Advertising in Winter Time," *Poster* 18, no. 2 (1927): 8.

5. Philip Chandler, "America on Wheels and Business," *Poster* 17, no. 10 (1926): 10.

6. John A. Jakle, *The Tourist: Twentieth-Century North America* (Lincoln: University of Nebraska Press, 1985), 103; Lewis Gannett, *Sweet Land* (New York: Doubleday, Doran, 1934), 5; Sinclair Lewis, *Free Air* (Lincoln: University of Nebraska Press, 1993). See also Wolfgang Sachs, *For the Love of the Automobile: Looking Back into the History of Our Desires* (Berkeley and Los Angeles: University of California Press, 1992), 94.

7. An evocative account of the phenomenon is illustrated in Sachs, *For the Love of the Automobile*, 166, through his extended quotation from Marcel Proust, *Remembrance of Things Past*, vol. 2 (New York: Random House, 1981), 109, which describes the fascination of the character Albertine, whose discovery of the distances and directions available to her by car is liberating but still rather unfathomable; she acknowledges that her understanding of the world was defined by the experience of space and time provided by train travel. The world experienced by car was a totally different arena.

On the experience of railroad travel and an examination of the social and historical impact of the new technology of the train, see Wolfgang Schivelbush, *The Railway Journey: Trains and Travel in the Nineteenth Century* (New York: Urizen, 1980; first published in German in 1978). Lynn Kirby explores the "perceptual paradigm" of the railway journey in relationship to film in *Parallel Tracks: The Railroad and Silent Cinema* (Durham, N.C.: Duke University Press, 1997); see esp. 6–8, 26–28. Anne Friedberg, in *Window Shopping: Cinema and the Postmodern* (Berkeley and Los Angeles: University of California Press, 1993), also examines the perception of movement and its relationship to consuming distances as commodities, as does Margaret Morse (see note 36, below), while Stephen Kern, in *The Culture of Time and Space, 1880–1918* (Cambridge, Mass.: Harvard University Press, 1983), addresses cultural innovations in painting and material culture that were attendant to the technological changes of industrialization.

8. Warren Belasco, *Americans on the Road: From Autocamp to Motel, 1910–1945* (Cambridge, Mass.: MIT Press, 1979), 19–39.

9. Elon Jessup, *The Motor Camping Book* (New York G. P. Putnam's Sons, 1921), 5, 2.

10. Winfield A. Kimball and Maurice H. Decker, *Touring with Tent and Trailer* (New York: Whittlesey House, 1937), 13. Frederic F. Van de Water confirmed this idea that the open road was salvation for white-collar workers tired of their disempowerment within corporate bureaucracies. He wrote that "the tale of men who, weary and worn out by office work, had taken to the road was almost endless. . . ." See Van der Water, *The Family Flivvers to Frisco* (New York: D. Appleton, 1927), 86. See also Marguerite S. Shaffer, *See America First: Tourism and National Identity, 1880–1940* (Washington, D.C.: Smithsonian Institution Press, 2001), 221–60; Marguerite S. Shaffer, "The Search for Identity in the Tourist Landscape," in *Seeing and Being Seen: Tourism and the American West*, ed. David M. Wrobel and Patrick T. Long (Lawrence: University Press of Kansas, 2001), 171–77; Belasco, *Americans on the Road*, 92–103.

11. See John Higham, "The Reorientation of American Culture in the 1890s," *Writing American History: Essays on Modern Scholarship* (Bloomington: Indiana University Press, 1970), 73–102; Harvey Green, *Fit for America: Health, Fitness, Sport and American Society* (New York: Pantheon, 1986), 219–58; Lears, *No Place of Grace*, 98–139. Specifically addressing the experiences of tourism, also see, see Belasco, *Americans on the Road*; Jakle, *The Tourist*; Dean MacCannell, *The Tourist: A New Theory of the Leisure Class* (New York: Schocken, 1976).

12. James Montgomery Flagg, *Boulevards All the Way—Maybe* (New York: George H. Doran, 1925), 138.

13. Lewis, *Free Air*. See also Shaffer, *See America First*, 249–50.

14. Lewis, *Free Air*, 45.

15. Belasco, *Americans on the Road*, 92.

16. A. L. Westgard, *Tales of a Pathfinder* (New York: A. L. Westgard, 1920), 167–68; Van de Water, *The Family Flivvers* 242. Van de Water expressed the same sentiments in other articles, writing that "having seen America, we are no longer New Yorkers or Easterners, but Americans." Frederic F. Van de Water, "The Education of the Tin-Can Tourist," *World's Work* 53, no. 2 (1926): 176.

17. Van de Water, *The Family Flivvers*, 93, 105, 106.

18. Belasco, *Americans on the Road*, 97, 145; Caroline Poole, *A Modern Prairie Schooner on the Transcontinental Trail: The Story of a Motor Trip* (San Francisco: n.p., 1919), 11; Flagg, *Boulevards All the Way*, 19. See also Joseph Interrante, "You Can't Go to Town in a Bathtub," *Radical History Review* 21 (1979): 151–68.

19. Gannett, *Sweet Land*, 30.

20. The narratives I reviewed are drawn from those documented by Carey Bliss, *Autos across America: A Bibliography of Transcontinental Automobile Travel, 1903–1940* (Austin, Tex.: Jenkins and Reese, 1982), and at the Beinecke Library, Yale University; additional titles are in the collection of the Huntington Library, San Marino, California. Kathleen Franz, "Narrating Automobility: Travelers, Tinkerers, and Technological Authority in the Twentieth Century" (Ph.D. diss., Brown University, 1999), 115, 136–37; *The Roadsides of North Carolina: A Survey* (Washington, D.C.: American Nature Association for the National Council for Protection of Roadside Beauty, 1930), 1; Leah Dilworth, "Tourists and Indians in Fred Harvey's Southwest," in *Seeing and Being Seen*, ed. Wrobel and Long, 142–64.

21. "How Many People Can Buy Motor Cars," *Automotive Manufacturer*, September 1921, 24; James Collins, "The Motor Car has Created the Spirit of Modern America," *Motor* 39 (1923): 186; Franz, "Narrating Automobility," 95–97; Flink, *Car Culture*, 156.

22. Blaine Brownell, "A Symbol of Modernity: Attitudes Toward the Automobile in Southern Cities in the 1920s," *American Quarterly* 24, no. 1 (1972): 35, quoting the *Atlanta Independent*, 25 August 1921; Franz, "Narrating Automobility," 118–19.

23. Jackson, *Crabgrass Frontier*, 161; Clay McShane, *Down the Asphalt Path: The Automobile and the American City* (New York: Columbia University Press, 1994), 135; George Kirkham Jarvis, "The Diffusion of the Automobile in the United States: 1895–1969" (Ph.D. diss., University of Michigan, 1972), 29, 95; David J. St. Clair, *The Motorization of American Cities* (New York: Praeger, 1986), 124–27; Reynold M. Wik, "The Early Automobile and the American Farmer," in *The Automobile and Culture*, ed. David Lewis and Laurence Goldstein (Ann Arbor: University of Michigan Press, 1980), 43; Flink, *Car Culture*, 147–48.

24. Michael L. Berger, *The Devil Wagon in God's Country: The Automobile and Social Change in Rural America, 1893–1929* (Hamden, Conn.: Archon, 1979), 52, 209–10; Wik, "The Early Automobile and the American Farmer," 43; Interrante, "You Can't Go to Town," 151–68. See also Norman Moline, *Mobility and the Small Town, 1900–1930* (Chicago: University of Chicago Press, 1971).

25. "It was not unusual," Robert and Helen Lynd wrote, "to see a family drive up to a relief commissary in 1935 to stand in line for its four-or five-dollar weekly food dole"; quoted in Flink, *Car Culture*, 154.

26. Richard Sterner, *The Negro's Share: A Study of Income, Consumption, Housing and Public Assistance* (New York: Harper and Brothers, 1943), 147–49.

27. John Steinbeck, *The Grapes of Wrath* (New York: Viking-Penguin, 1976), 95.

28. *Historical Statistics of the United States of the United States Colonial Times to 1970*, part 2 (Washington, D.C.: U.S. Bureau of the Census, 1975), 716, 718; Jackson, *Crabgrass Frontier*, 187; Michael Berkowitz, "A 'New Deal' for Leisure: Making Mass Tourism during the Great Depression," in *Being Elsewhere: Tourism, Consumer Culture, and Identity in Modern Europe and North America*, ed. Shelley Baranowski and Ellen Furlough (Ann Arbor: University of Michigan Press, 2001), 185–212.

29. See the photographs in Shades of L.A. Photograph Collection, History Division, Los Angeles Public Library; *James Van Der Zee* (New York: Abrams, 1993); illustrations in Evelyn Fairbanks, *The Days of Rondo: A Warm Reminiscence of St. Paul's Thriving Black Community in the 1930s and 1940s* (St. Paul: Minnesota Historical Society Press, 1999).

30. Robert Russa Moton, *What the Negro Thinks* (Garden City, N.Y.: Garden City, 1929), 42; Theodore Rosengarten, *All God's Dangers: The Life of Nate Shaw* (New York: Alfred A, Knopf, 1974), 249, 251.

31. In Los Angeles, for instance, public dissatisfaction with what were seen as the expensive, crowded, and inconvenient routes of traction companies was a factor leading to the demise of streetcar transportation. See Scott Bottles, *Los Angeles and the Automobile* (Berkeley and Los Angeles: University of California Press, 1987). On the battles of road and rail, also see Paul Barrett, *The Automobile and Urban Transit: The Formation of Public Policy in Chicago 1900–1930* (Philadelphia: Temple University Press, 1988); Mark Foster, *From Streetcar to Superhighway: American City Planners and Urban Transportation, 1900–1940* (Philadelphia: Temple University Press, 1981); Stephen Goddard, *Getting There: The Epic Struggle between Road and Rail in the American Century* (New York: Basic, 1994); and McShane, *Down the Asphalt Path*, 115–16.

32. See August Meier and Elliott Rudwick, "The Boycott Movement against Jim Crow Streetcars in the South," *Journal of American History* 55, no. 4 (1969): 766–67.

33. Quoted in Brownell, "A Symbol of Modernity," 35.

34. Phil Patton, *Open Road: A Celebration of the American Highway* (New York: Simon and Schuster, 1986), 20–22; Belasco, *Americans on the Road*, 7–24; George W. Pierson, *The Moving American* (New York: Alfred A. Knopf, 1973), 33–37.

35. Photograph of "Lewis Mountain Picnic Grounds for Negroes," in Donna R. Braden and Judith E. Endelman, *Americans on Vacation* (Dearborn, Mich.: Henry Ford Museum and Greenfield Village, 1990), 43; Franz, "Narrating Automobility," 127; Lillian Rhoades, "One of the Groups Middletown Left Out," *Opportunity: Journal of Negro Life*, March 1933, 76; "Vacation Days," *Crisis*, August 1912, 185–86; George S. Schuyler, "Traveling Jim Crow," *American Mercury*, August 1930, 432. I am grateful to Kathleen Franz for sharing references and ideas about African American travelers with me.

36. Raymond Williams, *Television: Technology and Cultural Form* (New York: Schocken, 1977), 26–27. Other experiences of mobile privatization are discussed in Friedberg, *Window Shopping*, 138–39; Shaun Moores, "Television, Geography, and 'Mobile Privatization,'" *European Journal of Communication* 8 (1993): 365–79; Margaret Morse, "An Ontology of Everyday Distraction: The Freeway, the Mall, and Television," in *Logics of Television: Essays in Cultural Criticism*, ed. Patricia Mellencamp (Bloomington: Indiana University Press, 1990), 193–221; and Thomas Streeter, *Selling the Air: A Critique of the Policy of Commercial Broadcasting in the United States* (Chicago: University of Chicago Press, 1996), 163, 287–89.

37. Frank E. Brimmer, "Nomadic America's $3,300,000,000 Market," *Magazine of Business* 52 (July 1927): 18; Frank E. Brimmer, "Nomadic America's Changing Spending Habits," *System: The Magazine of Business* 53 (April 1928): 445–47. Including auto purchases and other related expenses, Americans spent over ten billion dollars to travel approximately 141 billion miles in 1926. See Flink, *Car Culture*, 140.

38. A. W. Shaw, "The Underlying Trend of Business," *System: The Magazine of Business* 48 (November 1925): 523; "Makers and Measures of Prosperity," *Saturday Evening Post*, 9 March 1929, 30.

39. Shaw, "Underlying Trend," 527; William Trufant Foster and Waddill Catchings, "The Automobile—Key to Our Prosperity," *World's Work* 53, no. 2 (1926): 165–67; Clifton Reeves, "The Automobile Industry and its Wealth-Contributing Factors," *Annals of the American Academy of Political and Social Science* 115 (September 1924): 212–15.

40. John Rae, *American Automobile: A Brief History* (Chicago: University of Chicago Press, 1965), 105–20.

41. D. G. Baird, "Auto Manufacturers and Dealers Co-operate in Extensive Poster Campaigns," *Poster* 14, no. 6 (1923): 17. See also Baird, "'A Nation on Wheels,'" *Poster* 17, no. 3 (1926): 7.

42. Advertisements for Ivan B. Nordhem Company, "Pick Your Best Prospects thru Posting," *Poster* 13, no. 1 (1922): 77, and "Is it eye trouble—or what?" *Poster* 11, no. 2 (1920): 77.

43. Chandler, "America on Wheels," 9–10.

44. *Outdoor Advertising: A Primary Medium*, Chester H. Liebs, *Main Street to Miracle Mile: American Roadside Architecture* (Boston: Little, Brown, 1985), 21.

Chapter 3

1. The assertions that Americans were now an "outdoor population" were made in many publicity campaigns for outdoor advertising. See "The Truth about Outdoor Advertising," 2; K. H. Fulton, "Radio Address Broadcast over WPG and Network," in *The Industry Advances* (Chicago: OAAA, 1929), 21; Baird, "'A Nation on Wheels', 7; Chandler, "America on Wheels," 10. On the rise of mass leisure activities, see David Nasaw, *Going Out: The Rise and Fall of Public Amusements* (New York: Basic, 1993); Lary May, *Screening Out the Past: The Birth of Mass Culture and the Motion Picture Industry* (New York: Oxford University Press, 1980); William Leuchtenburg, *The Perils of Prosperity, 1914-1932* (Chicago: University of Chicago Press, 1993).

2. Leonard Dreyfuss, "The Advertising and Marketing of Tomorrow," *Poster* 14, no. 3 (1923): 12. On the competing benefits of radio and billboards, see Clarence B. Lovell, "Poster Advertising and Radio," *Poster* 16, no. 2 (1925): 10–12; R. Gilbert Gardner, "How Will Radio Activity Affect Advertising?" *Poster* 13, no. 5 (1922): 28; Fraser, *American Billboard*, 50. This emerged as a battle between boosters in each industry. Outdoor advertisers also criticized other "indoor" media; one favorite mode was to publicize examples of magazines and newspapers that "posterized" their advertisements by reducing text and enlarging the imagery or that depicted actual billboards within the advertising image itself. See "National Magazine Makes Comparison of Color Pages with Poster Boards," *Poster* 13, no. 5 (1922): 35, 61; Charles H. Gilbert, "When Poster Ideals Become Magazine Advertising," *Poster* 12, no. 6 (1921): 17–20; and Philip Chandler, "Outdoor Influence on 'Inside Mediums,'" *Poster* 17, no. 7 (1926): 15–18. Some even claimed that radio was an on-air poster; see Ethel M. Feuerlicht, "Poster Advertising—the Radio of Publicity," *Poster* 13, no. 6 (1922): 51.

3. Philip Chandler, "Giant Buying Power," *Poster* 17, no. 6 (1926): 34.

4. General Gasoline employed both women and men in its series of billboards featuring the sporting life: a woman tennis player is joined on the boards by a long distance jumper, a matador, and a

male skier. See L. Hoffman Pinther, "Descriptive Adjective Advertising," *Poster* 18, no. 6 (1927): 9–10, 31; interview by Maude I. G. Oliver with McClelland Barclay, "Stage Direction in Poster Design," *Poster* 19, no. 5 (1928), 16–18, 26.

5. On print ads see Roland Marchand, *Advertising the American Dream: Making Way for Modernity, 1920-1940* (Berkeley and Los Angeles: University of California Press, 1985).

6. "Ten Ways to Sell the Poster Idea," *Poster* 12, no. 12 (1921): 18.

7. C. H. Bristol, "Introducing Sunoco Motor Oil," *Poster* 11, no. 4 (1920): 10.

8. See for instance, Harry F. O'Mealia, "A Few Tips on Selling the City," *OAA News* 12, no. 8 (1922): 8.

9. See John Sears, *Sacred Spaces: American Tourist Attractions in the Nineteenth Century* (New York: Oxford University Press, 1989); Dona Brown, *Inventing New England: Regional Tourism in the Nineteenth Century* (Washington, D.C.: Smithsonian Institution Press, 1996); Leah Dilworth, *Imagining Indians in the Southwest: Persistent Visions of a Primitive Past* (Washington, D.C.: Smithsonian Institution Press, 1996); M. H. Dunlop, *Sixty Miles from Contentment: Traveling the Nineteenth Century American Interior* (New York: Basic, 1995).

10. Shaffer, *See America First*, 26–34, 74–76, 148, 156–60.

11. See Don E. Mowry, *Community Advertising: How to Advertise the Community Where You Live* (Madison, Wis.: Cantwell Press, 1924), 1–7 and Harold J. Ashe, "How Painted Display Boosts San Diego," *Poster* 19, no. 7 (1928): 20.

12. "Community Advertising," *Western Advertising*, 5 August 1938, 21–22; Tom Zimmerman, "Paradise Promoted: Boosterism and the Los Angeles Chamber of Commerce," *California History* 64, no. 1 (1985): 25–27.

13. Sinclair Lewis, *Babbitt* (New York: Modern Library, 1961), 28 and *Main Street* (New York: Modern Library, 1961), 400.

14. "Ten Ways," 19; Charles Finger, *Adventure under Sapphire Skies* (New York: William Morrow, 1931), 40.

15. Advertisement, *Poster* 11, no. 12 (1920): 81; see also *Poster* 14, no. 6 (1923): 4.

16. "Ten Ways," 19; Montague A. Tancock, "Selling City Improvement by Posters," *Poster* 13, no. 3 (1922): 31; Dwight S. Bayley, "Advertising Your City and Yourself," *Poster* 17, no. 6 (1926): 10; Emmett W. Rutledge, "Selling Cleveland to Clevelanders," *Poster* 17, no. 12 (1926): 17; N. M. McCready, "Yakima Discovers Itself," *Poster* 18, no. 10 (1927): 21; A. Leinard, "Waking Up a Community," *Poster* 20, no. 2 (1929): 21–22; J. Huber Denn, "Wilmington Made $10,000 Go a Long Way," *Poster* 20, no. 5 (1929): 25; "Allentown Community Campaign," *Poster* 19, no. 11 (1928): 6. See also Don Mowry, *Outdoor Community Advertising* (Madison, Wis.: American Community Advertising Association, 1928); Don Mowry, "Community and Outdoor Advertising," *Poster* 17, no. 7 (1926): 27–28, 32. The Rotary Club of New York initiated a nationwide poster campaign to boost business, which was sponsored by the Poster Advertising Association, donating $1,300,000 of space for 100,000 posters. See "Prosperity Campaign Stimulates National Optimism," *Poster* 14, no. 2 (1922): 15–16.

17. "Civic Advertising in Merrick," *Poster* 13, no. 8 (1922): 35, 45; Michael Kammen, *Mystic Chords of Memory: The Transformation of Tradition in American Culture* (New York: Vintage, 1993), 338.

18. Chandler, "Giant Buying Power," 5–6, 32; K. H. Fulton, "Application of Poster Advertising for Southern Manufacturers," *Poster* 12, no. 7 (1921): 15–16; C. O. Bridwell, "Merchandising in the Southwest with Poster Advertising," *Poster* 12, no. 7 (1921): 25–26; Clarence E. Bosworth, "Our Great Central Market," *Poster* 19, no. 8 (1928): 5; Robert Ray Aurner, "Outdoor Advertising for Real Estate," *Poster*, 17, no. 10 (1926): 5–8, 30–33.

19. "Rock City–Seventy Years of Family Fun," online at www.seerockcity/media; see also www.walldrug.com/history.

20. Philip Chandler, "The Romance Appeal in Outdoor Advertising," *Poster* 18, no. 3 (1927): 12–14. On Coral Gables, see William Frazer and John J. Guthrie Jr., *The Florida Land Boom: Speculation, Money and the Banks* (Westport, Conn.: Quorum, 1995), 95–99. For images of advertisements sponsored by the Miami Chamber of Commerce and by George Merrick featured on General Outdoor Advertising Company billboards in New York City, see the Billboard Photograph Collection at the New-York Historical Society.

21. Finger, *Adventures under Sapphire Skies*, 6.

22. Sears, *Sacred Spaces*.

23. Letitia Stockett, *America: First, Fast, and Furious* (Baltimore: Norman Remington, 1930), 48.

24. On the shopping experience, see Friedberg, *Window Shopping*.

25. Frank Brimmer, "Nomadic America's $3,300,000,000," 20-21.

26. Tourists seemed unwilling to accept that "fields and woods are a countryman's place of business." See Francis Dana, "Trippers and Trespassers," *Saturday Evening Post*, 18 July 1925, 8; Elizabeth Frazer, "The Destruction of Rural America," *Saturday Evening Post*, 9 May 1925, 39; Belasco, *Americans on the Road*, 74-76.

27. Belasco, *Americans on the Road*, 138. These same reactions to urban industrial growth contributed to the regionalist movement in the arts, literature, social sciences, and planning that hit its stride in the interwar years. See Robert Dorman, *Revolt of the Provinces: The Regionalist Movement in America, 1920-1945* (Chapel Hill: University of North Carolina Press, 1993).

28. Dona Brown addresses the way in which tourism helped to spread market relations "into the landscape, and even into regions of human consciousness," as "tourist industries brought natural scenery, leisure time, history, and even childhood memories and personal ancestry into the world of market transactions." Brown, *Inventing New England*, 10.

29. W. Livingston Larned, "Posters and the Winter Tourist," *Poster* 11, no. 2 (1920): 1.

30. Interestingly enough, Standard was one of the companies that agreed to remove its billboards from rural highways as a result of a letter-writing and publicity campaign by the anti-billboard National Roadside Council. Despite the fact that they were national users of outdoor advertising from an early date, they allied themselves to the women's cause with great fervor, sponsoring prizes and competitions for photos of "Scenic versus Sign-ic" locales and publishing booklets advocating sign removal. See "Scenic or Sign-ic Results," *Standard Oil Bulletin* 17, no. 7 (1929), and Kathleen Norris, *What Do You Want to See?* (San Francisco: Standard Oil Company of California, 1929).

31. "Quality Endures," *Poster* 13, no. 8 (1922): 48.

32. Shaffer, *See America First*, 178, 270-73. See also Paul S. Sutter, *Driven Wild: How the Fight against Automobiles Launched the Modern Wilderness Movement* (Seattle: University of Washington Press, 2002), 19-53.

33. L. P. Scoville, "Gulf Refining Company Brings Scenic Wonders to the Masses," *Poster* 15, no. 8 (1924): 10-11, 28-29; illustration, *Poster* 15, no. 11 (1924): 10.

34. Peter Blodgett, "Selling the Scenery: Advertising and the National Parks, 1916-1933," in *Seeing and Being Seen*, ed. Wrobel and Long, 289.

35. Reprints of "Outdoor Displays as Art Galleries," *Printers' Ink*, 19 February 1920; Tom Nokes, "Billboards are Defended as 'Public Art Galleries,'" *Johnstown Ledger*, 26 May 1922; interview with Lorado Taft by G. A. Nichols, "Taking Art to the People though Outdoor Advertising," *Printers' Ink Monthly*, OAA/Duke.

36. "Presentation of the Plan for the Formation of Outdoor Advertising Incorporated, March 23, 1931," section 2, 1, John W. Shleppey Outdoor Advertising Collection, McFarlin Library, University of Tulsa, Oklahoma; *1912-1952 Federal Litigations* (Chicago: OAAA, 1952), 32-39, OAA/Duke; Agnew, *Outdoor Advertising*, 35.

37. Michelle Bogart explains that magazines in the 1900s lagged behind posters in their "use of large, technically proficient and artistic magazine ads." See Bogart, *Artists, Advertising, and the Borders of Art*, 51. However, full color ads created, and often signed, by illustrators were by the 1920s the stock in trade of mass periodicals.

38. Chandler, "The Romance Appeal," 13.

39. Ibid., 12, 13.

40. Sachs, *For the Love of the Automobile*, 109.

41. On the idea of liminality, see Edith Turner and Victor Turner, *Image and Pilgrimage in Christian Culture: Anthropological Perspectives* (New York: Columbia University Press, 1978); Nelson Graburn, "Tourism: The Sacred Journey," in *Hosts and Guests*, ed. Valene Smith (Philadelphia: University of Pennsylvania Press, 1989), 21-36. Shaffer makes this point in *See America First*, 223, 242-43.

42. Sachs, *For the Love of the Automobile*, 155, 161.

43. At a time when the smokestack was seen as a symbol of progress and industrial productivity, urban reformers also began to criticize the physical effects of smoke pollution. On this conundrum, see David Stradling, *Smokestacks and Progressives: Environmentalists, Engineers, and Air Quality in America, 1881–1951* (Baltimore: Johns Hopkins University Press, 1999).

44. Many have addressed the idea of vision as appropriative, "imperialistic," or "magisterial," especially in terms of art and photography. See, for instance, John Berger, *Ways of Seeing* (London: Penguin, 1972); Susan Sontag, *On Photography* (New York: Farrar, Straus and Giroux, 1977); Alan Trachtenberg, *Reading American Photographs: Images as History* (New York: Noonday Press, 1990); Albert Boime, *Magisterial Gaze: Manifest Destiny and the American Landscape Painting* (Washington, D.C.: Smithsonian Institution, 1991); Angela Miller, *The Empire of the Eye: Landscape Representation and American Cultural Politics, 1825–1875* (Ithaca, N.Y.: Cornell University Press, 1993); and Mary Louise Pratt, *Imperial Eyes: Travel Writing and Transculturation* (New York: Routledge, 1992).

45. Tourism, in other words, served as an antidote to the anxieties and feelings of "weightlessness" that T. J. Jackson Lears describes as part of the modern experience; see Lears, *No Place of Grace*, 98–139. See also John Urry, *The Tourist Gaze: Leisure and Travel in Contemporary Society* (London: Sage, 1990); and Shaffer, *See America First*, 242–43, 248.

46. See Peter J. Schmitt, *Back to Nature: The Arcadian Myth in Urban America* (Baltimore: Johns Hopkins University Press, 1990).

47. Other uses of history in advertising are mentioned in Otis Pease, *The Responsibilities of Modern Advertising* (New Haven, Conn.: Yale University Press, 1958), 184; and Marchand, *Advertising the American Dream*, 260.

48. The campaign was heralded as "the largest outdoor advertising contract ever executed on a single idea" in the obituary for Irving Bromiley, who came up with the idea when he worked for O. J. Gude Company; *OAA News* 23, no. 4 (1933): 17; *OAA News* 25, no. 2 (1935): 1; Fraser, *American Billboard*, 58; letter from Joseph Blackstock, Director of Research, Patrick Media, to Tom Martin, Martin Outdoor Advertising, 31 January 1994, Clear Channel Archive; photo album compiled by Kerwin Fulton showing Book Boards for fifty-one different locales, OAA/Duke.

49. Like other history-oriented outdoor advertisements and tourist guidebooks, the campaign focused on colonial times, safely divorced from current political realities. In this, the advertisement was exemplary of larger impulses, such as the colonial revival style, the restoration of Colonial Williamsburg, and the placement of historic markers along roadsides. See Roderick Nash, *The Nervous Generation: American Thought, 1917–1930* (Chicago: Rand McNally, 1970), 75–77; and Kammen, *Mystic Chords of Memory*, 299–374.

50. C. Matlack Price, "Advertising an Idea by Means of Pictorial History," *Poster* 14, no. 2 (1923): 18–19; Plutarch, Jr., "Walter Whitehead," *Poster* 19, no. 12 (1928): 16.

51. The "Roads to Romance" billboards were part of a larger, cooperative advertising campaign that tied the posters to a radio program in which the Associated Gasoline motor-mates Jack and Ethyl (a play on ethyl gasoline) marry on the air and then go on a honeymoon tour of the Pacific Coast. See Augusta Leinard, "Selling Travel through Romance," *Poster* 20, no. 12 (1929): 9.

52. The national campaign included the line "Fisk Tires Civilize Savage Trails." See George L. Sullivan, "Fisk Tire Poster Pleases," *Poster* 10, no. 8 (1919): 41.

53. For instance, the Fred Harvey Company and the Atchison, Topeka, and Santa Fe Railway had marketed Indian culture in their promotionals since the 1890s, employing Western landscapists to do so. See Leah Dilworth, "Tourists and Indians," 145–46, 150–51, 159.

54. William Joseph Showalter, "The Automobile and the Pioneer," *Annals of the American Academy of Political and Social Science* 116 (November 1924): 25.

55. Warren Susman, "Communication and Culture," in *Mass Media between the Wars: Perceptions of Cultural Tension, 1918–1941*, ed. Catherine L. Covert and John D. Stevens (Syracuse, N.Y.: Syracuse University Press, 1984), xxvi–xxvii.

56. Michael Rogin, "Nature as Politics and Nature as Romance in America," in *Ronald Reagan, the Movie and Other Episodes in Political Democracy* (Berkeley and Los Angeles: University of California

Press, 1987), 169–89; Richard Slotkin, *Regeneration through Violence* (Middletown, Conn.: Wesleyan University Press, 1973); Henry Nash Smith, *Virgin Land: The American West as Symbol and Myth* (Cambridge, Mass.: Harvard University Press, 1978).

Chapter 4

1. On the dominant role played by copywriters, see Laird, *Advertising Progress*, 292.

2. Articles on poster design that advise artists and advertisers of optimal graphic strategies include: Frank H. Young, "Designing the Poster," *Magazine of Advertising Outdoors* 1, no. 10 (1930): 13–15, 19–23; "What Constitutes a Good Poster?" *Poster* 10, no. 11 (1919): 15–16; Leroy Fairman, "What a Poster Is and How to Make It," *Poster* 10, no. 11 (1919): 37–39; Burton Harrington, "What Is Poster Advertising?" *Poster* 14, no. 10 (1923): 3–4; Ethel Feuerlicht, "Doing 'Poster Duty,'" *Poster* 11, no. 8 (1920): 19; and "The Poster's the Thing," *Poster* 11, no. 3 (1920): 26. On the use of futurist and other modern design approaches, see John H. N. Adams, "Futurism Introduces the New Stoker," *Poster* 19, no. 4 (1928): 9; Alon Bement, "The Letter and Modernism," *Poster* 20, no. 1 (1929): 17–18; "Do You Want Modernism in Advertising Art?" *Poster* 20, no. 5 (1929): 13–16.

3. Stephen Kern attributes the phrase *aesthetics of speed* to the attempts of Italian futurist artists to "portray the impact of technology on human experience. . . . The Futurists also lost their heads over the new technology and proclaimed a 'new aesthetic of speed,' first announced by Marinetti. 'We say that the world's magnificence has been enriched by a new beauty; the beauty of speed.'" See Kern, *Culture of Time and Space*, 118–23.

4. See, for instance, Nash, *The Nervous Generation*.

5. Franz Engler and Claude Lichtenstein, *Streamlined: A Metaphor for Progress* (Baden, Switzerland: Lars Müller, 1990); Jeffrey L. Meikle, *Twentieth-Century Limited: Industrial Design in America, 1925-1939* (Philadelphia: Temple University Press, 1979); Steven Heller and Louise Fili, *Streamline: American Art Deco Graphic Design* (San Francisco: Chronicle, 1995).

6. Robert R. Updegraff captured the sentiments of the day in "The New American Tempo," in *The New American Tempo*, ed. Frederick C. Kendall (New York: Advertising and Selling, 1925), 1–15.

7. See for instance, *Outdoor Advertising and the Agency* (Chicago: National Outdoor Advertising Bureau, 1927), 49.

8. Edward S. LaBart, "Posting–A Dominant Force in Advertising," *OAA News* 11, no. 7 (1921): 32.

9. "Ten Ways," 17.

10. "Millions Cannot Read a Poster," *Poster* 10, no. 4 (1919): 33.

11. Leonard Dreyfuss, "The Advertising and Marketing of Tomorrow," *Poster* 14, no. 8 (1923): 12.

12. Baird, "'A Nation on Wheels,'" 7.

13. Franz Aust and Robert Harrison, *The Values of Art in Advertising* (Menasha, Wis.: George Banta, n.d.), 43.

14. W. Livingston Larned, *Illustration in Advertising* (New York: McGraw-Hill, 1925), 201, 208; Feuerlicht, "Doing 'Poster Duty,'" 19; "Putting Poster Punch in the Picture," *Poster* 11, no. 9 (1920): 32; "National Magazine Makes Comparison of Color Pages with Poster Boards," *Poster* 13, no. 5 (1922): 35, 61; Charles H. Gilbert, "When Poster Ideals Become Magazine Advertising," *Poster* 12, no. 6 (1921): 17–20; Chandler, "Outdoor Influence on 'Inside Mediums,'" 15–18.

15. Arthur Acheson, "Poster Publicity in the States," *Poster* 11, no. 2 (1920): 21; "New Ideals in Poster Art," *Poster* 11, no. 10 (1920): 32; David F. Noble, *America by Design: Science, Technology, and the Rise of Corporate Capitalism* (Oxford: Oxford University Press, 1977), 69–83.

16. Walter Dill Scott, quoted in Aust and Harrison, *The Values of Art*, 1.

17. On Lippmann, his ideas about democracy, and the relationship of his ideas to those of public relations specialist Edward Bernays, see Ewen, "Unseen Engineers: Biography of an Idea," *PR!*, 146–73.

18. Roland Marchand makes the point that advertisers commonly imagined themselves as superior in intellect to their audience in *Advertising the American Dream*, 69–72. Advertisers commonly employed the phrase "crystallizing public opinion," a phrase employed by Lippman that was also the title of a book by Bernays. See, for instance, "Address by Mr. John Sullivan, Secretary-Treasurer of the Association of National Advertisers Inc. before the Poster Advertising Association Convention at St. Louis, MO, July 15, 1920," *Bulletin* no. 81 (Poster Advert Association, 1920), OAA/Duke. Artist Jon

Brubaker, in an interview by Maude I. G. Oliver, "Is It the Individual Mind?" *Poster* 19, no. 4 (1928): 16–17, talks about "mass consciousness" as a "force that is terrifying in its magnitude and one which operates as an independent power, governing to a very large extent the motives thoughts, and acts of every individual." "Mass concepts, it is true, are deep-seated. They are so deep-seated, indeed, that the individual is compelled to conform to them. It is even true that, should he venture to oppose them openly, the mass may become a mob and stamp out his life." This idea of the mob mentality is also represented by Mrs. Harry Lilly in "The Economic Function of Art in Poster Advertising," *Poster* 16, no. 9 (1925): 16, who quotes Gustave LeBon's 1896 *The Crowd*. Le Bon, the mind of the crowd, and the relationship of these ideas to the field of public relations are discussed extensively by Stuart Ewen in *PR!*

19. Arthur I. Gates, "What Practical and Applied Psychology is Doing to Shorten the Distance between Human Minds," *Poster* 11, no. 9 (1920): 4.

20. Leonard Dreyfuss, "A Brief Survey of Poster Advertising," *Poster* 11, no. 2 (1920): 35.

21. Russell Burnett, "What Gets Your Attention Gets You," *OAA News* 25, no. 3 (1935): 5.

22. Burton Harrington, *Essentials of Poster Design* (Chicago: Poster Advertising Association, 1925), 2.

23. Quoted in Burton Harrington, "How the Poster Attracts the Eye," *OAA News* 18, no. 6 (1927): 7.

24. George French, "Advertising as a Factor in Modern Merchandising (Part VI)," *Poster* 13, no. 10 (1922), 19; "Poser of the Printed Picture," *Poster* 11, no. 1 (1920): 31.

25. Gates, " Practical and Applied Psychology," 43.

26. Ethel M. Feuerlicht, "'Look Like a Poster' Is New Appeal by New York Advertiser," *Poster* 13, no. 2 (1922): 27; Cy H. Davis, "Selling to Women through Poster Advertising," *Poster* 13, no. 3 (1922): 32; "To Whom Does Outdoor Advertising Appeal?" *OAA News* 18, no. 8 (1928): 15–17, 26.

27. Aline Norvell Handley, "How Posters Appeal to Me," *Poster* 18, no. 3 (1927): 16.

28. The Palmolive soap advertisement is reproduced in *Poster: Second Annual Design Number* 17, no. 9 (1926): insert following 48.

29. Augusta Leinard, "Women and Color Appeal in Advertising," *Poster* 18, no. 4 (1927): 8, 25.

30. Marchand, *Advertising the American Dream*, 34–35, 66–69, 131; Bogart, *Artists, Advertising, and the Borders of Art*, 69–70; Laird, *Advertising Progress*, 286–87; Henrietta Lee Coulling, "Woman in Advertising," *Poster* 17, no. 1 (1926): 26.

31. "The school boy of today is the doctor, lawyer or business man of tomorrow. . . . Attract him while he is a child and you will have less resistance to overcome some ten or fifteen years hence when you start out to sell him personally on your products"; see Donna E. Collister, "Pan-Gas in Picture and Poster," *Poster* 18, no. 2 (1927): 15. H. D. Kemperton, "What Little Miss Muffet Buys," *Poster* 12, no. 9 (1921): 28; E. L. Francis, "'Kid Copy'–An Asset," *Poster* 17, no. 1 (1926): 11. The assumption in "Millions Who Cannot Read," *Poster* 10, no. 4 (1919): 33, is that bright colors were especially appealing to illiterates and immigrants.

32. Edward Hardin, "Luring Film Fans with Posters," *Poster* 10, no. 8 (1919): 32; Collister, "Pan-Gas in Picture and Poster," 15; "Ten Ways," 18; Harrington, *Essentials of Poster Design*, 112–13.

33. Leonard Dreyfuss, "A Brief Survey of Poster Advertising," *Poster* 11, no. 2 (1920): 35.

34. Gates, "Practical and Applied Psychology," 4.

35. Jesse Frederick Steiner, *Americans at Play: Recent Trends in Recreation and Leisure Time Activities* (New York: McGraw-Hill, 1933), 108–12. Movies were from the beginning a working-class form of entertainment that gradually spread to more affluent classes. See May, *Screening Out the Past*.

36. Vachel Lindsay, "Hieroglyphics," *The Art of the Moving Picture* (New York: Macmillan Company, 1915), 171–88. Lindsay compares the photoplay and other early motion pictures to the early picture-alphabet of hieroglyphics as a means of criticizing its "primitive" mode of communication.

37. Frederick W. Kurtz, "Outdoor Advertising Joins the Arts," *Advertising and Selling*, January 1933, 24.

38. May, *Screening Out the Past*, 60.

39. At least, the standardized product and passive viewing was characteristic of the 1920s and later. May, *Screening out the Past* and Nasaw, *Going Out*, have explained that the immigrant-oriented and diversified film experience, complete with talking back to the movie screen in the early years of the nickelodeon, gave way to a more homogenous audience and film presentation in later years.

40. "Ten Ways," 18.

41. Susman, "Communication and Culture," xxvi.

42. Harrington, *Essentials of Poster Design*, 13–15. On the poster "close-up" see Matlack Price, "Posters and Realistic Style," *Poster* 14, no. 8 (1923): 24; and Feuerlicht, "Doing 'Poster Duty,'" 19.

43. One writer described the motorist's view of the modern pictorial poster, in contrast to the text laden billboard of yore, as "a flash from which there is no escape." See "Posters of Today," *Poster* 11, no. 9 (1920): 40.

44. Quoted in Fraser, *American Billboard*, 52.

45. Paul A. Merkle, "40 Miles an Hour," *Printers' Ink*, 28 April 1938, 18–19.

46. James Francis Tobin, "Commercial Art–Is It a Misnomer?" *Poster* 13, no. 6 (1922): 32.

47. Maude I. G. Oliver, "From Shipbuilding to Poster Art," *Poster* 19, no. 8 (1928): 8; Raymond Francis Yates, "Humanizing Technical Advertising," *Poster* 13, no. 3 (1922): 13–15.

48. See the Kuppenheimer clothing billboard reproduced in *Poster* 14, no. 11 (1923): facing 25, and Camel billboard in *Poster: Second Annual Design Number* 17, no. 9 (1926): following 48.

49. See, for instance, reproductions in John A. Schake, "Selling 'Oxydol' by Outdoor Advertising," *Poster* 17, no. 3 (1926): 13; *Poster* 15, no. 2 (1924): facing 17; H. S. McCauley, "The How and Why of Armour Advertising," *Poster* 15, no. 5 (1924): 13–16.

50. Robert E. Weems Jr., *Desegregating the Dollar: African American Consumerism in the Twentieth Century* (New York: New York University Press, 1998), 8; Richard Ohmann, *Selling Culture: Magazines, Markets, and Class at the Turn of the Century* (London: Verso, 1996), 255–66; Marchand, *Advertising the American Dream*, 192–94, 202–3.

51. Interview with McClelland Barclay by Maude I. G. Oliver, "Stage Direction in Poster Design," *Poster* 19, no. 5 (1928): 16.

52. Interview with Jon O. Brubaker by Maude I. G. Olivers, "Is it the Individual Mind?" *Poster* 19, no. 4 (1928): 16.

53. Samuel N. Holliday, "How Posters Should Be Built to Cover Selling Ideas in Design Now," *Poster* 11, no. 7 (1920): 42.

54. Bogart, *Artists, Advertising, and the Borders of Art*, 69–75.

55. Tobin, "Commercial Art–Is It a Misnomer?" 32; Bogart, *Artists, Advertising, and the Borders of Art*, 70; Marchand, *Advertising the American Dream*, 104–16.

56. "Walter Whitehead," *Poster* 19, no. 12 (1928): 15.

57. "Forty Miles an Hour," *Printers' Ink*, 28 April 1938, 19.

58. The great success of Burma-Shave in saving its ailing business through poetic postings inspired another couple to create a similar, serial style of advertising for their store, Wall Drug, in South Dakota. See www.walldrug.com/history.

59. Evelyn S. Dorman, "Burma-Shave," in Janice Jorgensen, ed., *Encyclopedia of Consumer Brands*, vol. 2 (Detroit: St. James Press, 1994), 88–90; Bill Vossler, *Burma-Shave: The Rhymes, the Signs, the Times* (St. Cloud, Minn.: North Star Press, 1997), 6–8; C. M. Odell, president of Burma-Shave, letter to the editor, "Burma-Shave's Road Signs," *Printers' Ink*, 11 July 1935, 14; Vincent R. Tortora, "Billions of Miles in Wayside Smiles," *Lion*, February 1998, 27–28; D. H. Seymour, "What Those Whimsical Signs Have Done for Burma-Shave," *Sales Management*, 27 December 1930, 502; see verses in Frank Rowsome, Jr., *The Verse by the Side of the Road* (Brattleboro, Vt.: Stephen Greene Press, 1965).

60. Vossler, *Burma-Shave*, 13–16, 31–43, 60–64, 86–95; "Bards of the Open Road," *Kiwanis Magazine*, May 1961, 38–39.

61. Dorman, "Burma-Shave," 90; Vossler, *Burma-Shave*, 30; William K. Zinsser, "Good-bye Burma Shave," *Saturday Evening Post*, 5 September 1964, 65–66.

Chapter 5

1. Jean Converse, *Survey Research in the United States: Roots and Emergence, 1860–1960* (Berkeley and Los Angeles: University of California Press, 1987), 87–161; Marchand, *Advertising the American Dream*, 75–76; Bogart, *Artists, Advertising, and the Borders of Art*, 153–54. In the 1940s, many outdoor advertising companies were sponsoring their own research studies. The Outdoor Advertising Institute (OAI), the industry marketing arm, commissioned a series of studies by Daniel Starch in the 1950s. See, for instance, Daniel Starch and Staff, *The Characteristics of Urban Outdoor Poster Readers* (New York:

OAI, c. 1956); *How You Can Win More Customers with Outdoor Advertising* (New York: OAI, 1959); Arthur D. Little, *A Study of Human Response to Visual Environments in Urban Areas* (n.p., n.d).

2. Aust and Harrison, *The Values of Art*, 5, 11, 18, 26, 43; Percy B. Eckhart, "Posters are Good Aesthetic Influence," *Magazine of Advertising Outdoors* 1, no. 10 (1930): 12.

3. Lilly, "The Economic Function of Art," 16.

4. On paintings reproduced on billboards as a "public service," see "Nativity Poster," *Poster* 20, no. 12 (1929): 26; "Expressions of Public Sentiment Reveal 'Blue Boy' Has Won Nation-wide Applause," *OAA News* 28, no. 5 (1938): 5. On the contested relationship of art and advertising, see Bogart, *Artists, Advertising, and the Borders of Art*, 79–124.

5. Kerwin H. Fulton, "The Advancement of Poster Advertising during the Last Twenty Years," *Poster* 14, no. 7 (1922): 11.

6. Fraser, *American Billboard*, 46.

7. Bogart explains that some illustrators, such as Maxfield Parrish, Jessie Willcox Smith, and J. C. Leyendecker had been working for publishing houses as well as creating posters and print ads since the turn of the century but that many others did not wish to be sullied by the connection to advertising. By the 1920s, publishers and elite magazines were not including as many illustrations and "the mass market magazines and advertisers became the primary patrons for illustrators." See Bogart, *Artists, Advertising, and the Borders of Art*, 48–49, 71.

8. Ibid., 111. The first annual design issue of the *Poster* began with the September 1925 issue; profiles of poster artists ran in *Poster* regularly throughout the 1920s.

9. Miss M. G. Webber, "Art Posters and the Association Members," *Poster* 10, no. 8 (1919): 33.

10. Tobin, "Commercial Art–Is It a Misnomer?" 32.

11. Gerrit A. Beneker, "Poster Art in Marketing Goods," *Poster* 12, no. 11 (1921): 55; advertisements for Foster and Kleiser, "The Future of Poster Art," *Poster* 11, no. 8 (1920): 43, and "A Discussion of the Design Problem," *Poster* 10, no. 10 (1919): 55.

12. Lilly, "The Economic Function of Art," 16.

13. "What Constitutes a Good Poster?" 15–16; Fairman, "What a Poster Is and How to Make It," 19, 39–40.

14. Harold R. Willoughby, "Maxfield Parrish–Poster Artist," *Poster* 13, no. 7 (1922): 18; "$3,000 Poster Advertises Hires Root Beer," *Poster* 12, no. 6 (1921): 35–37; William G. Sesser and Harry Weissberger, *Solving Advertising Art Problems* (New York: Advertising Artists, 1919), n.p.

15. Moreover, as Lorado Taft wrote, "the poster is a great avenue for American art . . . it can help develop rather than hinder an American school of art." Frank Alva Parsons, *The Art Appeal in Display Advertising* (New York: Harper and Brothers, 1921), xxv; L. I. Fleming, "The Romance and Art of the Poster," *Poster* 10, no. 12 (1919): 35.

16. "What Constitutes a Good Poster?" 15.

17. Fleming, "The Romance and Art of the Poster," 35; Dugald Shaw, "Material for History," *Poster* 16, no. 9 (1925): 13.

18. "The Poster's the Thing," *Poster* 11, no. 3 (1920): 26; "Barbarians?" *Poster* 16, no. 9 (1925): 14.

19. H. R. Willoughby, "W. G. Sesser, a European Artist Who Has Caught the American Idea," *Poster* 14, no. 6 (1923): 34.

20. H. R. Willoughby, "Herbert Paus," *Poster* 14, no. 1 (1923): 19; Harold R. Willoughby, "The Leyendecker Brothers," *Poster* 14, no. 3 (1923): 22.

21. The American achievements Coady enumerated ranged from "The Panama Canal, the Skyscraper and Colonial Architecture" to "Rag-time," "the Cake-walk," and "Krazy Kat." Robert J. Coady, "American Art," *Soil* 1 (January 1917): 55.

22. Matthew Josephson, "The Great American Billposter," *Broom* 3, no. 4 (1922): 305. Other articles in the magazine expressed the same convictions. Native American art was also discussed as being authentic sources, and advertising was presented as a modern day analogue.

23. Wanda Corn, *The Great American Thing: Modern Art and National Identity, 1915–1935* (Berkeley and Los Angeles: University of California Press, 1999), 3–40. For this and the following sections on American and European artists of the interwar period, I have drawn extensively on Wanda Corn's insightful study.

24. Calvin Coolidge, quoted in Bruce Barton, "The Silent Man on Beacon Hill: An Appreciation of Calvin Coolidge," *Woman's Home Companion*, March 1920, 11; Bruce Barton, *The Man Nobody Knows* (Stone Mountain, Georgia: GA Publishing, 1998); Frederick Lewis Allen, *Only Yesterday: An Informal History of the 1920s* (New York: Harper and Row, 1931), 146–54.

25. Corn, *The Great American Thing*, 135; Barbara Haskell, *The American Century: Art and Culture, 1900–1950* (New York: Whitney Museum of American Art/W. W. Norton, 1999), 153.

26. Wanda Corn, *In the American Grain: The Billboard Poetics of Charles Demuth* (Poughkeepsie, N.Y.: Vassar College, 1991); Corn, *The Great American Thing*, 193–237.

27. Corn, *The Great American Thing*, 204–208.

28. Ibid., 209, 346.

29. Blaise Cendrars, whose early visits to New York had inspired Francis Picabia, Marcel Duchamp, and others, called advertising one of the seven wonders of the world, exclaiming, "Have you thought about the sameness that would represent the streets, the squares . . . automobile roads, nature, without the countless posters, without the shop windows . . . without the illuminated signs . . . ?" See David Steel, "Surrealism, Literature of Advertising and the Advertising of Literature in France, 1910–1930," *French Studies* 41, no. 3 (1987): 283–84, 286–87; and Kirk Varnedoe and Adam Gopnik, *High and Low: Modern Art and Popular Culture* (New York: The Museum of Modern Art, 1990), 250–53. Apollinaire wrote in 1912, "Catalogues, posters, advertisements. . . . Believe me, they contain the poetry of our epoch"; quoted in Herbert Spencer, *Pioneers of Modern Typography* (London: Lund Humphries, 1969), 13. Cendrars said the same thing in his poem "Advertising = Poetry"; see Steel, "Surrealism," 285.

30. Quoted in Varnedoe, *High and Low*, 422 n. 64.

31. Corn, *The Great American Thing*, 122–25; Haskell, *The American Century*, 167–69.

32. Fernand Léger, "A New Realism–The Object?" *Little Review* 11 (1926): 7–8. One work by Gerald Murphy, *Boat Deck* (1923), was criticized for looking too much like "an immense billboard." See Corn, *The Great American Thing*, 121.

33. Haskell, *The American Century*, 170–71; Corn, *The Great American Thing*, 345–46; Patricia Hills, *Stuart Davis* (New York: Harry N. Abrams/Washington, D.C.: National Museum of American Art, Smithsonian Institution, 1996), 65.

34. Varnedoe, *High and Low*, 294. Barbara Zabel also talks about Davis's allusions as revealing the artist's "need to associate modern painting with a distinctively male enterprise, thus validating this mode of painting, still largely unappreciated in the United States"; see Zabel, "Stuart Davis's Appropriation of Advertising: The *Tobacco* Series, 1921–1924," *American Art* 5, no. 4 (1991): 63. In *Lucky Strike*, Davis playfully riffs on the French cubist still life by creating an all-American version. The tobacco, comics, and pipe also make a jocular contrast between the pipe-smoking intellectual and his modern, cigarette-toting counterpart, between leisurely paced café society and the factory line responsible for mass production and modern packaging, between elite and popular culture. See Corn, *The Great American Thing*, 346; and Zabel, "Stuart Davis," 57–67.

35. Bogart, *Artists, Advertising, and the Borders of Art*, 233.

36. Fraser, *American Billboard*, 50, 54, 61–64; Leonard G. Stevenson "Modern and Symbolic Outdoor Advertising Design," *Magazine of Advertising Outdoors*, November 1930, 15–18; clippings file, "Foster and Kleiser" folder, Clear Channel Archive; J. Asanger, "Contemporary Art in Outdoor Advertising: A Short Treatise by J. Asanger," February 1929, OAA/Duke. Otis Shepard's wife, Dorothy, also worked in the art department, and recalled that the latest design magazines were always floating around the office; see letter from James Fraser to Dorothy Shepard, Clear Channel Archive. On the circulation of European design journals in the United States in the 1920s, see Lorraine Wild, "Europeans in America," in *Graphic Design in America: A Visual Language History*, ed. Mildred Friedman (New York: Harry N. Abrams, 1989), 153, 159–60.

37. See, for instance, advertisements in *Poster* 18, no. 9 (1927), inside back cover; 19, no. 9 (1928): 78; 20, no. 2 (1929): 28; and 20, no. 6 (1929): 31.

38. General Outdoor Advertising was one such eastern counterpart to Foster and Kleiser that was far more conservative in its design, relying upon realism and resisting modern and European trends; see Fraser, *American Billboard*, 48, 54.

39. Adams, "Futurism Introduces the New Stoker," 9.

40. Young, "Designing the Poster," 20.

41. Augusta Leinard, "Achieving Tone as a Message," *Poster* 19, no. 10 (1928): 13.

42. Kern, *Culture of Time and Space*, 120.

43. Stevenson, "Modern and Symbolic Outdoor Advertising Design," 15.

44. Strauss, *Moving Images*, 67–69; clippings file, "Otis Shepard" folder, Clear Channel Archive; Tom Purvis, *Poster Progress* (London: The Studio, 1938), 80–81; [Phil Erbes], "Otis Shepard," 1950, Corporate Library, Wm. Wrigley Jr. Company, Chicago; Donna Harrison, "Otis and Dorothy Shepard," *Water Lines* 6, no. 3 (1991): 1, 4–8.

45. Green, *Modern Movements*, 213–14. Gilbert Seldes mentions "The streets of Paris are alive with billboards in the manner of Fernand Léger" in a March 10 article titled "Billboards and Poster," reprinted in *OAA News* 16, no. 4 (1926): 9.

46. See photographs for Star of the North railroad ads in the Billboard Photograph Collection at the New-York Historical Society; clippings file, "A. M. Cassandre" folder, Len Rubenstein, "Outdoor Advertising Comes of Age and Heads for New Highs," Ruth B. McDougall, "The Ad Men of the Twenties," all at Clear Channel Archive.

47. "History of Airbrush, Part 5, Between the Wars," ARTtalk.com, online at http://www.arttalk.com/artv1202-5.htm; Victor Margolin, "Chicago Graphic Design: A Brief History," http://www.aigachicago.org/html/pubs/featurebot.html; Fraser, *American Billboard*, 75; Strauss, *Moving Images*, 68, 71, 74.

48. Herbert Kerkow, "Lucian Bernhard," *Poster* 20, no. 10 (1929): 7.

49. Louis Musgrove, "Dynamic Symmetry and the Poster," *Poster* 18, no. 8 (1927): 37–39. George W. Kadel regularly published articles on dynamic symmetry in the 1930s. See, for instance, his "The Twenty-four Sheet Layout in Dynamic Symmetry," *Signs of the Times* 79, no. 4 (1935): 52–53, "Applied Dynamic Symmetry," *Signs of the Times* 79, no. 6 (1935): 21, "D.S. in the Twenty-four Sheet Poster," *Signs of the Times* 79, no. 9 (1935): 32. On streamlining and the Depression, see Meikle, *Twentieth-Century Limited*.

50. Ethel M. Feuerlicht, "Movement—An Indispensable Feature of the Successful Poster," *Poster* 10, no. 4 (1919): 29; "Points of Design That Make Posters Powerful," *Poster* 13, no. 5 (1922): 34; R. Fayerweather Babcock, "A Consideration of Shapes and Forms in Poster Composition," *Poster* 17, no. 11 (1926): 22; Aust and Harrison, *The Values of Art*, 14.

51. "Do You Want Modernism in Advertising Art? A Discussion," *Poster* 20, no. 5 (1929): 13–16; Lilly, "The Economic Function of Art," 16.

52. Interview with Andrew Loomis by Burton Harrington, "Tuning Art to Business," *Poster* 18, no. 1 (1927): 15; Dugald Shaw, "Material for History," *Poster* 16, no. 9 (1925): 13.

53. "Do You Want Modernism?" 15.

54. Fraser, *American Billboard*, 79.

55. Gasoline companies were especially logo-based in the 1920s and 1930s, as they sought to acclimate the public to their brand and what it looked like so that customers could find it on the road in the face of stiff competition. See for example, Supreme Auto Oil's "All Roads lead to the sign of the Orange Disc" and Chevrolet's "Everywhere—Chevrolet" in *Poster: Second Annual Design Number* (1926): color inserts following 16, and Independent Oil's "Buy at this sign" and Porter F. Leach, "The Story of the Spread Red Eagle," *Poster* (1926): 25–26, 34.

56. Fraser, *American Billboard*, 75; Walter Warde, *Poster Design* (San Francisco: Foster and Kleiser, 1947), 13–15.

57. Manuals and articles in the 1950s persistently advised that the silhouette and close-ups were key to the effective poster. See, for instance, *Essentials of Outdoor Advertising* (New York: Association of National Advertisers, 1958), 101–102; reprint of Garrett Orr "Designing for Posters," *Advertising Requirements*, 1957, Garrett Orr Papers, OAA/Duke.

Visualizing Distribution

1. Herbert Hoover, quoted in William Leach, *Land of Desire: Merchants, Money, and the Rise of a New American Culture* (New York: Vintage, 1993), 354. Hoover was regularly quoted in materials circulated by the outdoor advertising trade organizations; see, for instance, *The Pacific Coast as a Market*

for Commodities and the Outdoor Advertising Facilities Available in This Territory, 2d ed. (San Francisco: Foster and Kleiser, 1928), 4; "Outdoor Advertising, Inc., Releases the Urban Markets Study," *OAA News* 28, no. 10 (1938): 6; and "The Economic Importance of Advertising (Outline for an Address)" (Chicago: OAAA, Promotion and Relations Division, n.d.), n.p., OAA/Duke.

A good overview of Hoover's promotion of cooperative efforts between business and government in the 1920s is in Lynn Dumenil, *The Modern Temper: American Culture and Society in the 1920s* (New York: Hill and Wang, 1995), 35–40. Ellis W. Hawley takes Hoover's support of associations between businesses and trade groups as his subject in *Herbert Hoover and the Crisis of American Capitalism*, ed. J. Joseph Huthmacher and Warren I. Susman (Cambridge, Mass.: Schenkman, 1973), 4–13. The cooperative spirit was an element of what historians describe as the rise of corporate liberalism beginning in the progressive era and, according to some, continuing to the present. On corporate liberalism and its evolution, see Ellis W. Hawley, "The Discovery and Study of a 'Corporate Liberalism,'" *Business History Review* 52 (1978): 309–20; James Weinstein, *The Corporate Ideal in the Liberal State: 1900–1918* (Boston: Beacon Press, 1968); Alan Brinkley, *The End of Reform: New Deal Liberalism in Recession and War* (New York: Alfred A. Knopf, 1995); Noble, *America by Design*; Olivier Zunz, *Making America Corporate, 1870–1920* (Chicago: University of Chicago Press, 1990).

2. President's Conference on Unemployment, vol. 1, *Recent Economic Changes in the United States* (New York: McGraw-Hill, 1929), 272–73.

3. *Poster*, July 1921, 25; *Markets in Motion: The Wilbur Smith Study of Outdoor Advertising* (Chicago: OAAA, 1960).

Chapter 6

1. Before the 1870s, trademarks were employed mostly by patent medicines to promote their products. See Richard S. Tedlow, *New and Improved* (New York: Basic, 1990), 14; Laird, *Advertising Progress*, 17–19, 185, 187. See also Susan Strasser, *Satisfaction Guaranteed: The Making of the American Mass Market* (New York: Pantheon, 1989). The million-dollar national campaign introducing Uneeda Biscuit, by National Biscuit Company (later called Nabisco,) was the biggest of its time. Fox, *The Mirror Makers*, 39; Laird, *Advertising Progress*, 282–83.

2. Robert R. Clark, "No National Distribution without Advertising," *Printers' Ink*, 26 February 1925, 52.

3. S. N. Holliday, *The Story of Outdoor Advertising* (n.p, n.d), OAA/Duke.

4. Frank Presbrey, *History and Development of Advertising*, 339–41; Laird, *Advertising Progress*, 86.

5. Ohmann, *Selling Culture*, 11–30; Frank Luther Mott, *A History of American Magazines, 1885–1905* (Cambridge, Mass.: Harvard University Press, 1957), 18, 608–19; Theodore Peterson, *Magazines in the Twentieth Century* (Urbana: University of Illinois Press, 1956), 7; Pope, *Making of Modern Advertising*, 114.

6. Peterson, *Magazines*, 21, 27; Mott, *A History of American Magazines*, 16; Pease, *The Responsibilities of American Advertising*, 8–9; Pope, *Making of Modern Advertising*, 167–72.

7. Trade organizations collected a great deal of information on the growth of chain stores and frequently made parallels between the rise of the chain store and the rise of outdoor advertising, both of which were indebted to the automobile for their expanding markets. See files, "Case Study: Chain Stores," OAA/Duke. The practical necessity of massed selling was used to argue on behalf of chain-store development in the 1920s, which had begun to cause concern among many independent retailers. See, for instance, Walter S. Hayward, "The Chain Store and Distribution" and E. C. Sams, "The Justification of the Chain Store in Our Present System of Distribution," *Annals of the American Academy of Political and Social Science* 115 (September 1924): 220–25, 226–35. Contemporary accounts include Godfrey Lebhar, *Chain Stores in America 1859–1950* (New York: Chain Store Publishing, 1952); M. M. Zimmerman, *The Challenge of Chain Store Distribution* (New York: Harper and Brothers, 1931).

8. E. Meaker, "We Used Henry Ford's Principle," *System: The Magazine of Business* 48 (March 1925): 334.

9. Howard Thompson Lewis, "Distribution," *Annals of the American Academy of Political and Social Science* 149 (May 1930): 37. Edward A. Filene persuasively argued for mass methods in distribution, using the chain store as exemplar, in "Mass Buying and Mass Selling, Too," *Nation's Business*,

September 1924, 24–26; and "Mass Production Must Have Mass Consumption," *Magazine of Wall Street*, 25 January 1930, 520–22, 572–74.

10. Mrs. M.A. McCracy, "How I Built a Poster Plant on Pin Money," *OAA News* 12, no. 6 (1922): 10. See announcements and obituaries in *OAA News*, including: 9, no. 11 (1919): 10; 10, no. 2 (1920): 4; 10, no. 3 (1920): 10; 10, no. 5 (1920): 1, 4; 11, no. 9 (1920): 8; 10, no. 12 (1920): 1; 12, no. 1 (1922): 12; and 11, no. 2 (1921): 9, 10. See also obituaries compiled for a "who's who" in outdoor advertising, OAA/Duke. One announcement claimed the monthly income of his plant to be $630 per month; another described costs of employees (at $30–35/week), background (or blanking) paper (at $.15 per 24-sheet poster), posterboards (at $3.50–5.00 per foot), and brushes ($8.50), plus association dues, ground rents, and city license. See *OAA News* 10, no. 3 (1920): 10; and *OAA News* 10, no. 9 (1920): 8.

11. "Address by Mr. John Sullivan, Secretary-Treasurer of the Association of National Advertisers before the Poster Advertising Association Convention at St. Louis, MO, July 15, 1920," *Bulletin*, no. 81 (Chicago: Poster Advertising Association, 1920): 14–18, OAA/Duke.

12. W. W. Bell, "Association Progress," *OAA News* 12, no. 11 (1922): 13.

13. "The History of Organized Outdoor Advertising," *OAA News* 21, no. 1 (1931): 14; *Manual of the Outdoor Advertising Association of America* (Chicago: OAAA, 1926), 25.

14. Outdoor advertisers agreed in 1913 that advertising agencies were a detriment to the business, that they did not promote billboard advertising to their clients, and that they brought in a scant amount of business. See "Minutes of the Annual Meeting of the Poster Advertising Association, 1913," 97–100, and "Minutes of the Meeting of the Committee on Solicitors of the Poster Advertising Association, Atlantic City, N.J., July 7th, 1913," 4, 9, 11–13, OAA/Duke; Hower, *History of an Advertising Agency*, 426–27; and "Brief Outline of the History of Selling in the Outdoor Advertising Medium" (Chicago: OAAA, 30 July 1935), 1, OAA/Duke.

15. "Presentation of the Plan for the Formation of Outdoor Advertising Incorporated, March 23, 1931," sec. 2, 1, John W. Shleppey Outdoor Advertising Collection, McFarlin Library, University of Tulsa, Oklahoma; *1912–1952 Federal Litigations*, 32–39. Members of the outdoor association refused to pay commissions to advertising agencies, who were in effect competing with the outdoor industry representatives. See Agnew, *Outdoor Advertising*, 35.

16. Agnew, *Outdoor Advertising*, 37.

17. Ibid., 20–22; *Essentials of Outdoor Advertising*, 64–69; *The Purpose of NOAB* (Chicago: National Outdoor Advertising Bureau, n.d.); *Outdoor Advertising Organizations* (Johnstown, Pa.: Outdoor Advertising Association of Pennsylvania, 1936), 35–37; Pope, *Making of Modern Advertising*, 157; carbon copy of petition *USA v. General Outdoor Advertising Company, et al.*, 1927, OAA/Duke. The Cusack Company's founding year and assets are recorded in *United States Business History, 1602–1988*, comp. Richard Robinson (New York: Greenwood, 1990), 115.

18. *USA v. General*, 18–19. See also *1912–1952 Federal Litigations*.

19. *USA v. General*, 24–25, 26, 27, 28.

20. J. Walter Thompson Staff Meeting Minutes, 16 July 1929, 2–5, J. Walter Thompson Company Archives, John W. Hartman Center for Sales, Advertising, and Marketing History, Duke University, Durham, N.C. (hereafter JWT/Duke); "Brief Outline of the History of Selling," 2.

21. Outdoor Advertising Incorporated (OAI) did not take orders or directly place business with outdoor advertising companies on behalf of advertisers or agencies. Rather, it was a sales promotional organization, and provided research on previous campaigns, explained the best uses of paint and posters, and conducted market studies to show the use of outdoor advertising in specific markets. See *Report for Outdoor Advertising Incorporated of New York, N.Y.* (New York: Barrington Associates, 1937), 31–36; "Presentation of the Plan for the Formation of Outdoor Advertising Incorporated," sec. 3, 1–3; George W. Kleiser, "Welcoming address opening the Golden Anniversary Convention of OAAA," Los Angeles, 6 October 1941, 4, OAA/Duke; *Outdoor Advertising Organizations*, 38–41; Agnew, *Outdoor Advertising*, 16–18; "Brief Outline," 2–3; *1912–1952 Federal Litigations*, 22.

22. Arthur Siegel, "You Are Your Brother's Keeper," *OAA News* 20, no. 2 (1930): 11.

23. "The Responsibilities of a Salesman," *Poster* 11, no. 6 (1920): 45.

24. M. G. Webber, "Art Posters and Association Members," *Poster* 10, no. 8 (1919): 34.

25. Burton Harrington, "Why Poster Boards Bear the Imprint of Owner," *OAA News* 13, no. 9 (1922): 13.

26. *Foster and Kleiser Company Advertising Red Book,* Book No. 44, n.d., Clear Channel Archive; letter from Herbert Fisk, OAAA, to William Fricke, American Association of Advertising Agencies, New York, 10 October 1942, OAA/Duke; W. W. Workman, "President's Report," *OAA News* 14, no. 11 (1924): 2.

27. "The Economic Importance of Advertising" (Chicago: OAAA, Promotion and Relations Division, c. 1927), n.p., OAA/Duke.

28. Despite being popularly acclaimed, opposition to Burma-Shave signs also came from anti-billboard groups, to the extent that in 1933, the company sent a lawyer to visit with the leader of the opposition movement, Elizabeth Lawton. The company also organized farmers to oppose state legislation regulating outdoor advertising, which worked to the benefit of the OAAA too. Elizabeth Lawton, "Letter to the Members of the Ex Board," 3, Box 205, Albert Sprague Bard Papers, New York Public Library. "Plastic Statues Supplant Roadside Billboards," *Popular Mechanics* 64, no. 4 (1935): 561. See photographs of roadside advertising in Photograph Collection, History Division, Los Angeles Public Library. Mammoth roadside sculptures and advertising structures are the subjects of Karal Ann Marling, *The Colossus of Roads: Myth and Symbol along the American Highway* (Minneapolis: University of Minnesota Press, 1984).

29. Wilmot Lippincott, *Outdoor Advertising* (New York: McGraw-Hill, 1923), 56–57.

30. Letter to George Kleiser, President, OAAA, from J. B. Stewart, Vice President, Legal and Legislative Division, April 25, 1933; letter from Herbert Fisk to George Kleiser, April 18, 1933. In correspondence between Coca-Cola and the OAAA in February through April 1933, Coca-Cola expressed concerns that they would be taxed for doing business in the states in which they advertised. This was another imperative for Coca-Cola to turn over their campaigns to OAAA members rather than to lease and purchase their own sites for display. Memo dated September 30, 1932, concerning Tennessee House Bill, 1931, General Revenue Bill, Article III. All OAA/Duke.

31. *Why Not Tax the Rural Billboard?* (New York: National Committee for Restriction of Outdoor Advertising, 1928); *Civic Progress in Harrisburg: Billboards* (Harrisburg, Pa.: Municipal League of Harrisburg, 1923), n.p.; *Roadside Bulletin* 2, no. 3 (n.d.): 19. One group boasted that they removed fifteen thousand wood, tin, and paper "snipe" signs along fifteen hundred miles of road. See "Forum on Roadside Beauty held by Department of Conservation, New York State Federation of Women's Clubs, 19 April 1932, Park Central Hotel, New York," 5–6, OAA/Duke.

32. C. O. Bridwell, "The Use of Poster Advertising Effectively under 1921 Conditions," *Poster* 12, no. 9 (1921): 25; *Poster* 12, no. 1 (1921): 3; *OAA News* 13, no. 1 (1923): 5.

33. Charles Henry Mackintosh, "Poster Advertising a Factor in Retail Marketing," *Poster* 12, no. 11 (1921): 17; Harold L. Eves, "Small Towns: A Great Source of Business," *OAA News* 21, no. 10 (1931): 19; *The Main Street Plan or Small Town Market Coverage* (New York: Outdoor Advertising Incorporated, n.d.).

34. *OAA News* 13, no. 1 (1923): 6.

35. Report of the Joint Assembly and Senate Committee on the Scenic Preservation of State Highways," (Sacramento: California State Printing Office, 1931), 14–15.

36. L. P. Dickie, "Now in Florida," *Poster* 16, no. 1 (1925): 17.

37. *Poster* 17, no. 12 (1926): 16.

38. Mackintosh, "Poster Advertising," 17.

39. "Outdoor Interests Back Zoning as Answers to Women's Groups," *Sales Management*, 15 March 1939, 61.

40. "A Poster Salesman" and "Ten Ways to Sell the Poster Idea," *Poster* 12, no. 12 (1921): 17.

41. King Woodbridge, "The Uses of Outdoor Advertising," *OAA News* 22, no. 7 (1932): 27; "The Picture Gallery of the People," *Poster* 13, no. 1 (1922): 61.

42. See, for instance, Robert Benchley Amherst, "What the Dealer Thinks of Posters," *Poster* 12, no. 7 (1921): 35, 37; Leonard Dreyfuss, "A Brief Survey of Poster Advertising," *Poster* 11, no. 2 (1920): 34; C. King Woodbridge, "The Uses of Outdoor Advertising," *OAA News* 22, no. 7 (1932): 27.

43. W. Livingston Larned, "Posters That Make a Better Nation," *Poster* 11, no. 4 (1920): 3-4.

44. Advertisement for Outdoor Advertising Agency of America, "The Door to the Outdoor Market," *Poster* 14, no. 11 (1923): 2; *Outdoor Advertising* (Chicago: National Outdoor Advertising Bureau, 1923), 7.

45. Susan Strasser has written that for most of the nineteenth century, manufacturers generally sold to middlemen, who would distribute to the trade for sale to households. It was up to this wholesaler to open up "territory for manufactured goods; to the extent there was a national market before national marketing, it was created through sales, not advertising." See Strasser, *Satisfaction Guaranteed*, 35, 61. See also Pease, *The Responsibilities of American Advertising*, 6-7; Robert N. Mayer, *The Consumer Movement: Guardians of the Marketplace* (Boston: Twayne, 1989), 14; and Timothy Spears, "'All Things to All Men': The Commercial Traveler and the Rise of Modern Salesmanship," *American Quarterly* 45, no. 4 (1993): 525.

46. "A Poster Salesman"; "Ten Ways," 17.

47. The claim for advertising as "salesmanship on paper" is said to originate with Lord and Thomas advertising company agent John E. Kennedy in 1904; market research expert Daniel Starch intones virtually the same message, also echoing psychologist Walter Dill Scott, who had begun to work for advertisers in the 1890s and to publish widely on the subject in the 1900s. This chronology of usage is in Spears, "'All Things to All Men,'" 524-25. See also Walter Dill Scott, "The Psychology of Advertising," *Atlantic Monthly*, January 1904, 33-34.

48. "F.O.B. Keep Her Buying This Winter," address by Kerwin H. Fulton, president of Outdoor Advertising Incorporated, delivered at the American Bottlers of Carbonated Beverages Convention, Philadelphia, November 14, 1941, OAA/Duke; *The Pacific Coast as a Market*, 75.

49. French, "Advertising as a Factor in Modern Merchandising," 19; Leonard Dreyfuss, "A Brief Survey of Poster Advertising," *Poster* 11, no. 2 (1920): 35; C. O. Bridwell, "Merchandising in the Southwest with Poster Advertising," *Poster* 12, no. 7 (1921): 25. Bridwell also notes that since outdoor advertising doesn't provide other entertainment or edification, the industry has an even greater task to "hold the community's good will."

50. "The History of Outdoor Advertising," *OAA News* 21, no. 6 (1931): 20. See also *1912-1952 Federal Litigations*, 7; "The History of Outdoor Advertising," *OAA News* 21, no. 1 (1931): 13-14; *Manual of the Outdoor Advertising Association*, 12, 16.

Chapter 7

1. Miller McClintock, "Controlling Traffic to Speed Up Business," *System: The Magazine of Business* 50 (May 1927): 614.

2. See, for instance, *The Pacific Coast as a Market*.

3. Amherst, "What the Dealer Thinks," 37.

4. As one outdoor advertising commentator noted, "Passenger mileage of the private automobile rose from approx thirty billion miles . . . [in 1919] to a total of more than four hundred billion miles in 1930"; see Agnew, *Outdoor Advertising*, 148. "Even private enterprise–other than the outdoor advertising industry–has begun to evaluate traffic. . . . Oil companies count vehicular traffic at proposed and established locations for filling stations. Department and chain stores make counts of their own, inside and outside of their places of business." The same author explained that the Federal government also maintains traffic counting facilities through the Bureau of Public Roads. See Arthur Burnet, "Street Traffic and the Outdoor Market," *OAA News* 22, no. 6 (1932): 7; "Traffic Is the Moving Index of Social and Economic Relations," *OAA News* 25, no. 7 (1935): 7; and *The Pacific Coast as a Market*, 29, 47ff. Strasser, *Satisfaction Guaranteed*, 226, describes the practices of United Cigar Company to count sidewalk traffic when determining their store locations.

5. The problem was again noted in trade articles after the Second World War: "The expansion of urban areas, the phenomenal growth of metropolitan areas, cause a constant shift in the location of good sites. Changes in 'point of purchase' from downtown to outlying shopping centers, from densely built neighborhood concentration to the suburban store have complicated the problem. The dispersal of industry has scattered the traffic flow pattern." Reprint of Paul van Tassel Hedden, "Billboard Planning and Zoning," *Industrial Development*, January 1959, OAA/Duke.

6. William Ryan, "Traffic and Its Relation to Trade," *OAA News* 21, no. 8 (1931): 31.

7. Miller McClintock, "Remedies for Traffic Congestion," *Society of Automotive Engineers (S.A.E.) Journal* 23 (November 1928): 443.

8. L. R. Bissell, "Key Towns and Business Lanes," *OAA News* 18, no. 8 (1928): 10, 13.

9. *The Pacific Coast as a Market*, 5.

10. The *Market Data Hand Book of the United States* included information arranged by counties, such as population totals, manufacturing revenues, agricultural information, bank deposits and savings, automobile registrations, newspaper and magazine circulation figures, and numbers of wholesale and retail outlets, telephones, and electric customers. Also available was the market data in *Retail Shopping Areas*, published by the J. Walter Thompson advertising agency, and in *Trade Areas for Budgetary Control Purposes*, put out by another agency, Batten, Barton, Durstine, and Osborn. They included maps and census information that showed the buying power of residents within shopping areas, and could be used by retailers and advertisers to determine the purchasing powers and spending habits of people shopping in particular areas. See "Buying Power: Information Points Way to Successful Merchandizing," *OAA News* 20, no. 3 (1930): 10–11; "How the Wisconsin Association Made Its State Survey," *OAA News* 21, no. 12 (1931): 3; John Paver, "Organizing for Market Surveys by State Associations," *OAA News* 21, no. 11 (1931): 14–15; and Stuart Peabody, "How the Traffic Audit Bureau Operates," *Signs of the Times* 77, no. 3 (1934): 18, 48. *Industrial Digest* also published statistical information of use to OAAA members, compiled from Census data, showing the manufacturing activity of different regions. It included such information as the types of manufacturing industries, the numbers of wage earners, what they were paid, and what they bought. "The Middle West in Industry," *OAA News* 15, no. 7 (1925): 9; "Middle Atlantic States in Industry," *OAA News* 15, no. 8 (1925): 10; "Industries on the Pacific Coast," *OAA News* 15, no. 10 (1925): 6; "Zoning Maps," *OAA News* 12, no. 8 (1922): 3.

11. Arthur Burnet, "Street Traffic and the Outdoor Market," *OAA News* 22, no. 6 (1932): 34.

12. C. B. Lovell, "Market Value of Your Town," *OAA News* 15, no. 1 (1925): 14.

13. *OAA News* 23, no. 10 (1933): 7; Reyburn Hoffman, "Reasons and Methods for Making Traffic Counts," *Roads and Streets* 69 (November 1929): 409.

14. "The Market Place," *OAA News* 25, no. 7 (1935): 7.

15. Miller McClintock, "The Traffic Survey," *Annals of the American Academy of Politics and Social Science* 133 (September 1927): 8.

16. *America's Highways 1776–1976: A History of the Federal-Aid Program* (Washington, D.C.: U. S. Department of Transportation, Federal Highway Administration, 1976), 127; McClintock, "Interesting Features of Los Angeles' New Traffic Ordinance," *American City* 32, no. 3 (1925): 333; Harold M. Lewis and Ernest P. Goodrich, *Highway Traffic, Regional Survey*, vol. 3 (New York: Regional Plan of New York and Environs, 1927), 37.

17. Highway research sponsored by the federal government began in 1893 with the formation of the Office of Road Inquiry, in the Department of Agriculture. In 1916 it was renamed the Office of Public Roads and Rural Engineering; the title changed again in 1918 to Bureau of Public Roads, in 1939 to the Public Roads Administration, and in 1966 to the Department of Transportation in the Federal Highway Administration. The first comprehensive financial support for highway research was authorized by the Federal Highway Act of 1921. See *America's Highways*, 320–21.

18. In fact, McClintock's degree was in public administration, though his dissertation was on traffic control. A 1931 *Fortune* article delighted in calling him "the first man to be awarded a doctorate in traffic;" see McClintock, "Unfit for Modern Motor Traffic," *Fortune*, August 1936, 94; Edward Dimendberg, "The Will to Motorization," *October* 73 (summer 1995): 124–25; *The National Cyclopaedia of American Biography* 44 (Ann Arbor, Mich.: University Microfilms, 1967), 14. Edward Dimendberg was my original source of information on McClintock, and I am indebted to his work, which makes important comparisons between McClintock and Norman Bel Geddes's notions of frictionless traffic and the planning and construction of the Autobahn in Germany.

19. McClintock, "Unfit for Modern Motor Traffic," 85–92, 94, 96, 99; Miller McClintock, "Of Things to Come," *New Horizons in Planning: Proceedings of the National Planning Conference* (Chicago: American Society of Planning Officials, 1937), 34–35; Jeffrey L. Meikle, *Twentieth Century Limited*,

206–7; Jeffrey L. Meikle, *The City of Tomorrow: Model 1937* (New York: Pentagram Papers, 1983), 16–19, 27–28; "Transport: Four Frictions," *Time*, 3 August 1936, 41.

20. Meikle, *Twentieth-Century Limited*, 207; McClintock, "Unfit for Modern Motor Traffic," 85–94; Miller McClintock, *A Traffic Control Plan for Kansas City* (Kansas City, Mo.: Chamber of Commerce of Kansas City, 1930); "Street Traffic Control," *Electric Railway Journal* 72, no. 1 (1928): 12–16; Miller McClintock, "Parking—When, Where and Why?" *American City* 30, no. 4 (1924): 360–61; McClintock, "Interesting Feature," 333.

21. Meikle, *Twentieth-Century Limited*, 206–208; Dimendberg, "Will to Motorization," 122–28; Patton, *Open Road*, 73; *America's Highways*, 276–77.

22. *Newsweek*, 23 November 1942, 68. Surveys conducted from the air, and other traffic planning to accommodate air travel also appear in outdoor advertising journals and other traffic engineering journals, suggesting the ways in which engineers saw the ground and air as parallel. Aerial photography as a new surveying tool also suggests the ways in which they were seeking to visualize traffic comprehensively. See "Photographing Traffic from the Air," *Scientific American*, January 1938, 17; A. N. Johnson, "Aerial Survey of Highway Traffic," *Roads and Streets* 69 (August 1929): 298–99.

23. *Electric Railway Journal* 70, no. 2 (1927): 72–73. See also: "Traffic Flows," *Printers' Ink*, 19 January 1933, 79; "San Francisco Needs Street Traffic Control," *Electric Railway Journal* 71, no. 26 (1928): 1060–64; Miller McClintock, "The Traffic Survey," 9–18; "Detroit Survey: Develops Basic Traffic Data," part 1, *Electric Railway Journal* 71, no. 14 (1928): 570–74, and Part Two, 71, no. 15 (14 April 1928): 617–20.

24. Paul Barrett and Mark Rose, "Street Smarts: The Politics of Transportation Statistics in the American City," *Journal of Urban History* 25, no. 3 (1999): 405–12.

25. Press releases: "Traffic Planning," "Why Do Counties Need Traffic Engineers," "Why Do Small Cities Need Traffic Engineers," "Why Do Large Cities Need Traffic Engineers," and "The Traficounter Method," all c. 1936–39, John Paver Papers, OAA/Duke. These short articles promote the establishment of permanent positions for full-time traffic engineers in both small towns and big cities.

26. Harland Bartholomew, Frederick Law Olmsted, and Charles Henry Cheney, *A Major Traffic Street Plan for Los Angeles* (Los Angeles: Committee on Los Angeles Plan of Major Highways of the Traffic Commission of the City and County of Los Angeles, 1924), 67.

27. *America's Highways*, 122, 123, 240; "The Maine Highway Transportation Survey," *Public Roads* 6, no. 3 (1925): 45; "Highway Design for Motor Vehicles—A Historical Review, part 1: The Beginnings of Traffic Measurement," *Public Roads* 38, no. 3 (1974): 91; "Highway Design for Motor Vehicles—A Historical Review, part 2: The Beginnings of Traffic Research," *Public Roads* 38, no. 4 (1975): 163–64; A. L. I. Hewes, "Development of Highway Traffic in California," *Proceedings of the American Society of Civil Engineers* 51, no. 2 (1925): 377–78.

28. *America's Highways*, 163. This is a more complicated story than is possible to recount here. See Barrett and Rose, "Street Smarts," 405–33, where the authors trace the use of traffic surveys and the planning of routes according to "demand" lines from streetcar engineers in the 1910s to interstate plans in the 1940s and 1950s to interstate construction thereafter. *Toll Roads and Free Roads*, a report of the Bureau of Public Roads based on surveys from 1938 and 1939, also recommends the routes for expressways according to "recognized popular routes of travel." The bias toward expanding existing traffic routes was short sighted, ignoring the idea that roads in new areas would create their own new demands. See *Toll Roads and Free Roads* (Washington, D.C.: Bureau of Public Roads, 1939), 15. See also Patton, "The Triumph of the Engineers," *Open Road*, 143–51; and Bruce Seely, *Building the American Highway System: Engineers as Policy Makers* (Philadelphia: Temple University Press, 1987).

29. E. H. Holmes, "Procedures Employed in Analyzing Passing Practices of Motor Vehicles," *Public Roads* 19, no. 11 (1939): 209–12, 221; "Motor Tourist Traffic in Michigan," *Public Roads* 13, no. 1 (1933): 197–200.

30. Lewis and Goodrich, *Highway Traffic*, 60; "Detroit Street Traffic Survey," *Electric Railway Journal* 70, no. 18 (1927): 823; McClintock, "Controlling Traffic to Speed Up Business," 616.

31. Barrett and Rose, "Street Smarts," 413.

32. "How Fifteen Members Put Their Business on a Twentieth Century Basis," *OAA News* 14, no. 11 (1923): 10.

33. *The Pacific Coast as a Market*, 14, 15.

34. "Where is Your Population?" *OAA News* 18, no. 7 (1928): 16.

35. "The Scientific Age of Advertising," *OAA News* 15, no. 2 (1925): 4; William Irvin, "Distribution and the Outdoor Medium," *OAA News* 16, no. 7 (1926): 1; Lee H. Bristol, "Why Business Needs a Distribution Director," *Advertising Outdoors*, May 1931, 18; "Research–Is It a Fad?" *Advertising Outdoors*, June 1931, 9–11, 39.

36. "A Brief History of TAB," n.d., OAA/Duke. Francis Hanks, "Education to Aid Outdoor Advertising," *Printers' Ink*, 19 June 1924, 93. "University Researches Industry," *OAA News* 14, no. 9 (1924): 17. The five-year plan that the OAAA embarked upon in 1925 was the result of the studies conducted by the Barney Link Fellowship.

37. In 1937, a summer school at Notre Dame University was established, called the School of Outdoor Advertising. By 1941, Notre Dame and the OAAA established the Outdoor Advertising Foundation to raise funds supporting research and training programs. See "Outdoor Advertising Foundation Fund Tops $15,000 Two Years ahead of Schedule" (1949), OAA/Duke.

38. "A Brief History of TAB," 1; Agnew, *Outdoor Advertising*, 18–20.

39. Stuart Peabody, "A Buyers' Guide for National Advertisers–The Traffic Audit Bureau," *Signs of the Times* 75, no. 4 (1933): 8.

40. "NOAB Information Desk," John Paver Papers, OAA/Duke.

41. *OAA News* 17, no. 8 (1927): 3; John Paver, "Organizing for Market Surveys by State Associations," *OAA News* 21, no. 11 (1931): 14–15.

42. *OAA News* 22, no. 11 (1932): 51.

43. "Private Property Is the Basis of Society and Business . . . ," *Signs of the Times* 75, no. 4 (1933): 58–59; "Traffic Studies by the Erskine Bureau," *Signs of the Times* 78, no. 1 (1934):17; "ANA Traffic Studies May Develop New Sales Quota Yardstick," *Sales Management*, 15 June 1934, 65.

44. A. R. Burnet, "Traffic Buying Power in Motion," *OAA News* 23, no. 10 (1933): 6–7; "Paver Describes Erskine Research for Present Year," *OAA News* 23, no. 11 (1933): 15; John Paver, "The Movement of People," *OAA News* 23, no. 12 (1933): 6.

45. Miller McClintock, "Traffic and Trade Relationship to be Shown by Harvard Research," *OAA News* 22, no. 4 (1932): 20.

46. See Miller McClintock and John Paver, *Traffic and Trade: An Introduction to the Analysis of the Relationship between the Daily Habitual Movement of People and Their Trade Activities in Markets* (New York: McGraw-Hill, 1935); *Markets in Motion*. The Bureau of Public Roads also conducted various traffic planning studies to collect information on drivers, driving patterns, and destinations beginning in the 1940s; see Dimendberg, "The Will to Motorization," 92.

47. See typescript of the summary report by Miller McClintock and John Paver, presented to the OAAA, "Traffic and Trade," 1933, OAA/Duke.

48. *Sales Management*, 15 June 1937, 1184; "A Brief History of TAB," 1. "Millions of dollars spent in relocating panels give better display than ever before," one avid supporter of the survey results gushed. "Average panels per location is now down to 1.7." Kerwin Fulton, *OAA News* 30, no. 4 (1940): 8. The incentive for such investment in a "better display" with fewer billboards may have come through the calibration of the Net Advertising Circulation (NAC) as part of the traffic surveys, which modified gross circulation figures to take into account the effectiveness of the board. *OAA News* 23, no. 8 (1933): 7. The NAC rated the billboard structure and then modified the circulation figures in order to ascertain that nationwide billboard values remained consistent and equivalent. It also made outdoor circulation figures comparable with the print media's Audit Bureau of Circulation figures.

49. William B. Ryan, "Traffic and Its Relation to Trade," *OAA News* 23, no. 8 (1933): 30.

50. McClintock, *Traffic and Trade*, 49, 77, 81, 85; "Traffic Research," *Signs of the Times* 74, no. 4 (1933): 42; Agnew, *Outdoor Advertising*, 150–51.

51. Other agencies interested in traffic data include the Department of Public Roads, real estate boards, department and chain stores, petroleum industries (for locating gas stations), city and regional planning bodies, and others. Ryan, "Traffic and its Relation to Trade," 30.

52. Typescript, McClintock and Paver, "Traffic and Trade," 42.

53. "ANA Traffic Studies May Develop New Sales Quota Yardstick," *Sales Management*, 15 June 1934, 606.

54. "Advertising and Selling Presents Tribute to Progress of Medium," *OAA News* 30, no. 2 (1941): 7; "Outdoor Interests Back Zoning as Answers to Women's Groups," *Sales Management*, 15 March 1939, 61; *Keeping You Posted* (New York: National Outdoor Advertising Bureau, n.d.), n.p.

55. Frederic R. Gamble, "The Agency Viewpoint toward Outdoor Advertising's Traffic Audit Bureau," *Signs of the Times* 77, no. 4 (1934): 9.

56. "Fulton Tells of Big Pickup in Outdoor Volume," *OAA News* 24, no. 2 (1934): 6.

57. "Poster Patter," *Signs of the Times* 74, no. 3 (1933): 72.

58. The OAAA recommended minimum circulation for maintaining billboards at 1,000 gross circulation per twelve hours, which had serious implications for the 14,000 towns with OAAA membership with insufficient readership. These approximately 100,000 boards would have to be reoriented, either removed or placed with "angled individual panels with long approach distances." See "Greeley Explains Bulletin's Value," *OAA News* 24, no. 6 (1934): 4.

59. "Bristol Reveals Plans to Extend TAB Principles," *OAA News* 25, no. 5 (1935): 5.

Chapter 8

1. "Advertising & Selling Presents Tribute to Progress of Medium," *OAA News* 31, no. 2 (1941): 7. This visual training included showing "the customer a picture of his package, so he will know what to look for in the store."

2. Self-service shopping was significantly different from prior experiences, as there was no clerk to ask about or suggest a product. This made the package and the brand all the more important. Kerwin H. Fulton, "Advertising Today," *OAA News* 30, no. 4 (1940): 1.

3. C. King Woodbridge, "The Uses of Outdoor Advertising," *OAA News* 22, no. 7 (1932): 27.

4. Harold L. Eves, "Electrical Advertising," *OAA News* 20, no. 6 (1930): 8–9. Eight years earlier, another article claimed that just 20 percent of the poster boards are illuminated, and extolled how expanding this service would benefit the outdoor advertising industry. H. C. Price, "Blaze of Color to Usher in National Movement to 'Electrify America,'" *Poster* 13, no. 10 (1922): 34.

5. Rose, *Cities of Light and Heat*, 1–2. See also David Nye, *Electrifying America: Social Meanings of a New Technology* (Cambridge, Mass.: MIT Press, 1990), 29–73; Wolfgang Schivelbusch, *Disenchanted Night: The Industrialization of Light* (Berkeley and Los Angeles: University of California Press, 1988).

6. The Wrigley tropical fish spectacular cost $8,000 per month on an eight-year contract. Some advertisers felt the signs in Times Square had limited impact on actual sales, since visitors to the site were tourists, and were not there to buy the gum or washing machines advertised. They acknowledged, however, that these spectaculars did bring the manufacturer great attention nevertheless. "Representatives' Meeting–Friday, July 6, 1928," 15, JWT/Duke; "World's Largest Electrical Unit Begins Operation," *OAA News* 26, no. 4 (1936): 1; "The World's Largest Spectacular," *Signs of the Times* 82, no. 4 (1936): 7–9; "A Brief History of Electric Advertising Displays," *Printers' Ink Monthly*, March 1931, 94–96. See William Taylor, ed., *Inventing Times Square: Commerce and Culture at the Crossroads of the World* (New York: Russell Sage Foundation, 1991); Nye, *Electrifying America*, 73–84; Leach, *Land of Desire*, 340–48; Tama Starr and Edward Hayman, *Signs and Wonders* (New York: Currency-Doubleday, 1998), 88–131.

7. Paul S. Clapp, "Electric Power Transforms Main Street," *The Magazine of Wall Street*, 29 June 1929, 422–423; Nye, *Electrifying America*, 54–57.

8. Lewis, *Main Street*, 400.

9. H. H. Magdsick, "Building Prosperity Avenue," *Transactions of the Illuminating Engineering Society*, May 1930, 451–53.

10. Ibid.; emphasis added. To fulfill this goal, some urged that companies lobby for the standardization of ordinances governing the extent to which light could be projected. See Tracy Simpson, "Advertising Value of Electric Signs and Billboards," *Journal of Electricity*, 1 June 1924, 414.

11. Rose, *Cities of Light and Heat*, 665.

12. Posters were also put to use by the National Electric Light Association for an educational campaign to "Electrify America!" Lithographed posters covering the lighting and appliance field were offered to central power stations in the fifteen thousand towns and cities in the United States and Canada with service. H. C. Price, "Blaze of Color," 32–34.

13. Irving Fisher, "The Decentralization and Suburbanization of Population," *Annals of the American Academy of Political and Social Sciences* 118 (March 1925): 96.

14. Clapp, "Electric Power," 422–23.

15. On the expansion of downtown shopping areas, although not specifically on the role of electricity, see Longstreth, *City Center to Regional Mall*, esp. 3–79; Longstreth, "Silver Spring: Georgia Avenue, Colesville Road, and the Creation of an Alternative 'Downtown' for Metropolitan Washington," in *Streets: Critical Perspectives on Public Space*, ed. Zeynep Celik, Diane Favro, and Richard Ingersoll (Berkeley and Los Angeles: University of California Press, 1994), 247–58. On air conditioning in Ralph's supermarkets, Longstreth, *The Drive-in, the Supermarket, and the Transformation of Commercial Space in Los Angeles, 1914–1941* (Cambridge, Mass.: MIT Press, 1999), 118.

16. Ronald C. Tobey, *Technology as Freedom: The New Deal and Electrical Modernization of the American Home* (Berkeley and Los Angeles: University of California Press, 1996), 2, 5. Tobey also notes that such electrical appliances as refrigerators weren't widely distributed until the Depression (19).

17. See for instance, Allen Addicks, "The Significance of National Advertising to the Industry," *Gas Age-Record*, 9 July 1932, 31–33. In 1932, the American Gas Association "announced 'plans for the institution of a national advertising and promotional campaign for the stimulation of a greater use of gas and gas-burning appliances, involving the expenditure of approximately $6,000,000 in excess of current advertising expenditures, over a period of the next three years,'" 31. See also Lee S. Arthur, "Advertising That Has Taught Consumers Better Buying Habits," *Printers' Ink Monthly*, December 1923, 23–26; I. Lippincott, "Advertising as a Creative Force, *Poster* 13, no. 8 (1922): 29–30; Vergil D. Reed, "Carrying Industrial Product's Story through to Consumer," *Printers' Ink*, 15 September 1932, 51–56.

18. Mayer, *The Consumer Movement*, 20.

19. Leach, *Land of Desire*, 39–41, 55–70.

20. See *Poster* 17, no. 11 (1927): 4; *Poster* 17, no. 2 (1927): 3; and *Poster* 16, no. 10 (1926): 4.

21. Fulton, "Advertising Today," 10.

22. Simpson, "Advertising Value," 413.

23. "Electricity for Publicity," *Electrician*, 15 February 1924, 197.

24. Toward this end, sign manufacturers marketed special projectors and reflectors to be mounted on the billboards or on adjacent buildings. They found that "the best results are obtained by the use of specially built, porcelain enameled, steel, angle reflectors well out in front and above the board." These became the standard for the OAAA and were marketed through their trade journals and promotional materials. See Simpson, "Advertising Value," 413. Psychologists suggested that advertisements using pictures were like film, able to hit the mind direct through the eye. Electricity made the outdoor advertisement even more filmic.

25. Ibid.

26. "Brown Says Third Dimensional Bulletins Are Here to Stay," *OAA News* 24, no. 10 (1934): 4.

27. *Outdoor Advertising–the Modern Marketing Force* (Chicago: OAAA, 1928), 9, 47.

28. "Chevrolet Places Clock Bulletins," *OAA News* 26, no. 10 (1936): 10; *Chevrolet: Enterprising and Consistent* (New York: Outdoor Advertising Incorporated, n.d.); R. S. Fulton, "Advertising Clocks," *Signs of the Times* 82, no. 1 (1936): 24–25; P. E. Van Horn, "Tools for Painted Display," *Signs of the Times* 76, no. 3 (1934): 21; "The Complete Story about the New Sunkist Campaign," *Signs of the Times* 75, no. 4 (1933): 12; Augusta Leinard, "Electric Clocks Mark S & W Time," *Advertising Outdoors*, May 1931, 7. Leinard was aluding to another clock campaign, by S & W Coffee, which used the slogan "S & W Time is all the time." Only a few ads actually incorporated the clock into their advertising content in this way. S & W advertised on billboards from Canada to Mexico. In fact, their only advertising took place on the radio and outdoors (7–8).

29. Special Scotchlite and other reflectorized materials added to the impact of the electrified ads. See Van Horn, "Tools for Painted Displays," 21. See also "Bulletin Reports Stock Trend out of Doors," *OAA News* 26, no. 8 (1936): 12.

30. Marsh, *Suburban Lives*, xiii-xiv. A photograph of the Bullock's third-dimensional bulletin is reproduced in Sally Henderson, *Billboard Art* (San Francisco: Chronicle, 1980), 36.

31. Arthur, "Advertising That Has Taught Consumers," 24.

32. Quoted in "Model Bedrooms in Streamliners Prove Effective," *OAA News* 28, no. 12 (1938): 12.

33. *OAA News* 28, no. 5 (1938).

34. Arthur, "Advertising That Has Taught Consumers," 24.

35. Dolores Hayden, *Redesigning the American Dream: The Future of Housing, Work, and Family Life* (New York: W.W. Norton, 1984), 34; Janet Hutchison, "Building for Babbitt: The State and the Suburban Home Ideal," *Journal of Policy History* 9, no. 2 (1997): 184–210.

36. *OAA News* 26, no. 2 (1936): 3.

37. Norman B. Terry, "Display Windows in Billboards Produce Results," *Gas Age-Record*, 28 December 1929, 957–58.

38. Oliver and Barclay, "Stage Direction in Poster Design," 16–18, 26; "Selling the Movies on the Outdoor Medium," *Poster* 17, no. 8 (1926): 27; Eldridge Peterson, "Evolution of a Poster," *Printers' Ink Monthly*, January 1936, 18.

39. "Selling the Movies," 28. On the relationship between outdoor advertising and the movies see also Philip Chandler, "Poster Advertising and Motion Pictures," *Poster* 15, no. 5 (1924): 17–20, 32; Jerry Lynott, "The Sky's the Limit," *Impressions* (Scranton, Pa.: Patrick Media Group), May 1988, 28.

40. Lynott, "The Sky's the Limit," 29.

41. "MGM Increases Use of Posters 2nd Year in Row," *OAA News* 26, no. 8 (1936): 4.

42. Zukor explained that a printed notice would appear on a selection of posters, offering a free gift to all who requested it at the movie theater. The quantity of gift requests was his test of the effectiveness of the poster. See Lynott, "The Sky's the Limit," 28–29.

43. To overcome the perception that Carthay Center was too far to go from Hollywood, especially when most people expected to go downtown for a movie, the theater used billboards extensively, including the tag line "10 Minutes to Carthay Circle Theatre." John Cator, "Chasing the Distance Bogy," *Poster* 20, no. 2 (1929): 17–18.

44. "Hollywood Gave This Unusual Bulletin a Studio Premiere," *OAA News* 22, no. 9 (1932): 34; Lynott, "The Sky's the Limit," 30.

45. Richard Longstreth mentions the gala openings and events that Los Angeles drive-in markets hosted, which bear similarity to those held at billboard sites. Both also used the ready pool of actors and actresses in the area. See Longstreth, "The Forgotten Arterial Landscape: Photographic Documentation of Commercial Development along Los Angeles Boulevards during the Interwar Years," *Journal of Urban History* 233, no. 4 (1997): 455.

46. "C-R-A-S-H—It's a Strike," *OAA News* 23, no. 6 (1933): 6. G & W Whiskey staged a similar "coming-out party" for their new board, which featured an animated cut-out figure of a bartender shaking cocktails at a sleekly designed modern bar. "Folks, Meet 'Adolph,'" *OAA News* 25, no. 10 (1935): 3.

47. *OAA News* 26, no. 7 (1936): 1.

48. Longstreth, *The Drive-in, the Supermarket*, 118.

49. "Show-case Bulletin Scores a Hit for Indianapolis Ford Dealers," *OAA News* 25, no. 12 (1935): 10.

50. Liebs, *Main Street to Miracle Mile*, 82–86.

51. "Views in the News" *Signs of the Times* 79, no. 3 (1935): 57; "Super Structure," *Signs of the Times* 79, no. 4 (1935): 66; advertisement, *Signs of the Times* 79, no. 4 (1935): 37.

52. Meikle, *Twentieth-Century Limited*, 4; "That Growing Demand among Advertisers and Agencies for Streamlined Structures," *Signs of the Times* 81, no. 4 (1935): 12; "Streamlined Outdoor Structures," *Signs of the Times* 82, no. 3 (1936): 10; advertisement for streamline designed bulletin by Dick and Anderson, Knoxville, Tennessee, *Signs of the Times* 79, no. 7 (1935): 29.

53. "That Growing Demand," 13.

54. See, for instance, Foster and Kleiser streamliners in "Modern Painted Bulletins," *Signs of the Times* 89, no. 3 (1938): 22–23.

55. Meikle, *Twentieth-Century Limited*, 154.

56. Fisk Tire's was the first national campaign to use the Streamliner (embellished with new reflecting discs, said to have a reflecting light equal to a five-watt light bulb), from "Pines to Palms," "Portland [Maine] to Portland [Oregon]." See "After Thirteen Years . . . ," *Signs of the Times* 88, no. 4 (1938): 11–12; advertisement for Fisk Tire Company in *Signs of the Times* 89, no. 1 (1938): 27.

57. Agnew, *Outdoor Advertising*, 28; J. M. Jones, "Walker and Co. Celebrates Its Golden Anniversary," *OAA News* May 1935, 7.

58. See, for instance, the images of the Minneapolis-area display for Bouttells department store, "Two Windows Featured," *Signs of the Times* 74, no. 4 (1933): 46–47.

59. Longstreth, *The Drive-in, the Supermarket*, 48, 62–63, 105–106; M. Jeffrey Hardwick, "Creating a Consumer's Century: Urbanism and Architect Victor Gruen, 1938–1968" (Ph.D. diss., Yale University, 2000), 87 (forthcoming as *The Mall Maker: Victor Gruen, Architect of an American Dream* [Philadelphia: University of Pennsylvania Press, 2003]); John A. Jakle and Keith A. Sculle, *The Gas Station in America* (Baltimore: Johns Hopkins University Press, 1994), 146.

60. Meikle, *Twentieth-Century Limited*, 119.

61. "Main Street, U.S.A.," *Architectural Forum* 70 (1939): 85; Horace Ginsbern, "In Store-Front Displays," *Signs of the Times* 77, no. 3 (1934): 11; Morris Lapidus, "Where the Sign Begins . . . ," *Signs of the Times* 78, no. 1 (1934): 11; William F. Rooney, "Electrical Displays," *Signs of the Times* 73, no. 2 (1933): 10.

62. Jakle and Sculle, *Gas Station*, 146.

63. Liebs, *Main Street to Miracle Mile*, 40. Liebs traces the development of roadside architecture from the nineteenth-century commercial strip to the 1980s. See also Richard Longstreth, "Don't Get Out: The Automobile's Impact on Five Building Types in Los Angeles, 1921–1941," *Arris: Journal of the Southeast Chapter of the Society of Architectural Historians* 7 (1996): 32–56; Longstreth, *City Center to Regional Mall*; and Longstreth, *The Drive-In, the Supermarket*.

64. F. A. Radford built Wigwam Villages in Kentucky, Louisiana, Florida, Alabama, Alabama, and California in the 1930s, all with neon signs flashing "eat and sleep in a wigwam." See J. J. C. Andrews, *The Well-Built Elephant and Other Roadside Attractions* (New York: Congdon and Weed, 1984), 96–100; [James Agee], "The Great American Roadside," *Fortune*, September 1934, 56, 62–63; Jakle and Sculle, *Gas Station*, 158–60; Liebs, *Main Street to Miracle Mile*, 50–53; John Margolies, *Pump and Circumstance: Glory Days of the Gas Station* (Boston: Little, Brown, 1993), 34–35ff; Marling, *The Colossus of Roads*, 66–67; Belasco, *Americans on the Road*, 159. Marling and Belasco, in particular, discuss the escapism and the tourist experience.

65. Jim Heimann, *California Crazy and Beyond: Roadside Vernacular Architecture* (San Francisco: Chronicle Books, 2001), is devoted to this genre of architecture. In the 1930s, giant oranges were built in Florida, California, and even upstate New York. The Big Cone was a twenty-five-foot-high upside-down ice cream cone built in 1928 in Santa Ana, California; a chain of similar buildings sprang up in Ohio around that time as well. One teapot in Tacoma, Washington, served something else in its teacups—it was a speakeasy for awhile. See Andrews, *Well-Built Elephant*, 32, xi, 63. Eight twenty-foot-high shell-shaped stations were built in Winston-Salem between 1930 and 1933. See Jakle and Sculle, *Gas Station*, 194, 199; Marling, *Colossus of Roads*, 74; Daniel Vierya, *An Architectural History of America's Gas Stations* (New York: Collier Macmillan, 1979), 18–19; and Andrews, *Well-Built Elephant*, 2.

66. Marling, *Colossus of Roads*, 9–16; Heimann, *California Crazy*, 162.

67. "The Great American Roadside," 172. On the attribution of this article to Agee, see Judith Keller, "Evans and Agee: 'The Great American Roadside' (*Fortune* 1934)," *History of Photography* 16 (1992): 170–71.

68. David Gebhart, "Introduction," in Heimann, *California Crazy*, 5, 15.

69. Heimann, *California Crazy*, 11; Vierya, *An Architectural History*, 14–15, 26, 59; Jakle and Sculle, *Gas Station*, 146, 149.

70. Liebs, *Main Street to Miracle Mile*, makes this point in relation to supermarkets, 129.

71. Hardwick, "Creating a Consumer's Century," 98.

Chapter 9

1. J. C. Nichols, "The Planning and Control of Outlying Shopping Centers," *Journal of Land and Public Utility Economics*, January 1926, 17; John Ihlder, "The Automobile and Community Planning," *Annals of the American Academy of Political and Social Sciences* 116 (November 1924): 199–205.

2. My use of the term *strip* is consistent with what Chester Liebs has traced to the turn-of-the-century "taxpayer strips." These were linear commercial corridors comprised of single rows of one-story shop fronts that were conceived as temporary structures to produce enough revenue to pay taxes and

retain the property for more profitable development at a later time. Liebs, *Main Street to Miracle Mile*, 12–16ff, 229. See also Ebner, "Re-reading Suburban America." Richard Longstreth's detailed studies of Los Angeles in *City Center to Regional Mall* have been useful in understanding the birth of the commercial strip as well. Other scholarly works that address decentralization, though as a post–World War II phenomenon, are Berry and Cohen, "Decentralization of Commerce and Industry"; Jakle and Mattson, "The Evolution of a Commercial Strip"; Boal and Johnson, "The Functions of Retail and Service Establishments on Commercial Ribbons."

3. See, for instance, the use of phrases "shoe-string" and "ribbon" slums in "Well done, California!" *Sunset*, August 1939, 14; *The National Committee for Restriction of Outdoor Advertising: What It Is and What It Seeks to Do* (New York: National Committee for Restriction of Outdoor Advertising, n.d.), n.p.; Albert S. Bard, "Progress in Billboard Control," in *American Civic Annual*, vol. 3, ed. Harlean James (Washington, D.C.: American Civic Association, 1931), 196; Alfred Bettman, Robert Whitten, E. P. Goodrich, "Roadside Improvement: A Report of the American City Planning Institute," *City Planning* 9, no. 4 (1933): 181–86.

4. Longstreth, *The Drive-In, the Supermarket*, 37–38, 72; Clarence S. Stein and Catherine Bauer, "Store Buildings and Neighborhood Shopping Centers," *Architectural Record* 75 (February 1934): 184.

5. Green Bay, Wisconsin, is one example of zoning to keep auto-related and grocery store business from residential districts in 1925; Champaign, Illinois, sought to use excess commercial zoning to stabilize property values, and implemented commercial zoning in 1926. See Jakle and Sculle, *Gas Station*, 187, 215.

6. Stein and Bauer, "Store Buildings," 187.

7. Bartholomew, quoted in Stein and Bauer, "Store Buildings," 187. See also Harland Bartholomew, "Business Zoning," *Annals of the American Academy of Political and Social Science* 155 (May 1931): 101–2; Bartholomew, *Urban Land Uses* (Cambridge, Mass.: Harvard University Press, 1932), 71–71. A list of Bartholomew's urban plans appears in Eldridge Lovelace, *Harland Bartholomew: His Contributions to American Urban Planning* (Urbana: University of Illinois, Department of Urban and Regional Planning, 1993), A-20. On his city planning see Marina Moskowitz, "Standard Bearers: Material Culture and Middle-Class Communities at the Turn of the Twentieth Century" (Ph.D. diss., Yale University, 1999).

8. F. T. Hopkins, *The Roadside Advertising Controversy* (Chicago: National Outdoor Advertising Bureau, 1938), n.p., OAA/Duke.

9. Longstreth, "The Forgotten Arterial Landscape," 439, 454; Longstreth, *City Center to Regional Mall*, figs. 44, 66, 94. See Wilshire, Vermont, Western, and Sunset street scenes in the Photograph Collection, History Department, Los Angeles Public Library and in the Dick Whittington and Title Insurance and Trust Company photograph collections, Regional History Collection, University of Southern California, Los Angeles (hereafter Regional History/USC). (In the Whittington collection, see, for instance, photographs numbered 8-75-22, 3-54-5, 811-127-1, and A10-17-4; in the Title Insurance collection, see 1-1-1-424, 1-1-1-425, 1-1-1-430.)

10. "Economic Utility of Poster Panels," *OAA News* 15, no. 4 (1924): 17.

11. James C. Klemos, "Taking the Kinks out of Operating," *OAA News* 15, no. 2 (1924): 13–14.

12. Walter Foster, "Leasing and Maintenance of Poster Advertising," *OAA News* 14, no. 1 (1923): 9.

13. Klemos, "Taking the Kinks Out," 3.

14. Ibid.

15. Walter Foster explained his practice of leasing but not using space as "protection to keep anyone else from leasing it or building on it. . . . we set up a fund for protection." Ibid., 8; see also "Outdoor Advertising Company Takes the Count," *Civic Comment*, March–April 1931, 13, OAA/Duke.

16. Heiman, *California Crazy*, 50.

17. Heiman, *California Crazy*, 45, 50; Longstreth, *The Drive-In, the Supermarket*, 69.

18. Jakle and Sculle, *Gas Station*, 55, 58, 183.

19. Ibid., 135–36, 209, 227; Longstreth, *The Drive-In, the Supermarket*, 69.

20. Tedlow, *New and Improved*, 238; Longstreth, *The Drive-in, the Supermarket*, 78, 92.

21. Tedlow, *New and Improved*, 238; Longstreth, *The Drive-In, the Supermarket*, 110.

22. Reprint of Donald Curtiss, "Super Markets and Self-Service Stores," *Advertising and Selling*, June 1940, OAA/Duke.

23. Ibid. See also reprint of Edward Pachuta, "Building Brand Identification through Outdoor Advertising," *Quick Frozen Foods*, March 1958, OAA/Duke; Press Release from Vincent V. Van Beuren, OAI, "The Outdoor Supermarket Alliance: How Outdoor Serves Advertisers in the Self-Service Field," 27 January 1958, 2, OAA/Duke.

24. "Outdoor Vies for More Sales, Fewer Curbs," *Printers' Ink*, 5 June 1959, 50.

25. Liebs, *Main Street to Miracle Mile*, 60, 90.

26. W.C. Wall, "A 'New Look' for Signs, Too," *Signs of the Times*, September 1948, 26; "Outdoor Vies for More Sales," 50; "Highlights in the Poster and Painted Display Medium (By Decades)," n.d., 2–4, Clear Channel Archive. Many issues of *Signs of the Times* in this period document the technological advances in plastics, such as the use of backlit Plexiglas boxes.

27. C. D. McCormick, *Advertising and Selling*, February 1947, 60; see blueprints and patent applications for the Loewy billboard frame, OAA/Duke. Gannett Outdoor Advertising made one of the first notable changes to the Loewy panel, introducing the "Trim Panel," which replaced the one-foot-wide curved frame with a mere 1.5-inch border. See Fraser, *American Billboard*, 157.

28. The ease with which billboards could be installed, dismantled, and moved around with the boom truck also led to the practice of sign rotation; advertisers could move and reuse the same signs all over town, guaranteeing the kinds of saturation that traffic and trade surveys had proven necessary. See *Outdoor 101* (New York: Institute of Outdoor Advertising, n.d.), 12; Henderson, *Billboard Art*, 54.

29. Stein and Bauer, "Store Buildings and Neighborhood Shopping Centers," 175–83; Longstreth, *The Drive-in, the Supermarket*, 156; Hardwick, "Creating a Consumer's Century," 142–43.

"The Billboard War"

1. *Ribbons of Gold* was a 1955 promotional booklet produced by Foster and Kleiser (OAA/Duke) to sell the highways and bridges in the Bay Area to potential users of outdoor advertising. The phrase perfectly describes attitudes of outdoor advertisers to highways in the preceding decades, beginning with the growth of automobile travel, too. "Ribbon" and "shoe-string slums" appear in literature pertaining to roadside beauty and town planning in the 1930s, though it had earlier roots in "taxpayer strips." See Liebs, *Main Street to Miracle Mile*, 23–25; "Well done, California!" 14; *The National Committee for Restriction of Outdoor Advertising*; Bard, "Progress in Billboard Control," 196; Bettman, Whitten, and Goodrich, "Roadside Improvement,"181–86.

2. Paula Baker, "The Domestication of Politics: Women and American Political Society, 1780–1920," *American Historical Review* 89, no. 3 (1984): 620–47; Barbara Welter, "The Cult of True Womanhood," *Dimity Convictions: The American Woman in the Nineteenth Century* (Athens: Ohio University Press, 1976), 21–41; Daniel Scott Smith, "Family Limitation, Sexual Control, and Domestic Feminism in Victorian America," in *Clio's Consciousness Raised: New Perspectives in the History of Women*, ed. Mary Hartman and Lois Banner (New York: Harper Colophon, 1974); Linda Kerber, "Separate Spheres, Female Worlds, Woman's Place: The Rhetoric of Women's History," *Journal of American History* 75 (June 1988): 9–39.

3. Quoted in Robin Muncy, *Creating a Female Dominion in American Reform, 1890–1935* (New York and Oxford: Oxford University Press, 1991), 36. Temperance leader France Willard called women's social reform work "municipal housekeeping" and described it as bringing "the home into the world" and making "the world more homelike"; quoted in Sheila Rothman, *Woman's Proper Place: A History of Changing Ideals and Practices* (New York: Basic, 1978), 67. As urban historian Maureen Flanagan and others have shown, this does not mean that women involved in municipal work were apolitical. Rather, the metaphor of the home served to bring women together and into the public realm of politics with a specific purpose, of treating the city with the same heartfelt interest with which they treated the home. This was in contrast to the pecuniary interests of men invested in the business matters of city politics. See Maureen A. Flanagan, *Seeing with Their Hearts: Chicago Women and the Vision of the Good City, 1871–1933* (Princeton, N.J.: Princeton University Press, 2002); Flanagan, "Gender and Urban Political Reform in Chicago: The City Club and the Woman's City Club of Chicago in the Progressive Era," *American Historical Review* 95, no. 4 (1990): 109–30; Flanagan, "The City Profitable and the City Livable: Environmental Policy, Gender, and Power in Chicago in the 1910s," *Journal of Urban History* 22, no. 2 (1996): 163–90; Suellen Hoy, "Municipal Housekeeping: The

Role of Women in Improving Urban Sanitation Practices, 1870–1917," in *Pollution and Reform in American Cities, 1870–1930*, ed. Martin V. Melosi (Austin: University of Texas Press, 1980), 173–98; Stradling, *Smokestacks and Progressives*.

4. *Corporate liberalism* describes the complex socioeconomic forces at work in reconciling democratic notions of private property, individualism, and free enterprise with scientific and engineering technologies. Historians have used the term in relationship to industrial change in the decades around the turn of the century and the ways in which the controlling elements of scientifically managed work (mass production) were increasingly complemented by mass leisure and consumption. Some have said that the policies attendant to the ideas of corporate liberalism underlay New Deal policies as well as policy in years since. The term appeared first in Martin J. Sklar, "Woodrow Wilson and the Political Economy of Modern United States Liberalism," *Studies on the Left* 1, no. 3 (1960): 17–47; see also his *The Corporate Reconstruction of American Capitalism, 1890–1916: The Market, the Law, and Politics* (Cambridge: Cambridge University Press, 1988). On the "culture of abundance" that is part of corporate liberalism, see Warren Susman, "Toward a History of the Culture of Abundance," in *Culture as History: The Transformation of American Society in the Twentieth Century* (New York: Pantheon, 1984), xix–xxx. Overviews of the literature on corporate liberalism and its evolution include Ellis W. Hawley, "The Discovery and Study of a 'Corporate Liberalism,'" *Business History Review* 52 (Autumn 1978): 309–20; J. Joseph Huthmacher and Warren Susman, eds., *Herbert Hoover and the Crisis of American Capitalism* (Cambridge, Mass.: Schenkman, 1973); James Weinstein, *The Corporate Ideal in the Liberal State: 1900–1918* (Boston: Beacon Press, 1968); Alan Brinkley, *The End of Reform: New Deal Liberalism in Recession and War* (New York: Alfred A. Knopf, 1995); David F. Noble, *America by Design: Science, Technology, and the Rise of Corporate Capitalism* (New York: Alfred A. Knopf, 1977); Olivier Zunz, *Making America Corporate, 1870–1920* (Chicago: University of Chicago Press, 1990).

5. The "scornful" naming of "scenic sisters" and the "war" is summarized in reprint of Albert S. Bard, "Winning the Billboard War," *National Municipal Review* 30, no. 7 (1941): 2, OAA/Duke. The term *billboard war* was commonly used to describe roadside reform efforts, as is noted in James P. Taylor in his address to the Vermont Federation of Women's Clubs; see, *Hospitality de Luxe: Pomp of Highways and Glory of Roadsides* (Burlington, Vt.: Lane Press, 1929), n.p, OAA/Duke.

6. By *extralegal* I mean coercive activities such as boycotts, public protests, defacement of signs in areas zoned against billboards or as yet unregulated.

Chapter 10

1. Landscape architect Warren H. Manning began the American Park and Outdoor Art Association (APOAA) in 1897 with laypeople, professional landscape architects, park superintendents, and park commissioners, all dedicated to good taste in landscape and park development. Miss Jesse M. Good was the national organizer for the National League of Improvement Associations, which was formed in 1900; Charles Zueblin became its president and changed the name to the American League for Civic Improvement (ALCI) the following year. The group made outdoor art and beauty as well as town planning and civic improvement its goals. Initially, the APOAA segregated its female members in the Women's Auxiliary; after the joining of the ALCI and APOAA to form the American Civic Association (ACA), a separate Woman's Outdoor Art League continued. See Wilson, "J. Horace McFarland and the City Beautiful Movement"; Ernest Morrison, *J. Horace McFarland: A Thorn for Beauty* (Harrisburg, Pa.: Commonwealth of Pennsylvania, Pennsylvania Historical and Museum Commission, 1995), 90; Jon A. Peterson, "The City Beautiful Movement: Forgotten Origins and Lost Meaning," *Journal of Urban History* 2, no. 4 (1976): 421–23; Daphne Spain, *How Women Saved the City* (Minneapolis: University of Minnesota Press, 2001), 54–57; and Daniel Bluestone, "Roadside Blight and the Reform of Commercial Architecture," in *Roadside America: The Automobile in Design and Culture*, ed. Jan Jennings (Ames: Iowa State University Press and the Society for Commercial Archeology, 1990), 171–72. The existence of segregated women's groups within these organizations and their dedication to civic improvement reveal larger distinctions and imperatives for dividing women amateurs from male professionals. For more on the role of women in civic improvement organizations and in the City Beautiful movement, see Bonj Szczygiel, "'City Beautiful' Revisited: An Analysis of Nineteenth-Century Civic Improvement Efforts," *Journal of Urban History* 29, no. 2 (2003): 107–32.

2. Eugenie Ladner Birch, "From Civic Worker to City Planner: Women and Planning, 1890–1980," in *The American Planner: Biographies and Recollections*, ed. Donald A. Krueckeberg (New York: Methuen, 1983), 398–99; Peterson, "The City Beautiful Movement," 422–24. See also Karen Blair, *The Torchbearers: Women and Their Amateur Arts Associations in America, 1890–1930* (Bloomington and Indianapolis: Indiana University Press, 1994), 94–102. William H. Wilson does not focus on gender issues but does mention women's presence in a variety of civic improvement societies engaged in anti-billboard activities in his "The Billboard," 402, 404, 410.

3. M. Christine Boyer, *Dreaming the Rational City: The Myth of American City Planning* (London and Cambridge, Mass.: MIT Press, 1983), 14–46. See also Paul Boyer, *Urban Masses and Moral Order in America, 1820–1920* (Cambridge, Mass.: Harvard University Press, 1978).

4. Wilson, "The Billboard," 415.

5. "Trying to Draw the Line," *Brooklyn Eagle*, 3 April 1892, 20; "Indecent Posters," *Billboard* 10, no. 5 (1898): 13; "Will it come to this?" *Billposter* 4, no. 2 (1899): 19; Baldwin, *Domesticating the Street*, 60–61.

6. Schultz, "Legislating Morality," 37–44; Bogart, *Artists, Advertising, and the Borders of Art*, 92–100. On the transition from scarcity to abundance, see Lears, "From Salvation to Self Realization"; Warren Susman, "'Personality' and the Making of Twentieth-Century Culture."

7. Schultz, "Legislating Morality," 37, 39; Bogart, *Artists, Advertising, and the Borders of Art*, 100; Wilson, "The Billboard." 400–401. These ideas are also consistent with what Paul Boyer puts forth in *Urban Masses*.

8. Morrison, *J. Horace McFarland*, 89, 95.

9. Boyer, *Urban Masses*, 179, 221, 261–276. See also William H. Wilson, *The City Beautiful Movement* (Baltimore: Johns Hopkins University Press, 1989); Susan Marie Wirka, "The City Social Movement: Progressive Women Reformers and Early Social Planning," in *Planning the Twentieth-Century American City*, ed. Mary Corbin Sies and Charles Silver (Baltimore: Johns Hopkins University Press, 1996), 55–76.

10. James Gilbert, *Perfect Cities: Chicago's Utopias of 1893* (Chicago: University of Chicago Press, 1991); Alan Trachtenberg, *Incorporation of America: Culture and Society in the Gilded Age* (New York: Hill and Wang, 1982); Christine Boyer, *Dreaming the Rational City*; Wilson, *City Beautiful*, 75–95.

11. Burnham's work in planning Chicago, Washington, D.C., and the Chicago Columbian Exposition served as great means of publicizing the principles of City Beautiful, which were rooted in the earlier work of municipal improvement leagues as well as the work of landscape architect Frederick Law Olmsted. See Thomas S. Hines, *Burnham of Chicago: Architect and Planner* (Chicago: University of Chicago Press, 1979), 312–46; Spain, *How Women Saved the City*, 49–53; Wilson, *City Beautiful*, 44; Szczygiel, "'City Beautiful' Revisited," 107–9.

12. Szczygiel, "'City Beautiful' Revisited," 125. Women in civic reform is the focus of *American City* 6, no. 6 (1912).

13. Mary Ritter Beard, *Women's Work in Municipal Reform* (New York: Arno Press, 1972), 318.

14. Ibid., 298–99; Morrison, *J. Horace McFarland*, 96. Richard Watrous, secretary of the ACA made a similar claim in 1909, attributing to women "the enthusiasm, the untiring efforts and practical suggestions" and "the splendid headway attained by general improvement propaganda." See Birch, "From Civic Worker to City Planner," 403.

15. Wirka, "The City Social Movement," 55–76.

16. Karen Blair, *The Clubwoman as Feminist: True Womanhood Redefined, 1868–1914* (New York: Holmes and Meier, 1980), 90, 93. In the antebellum years, women gathered together for purposes seemingly apolitical. New York journalist Jane Croly founded a club in 1868, whose name, "Sorosis" was chosen by the women from a "botanical dictionary [which described the reference to] plants with an aggregation of flowers that bore fruit"; see Blair, *Clubwoman*, 20. The flowery name belied a serious purpose: career women working on behalf of women's education and professionalization. Several decades later, Jane Addams traced the development of women's clubs and their interests in a 1914 address to the General Federation of Women's Clubs (GFWC): "The clubs of this Federation early learned through their philanthropies that in loving-kindness there is a great salvation; through their study of poesy and art, that in beauty there is truth; are not they now adding the third dictum that in

the understanding of life lies the path to social progress?" See Mildred White Wells, *Unity in Diversity: The History of the General Federation of Women's Clubs* (Washington, D.C.: General Federation of Women's Clubs [GFWC], 1953), 198.

17. See, for instance, Muncy, *Creating a Female Dominion*; and Flanagan, *Seeing with Their Hearts*.

18. Blair, *Torchbearers*, 32, 98; Wells, *Unity in Diversity*, 198.

19. About women's municipal reform, Mary Beard wrote, in 1915, "Nor, as we have seen, is this movement for civic betterment confined to the greater cities. In thousands of out-of-the-way places which hardly appear on the map, unknown women with large visions are bent on improving their minds for no mere selfish advancement but for the purpose of equipping themselves to serve their little communities. . . . These local associations are federated into state and national associations." See Beard, *Women's Work*, 318. Blair also describes the stated intentions of clubwomen in 1906 to create Municipal Art Commissions "in towns of every size"; see Blair, *Torchbearers*, 94. The regionalist writer Zona Gale was among those small-town women who became involved in reform, publishing *Civic Improvement in Little Towns* (Washington, D.C.: American Civic Association, 1915); on Gale, see Julia Ehrhardt, *Writers of Conviction: The Personal Politics of Zona Gale, Dorothy Canfield Fisher, Rose Wilder Lane, and Josephine Herbst* (Columbia: University of Missouri Press, 2004).

20. Lewis, *Main Street*, 11.

21. Reformers drew ranks from the GFWC, the American Federation of Arts, the Outdoor Art League, Municipal Societies, the American Civic Association, the American Nature Association, and the Garden Club of America. Blair argues that art clubwomen saw that wilderness preservation was becoming a popular idea and thought this cause offered broadening possibilities to them too. They were "perhaps hopeful that if they supported the lovers of natural beauty, their projects would be supported in turn. . . . Members of the art clubs, then, stepped into the world of nature lovers and worked alongside their civic minded sisters to protect the natural environment." See Blair, *Torchbearers*, 100.

Like other civic reformers, the roadside reformers were predominantly white women, married to middle-class professional men; see Blair, *Torchbearers*, 3, 100; and Bluestone, "Roadside Blight," 172.

22. Wells, *Unity and Diversity*, 193–94.

23. "Funeral Services Conducted for Mrs. Elizabeth Lawton," *Glens Falls, N.Y., Times*, 8 July 1952, and other untitled obituaries, OAA/Duke; Roger William Riis, "The Billboards Must Go–II," *Reader's Digest*, November 1938, 81; Birch, "From Civic Worker to City Planner," 414.

24. "Report by Mrs. Elizabeth B. Lawton, Seventeenth Biennial Convention, Los Angeles, 1924," 415, "Women's Clubs against Billboards," *American Magazine of Art*, 2 July 1922, "To Eliminate Billboards," *Paterson Press Guardian*, 1 August 1922, and *American Magazine of Art*, November 1922, OAA/Duke; *General Federation News* 3, no. 1 (1922): 22.

25. "Official Minutes of the Board of Directors Meeting, GFWC, Washington, D.C., Wednesday, January 9, 1924," 370, "Big Advertisers Drop Billboards as Public Indignation Gains Force," *American Press*, March 1924, 5, and "Report by Mrs. Elizabeth B. Lawton, Seventeenth Biennial Convention," 415, OAA/Duke; "Billboards on the Move," *Civic Comment* 8 (28 June 1924): 12; Elizabeth Lawton, "Protecting the Scenery from Billboards," in *American Civic Annual*, ed. Harlean James (Washington, D.C.: American Civic Association, 1929), 144. Regarding the GFWC, see Blair, *Torchbearers*, 39; Anne M. Evans, "Women's Rural Organizations and Their Activities," *United States Department of Agriculture Bulletin No. 719* (Washington, D.C.: Government Printing Office, 1918), 1.

26. *Roadside Bulletin* 2, no. 6 (1934): 1. (Hereafter, *Roadside Bulletin* will be abbreviated as *RB*; please note that these journals were not published with regularity and often did not print the month or year of publication.)

27. William C. Hunt recognized the threat posed by Mrs. Lawton, whom he described as "a human comet," for her use of the "powerful agencies of publicity"; See Hunt, "Popularization of Poster Advertising," *OAA News* 14, no. 8 (1924): 9.

28. This comment was scrawled on a page with obituary clippings dated July 1952, OAA/Duke. Edward C. Donnelly described her activities as "pernicious, unfounded and constantly harassing" (letter to H. E. Fisk, 23 July 1941), while J. B. Stewart called her the "arch enemy" of outdoor activities (letter to Tom Griffith, Griffith Advertising Agency, 3 May 1940), OAA/Duke.

29. Letter from Mrs. C. Oliver Iselin, NRC, to Library of the Department of City Planning and Landscape Architecture, Harvard University, February 1955, Loeb Library, Graduate School of Design, Harvard University (hereafter, Loeb/Harvard). The dissolution letter claimed that state garden clubs and the Keep America Beautiful movement were doing the same work, so the NRC was no longer necessary.

30. *The National Committee for Restriction of Outdoor Advertising*; *Save the Beauty of America: The Landscape is No Place for Advertising* (Washington, D.C.: GFWC, Department of Art, Billboard Restriction Committee, n.d.), n.p.; "Billboards on the Move," 12.

31. Mrs. W. L. Lawton, *Digest of Address on Billboard Campaign, Delivered at the Biennial (Los Angeles, Cal.) Art Day, June 11, 1924* (New York: National Committee for Restriction of Outdoor Advertising, 1924), n.p.; Wells, *Unity in Diversity*, 197.

32. "Recent Roadside Improvement," in *American Civic Annual*, vol. 3, ed. Harlean James (Washington, D.C.: American Civic Association, 1931), 162. "What is the Policy of the General Federal of Women's Clubs on Billboard Restriction?" Box 21, Albert Sprague Bard Papers, New York Public Library (hereafter, Bard Papers).

33. James P. Karp, "The Evolving Meaning of Aesthetics in Land-Use Regulation," *Columbia Journal of Environmental Law* 15, no. 2 (1990): 310.

34. *City of Passaic v. Patterson Bill Posting, Advertising and Sign Painting Co.*, 72 N.J.L. 285, 62 A. 267 (1905); *Varney and Green v. Williams* 155 Cal. 318 (1909); *St. Louis Gunning Advertising Co. v. St. Louis* 231 U.S. 761 (1913); *Thomas Cusack Co. v. City of Chicago* 242 U.S. 526 (1917). Dozens of articles published by the NRC and the American Civic Association bemoan the courts' shortsightedness in granting aesthetics primary attention. Articles that spell out the legal limitations include Everett L. Millard, "Legal Handicaps in the Billboard Problem," *American City* 12, no. 3 (1915): 254–55; "Aesthetic Considerations and Billboard Zoning," *Journal of Land and Public Utility Economics*, May 1931, 208–10; Andrew Wright Crawford, *Important Advances toward Eradicating the Billboard Nuisance*, 2d ed. (Washington, D.C.: American Civic Association, 1920), 10. As a way around the exclusion of aesthetics from the police power, the American Civic Association, one of the organizations for which the NRC served as a clearinghouse, suggested that each state amend its constitution so that the "'rule of reason' now applicable to legislation under the police power for the protection of the ear and nose to be likewise applicable to acts for the protection of the eye." Their contention was, "If we can get rid of John Barleycorn by a constitutional amendment, we can similarly get rid of Billy Billboard. Indeed, John used to be one of Billy's best customers. . . !" Crawford, *Important Advances*, 14–15; "Fairfield County," 5, Box 20, Bard Papers.

Aesthetics, standing alone, was the basis for the exercise of the police power, beginning with the Supreme Court's decision in *Berman v. Parker* 348 U.S. 26 (1954), which authorized urban renewal projects based on the idea that "the concept of public welfare is broad and inclusive. The values it represents are spiritual as well as physical, aesthetic as well as monetary." *People v. Stover* 191 N.E. 2d 272 (1963) continued the trend. Secondary sources on the legal regulation of outdoor advertising include: John Costonis, "Law and Aesthetics: A Critique and a Reformulation of the Dilemmas," *Michigan Law Review* 80, no. 3 (1982): 355–461; J. Barry Cullingworth, "Aesthetics in U.S. Planning: From Billboards to Design Controls," *Town Planning Review* 62, no. 4 (1991): 399–413; Daniel R. Mandelker and William R. Ewald, *Street Graphics and the Law* (Washington, D.C., and Chicago: Planners Press, American Planning Association, 1988). A philosophical and legal overview of aesthetics, zoning, and planning is Samuel Bufford, "Beyond the Eye of the Beholder: A New Majority of Jurisdictions Authorize Aesthetic Regulation," *UMKC Law Review* 48, no. 2 (1980): 126–66; Karp, "The Evolving Meaning of Aesthetics in Land-Use Regulation," 307–28.

35. "Big Advertisers Drop Billboards as Public Indignation Gains Force," *American Press*, March 1924, 5, and reprint, Mrs. W. L. Lawton, "Rural Billboard Advertising Increasingly Viewed as Menace to Outdoor Beauty," *General Federation News*, March 1929, OAA/Duke. J. Horace McFarland agreed that public opinion could ultimately abolish billboards, writing, "It is, as is everything in America, 'up to the people.'" See J. Horace McFarland, "The Billboard and the Public Highways," *Annals of the American Academy of Political and Social Science* 116 (November 1924): 95.

36. Albert Bard was uniquely suited to work with the National Roadside Council, since he was an

active member of the New York City Club and the Municipal Art Society, serving as Secretary of The Mayor's Billboard Advertising Commission of the City of New York in 1913. Boxes 20, 21, 30, Bard Papers; *Report of the Mayor's Billboard Advertising Commission*; Bogart, *Artists, Advertising, and the Border of Art*, 90, 96, 335 n. 88.

37. Lewis, *Main Street*, 404.

38. Bogart, *Artists, Advertising, and the Border of Art*, 101–2.

39. "Knocking a Nuisance–Signboards or Scenery, Which?" *Philadelphia Record*, 13 April 1924, 8–9.

40. *RB* 1, no. 6 (c. 1931): 17; *RB* 1, no. 2 (c. 1930): 16.

41. *RB* 2, no. 4 (1933): 15, 21. The Pennsylvania Roadside Council established the "blot of the month" club in 1939; reprint of Elizabeth B. Lawton and Walter L. Lawton, "Pennsylvania Tries Cooperation to Solve the Roadside Problem," *Nature Magazine*, January 1942, Loeb/Harvard. The erection of lattices to block billboards was the subject of a New York case in which the court allowed the New York Superintendent of Public Works to erect a lattice screen to block motorists' view of a billboard at a curve in the road since the billboard was both "obnoxious" and a "public nuisance." The case had additional significance for the secondary importance it paid to aesthetics: "Beauty may not be queen, but she is not an outcast beyond the pale of protection or respect. She may at least shelter herself under the wing of safety, morality, or decency." Furthermore, the court stated, "No adjacent owner has the vested right to be seen from the street in his backyard privacy." See *Perlmutter v. Greene* 182 N.E. 5 (1932); Cullingworth, "Aesthetics in U.S. Planning," 401; *RB* 2, no. 3 (c. 1933): 2–4. Another story was about a neighbor who was incensed by the huge ad that he could read from his property. He "blanketed the board with a canvas sign reading: 'I favor products not advertised on the landscape.'" *RB* 2, no. 1 (n.d.): 2.

42. *RB* 2, no. 1 (n.d.): 4; *RB* 1, no. 4 (1931): 3.

43. Lawton, "Protecting the Scenery from Billboards," *American Civic Annual*, ed. Harlean James (Washington, D.C.: American Civic Association, 1929), 145–46.

44. Blair, *Torchbearers*, 101; *The National Committee for Restriction of Outdoor Advertising*; *RB* 1, no. 4 (1931): 3.

45. *RB* 1, no. 4 (1931): 3; *RB* 1, no. 3 (n.d.): 23; "Another Sticker Joins the Ranks," *Civic Comment*, March–April 1931, and "Topics of the Times: A Buyers' Strike against Billboards," *New York Times*, 19 November 1929, OAA/Duke.

46. "A White List," *Garden Glories* (Garden Club of Illinois) 4, no. 6 (1932), OAA/Duke.

47. *RB* 1, no. 6 (c. 1931): 4. The tactics of the NRC compared with those of predecessors such as Florence Kelley and the National Consumers League (NCL), formed in 1899, which similarly used "white lists." See Rosalind Rosenberg, *Divided Lives: American Women in the Twentieth Century* (New York: Hill and Wang, 1992), 40; and Jacqueline K. Dirks, "Righteous Goods: Women's Products, Reform Publicity, and the National Consumers' League" (Ph.D. diss., Yale University, 1996).

48. "Billboards on the Move," 12. It was the women's job to "arouse men to public duties and to aesthetic considerations," claimed James P. Taylor in *Hospitality de Luxe*, n.p.

49. "Is an Assault on Advertising Under Way?" *Printers' Ink*, 17 April 1924, 54; "Standard Oil Champions Beauty," *Brooklyn Eagle*, 13 April 1924, 2.

50. "Standard Oil Quits Billboards in East and 2,200 in the West," *American Press*, May 1924, 1–2; "Big Advertisers Drop Billboards as Public Indignation Gains Force," *American Press*, March 1924, 5; "Knocking a Nuisance–Signboards or Scenery, Which?" *Philadelphia Record*, 13 April 1924, 8–9; "Standard Oil Champions Beauty," *Brooklyn Eagle*, 13 April 1924, 2.

51. *RB* 2, no. 4 (1933), 1, 25.

52. Norris, *What Do You Want to See?*; Foster and Kleiser office memorandum from Mr. Lomax to Mr. Barry, 20 November 1929, OAA/Duke; "'Scenic or Sign-ic'–Results," *Standard Oil Bulletin* 17, no. 7 (1929): 1–9, 15–16.

53. "'Marvelous Marin' Pulls Down Own Billboards," *California Highways and Public Works*, December 1929, 16; Gabrielle Barnett, "Drive-by Viewing: Redwoods, Cars, and Visual Consciousness" (paper presented at the annual meeting of the American Society of Environmental History, 2002).

54. Mrs. Charles N. Felton, "Keep Scenic Highways Scenic," *California Highways and Public*

Works, February 1930, 15, 17; C. C. Carleton, "Zoning for Control of Building along the California State Highway System," *California Highways and Public Works*, January 1936, 16; George B. Ford, "A Program for Roadside Improvement," in *American Civic Annual*, vol. 2, ed. Harlean James (Washington, D.C.: American Civic Association, 1930), 184–87; Birch, "From Civic Worker to City Planner," 491. Years later another Rockefeller—Laurence—would offer support for another incarnation of the same cause, Lady Bird Johnson's beautification campaigns. See Lewis Gould, *Lady Bird Johnson and the Environment* (Lawrence: University Press of Kansas, 1988), 69–70.

55. Advertisers were quick to come to the defensive; see, for instance, "Is an Assault on Advertising Under Way?" 54–55, 61, 64.

56. Frank H. McKee, "Scenic Highways and Billboards," *California Highways and Public Works*, December 1929, 12–13; *Report of the Joint Assembly and Senate Committee on the Scenic Preservation of State Highways* (Sacramento: California State Printing Office, 1931); Elizabeth Lawton, "Roadside Surveys in the Pacific Coast States," in *American Civic Annual*, vol. 3, ed. Harlean James (Washington, D.C.: American Civic Association, 1931), 175–76.

57. Carleton, "Zoning for Control of Building," 19.

58. Typescript of speech and slide show by Frank C. Balfour, "Battle of the Billboards in California," presented before the Right of Way Committee, American Association of State Highway Officials' Thirty-Seventh Annual Convention, Omaha, Nebraska, 23–26 October 1951, 6, Regional History/USC.

59. J. M. Call, "California's Experience in Regulating Advertising Signs along Highways," *California Highways and Public Works*, November–December 1934, 10.

60. *Los Angeles Herald Examiner*, 6 July 1951, Regional History/USC; Alice Spalding Brown, *History of the Outdoor Circle* (Honolulu: n.p., 1962); Josephine L. Campbell, *How Hawaii Erased a Blot* (Honolulu: Outdoor Circle, n.d.); Fred C. Kelly, "How Hawaii Abolished Objectionable Signs: Boycott versus Billboard," *Reader's Digest*, February 1937, 39; Balfour, "Battle of the Billboards in California," 14–16.

61. See, online, http://outdoorcircle.org. The other states that have banned billboards are Alaska, Maine, and Vermont.

62. *Progress in 1925: National Committee for Restriction of Outdoor Advertising* (New York: National Committee for Restriction of Outdoor Advertising, 1925), 3–4.

Chapter 11

1. "Funeral Services Conducted for Mrs. Elizabeth Lawton."

2. Letter from George Kleiser, President, OAAA, to Mr. I. W. Digges, Secretary, Outdoor Advertising Inc., 8 August 1931 and 19 August 1931, and National Roadside Council, *What It Is—What It Does*, December 1938, OAA/Duke. The Lawtons' surveys that were conducted from 1923 through 1938 were published in the *Roadside Bulletin* and often as their own publications. James Taylor, in *Hospitality de Luxe*, comments that from 1926 to 1929, Mrs. Lawton traveled thirty thousand miles conducting surveys. When Lawton's "Approaches to the Federal City" was published in 1930, the *Civic Comment* reported that there was great press coverage, with the *Evening Star* publishing from "one to three articles almost every day." See "The Federal City Roadside Campaign," *Civic Comment* 32 (January–February 1931): 3.

3. Hopkins, *The Roadside Advertising Controversy*. Leonard Dreyfuss of the OAAA chastised club-women for not appropriately studying the outdoor advertising industry. He believed that women merely went to flower shows and signed cards protesting advertising, without knowing quite what they were signing. See "Forum on Roadside Beauty," Department of Conservation, New York State Federation of Women's Clubs, Park Central Hotel, New York, 19 April 1932, 18, OAA/Duke.

4. The quote is from *An Appeal to Chambers of Commerce and Civic Organizations* (New York: National Roadside Council, n.d.), n.p.

5. *Save the Beauty of America*.

6. *RB* 1, no. 2 (c. 1930): 2; *RB* 1, no. 3 (n.d.): 6.

7. Thomas Cole, "Essay on American Scenery" (1835), in *The American Landscape: A Critical Anthology of Prose and Poetry*, ed. John Conron (New York: Oxford University Press, 1973), 568–78.

On landscape painting, the picturesque, and the sublime, see David Miller, ed., *American Iconology* (New Haven, Conn.: Yale University Press, 1993); William H. Truettner and Alan Wallach, eds., *Thomas Cole: Landscape into History* (New Haven, Conn.: Yale University Press/ Washington, D.C.: Smithsonian Institution, National Museum of American Art, 1994); Barbara Novak, *Nature and Culture: American Landscape and Painting, 1825–1875*, rev. ed. (New York: Oxford University Press, 1995); George A. Thompson, ed., *Landscape in America* (Austin: University of Texas Press, 1995). On ideas about nature and industrial technology, see John Kasson, *Civilizing the Machine: Technology and Republican Values in America* (New York: Grossman, 1976); Leo Marx, *Machine in the Garden: Technology and the Pastoral Ideal in America* (London: Oxford University Press, 1964).

8. Billboard and Roadside Committee, *Calendar 1928: The Garden Club of America*, OAA/Duke; cartoons referencing William Cullen Bryant and landscape painter John Constable in Elizabeth Lawton, "Protecting the Scenery from Billboards," in *American Civic Annual*, ed. Harlean James (Washington, D.C.: American Civic Association, 1929), 143, 146. Cartoons such as " If you wish to enjoy American scenery go prepared," on the cover of the 1925 GFWC pamphlet *Save the Beauty of America,* show the landscape beyond the billboard comprised of farmland and rolling hillsides dotted with trees. Others preferred more sublime scenery of native wilderness, as in the cartoon of "The Old Indian Trail, Yesterday and . . . Today," *The State Highways: The Lesson of the Mohawk Trail* (Boston: Massachusetts Forestry Association, n.d.), n.p., Loeb/Harvard.

9. *RB*, 2, no. 6 (1934): 8–9; Elizabeth Lawton, "Notes from Here and There on Roadside Development," in *American Civic Annual*, vol. 5, ed. Harlean James (Washington, D.C.: American Civic Association, 1934), 177–78. Marguerite S. Shaffer examines the ways guidebooks, travel narratives, and tourist mementos taught audiences how to look at scenery, and how to imagine themselves as part of the nation at large through those activities in *See America First.*

10. Ibid., 277.

11. On the cultural construction of nature and wilderness, see Nash, *Wilderness and the American Mind*; Machor, *Pastoral Cities*; Rogin, "Nature as Politics and Nature as Romance in America"; Slotkin, *Regeneration through Violence*; Smith, *Virgin Land*; Perry Miller, *Errand into the Wilderness* (Cambridge, Mass.: Harvard University Press, 1964); and Miller, *Nature's Nation* (Cambridge, Mass.: Belknap Press of Harvard University, 1967).

12. "Forum on Roadside Beauty," 26.

13. *RB* 2, no. 4 (1933): 3.

14. *RB* 2, no. 3 (c. 1933): 8. Speech of Mrs. W. L. Lawton, given at University of Illinois–Urbana, August 7, 1931, 2, OAA/Duke. The Bureau of Public Roads offered the statistic that sixty percent of all travel in Illinois was nonbusiness travel. *RB* 1, no. 6 (c. 1931): 1.

15. Elizabeth Lawton, "Florida behind the Billboards," *Nature Magazine*, May 1940, 277; emphasis added. The comparison of roadside views to window displays was common. Albert Bard thought that highways free of commercialism were a way to showcase a state. One highway commissioner wrote, "'[T]o the majority of motorists our roadsides are our show windows, and they stop and visit with us only as our window display proves attractive to them.'" They needed only to be "relieved of the motley collection of exhibits which often obscure the view," another booster cried. *Roadside Improvement*, supplement to *Planning and Civic Comment* 4, no. 4 (October-December 1938): 2; *The Roadsides of Oregon: A Survey* (Washington, D.C.: American Nature Association for the National Council for Protection of Roadside Beauty, 1930), 4. Perhaps by describing landscape views as valuable commodities and the road as a site of mass consumption, reform-minded men or those appealing to them could rationalize beauty as more than the domain of clubwomen and "long-haired dreamers." George B. Ford, "What Makes 'the City Beautiful,'" in *Planning Problems of Town, City and Region: Papers and Discussions at the Twenty-first National Conference on City Planning* (Philadelphia: William F. Fell, 1929), 171.

16. Lawton, "Notes from Here and There," 177–78.

17. Ibid.; *RB* 1, no. 2 (c. 1930): 20.

18. Timothy Mark Davis, "Mount Vernon Memorial Highway and the Evolution of the American Parkway" (Ph.D. diss., University of Texas at Austin, 1997), 86–87.

19. McShane, *Down the Asphalt Path*, 32–35; Patton, *Open Road*, 67–69;

20. In the 1930s parkway construction included the Saw Mill River, Hutchinson, and Cross County Parkways in Westchester County, New York; the Merritt Parkway in Connecticut; the Mount Vernon Memorial Highway in Virginia; the Blue Ridge Parkway in Virginia and North Carolina; and the Natchez Trace Parkway in Mississippi. See Davis, "Mount Vernon Memorial Highway," 191; *America's Highways*, 133, 137, 139.

21. Davis, "Mount Vernon Memorial Highway," 187; also see Bruce Radde, *The Merritt Parkway* (New Haven, Conn.: Yale University Press, 1993).

22. Lawton, "Notes from Here and There," 179. When, in 1937, the "freeway" concept was first being suggested (in Rhode Island and New York), roadside reformers saw its value as similar to parkways but with more problems. Like parkways, freeways were intended to be limited in access, but without such wide rights of way. Also like parkways, they seemed too expensive and difficult to build on a national basis. Flavel Shurtleff, counsel of the American Planning and Civic Association, wrote, "The freeway will help, if it is wide enough to make billboards on private property unreadable; otherwise, it should be supplemented by control of private property uses along its borders"; see Shurtleff, "Roadside Conditions," in "Summary of the Joint Conference on Roadside Improvement," *Planning Broadcasts* (American Planning and Civic Association), December 1938, 3, 4, 10. The freeway idea is discussed in Edward M. Bassett, "Zoning Round Table," *Planning and Civic Comment* 3, no. 2 (1937), 25.

23. Davis, "Mount Vernon Memorial Highway," 86–87, 417.

24. Lawton, "Notes from Here and There," 179; *Roadside Improvement* supplement, 5.

25. Elizabeth Lawton, "Summary of Proceedings of Second Joint Conference on Roadside Improvement," *Planning Broadcasts*, January 1941, 8, 22.

26. Davis, "Mount Vernon Memorial Highway," 187.

27. Ralph Waldo Emerson, "Nature" (1836), in *The American Landscape: A Critical Anthology of Prose and Poetry*, ed. John Conron (New York: Oxford University Press, 1973), 580.

28. Charlotte Rumbold, "Beyond the Billboards Lies America," *Clevelander* 6 (June 1931): 2; "Who Owns the Landscape," *New York Herald Tribune*, quoted in *RB* 1, no. 6 (c. 1931): 1.

29. On the appropriative powers of vision or the spectators' gaze, see, for instance, Berger, *Ways of Seeing*; Sontag, *On Photography*; Boime, *Magisterial Gaze*; Miller, *The Empire of the Eye*; and Pratt, *Imperial Eyes*. Alan Trachtenberg addresses this in terms of Clarence King's descriptions of the Sierra Nevadas in *Reading American Photographs: Images as History* (New York: Noonday Press, 1990), 119–63.

30. Mrs. W. L. Lawton, "Regulation of Outdoor Advertising," in *Planning Problems of Town, City and Region: Papers and Discussions at the Eighteenth National Conference on City Planning* (Philadelphia: William Fell, 1926), 87.

31. Lawton, "Roadside Surveys in the Pacific Coast States," 176.

32. McFarland, "The Billboard and the Public Highways," 101.

33. *RB* 2, no. 4 (1933): 26.

34. Lawton, *Digest of Address on Billboard Campaign*.

35. Paul Sann, *The Lawless Decade* (New York: Crown, 1957), 86.

36. Arthur Pack, of the American Nature Association, spoke for the group, exclaiming, "'Buy, buy, buy. . . !' is a sound argument up to a certain point, at least in these days of depression and fear, but to the gods of buying and selling must we sacrifice everything?" "Forum on Roadside Beauty," 11.

37. *RB* 1, no. 3 (n.d.): 13.

38. Anna Steese Richardson, "Beauty or Billboards?" *Woman's Home Companion*, September 1931, 25, 59; *RB*, 2, no. 4 (1933), 1, 6.

39. Hopkins, *The Roadside Advertising Controversy*. "Don't forget, ladies," another billboard advocate wrote, in case the reformers weren't sympathetic to farmers, that "in about 80% of cases these rentals are paid to women. . . . Much of this property would otherwise stand idle and the rental paid by the poster men is very much appreciated, because it helps to pay the taxes." Holliday, *The Story of Organized Outdoor Advertising*.

40. "Conference on Roadside Business and Rural Beauty," Chamber of Commerce, Washington, D.C., 8 January 1931, 34ff, OAA/Duke; *RB* 1, no. 3 (n.d.): 19.

Jackson Lears, "Packaging the Folk: Tradition and Amnesia in American Advertising, 1940," in *Folk Roots, New Roots: Folklore in American Life*, ed. Jane S. Becker and Barbara co (Lexington, Mass.: Museum of Our National Heritage, 1988), 106–7.

42. McFarland, "The Billboard and the Public Highways," 95.

43. *RB* 1, no. 6 (c.1931): 7.

44. *The Roadsides of Oregon: A Survey*, 8, 11; *The Roadsides of North Carolina*, 11.

45. Joseph Lee, "Hot Dog in the Manger," letter to the editor, *The Boston Herald*, 31 March 1928, OAA/Duke; Struthers Burt, "Obscenic Scenery," *Saturday Evening Post*, 18 June 1932, 14.

46. *RB* 1, no. 2 (c.1930): 13, 16; *National Roadside Council: What It Is and What It Does* (New York: National Roadside Council, 1939), n.p.

47. Downer, quoted in Davis, "Mount Vernon Memorial Highway," 167; Burt, Obscenic Scenery," 14; *Save the Beauty of America*.

48. See, for instance, Schmitt, *Back to Nature*; Lears, *No Place of Grace*; Jeffrey L. Meikle, "Domesticating Modernity," in *Designing Modernity: The Art of Reform and Persuasion*, ed. Wendy Kaplan (New York: Thames and Hudson, 1995); Lawrence W. Levine, "Progress and Nostalgia: The Self Image of the Nineteen Twenties," in *The Unpredictable Past: Explorations in American Cultural History* (New York: Oxford University Press, 1993), 189–205.

49. *RB*, 2, no. 1 (n.d.): 7; "What Attracts the Tourist to Your Town?" OAA/Duke; *RB*, 1, no. 2 (c. 1930): 4.

Chapter 12

1. "Ten Ways,"18. A similar point is the subject of W. Livingston Larned, "Posters and the Winter Tourist," *Poster* 11, no. 2 (1920): 1.

2. On the renewed fears of overproduction/underconsumption and attempts to "rationalize" distribution in the 1920s and 1930s see Benjamin Kline Hunnicutt, "The New Economic Gospel of Consumption," *Work without End: Abandoning Shorter Hours for the Right to Work* (Philadelphia: Temple University Press, 1988), 37–65; Gary Cross, *Time and Money: The Making of Consumer Culture* (New York: Routledge, 1993), 15–46; Daniel Horowitz, *The Morality of Spending: Attitudes toward the Consumer Society in America, 1875–1940* (Baltimore: Johns Hopkins University Press, 1985), 135ff.

3. Hopkins, *The Roadside Controversy*.

4. Reprint of "To the Ladies," *Printers' Ink*, 8 May 1924, OAA/Duke.

5. *One Hundred Reformers versus 25,000 Wage Earners* (New York: OAAA, c. 1936), n.p.

6. Lavinia Engle, "Billboard Tax Law in Maryland," in *American Civic Annual*, vol. 3, ed. Harlean James (Washington, D.C.: American Civic Association, 1931), 199.

7. *One Hundred Reformers versus 25,000 Wage Earners*.

8. Franz Aust, "The Democratization of Art," *Poster* 15, no. 12 (1924): 8.

9. Hopkins, *The Roadside Controversy*.

10. "That Truth May Prevail in Our Schools," *The Instructor*, n.d; and *Confidential Bulletin*, no. 3 (15 April 1939); both OAA/Duke. See also *Ad Andy in Outdoorland* coloring book (San Francisco: Foster and Kleiser, n.d.), Clear Channel Archive.

11. Holliday, *The Story of Organized Outdoor Advertising*. On the broad reach of the medium to illiterate and immigrant populations, see "Ten Ways," 17; Leonard Dreyfuss, "The Advertising and Marketing of Tomorrow," *Poster* 14, no. 8 (1923): 12; Arthur Acheson, "Poster Publicity in the States," *Poster* 11, no. 2 (1920): 21; "New Ideals in Poster Art," *Poster* 11, no. 10 (1920): 32; and Leonard Dreyfuss, "A Brief Survey of Poster Advertising," *Poster* 11, no. 2 (1920): 35.

12. Bogart, *Artists, Advertising, and the Border of Art*, 114.

13. Aust, "The Democratization of Art," 8. Aust was a Barney Link Advertising Research Fellow in 1929–30.

14. Loredo Taft, "Bring Art to the 'Home Towns," *Poster* 15, no. 12 (1924): 2; Aust, "The Democratization of Art," 4–5, 8.

15. "Expressions of Public Sentiment Reveal 'Blue Boy' Has Won Nation-wide Applause," *OAA News* 28, no. 5 (1938): 5; advertisement for Continental Lithography, *Western Advertising*, February 1933, 71. Billboards as the art gallery or picture gallery of the masses were phrases used frequently by

spokesmen and women for outdoor advertising. See, for instance, Charles W. Duncan, "The Picture Gallery of the People," *Poster* 14, no. 2 (1922): 41; Gerrit A. Beneker, "Poster Art in Marketing Goods," *Poster* 12, no. 11 (1921): 54.

16. Letters from Judge Frost to Al Norrington, Promotion and Research Committee, Poster Advertising Association, 10 October 1924, and Norrington to Mrs. Harry Lilly, 1 November 1924, OAA/Duke; *General Federation News*, July–August 1922, 22; "Three Campaigns Backed by Fine Arts Department," *General Federation News*, June–July 1923, 11.

17. The common first line of articles on poster artists described their businesslike office-studio. See I. G. Oliver, "Jon Brubaker," *Poster* 19, no. 4 (1928): 16–17 (whose studio was a "modern surrounding . . . not Greenwich Village at all"); Augusta Leinard, "Otis Shepard: Man and Artist," *Poster* 20, no. 7 (1929): 16; H. R. Willoughby, "Herbert Paus," *Poster* 14, no. 1 (1923): 19; "November Cover by Charlotte Malsbary," *Poster* 10, no. 11 (1919): 21. There were other objectives fulfilled by asserting the masculinity of the commercial artists. It gave weight and substance to an enterprise perceived by many to imply frivolity, irrationality, and a distinctive lack of business sense, and gave license to admen's claims that they had a productive role in society and the economy. Also, by showing the commercial illustrator to be a worker, not just an artist, the industry was allying itself with the causes of labor in a way that was easy and carried little real obligation.

18. Reprint of James O'Shaughnessy, "The Meal Ticket of American Art," *Printers' Ink*, 24 April 1924, OAA/Duke.

19. Ethel M. Feuerlicht, "Poster Work Teaches Women to Be Self Supporting," *Poster*, December 1920, 25–26; E. Walter Osborne, "'A Woman's Place' in Poster Advertising," *Poster*, December 1920, 17–18.

20. Aust and Harrison, *The Values of Art*, 3, 11.

21. See business cards and letterheads in scrapbook kept by R. B. Shleppey, c. 1890, John W. Shleppey Outdoor Advertising Collection, McFarlin Library, University of Tulsa, Oklahoma; Bogart, *Artists, Advertising, and the Borders of Art*, 114.

22. "Highlights in the poster and painted display medium (by decade)," n.d., and sales brochure for Thompson Poster Green, December 1947, OAA/Duke. In the 1930s and 1940s, the OAAA realized the cache that came with hiring from the big names of the newly emerged field of industrial design; they patented a Streamliner billboard frame, and hired Raymond Loewy to design another. See blueprints and patent applications, OAA/Duke.

23. Reprint of Franz Aust, "How Outdoor Advertising Can Be Part of the Natural Landscape," *Printers' Ink*, 24 April 1924, OAA/Duke.

24. *RB* 1, no. 6 (c.1931), 20; *RB* 2, no. 2 (n.d.): 3.

25. *Foster and Kleiser Company Gardens* (San Francisco: Foster and Kleiser, 1930), and *"Come into the Garden with Us"* (San Francisco: Foster and Kleiser, 1930), Clear Channel Archive. Other examples of sign parks nationwide are represented in *Beauty and Utility in Outdoor Advertising* (Chicago: OAAA, n.d.); John Whitmer, "A Cooperative Community Development," *OAA News* 19, no. 10 (1929): 26; "Landscaping the Panel Location, *OAA News* 16, no. 10 (1926): 10.

26. *"Come into the Garden with Us".* The "lizzies" were produced between 1923 and 1931, until the cost became prohibitive. TAB Annual Meeting and Management Conference, January 1978, file: Bulletin Structures, Clear Channel Archive.

27. "Wilder Aids Civic Plans," *OAA News* 13, no. 1 (1923): 21; "How Association Members Improve Rundown and Unsightly Sections," *Poster* 14, no. 2 (1923): 20–21; Harris Wescott, "If Standardized Outdoor Advertising Did Not Exist!" *Poster* 19, no. 3 (1928): 8–11. During 1944, more than 5,743 Victory Gardens flourished on ground provided by the General Outdoor Advertising Company. See *5743 Victory Gardens* (n.p.: General Outdoor Advertising, c. 1944), OAA/Duke. The garden usage of the land around the billboard structures is especially notable given the historic legal case in 1911 (*St. Louis Gunning Co. v. City of St. Louis*) that claimed the space behind billboards offered a hiding place for prostitutes and miscreants, and was constantly used as privies and dumping grounds for all kinds of waste. Costonis, "Law and Aesthetics," 162–63.

28. Aust, "Democratization in Art," 4–5.

29. O'Shaugnessy, "Meal Ticket"; Aust, "How Outdoor Advertising Can Be Part."

30. Unsigned, unattributed letters from Johnstown, Pa., to Gordon H. Seymour, Springfield, Mass., 13 November 1920, and to J. H. Brinkmeyer, president of Poster Advertising Association, 29 April 1922, OAA/Duke. Leonard Dreyfuss also proposed the formation of a "Sisterhood of the Poster Advertising Association," in an article by that name. He thought that if all else failed, the women would at least enhance the "entertainment features" of association meetings. *OAA News* 10, no. 12 (1920): 10.

31. Letter to Brinkmeyer, 29 April 1920.

32. Ibid.; Minutes, Thirty-Sixth Annual Convention, OAAA, Atlanta, October 18 to 23, 1926, vol. 1: 41–46, OAA/Duke.

33. Their early activities included lobbying the New York City Planning Commission to express their opposition to proposed zoning resolutions. See *Woman's Fact-Finding Roadside Association* (n.p.: n.p., n.d), OAA/Duke.

34. Letter from Freda Dixon, director, Women's Division, OAAA, to the Committee Members of the Outdoor Advertising Women of America, n.d., membership pamphlet for the *Outdoor Advertising Women of America* (Chicago: OAAA Women's Division, n.d.), and issues of *Newsletter of the Outdoor Advertising Women of America*, 1961–1963, OAA/Duke.

35. Their success may be judged by the comments of Elizabeth Lawton, who, in describing the strength of the billboard lobby, claimed it had "many friends in court," was firmly entrenched in "practically every civic group of prominence" and chambers of commerce, and had infiltrated all of the garden and women's clubs ("where, in some cases, the wives of billboard men, or of large billboard users, hold key positions and influence club policies"), to the extent that many legislators and club members were afraid to raise the subject of roadside control. See Lawton, "Florida behind the Billboards," 283.

36. In 1933, Coca-Cola, for instance, decided to use permits in order to assure that their ads were only posted on legitimately rented outdoor advertising spaces in keeping with local desires. The permits were to ensure that snipe ads weren't posted on trees, fences, and the like. See letter to George Kleiser, president, OAAA, from J. B. Stewart, vice president, Legal and Legislative Division, OAAA, 25 April 1933; letter from Herbert Fisk to George Kleiser, 18 April 1933, OAA/Duke. Morton Salt apparently did not follow this scheme, at least if Elizabeth Lawton's surveys of roadsides were correct. She noted the predominance of these small metal signs tacked everywhere. So did the group of Seattle, Washington, women who set out to remove the snipe signs on the highway between Seattle and Pierce King County. They remarked upon the difficulty they had removing the "Morton Salt–It Pours" tin signs, which "were nailed in profusion on every log and almost every fence. In most cases, the new sign had been fastened over an old sign and we found them as thick as five deep." *RB* 2, no. 3 (c. 1933): 19. By the time the United States started to mobilize for war, in 1942, the tin and sheet iron snipe signs met their demise, as they were removed for scrap metal. See "Urges Collection of Roadside Signs for Defense Scrap," *Atlanta Journal*, 27 January 1942, OAA/Duke.

37. Clubwomen acknowledged their lobbying for license fees and enforcement of existing regulations would drive the small, independent operators out of business, perhaps to the advantage of the largest outdoor advertisers. "Shall Our Roadsides Be Scenic or Signic?" in *Billboards Destroy Motoring Joy: Billboard Primer* (n.p.: Garden Club of Virginia, c. 1936), n.p. Stella Minick, "Report of Work Done by the Garden Club of Waynesboro in Reference to Roadside Improvement," 2 October 1939, OAA/Duke. See also "Conference on Roadside Business and Rural Beauty," 8 January 1931, 29.

38. "Conference on Roadside Business and Rural Beauty," 8 January 1931, 40; Hopkins, *The Roadside Advertising Controversy*.

39. See *1912–1952 Federal Litigations*. The consolidation of the outdoor advertising industry is similar to that of many other industries at the height of the trade association movement in the 1920s. See Ellis W. Hawley, "Herbert Hoover, the Commerce Secretariat, and the Vision of an 'Associative State,' 1921–1928," *Journal of American History* 61 (June 1974): 116–40.

40. Ewen, *PR!* 304–5, 311–20; James Guimond, *American Photography and the American Dream* (Chapel Hill: University of North Carolina Press, 1991), 114–16; "Posters Hail 'The American Way' From Coast to Coast," *OAA News* 27, no. 1 (1937): 3.

41. Guimond, *American Photography and the American Dream*, 112–14.

42. See, for instance, *Association News* 22 (1932): 38–39.

Chapter 13

1. Lawton, *Digest of Address on Billboard Campaign.*

2. Struthers Burt, "Beauty and Billboards are not Compatible," in *American Civic Annual*, vol. 3, ed. Harlean James (Washington, D.C.: American Civic Association, 1931), 184.

3. On the 1931 meetings, see the transcripts of "Conference on Roadside Business and Rural Beauty," Chamber of Commerce, Washington, D.C., 8 January 1931, and 10 April 1931, OAA/Duke. In 1932, under the auspices of the Department of Conservation of the New York Federation of Women's Clubs, another conference was called, with many of the same members as had attended the meetings of the previous year. As the billboard reformers presented their plans for zoning, the members of the outdoor advertising industry and the real estate industry refuted every one of their points, instead advocating that the reformers help the industry to self-regulate. See transcripts of the "Forum on Roadside Beauty." On the various zoning plans the NRC put forth, see *National Roadside Council: What It Is–What It Does* (New York: National Roadside Council, c. 1939), n.p.; Bard, "Winning the Billboard War," 1–4; *RB* 2, no. 3 (c. 1933): 55–60.

4. *The Roadsides of California: A Survey* (Washington, D.C.: American Nature Association for the National Council for Protection of Roadside Beauty, n.d.), 46–47.

5. "Conference on Roadside Business and Rural Beauty," 8 January 1931, 33, 72. See also Lawton, "Roadside Surveys in the Pacific Coast States," 177; reprint of "Will California Outsmart Florida?" *Florida*, February 1940, n.p., Loeb/Harvard; Lawton, "Notes from Here and There," 180.

6. Bettman, Whitten, and Goodrich, "Roadside Improvement," 182–83.

7. Elizabeth Lawton, "County Zoning as a Solution," *Roadsides of California*, 45–46.

8. Reprint of Albert S. Bard, "Highway Zoning," *Westchester Countryside*, winter 1937, OAA/Duke.

9. *Roadside Improvement*, supplement, 4. See also Edward Bassett, "Billboards," *Planning and Civic Comment* 1, no. 2 (1935): 18.

10. OAAA Memorandum Re: Proposed Legislation Restricting Use of Farm Lands, 7, OAA/Duke.

11. *RB* 1, no. 3 (n.d.): 12.

12. Letter from James Lakin, West Virginia Poster Advertising Company, to W. W. Bell, OAAA, Chicago, 13 January 1926, OAA/Duke.

13. *The Roadside Advertising Controversy* (New York: NYC Federation of Women's Clubs, 1939), n.p.

14. Letter from Elizabeth Lawton to Arthur Pack, American Nature Association, April 22, 1932, file: General Correspondence 1932, Box 20, Bard Papers.

15. On Herbert Nelson's proposed bill, his acclaim for billboards, and conference discussions of eminent domain (compensation for the loss of business arising from limitations upon property use), see "Sale of 'Right to View' Proposed as Billboard Solution," *California Highways and Public Works*, May 1931, 9; transcript of "A Conference on Roadside Business and Rural Beauty," 10 April 1931, 13–20, 23–50, and the NAREB and OAAA-sponsored booklet, *A Conference on Roadside Business and Rural Beauty*, 1931, 4, 6, OAA/Duke. A later variation of Nelson's bill that was promoted by the OAAA was called the "Tentative Plan."

16. Letter from Herbert Nelson to Elizabeth Lawton, 21 October 1939, reproduced as "Do Billboards Depreciate Real Estate Value?" *National Roadside Council News Letter*, and letter from A. E. Germer, Manager, Department of Public Relations to Members of the OAAA, 3 January 1940, OAA/Duke; Bard, "Winning the Billboard War," 2, 4; Thomas C. Desmond, "Women at Work: Cleaning Up the Roadsides," *Bulletin: National Council of State Garden Clubs*, November 1941, 22; *Decentralization: What Is It Doing to Our Cities?* (Chicago: Urban Land Institute, 1940).

17. Bard, "Winning the Billboard War," 4.

18. *Roadside Protection, A Study of the Problem and A Legislative Guide* (Washington, D.C.: American Automobile Association, 1941), 12–13; *America's Roadsides: A Practical Program for Replacing Confusion and Chaos with Sane and Orderly Development* (Washington D.C.: American Automobile Association, 1940). The AAA first appointed a committee to study roadside protection in 1936. Ironically, they continued to use billboards to advertise well after the committee began its work; for instance, the Automobile Club of Southern California spent over $15,000 dollars on outdoor advertising in 1938. The AAA received letters from clubwomen asking them to cease using billboards, but

refused to comply. *Roadside Improvement*, supplement, 7; "Historical Materials," *Digest of Minutes of Board of Directors* 8 (1 December 1938), 124, Automobile Club of Southern California Archives.

19. Bard, "Winning the Billboard War," 2; Elizabeth B. and Walter L. Lawton, "The Story of a Highway," *Nature Magazine*, May 1941, 263.

20. "Progress in Highway Protection Secured through County and Town Zoning," *RB*, December 1946, 1.

21. "Outdoor Interests Back Zoning as Answers to Women's Groups," *Sales Management*, 15 March 1939, 60–61. The OAAA formed alliances with three national groups: the Highway Property Owners Association was started in 1940, with branches organized in states where roadside control bills were proposed; the Roadside Business Association was formed in 1945 by the American Highway Sign Association; and the Conference of Roadside Business and Property Owners, which was a group representing national trade associations for a variety of businesses, met sporadically in the 1940s. Billboard men were the top officers in each of these groups. Lawton, "The Story of a Highway," 264; "Information Bulletin: Report on Conferences of Roadside Business Groups," 4 August 1948 and 6 October 1948, OAA/Duke.

22. Desmond, "Women at Work," 21–22.

23. Hilda Fox, "Public Education First," *RB*, December 1946, 30, 33.

24. "Questions and Answers on Roadside Zoning," in *Protecting Our Roadsides for Permanency or 'The Auto Graveyard'–Which?* (n.p.: Associated Clubs of Virginia for Roadside Development, 1941), n.p.

25. *RB*, December 1946, 27, 30, 33.

26. From 1937 to 1941, the average death rate on America's highways climbed above 30 in 100,000 for the first time; by the late 1930s numerous state highway departments were studying how to improve highway safety and federal appropriations were being made to aid the situation. In 1947 President Truman hosted a highway safety conference that received much attention in the OAAA and reformers' publications. See *Accident Facts* (Washington, D.C.: National Safety Council, 1991); William Kaszynski, *The American Highway: The History and Culture of Roads in the United States* (Jefferson, N.C.: McFarland, 2000), 111–12.

27. "Safety Conference Moves for Strong 1947 Program," *OAA News* 38, no. 6 (1947): 3; *RB*, January 1947, 13.

28. The various studies cited by the OAAA are reviewed in *Presenting the Truth about Outdoor Advertising* (Chicago: OAAA, 1957), 20–21.

29. *Sunset*, August 1939, 13.

30. [Elizabeth B. Lawton], "A Motorist's View–U.S. Route 1 from Maine to Florida," Loeb/Harvard; Lawton, "The Story of a Highway," 262, 264.

31. On World War I and advertising, see Creel, *How We Advertised America*; *Poster: War Souvenir Edition*; Pope, "The Advertising Industry and WWI," 5, 15–17; Ewen, *PR!* 104–27. On World War II and outdoor advertising industry efforts, see "War Activities Souvenir Edition," *OAA News* 35, no. 4 (1945); *Outdoor Advertising a Channel of Communication with the Public* (Chicago: OAAA, 1942); and *Outdoor Advertising a Channel of Communication in the War Effort* (Chicago: OAAA, 1943). See also William Bird, *Design for Victory* (Washington, D.C.: Smithsonian Institution Press, 1998) and Lawrence Samuel, *Pledging Allegiance: American Industry and the Bond Drive of World War II* (Washington, D.C.: Smithsonian Institution Press, 1997).

32. During the war, federal aid for highway construction was limited to roads necessary for military defense, though plans were developed for a national highway system; the Federal-Aid Highway Act of 1944 proposed an interstate system but not details on funding it, which would only come in the 1950s. See Richard F. Weingroff, *Public Roads* (Washington, D.C.: USDOT/FHWA, 1996); Federal-Aid Highway Act of 1956, Public Law 627, 23 USC 48; and Kaszynski, *The American Highway*, 170–71.

33. *Advertising Agency Magazine*, 17 January 1958, 15; Robert Moses, "Salvo in the Billboard Battle," *New York Times Magazine*, 16 March 1958, 16.

34. Senator Richard L. Neuberger, "Outdoor Advertising: A Debate," *Saturday Review*, 9 November 1957, 10–12; "The Billboard Battle," *Time*, 1 April 1957, 84; Richard Thruelsen, "Where Are Those Superhighways?" *Saturday Evening Post*, 14 December 1957, 62–63; *Federal Control of Outdoor*

Advertising: Text of Senate and House Debate March 24–April 3, 1958 (Chicago: OAAA, 1958), 1–2; Maurine Neuberger, "The View from the Highway," *Country Beautiful* 2, no. 6 (1963), 23; "Outdoor Ad Business Shows Signs of Life," *Wall Street Journal*, 8 July 1964, 28; Gould, *Lady Bird Johnson*, 138, 140; Philip Tocker, interview by Lewis Gould, 3 July 1984, 4, OAA/Duke.

Senator Kerr addressed the OAAA Convention in 1957, and explained that his opposition to the Neuberger bill to prohibit billboard advertising rested on state rights and economic principles (in which it is the right of Americans to profit from highway development); he claimed to know neither how to spell the word aesthetics nor what it meant. "Address by the Honorable Robert S. Kerr to the members of the OAAA at their Sixtieth Annual Convention, New Orleans, Louisiana, November 13, 1957," 4–8, OAA/Duke.

35. Gould, *Lady Bird Johnson*, 167.

36. Charles Stevenson, "The Great Billboard Scandal of 1960," *Reader's Digest* (1960), 152–53, OAA/Duke.

37. "Outdoor Criticism," *Advertising Agency Magazine*, 17 January 1958, 23; Foster and Kleiser interoffice correspondence from J. W. Fontana, director of public relations, to all branch managers, re: Union Oil Company, 4 December 1956, Clear Channel Archive.

38. Neuberger, "View from the Highway," 23.

39. Gould, *Lady Bird Johnson*, 140.

40. Stevenson, "The Great Billboard Scandal of 1960," 150.

41. *Beauty for America: Proceedings of the White House Conference on Natural Beauty* (Washington, D.C.: Government Printing Office, 1965), 250–51.

42. Gould, *Lady Bird Johnson*, 142, 157.

43. "Notes and Comments: The Message on Natural Beauty," *Landscape* 14, no. 3 (1965): 1.

44. Ada Louise Huxtable, "Planning for Beauty," *New York Times*, 24 May 1965, 28.

45. Gould, *Lady Bird Johnson*, 153, 188. Gould describes the discomfort that Lady Bird Johnson and male members of the administration felt with "feminine aura" of beautification, which sounded "cosmetic and trivial and . . . prissy" (60–61).

46. "The Conference Call (Message from the president to the United States of Congress, February 8, 1965," in *Beauty for America: Proceedings of the White House Conference on Natural Beauty* (Washington, D.C.: Government Printing Office, 1965), 1–3. The messages of Lady Bird Johnson and conference chairman Laurence Rockefeller that introduced the conference used the same tropes of nature and focused on "the places where most people live and work—our cities and the suburbs and countryside around them" (17–22).

47. "Remarks of the President to the Delegates to the Conference on Natural Beauty (as Actually Delivered), May 25, 1965," 6, Beautification Files: White House Conference on Natural Beauty, White House Social Files, Box 14, Lyndon B. Johnson Library.

48. Elizabeth Brenner Drew, "Lady Bird's Beauty Bill," *Atlantic Monthly*, December 1965, 68–71; "LBJ's Plan for Roads: Beauty–Or No Money," *U.S. News and World Report*, 7 June 1965, 62–77.

49. Gould, *Lady Bird Johnson*, 150ff.

50. Shelby Scates, "Billboards–Great Society Grapples Great Issues," *Argus* (Seattle) 72, no. 26 (1965), 1; reprint of "What President Johnson's Proposed Federal Billboard Control Bill Will Mean to the Standardized Outdoor Advertising Medium," *Advertising Age*, 31 May 1965, OAA/Duke; Gould, *Lady Bird Johnson*, 152.

51. Gould, *Lady Bird Johnson*, 144, 152; Tocker interview, 3 July 1984, 16, and 1 August 1984, 1–2, OAA/Duke.

52. In contrast to the Bonus Act of 1958, the HBA withheld funds to states that did not comply. *Highway Beautification Act of 1965* (San Francisco: Foster and Kleiser, 1965).

53. Drew, "Lady Bird's Beauty Bill," 70; letter from Helen Reynolds, California Roadside Council, to Rex Whitton, Federal Highway Administrator, 19 October 1966, 2–4, OAA/Duke; James Nathan Miller, "The Great Billboard Double-Cross," *Reader's Digest*, June 1985, 84–85.

54. Vermont was one such case, and refused to compensate sign owners for removal of signs on primary roads, preferring to settle claims one by one as they arose. "Vermont's New Signs of the Times," *Innovations* (Council of State Governments, 1979), 2.

55. Letter to the editor of the *Atlantic Monthly* from Helen Reynolds, California Roadside Council, 15 December 1965, Beautification Files: White House Conference on Natural Beauty, White House Social Files, Box 14, Lyndon B. Johnson Library.

56. Ibid.

57. Miller, "The Great Billboard Double-Cross," 86; Kent MacDougall, "Outdoor Ad Business Shows Signs of Life after Slumping to 11-Year Low Last Year," *Wall Street Journal*, 8 July 1964, 28.

58. Charles F. Floyd and Peter J. Shedd, *Highway Beautification: The Environmental Movement's Greatest Failure* (Boulder, Colo.: Westview Press, 1979); Miller, "The Great Billboard Double-Cross," 83–90.

59. Drew, "Lady Bird's Beauty Bill," 70.

60. Miller, "The Great Billboard Double-Cross," 86–87.

61. Reprint of Bernard Johnson, "Vermont Acts to Ban Billboards and Signs," *New York State Planning News* 32, no. 4 (Central Planning Office, Montpelier, Vermont, 1968).

62. Tocker interview, 1 August 1984, 2.

63. Letter from John W. Primrose, West Kentucky Advertising Company, to Frank Blake, OAAA, 1 June 1965, OAA/Duke.

Losers and Winners

1. "Green Tunnel vs. Billboard," *Life*, 11 March 1957, OAA/Duke.

2. Ruth Knight, "Bless Those Billboards," *The Kiwanis Magazine*, summer 1964, 52–53.

3. "Green Tunnel vs. Billboard."

4. "Battle of the Billboards," *New York Times*, 24 March 1957, OAA/Duke.

5. Robert Moses, quoted in *Advertising Agency*, 15; Vance Packard, "America the Beautiful–And Its Desecrators," *Atlantic Monthly*, August 1961, 51–55; Peter Blake, *God's Own Junkyard: The Planned Deterioration of America's Landscape* (New York: Holt, Rinehart, and Winston, 1964).

6. Letter from Frank Blake, OAAA, to George E. Burket, Mid-State Advertising Corporation, February 25, 1964, OAA/Duke.

Conclusion

1. Pop artist James Rosenquist worked as a sign painter, first painting Phillips 66 gasoline signs in Iowa, then painting billboards for General Outdoor Advertising in Minneapolis, then working for Artkraft Strauss in New York's Time Square in the 1950s. See Judith Goldman, *James Rosenquist* (New York: Viking-Penguin, 1985), 19–20, 22–25; and "Billboard Painter, Local 230, Is Broadway's Biggest Artist," *Democrat* (Durant, Okla.), 6 June 1960, reproduced in *James Rosenquist* (Toronto: National Gallery of Canada, 1968). Andy Warhol was a commercial illustrator for magazines such as *Harper's* and designed window displays in the 1950s. See Donna De Salvo, ed., *"Success Is a Job in New York . . . ": The Early Art and Business of Andy Warhol* (New York: Grey Art Gallery, New York University/Pittsburg: Carnegie Museum of Art, 1989) and Klaus Honnef, *Andy Warhol, 1928–1987: Commerce into Art* (Cologne: Benedikt Taschen Verlag, 1993).

2. Robert Venturi, Denise Scott Brown, and Steven Izenour, *Learning from Las Vegas* (Cambridge, Mass.: MIT Press, 1972).

3. Blake, *God's Own Junkyard*.

4. Venturi, Brown, and Izenour, *Learning from Las Vegas*, 76. Photographs from Blake's book are also reproduced in Robert Venturi, *Complexity and Contradiction in Architecture* (New York: Museum of Modern Art, 1966), 54–55.

5. Susan Sontag, "Notes on Camp," in *Against Interpretation* (New York: Anchor, 1986), 288.

6. Andy Warhol, *America* (New York: Harper and Row, 1985). This is a revealing book, insofar as it is a pointed political and socioeconomic critique. This is not to say, however, that Warhol impugned money making or consumer culture. As Sharon Zukin has written, he had an "ironic acceptance of capitalism" and "a willingness to use [commercial culture] and profit from it"; see Zukin, "Billboards Are Public Art in the Money Economy," in *Wall Power* (Philadelphia: Institute of Contemporary Art, University of Pennsylvania, 2000), n.p.

7. See www.scenic.org.

8. "Billboard Bandit," *Time*, 22 March 1971, 48; Susan Leibovitz Steinman, "Directional Signs: A Compendium of Artists' Works," in *Mapping the Terrain: New Genre Public Art*, ed. Suzanne Lacy (Seattle: Bay Press, 1995), 250–51.

9. "Billboard Firms Lure New Ads as Tobacco, Liquor Sales Slide," *Wall Street Journal*, 7 May 1987, 1; clippings file, "100 Largest National Accounts in Outdoor Advertising" folder, Clear Channel Archive.

10. Richard W. Pollay, Jung S. Lee, and David Carter-Whitney, "Separate, But Not Equal: Racial Segmentation in Cigarette Advertising," *Journal of Advertising* 21, no. 1 (1992): 46; Jacqueline L. Stoddard et al., "Targeted Tobacco Markets: Outdoor Advertising in Los Angeles Minority Areas," *American Journal of Public Health* 87, no. 7 (1997): 1232–33.

11. Pfleger counted three tobacco and liquor billboards in a nearby white neighborhood of similar size, while his black neighborhood had 118. Janice Castro, "Volunteer Vice Squad," *Time*, 23 April 1990, 60–61; Christina Duff, "Inner-City Priest Wins Acquittal after Having Defaced Billboards," *Wall Street Journal*, 5 July 1991, B2; Pollay, "Separate But Not Equal," 46. Artist David Hammons found in Charleston, S.C., where billboards were prohibited from residential neighborhoods, that 75 percent of illegal billboards were located in black areas, with 25 percent of those billboards promoting tobacco and alcohol. See Mary Jane Jacob, ed., *Places with a Past: New Site Specific Art at Charleston's Spoleto Festival* (New York: Rizzoli/Charleston: Spoleto Festival USA, 1991), 188.

12. Stephanie Strom, "Billboard Owners Switching, Not Fighting," *New York Times*, 4 April 1990, B1; Alison Fahey and Judann Dagnoli, "PM Ready to Deal with Outdoor Ad Foes," *Advertising Age* 61, no. 25 (18 June 1990): 3; Taylor and Chang, "History of Outdoor Advertising Regulation," 56–57. Although no longer called the "Code of Advertising Practices," the OAAA urges its members to follow a code of ethics, to maintain a diversified roster of advertisements, and to use empty space for public service campaigns; see www.oaaa.org.

13. "Billboard Firms Lure New Ads," 1.

14. Sally Goll Beatty, "Pact Could Send Marlboro Man into the Sunset," *Wall Street Journal*, 17 April 1997, B1; Linda Sandler, "Heard on the Street: Possible New Curbs on Cigarette Ads May Put Pressure on Some Firms That Get Revenue," *Wall Street Journal*, 21 April 1997, C2. The Master Settlement Agreement is available online at www.naag.org/issues/tobacco.

15. "Ads for Cigarettes, Alcohol Are Banned by Chicago Council," *Wall Street Journal*, 12 September 1997. In 2001, the Supreme Court struck down regulations prohibiting tobacco advertisements as a violation of the First Amendment, thereby invalidating local ordinances in New York, Chicago, Los Angeles, and other California cities. David Savage, "Justices Say States, Cities Can't Limit Tobacco Ads," *Los Angeles Times*, 29 June 2001, A25–26.

16. Zukin, "Billboards Are Public Art." Offensive ads aren't limited to minority neighborhoods. The affluent West Side community of Los Angeles recently objected to a billboard for Tha Row Records, which featured "a cartoon character sitting on the toilet and a corresponding vulgarity." It was put up against the wishes of the billboard owner, who was denied access to the structure by Tha Row, which owned the building. See Seema Mehta, "Council Told Law Is on the Side of Billboard," *Los Angeles Times*, 26 June 2002, B5.

17. On the terminology of "correcting" or altering advertisements, see Timothy Drescher, "The Harsh Reality: Billboard Subversion and Graffiti," *Wall Power* (Philadelphia: Institute of Contemporary Art, University of Pennsylvania, 2000), n.p. In the 1930s, *Ballyhoo* magazine similarly mocked the strategies of advertisers with their "revised" versions of popular ads. See Marchand, *Advertising the American Dream*, 312–14.

18. Drescher, "The Harsh Reality," 15; Klein, *No Logo*, 282, 289, 293; Billboard Liberation Front and Friends, *The Art and Science of Billboard Improvement*, second ed. (San Francisco: Billboard Liberation Front, 2000). Online sources can be found at www.adbusters.org; www.graffiti.org/ron_english; and www.billboardliberation.com.

19. Klein, *No Logo*, 281, 284; Liz Mcquiston, *Graphic Agitation: Social and Political Graphics since the Sixties* (London: Phaidon, 1993), 182.

20. Tom Frank, *Conquest of Cool: Business Culture, Counterculture, and the Rise of Hip Consumerism* (Chicago: University of Chicago Press, 1997).

21. Gail Edmondson, "Diesel is Smokin', " *Business Week*, 20 January 2003, 26; Klein, *No Logo*, 17, 297–99. On earlier campaigns, such as the 1994 Chrysler Plymouth Neon billboard, which added graffiti to its billboards to take on the looked of a pirated advertisement, see the articles online at www.billboardliberation.com/media/co.opt.html.

22. "BP–Back to Petroleum," *Review–Institute of Public Affairs* 55, no. 1 (2003): 13–14; Cait Murphy, "Is BP beyond Petroleum? Hardly," *Fortune* 30 September 2002, 44–46.

23. Ann Goldstein, ed., *Barbara Kruger* (Los Angeles: Museum of Contemporary Art/Cambridge Mass.: MIT, 1999); Kate Linker, *Love for Sale: The Words and Pictures of Barbara Kruger* (New York: Harry N. Abrams, 1990); W. J. T. Mitchell, "An Interview with Barbara Kruger," in *Art and the Public Sphere* (Chicago: University of Chicago Press, 1990), 235–48; bell hooks, "Subversive Beauty: New Modes of Contestation," in *Felix Gonzalez-Torres* (Los Angeles: Museum of Contemporary Art, 1994), 45–49; Nancy Spector, *Felix Gonzalez-Torres* (New York: Guggenheim Museum, 1995); Richard Meyer, "This is to Enrage You: Gran Fury and the Graphics of AIDS Activism," in *But Is It Art? The Spirit of Art as Activism*, ed. Nina Felshin (Seattle: Bay Press, 1995), 51–83. For a survey of art on billboards, see *Billboard: Art on the Road* (North Adams, Mass.: Mass MoCA/Cambridge, Mass.: MIT Press, 1999).

24. Marc Gunther, "The Great Outdoors," *Fortune*, 1 March 1999, 150–52; Kate Fitzgerald, "Slide Over to the Slow Lane," *Advertising Age*, 9 July 2001, S1; Theresa Howard, "Marketers Rediscover the Power, Creative Potential of Billboards," *USA Today*, 19 July 2001, 3B.

25. Christopher Gray, "Signs of the Times," *Avenue*, October 1990, 111; Bogart, *Artists, Advertising, and the Borders of Art*, 92; Zukin, "Billboards Are Public Art."

26. Ted Shaffrey, "Another 15 Minutes of Fame," *Los Angeles Times*, 8 July 2001, P3.

27. Marc Gunther, "The Great Outdoors," *Fortune*, 1 March 1999, 152; Howard, "Marketers Rediscover the Power," 3B.

28. John Werner Kluge, president of Metromedia, had set out to nationalize the holdings of Foster and Kleiser by purchasing General Outdoor of Chicago and New York, then Packer Outdoor in Ohio, and other companies. In 1965 Metromedia became the largest outdoor advertising operation in the world. Karl Eller began buying small companies across different media in the 1960s and 1970s, and by 1978 merged his Combined Communications with Gannett. See Lawrence M. Hughes, "Rooter for the 'Mets,'" *Sales Management*, 6 November 1964, 42–46; Gail Bellas, *Wilshire Business* 38, no. 5 (1972): 12; John Quirt, "Gannett's Prize Catch," *Fortune*, 5 June 1978, 142–43; clippings file, "Karl Eller" folder, Clear Channel Archive.

29. News Release by Eller Media Company, 25 February 1997, and clippings file, "Karl Eller" folder, Clear Channel Archive; Rhonda L. Rundle, "Outdoor Systems' Gannett Deal Is a Large Sign of Moreno's Ascent," *Wall Street Journal*, 11 July 1996, B6; Mark Hudis, "All the Signs Point Up," *Mediaweek*, 15 July 1996, 6; Debra Sparks, "Musical Billboards," *Financial World*, 18 February 1997, 48–51; Joan Harrison, "A Face Lift for a Drab Industry," *Mergers and Acquisitions* 31, no. 6 (1997): 46–47.

30. Gunther, "The Great Outdoors," 150; Katy Bachman, "To Infinity and Beyond," *Mediaweek*, 31 May 1999, 8.

31. John Kluge brought the new digital painting system to the market and his Metromedia Technologies led the field in large-scale imaging. See Lee Kerry, "It's All Outdoor," *Adweek*, 29 February 1988, 16; Gunther, "The Great Outdoors," 54; Rundle, "Outdoor Systems' Gannett Deal," B6; Sparks, "Musical Billboards," 48–51.

32. Gunther, "The Great Outdoors," 150; Rundle, "Outdoor Systems' Gannett Deal," B6; William P. Barrett, "The Phoenix of Phoenix," *Forbes*, 1 January 1996, 45; Sparks, "Musical Billboards," 49; Dwain R. Stoops, "Billboard Valuation: Fundamental Asset Allocation Issues," *Appraisal Journal* 71, no. 2 (2003): 159. It was no coincidence that outdoor companies were snatched up by firms with large interests in radio just as it was deregulating, given the parallels between the two industries, both of which rely upon reaching audiences in their cars. See Hudis, "All the Signs Point Up," 6; Bachman, "To Infinity," 8; and Katy Bachman, "Smaller is Better," *Mediaweek*, 24 September 2001. Although it is difficult to build new billboards, the OAAA has made deals to swap out existing billboards, removing some locations while putting up billboards in other, more lucrative spots, sometimes resulting in an overall reduction in the total number of billboards; Nancy Fletcher, OAAA president, conversation with author, Los Angeles, 11 July 2002.

33. Bachman, "Smaller is Better," 24; Nancy Fletcher conversation, 11 July 2002.

34. Kate Fitzgerald, "Financial Overview," *Outdoor Advertising Magazine* 12, no. 3 (2003): 8–9; Fitzgerald, "Slide Over," S1; Tony Case, "Outdoor Signs of the Times," *Mediaweek*, 30 September 2002, 6.

35. Lowry Mays, "The Media Revolution," keynote address, OAAA/TAB National Convention, 9 June 2003, Washington, D.C.

36. Bill Gates, *The Road Ahead* (New York: Penguin, 1995), 6–7, 103–10, 116, 180–81.

37. Andrew Ross writes that the use of the terms *network* and *Web* rather than *superhighway* represents the rise of more "ecologically resonant" metaphors and that "the organic, interconnected world of natural, self-regulating communities and networked information technologies is replacing the obsolete, rigid, linear structure of megamachine civilization built for privatized mobility." Of course, both are built for privatized mobility, as is now clear. See Ross, *Real Love: In Pursuit of Cultural Justice* (New York: New York University Press, 1998), 31.

38. Reed Tucker, "Would You Put Your Ad Here?" *Fortune*, 17 March 2003, 42.

39. "For Media Buyers Who Want to Get a Head," *B to B* (Chicago), 5 May 2003, 8.

40. David Lipin, "New Medium Sticks," *Adweek*, 22 May 2000, 4; Erik Gruenwedel, "Street Fighters," *Adweek*, 7 August 2000, 36–38; Charles Pappas, "Ad Nauseam: Ad Creep," *Advertising Age*, 10 July 2000, 16, 18; Chris Powell, "A New Kind of Outdoor Project," *Marketing Magazine* 10 March 2003, 4; Warren Berger, "Guerrilla Monsoon: Future of Guerrilla Advertising," OAAA/TAB National Convention, 10 June 2003, Washington, D.C.

41. Since the ads that wrap around buses make it virtually impossible to see inside, some cities, in the aftermath of September 11, 2001, have questioned what hazards they pose. Doug Hanchett, "Ban of Bus Window Ads," *Boston Herald*, 14 February 2002, 25.

42. Case, "Outdoor Signs of the Times," 6; Katy Bachman, "O-town Takes a Cut of New Arena Outdoor Ad Revenue," *Mediaweek*, 18 November 2002, 12; Gunther, "The Great Outdoors," 57; Brad Edmundson, "In the Driver's Seat," *American Demographics*, March 1998, 47.

43. I am grateful to Reuben Taylor for bringing this to my attention. Michael Burgi, "Signs of the Times," *Mediaweek*, 4 March 1996, 14; John Consoli, "Virtual Ads to Set the Pitch," *Mediaweek*, 22 March 1999, 12; Glen Dickson, "NFL to Kick Off Virtual Billboards," *Broadcasting and Cable*, 11 August 1997, 41; Pappas, "Ad Nauseam: Ad Creep," 16, 18.

44. Sandra Yin, "Counting Eyes on Billboards," *American Demographics*, December 2002–January 2003, 11; Bob McCann, "Leveraging GPS: Passive Audience Measurement for Outdoor," OAAA/TAB National Convention, 9 June 2003, Washington, D.C.

45. See www.oaaa.org/outdoor; and "Getting into Outdoor," *Marketing Week*, 30 January 2003, 39. New digital-ink billboards can be networked together and changed instantly to take into account viewer reaction, time of day, location, sales results, or current events. See "Ford Tests Digital Ink Billboards in Clear Channel Tie," *Marketing* (London), 3 April 2003, 7; Chris Powell, "Digital Ink Makes Billboards Flexible," *Marketing Magazine* (Toronto), 14 April 2003, 4; "Magink Digital-Ink Billboards Heralded as the Future of Outdoor Advertising," *Business Wire*, 30 April 2003; Kathy Prentice, "Taxi! Taxi! I have a message for you!," *Media Life*, 16 April 2001 (online at www.medialifemagazine.com/news2001/april01/apr16).

BIBLIOGRAPHY

Archives

Automobile Club of Southern California Archives
Clear Channel Outdoor, Los Angeles
John W. Hartman Center for Sales, Advertising, and Marketing History, Duke University
John W. Shleppey Outdoor Advertising Collection, McFarlin Library, University of Tulsa
Loeb Library, Graduate School of Design, Harvard University
Los Angeles Public Library, Photograph Collection
Lyndon Baines Johnson Library and Museum
National Museum of American History, Smithsonian Institution
New-York Historical Society Print, Photograph, Architecture, and Ephemera Collections
New York Public Library, Albert Sprague Bard Papers
Regional History Collections, University of Southern California

Select Periodicals

Advertising Outdoors
American Civic Association Annual
Billboard Advertising (continued by *Billboard*)
Billposter–Display Advertising (continued by *Billposter and Distributor*)
Brooklyn Eagle
Broom
California Highways and Public Works
Civic Comment (continued by *Planning and Civic Comment*)
Fortune
General Federation News (General Federation of Women's Clubs)
Los Angeles Times
Magazine of Business (also called *System: The Magazine of Business*)
Nature Magazine (American Nature Association)
New York Times
Outdoor Advertising Association News
Poster
Printers' Ink
Public Roads
Roadside Bulletin (National Roadside Council)
Sales Management

Signs of the Times
Western Advertising

Books and Articles

Agnew, Hugh. *Outdoor Advertising*. New York: McGraw-Hill, 1938.

Alexandre, Arsène, M. H. Spielmann, H. C. Bunner, and August Jaccaci. *The Modern Poster*. New York: Charles Scribner's Sons, 1895.

Allen, Frederick Lewis. *Only Yesterday: An Informal History of the 1920s*. New York: Harper and Row, 1931.

America's Highways, 1776–1976: A History of the Federal-Aid Program. Washington, D.C.: U.S. Department of Transportation, Federal Highway Administration, 1976.

America's Roadsides: A Practical Program for Replacing Confusion and Chaos with Sane and Orderly Development. Washington D.C.: American Automobile Association, 1940.

An Analysis and Review of the Highway Advertising Situation. San Francisco: Foster and Kleiser, 1928.

An Appeal to Chambers of Commerce and Civic Organizations. New York: National Roadside Council, n.d.

Andrews, J. J. C. *The Well Built Elephant and Other Roadside Attractions*. New York: Congdon & Weed, 1984.

Aust, Franz, and Robert S. Harrison. *The Values of Art in Advertising*. Menasha, Wis.: George Banta, n.d.

Bailey, Kristin Szylvian. "Fighting 'Civic Smallpox': The Civic Club of Allegheny County's Campaign for Billboard Regulation, 1896–1917." *Western Pennsylvania Historical Magazine* 70, no. 1 (1987): 3–28.

Baker, Paula. "The Domestication of Politics: Women and American Political Society, 1780–1920." *American Historical Review* 89, no. 3 (1984): 620–47.

Baldwin, Peter C. *Domesticating the Street: The Reform of Public Space in Hartford, 1850–1930*. Columbus: Ohio State University Press, 1999.

Bard, Albert S. "Winning the Billboard War." *National Municipal Review* 30, no. 7 (1941): 409–11.

Barnett, Gabrielle. "Drive-by Viewing: Redwoods, Cars, and Visual Consciousness." Paper delivered at the Annual Meeting of the American Society of Environmental History, 2002.

Barnum, P. T. *Struggles and Triumphs, Or, Forty Years' Recollections of P. T. Barnum*. New York: Penguin, 1981.

Barrett, Paul. *The Automobile and Urban Transit: The Formation of Public Policy in Chicago 1900–1930*. Philadelphia: Temple University Press, 1988.

Barrett, Paul, and Mark Rose. "Street Smarts: The Politics of Transportation Statistics in the American City." *Journal of Urban History* 25, no. 3 (1999): 405–33.

Bartholomew, Harland. *Urban Land Uses*. Cambridge, Mass.: Harvard University Press, 1932.

Bartholomew, Harland, Frederick Law Olmsted, and Charles Henry Cheney. *A Major Traffic Street Plan for Los Angeles*. Los Angeles: Committee on Los Angeles Plan of Major Highways of the Traffic Commission of the City and County of Los Angeles, 1924.

Barton, Bruce. *The Man Nobody Knows*. Stone Mountain, Ga.: GA Publishing, Inc., 1998.

Beard, Mary. *Women's Work in Municipal Reform*. New York: Arno Press, 1972.

Beauty and Utility in Outdoor Advertising. Chicago: Outdoor Advertising Association of America, n.d.

Beauty for America: Proceedings of the White House Conference on Natural Beauty. Washington, D.C.: Government Printing Office, 1965.

Belasco, Warren. *Americans on the Road: From Autocamp to Motel*. Cambridge, Mass.: MIT Press, 1979.

Belin, Alletta, Mercedes R. Bilotto, and Thaddeus Carhart. *A Legal Handbook for Billboard Control*. Stanford, Calif.: Stanford Environmental Law Society, 1976.

Berger, John. *Ways of Seeing*. London: Penguin, 1972.

Berger, Michael. *The Devil Wagon in God's Country: The Automobile and Social Change in Rural America, 1893–1929*. Hamden, Conn.: Archon, 1979.

Berkowitz, Michael. "A 'New Deal' for Leisure: Making Mass Tourism during the Great Depression."

In *Being Elsewhere: Tourism, Consumer Culture, and Identity in Modern Europe and North America*, edited by Shelley Baranowski and Ellen Furlough. Ann Arbor: University of Michigan Press, 2001.

Berry, Brian L. "Ribbon Developments in the Urban Business Pattern." *Annals, Association of American Geographers* 49 (March 1959): 145–55.

Berry, Brian L., and Yehoshua Cohen. "Decentralization of Commerce and Industry: The Restructuring of Metropolitan America." In *The Urbanization of the Suburbs*, edited by Louis Masotti and Jeffrey Hadden. Beverly Hills: Sage, 1973.

Billboard: Art on the Road. North Adams, Mass.: Mass MoCA/Cambridge, Mass.: MIT Press, 1999.

The Billboard: A Blot on Nature and a Parasite on Public Improvements. New York: New York Roadside Improvement and Safety Committee, 1939.

Birch, Eugenie Ladner. "From Civic Worker to City Planner: Women and Planning, 1890–1980." In *The American Planner: Biographies and Recollections*, edited by Donald A. Krueckeberg. New York: Methuen, 1983.

Bird, William L., Jr., and Harry R. Rubenstein. *Design for Victory: World War II Posters on the American Home Front*. New York: Princeton Architectural Press, 1998.

Blair, Karen. *The Clubwoman as Feminist: True Womanhood Redefined, 1868–1914*. New York: Holmes and Meier, 1980.

——. *The Torchbearers: Women and Their Amateur Arts Association in America, 1890–1930*. Bloomington: Indiana University Press, 1994.

Blake, Peter. *God's Own Junkyard: The Planned Deterioration of America's Landscape*. New York: Holt, Rinehart, and Winston, 1964.

Bliss, Carey. *Autos across America: A Bibliography of Transcontinental Automobile Travel, 1903–1940*. Austin, Tex.: Jenkins and Reese, 1982.

Blodgett, Peter. "Selling the Scenery: Advertising and the National Parks, 1916–1933." In *Seeing and Being Seen: Tourism and the American West*, edited by David M. Wrobel and Patrick T. Long. Lawrence: University Press of Kansas, 2001.

Bluestone, Daniel. "Roadside Blight and the Reform of Commercial Architecture." In *Roadside America: The Automobile in Design and Culture*, edited by Jan Jennings. Ames: Iowa State University Press, and the Society for Commercial Archeology, 1990.

Boal, F. N., and D. B. Johnson. "The Functions of Retail and Service Establishments on Commercial Ribbons." In *International Structure of the City*, edited by Larry S. Bourne. New York: Oxford University Press, 1971.

Bogart, Michelle. *Artists, Advertising, and the Borders of Art*. Chicago: University of Chicago Press, 1995.

Boime, Albert. *Magisterial Gaze: Manifest Destiny and the American Landscape Painting*. Washington, D.C.: Smithsonian Institution Press, 1991.

Bottles, Scott. *Los Angeles and the Automobile: The Making of the Modern City*. Berkeley and Los Angeles: University of California Press, 1987.

Boyer, M. Christine. *Dreaming the Rational City: The Myth of American City Planning*. Cambridge, Mass.: MIT Press, 1983.

Boyer, Paul. *Urban Masses and Moral Order in America, 1820–1920*. Cambridge, Mass.: Harvard University Press, 1978.

Braden, Donna R., and Judith E. Endelman. *Americans on Vacation*. Dearborn, Mich.: Henry Ford Museum and Greenfield Village, 1990.

Breitenbach, Edgar. *The American Poster*. Washington, D.C.: American Federation of Arts, 1969.

Brinkley, Alan. *The End of Reform: New Deal Liberalism in Recession and War*. New York: Alfred A. Knopf, 1995.

Brown, Alice Spalding. *History of the Outdoor Circle*. Honolulu: n.p., 1962.

Brown, Dona. *Inventing New England: Regional Tourism in the Nineteenth Century*. Washington, D.C.: Smithsonian Institution Press, 1996.

Brownell, Blaine. "A Symbol of Modernity: Attitudes toward the Automobile in Southern Cities in the 1920s." *American Quarterly* 24, no. 1 (1972): 20–44.

Bufford, Samuel. "Beyond the Eye of the Beholder: A New Majority of Jurisdictions Authorize Aesthetic Regulation." *UMKC Law Review* 48, no. 2 (1980): 126–66.

Calkins, Earnest Elmo. *Business the Civilizer*. Boston: Little, Brown, 1928.

Campbell, Josephine L. *How Hawaii Erased a Blot*. Honolulu: Outdoor Circle, n.d.

City Planning Procedure. Washington, D.C.: American Civic Association, 1926.

Civic Improvement in Your Town: A Program and Plan of Procedure. Washington, D.C.: American Civic Association, 1927.

Civic Progress in Harrisburg: Billboards. Harrisburg, Pa.: Municipal League of Harrisburg, 1923.

Cole, Thomas. "Essay on American Scenery" (1835). In *The American Landscape: A Critical Anthology of Prose and Poetry*, edited by John Conron. New York: Oxford University Press, 1973.

Constantine, Mildred, ed. *Word and Image*. New York: Museum of Modern Art/Greenwich, Conn.: New York Graphic Society, 1968.

Converse, Jean. *Survey Research in the United States: Roots and Emergence, 1860–1960*. Berkeley and Los Angeles: University of California Press, 1987.

Corn, Wanda. *The Great American Thing: Modern Art and National Identity, 1915–1935*. Berkeley and Los Angeles: University of California Press, 1999.

——. *In the American Grain: The Billboard Poetics of Charles Demuth*. Poughkeepsie, N.Y.: Vassar College, 1991.

Costonis, John. *Icons and Aliens: Law, Aesthetics, and Environmental Change*. Urbana: University of Illinois, 1989.

——. "Law and Esthetics: A Critique and Reformulation of the Dilemmas." *Michigan Law Review* 80, no. 3 (1982): 355–461.

Crawford, Andrew Wright. *Important Advances toward Eradicating the Billboard Nuisance*. 2d ed. Washington, D.C.: American Civic Association, 1920.

Crawford, Margaret, and Martin Wachs, eds. *The Car and the City: The Automobile, the Built Environment, and Daily Urban Life*. Ann Arbor: University of Michigan Press, 1992.

Creel, George. *How We Advertised America*. New York: Arno Press, 1972.

Cross, Gary. *Time and Money: The Making of Consumer Culture*. New York: Routledge, 1993.

Cullingworth, J. Barry. "Aesthetics in U.S. Planning: From Billboards to Design Controls." *Town Planning Review* 48, no. 2 (1991): 399–414.

——. *Political Culture of Planning: American Land Use Planning in Comparative Perspective*. London: Routledge, 1993.

Davis, Timothy Mark. "Mount Vernon Memorial Highway and the Evolution of the American Parkway." Ph.D. diss., University of Texas, Austin, 1997.

Decentralization: What Is It Doing to Our Cities? Chicago: Urban Land Institute, 1940.

De Salvo, Donna, ed. *"Success is a Job in New York . . .": The Early Art and Business of Andy Warhol*. New York: Grey Art Gallery, New York University/Pittsburgh: Carnegie Museum of Art, 1989.

Dilworth, Leah. *Imagining Indians in the Southwest: Persistent Visions of a Primitive Past*. Washington, D.C.: Smithsonian Institution Press, 1996.

——. "Tourists and Indians in Fred Harvey's Southwest." In *Seeing and Being Seen: Tourism and the American West*, edited by David M. Wrobel and Patrick T. Long. Lawrence: University Press of Kansas, 2001.

Dimendberg, Edward. "The Will to Motorization." *October* 73 (summer 1995): 91–137.

Dirks, Jacqueline. "Righteous Goods: Women's Products, Reform Publicity, and the National Consumer's League." Ph.D. diss., Yale University, 1996.

Dorman, Evelyn S. "Burma-Shave." In *Encyclopedia of Consumer Brands*, edited by Janice Jorgensen. Detroit: St. James Press, 1994.

Dorman, Robert. *Revolt of the Provinces: The Regionalist Movement in America, 1920–1945*. Chapel Hill: University of North Carolina Press, 1993.

Drescher, Timothy. "The Harsh Reality: Billboard Subversion and Graffiti." In *Wall Power*. Philadelphia: Institute of Contemporary Art, University of Pennsylvania, 2000.

Dumenil, Lynn. *The Modern Temper: American Culture and Society in the 1920s*. New York: Hill and Wang, 1995.

Dunlop, M. H. *Sixty Miles from Contentment: Traveling the Nineteenth Century American Interior*. New York: Basic, 1995.

Ebner, Michael. "Re-reading Suburban America: Urban Population Deconcentration, 1810–1980." In *American Urbanism*, edited by Howard Gillette Jr. and Zane L. Miller. New York: Greenwood, 1987.

Ehrhardt, Julia. W*riters of Conviction: The Personal Politics of Zona Gale, Dorothy Canfield Fisher, Rose Wilder Lane, and Josephine Herbst*. Columbia: University of Missouri Press, 2004.

Emerson, Ralph Waldo. "Nature" (1836). In *The American Landscape: A Critical Anthology of Prose and Poetry*, edited by John Conron. New York: Oxford University Press, 1973.

Engler, Franz, and Claude Lichtenstein. *Streamlined: A Metaphor for Progress*. Baden, Switzerland: Lars Müller, 1990.

Essentials of Outdoor Advertising. New York: Association of National Advertisers, 1958.

Evans, Anne M. "Women's Rural Organizations and Their Activities." *United States Department of Agriculture*, Bulletin No. 719. Washington, D.C.: Government Printing Office, 1918.

Ewen, Stuart. "Advertising and the Development of Consumer Society." In *Cultural Politics in Contemporary America*, edited by Ian Angus and Sut Jhally. New York and London: Routledge, 1989.

——. *Captains of Consciousness: Advertising and the Social Roots of the Consumer Culture*. New York: McGraw-Hill, 1976.

——. *PR! A Social History of Spin*. New York: Basic, 1996.

Fairbanks, Evelyn. *The Days of Rondo: A Warm Reminiscence of St. Paul's Thriving Black Community in the 1930s and 1940s*. St. Paul: Minnesota Historical Society Press, 1999.

Federal Control of Outdoor Advertising. Chicago: Outdoor Advertising Association of America, 1958.

Felix Gonzalez-Torres. Los Angeles: Museum of Contemporary Art, 1994.

Fifty Years of Outdoor Advertising, 1901–1951. San Francisco: Foster and Kleiser Company, 1951.

Finger, Charles. *Adventure under Sapphire Skies*. New York: William Morrow, 1931.

Fisher, Irving. "The Decentralization and Suburbanization of Population." *Annals of the American Academy of Political and Social Sciences* 118 (March 1925): 96.

Fishman, Robert. *Bourgeois Utopias: The Rise and Fall of Suburbia*. New York: Basic, 1987.

Flagg, James Montgomery. *Boulevards All the Way—Maybe*. New York: George H. Doran, 1925.

Flanagan, Maureen A. "The City Profitable and the City Livable: Environmental Policy, Gender, and Power in Chicago in the 1910s." *Journal of Urban History* 22, no. 2 (1996): 163–90.

——. "Gender and Urban Political Reform in Chicago: The City Club and the Woman's City Club of Chicago in the Progressive Era." *The American Historical Review* 95, no. 4 (1990): 109–30.

——. *Seeing with Their Hearts: Chicago Women and the Vision of the Good City, 1871–1933*. Princeton, N.J.: Princeton University Press, 2002.

Flink, James. *America Adopts the Automobile*. Cambridge, Mass.: MIT Press, 1970.

——. *The Automobile Age*. Cambridge, Mass.: MIT Press, 1988.

——. *The Car Culture*. Cambridge, Mass.: MIT Press, 1975.

Flint, Richard W. "The Circus." *Quarterly Journal of the Library of Congress* 40, no. 3 (1983): 204–24.

Floyd, Charles F., and Peter J. Shedd. *Highway Beautification: The Environmental Movement's Greatest Failure*. Boulder, Colo.: Westview Press, 1979.

Ford, George B. "What Makes 'The City Beautiful.'" In *Planning Problems of Town, City and Region: Papers and Discussions at the Twenty-first National Conference on City Planning*. Philadelphia: William F. Fell, 1929.

Foster and Kleiser Company Gardens. San Francisco: Foster and Kleiser, 1930.

Foster, George G. *New York by Gas-light*. Berkeley and Los Angeles: University of California Press, 1990.

Foster, Mark. *From Streetcar to Superhighway: American City Planners and Urban Transportation, 1900–1940*. Philadelphia: Temple University Press, 1981.

Fox, Charles Philip, and Tom Parkinson. *Billers, Banners and Bombast: The Story of Circus Advertising*. Boulder, Colo.: Pruett, 1985.

Fox, Stephen. *The Mirror Makers: A History of American Advertising and Its Creators*. New York: William Morrow, 1984.

Frank, Tom. *The Conquest of Cool*. New York: Pantheon, 1997.

Franz, Kathleen. "Narrating Automobility: Travelers, Tinkerers, and Technological Authority in the Twentieth Century." Ph.D. diss., Brown University, 1999.

Fraser, James. *The American Billboard: One Hundred Years*. New York: Harry N. Abrams, 1991.

Frazer, William, and John J. Guthrie, Jr. *The Florida Land Boom: Speculation, Money and the Banks*. Westport, Conn.: Quorum, 1995.

Friedberg, Anne. *Window Shopping: Cinema and the Postmodern*. Berkeley and Los Angeles: University of California Press, 1993.

Frost, E. Allen. *Outdoor Advertising . . . Its Genesis, Development and Place in American Life*. Chicago: Outdoor Advertising Association of America, 1940.

Fulton, K. H. "Radio Address Broadcast over WPG and Network." *The Industry Advances*. New York: Outdoor Advertising Association of America, 1929.

Gannett, Lewis. *Sweet Land*. New York: Doubleday, Doran, 1934.

Gates, Bill. *The Road Ahead*. New York: Penguin, 1995.

Gilbert, James. *Perfect Cities: Chicago's Utopias of 1893*. Chicago: University of Chicago Press, 1991.

Goddard, Stephen. *Getting There: The Epic Struggle between Road and Rail in the American Century*. New York: Basic, 1994.

Goldman, Judith. *James Rosenquist*. New York: Viking, 1985.

Goldstein, Ann, ed. *Barbara Kruger*. Los Angeles: Museum of Contemporary Art/Cambridge, Mass.: MIT Press, 1999.

Goodrum, Charles, and Helen Dalrymple. *Advertising in America: The First Two Hundred Years*. New York: Harry N. Abrams, 1990.

Gould, Lewis L. *Lady Bird Johnson and the Environment*. Kansas: University of Kansas Press, 1989.

Graburn, Nelson. "Tourism: The Sacred Journey." In *Hosts and Guests*, edited by Valene Smith. Philadelphia: University of Pennsylvania Press, 1989.

Green, Harvey. *Fit for America: Health, Fitness, Sport and American Society*. New York: Pantheon Books, 1986.

Guimond, James. *American Photography and the American Dream*. Chapel Hill: University of North Carolina Press, 1991.

Gutfreund, Owen D. "Twentieth Century Sprawl: Accommodating the Automobile and the Decentralization of the United States." Ph.D. diss., Columbia University, 1998.

Hardwick, M. Jeffrey. *Mall Maker: Victor Gruen, Architect of an American Dream*. Philadelphia: University of Pennsylvania Press, 2003.

Harrington, Burton. *Essentials of Poster Design*. Chicago: Poster Advertising Association, 1925.

Harris, Neil. "Iconography and Intellectual History: The Halftone Effect." *Cultural Excursions: Marketing Appetites and Cultural Tastes in Modern America*. Chicago: University of Chicago Press, 1990.

Haskell, Barbara. *The American Century: Art & Culture, 1900–1950*. New York: Whitney Museum of American Art/W. W. Norton, 1999.

Hawley, Ellis. "The Discovery and Study of a 'Corporate Liberalism.'" *Business History Review* 52 (autumn 1978): 309–20.

——. "The New Deal and Business." In *The New Deal*, edited by John Braemen, Robert H. Bremner, and David Brody. Columbus: Ohio State University Press, 1975.

Hayden, Dolores. *Building Suburbia: Green Fields and Urban Growth, 1820–2000*. New York: Pantheon, 2003.

——. *Redesigning the American Dream: The Future of Housing, Work, and Family Life*. New York: W.W. Norton, 1984.

Hayward, Walter S. "The Chain Store and Distribution." *Annals of the American Academy of Political and Social Science* 115 (September 1924): 220–25.

Heimann, Jim. *California Crazy and Beyond: Roadside Vernacular Architecture*. San Francisco: Chronicle Books, 2001.

Heller, Steven, and Louise Fili. *Streamline: American Art Deco Graphic Design*. San Francisco: Chronicle Books, 1995.

Henderson, Sally. *Billboard Art*. San Francisco: Chronicle Books, 1980.

Henkin, David M. *City Reading: Written Words and Public Spaces in Antebellum New York*. New York: Columbia University Press, 1998.

Higham, John. "The Reorientation of American Culture in the 1890s." *Writing American History: Essays on Modern Scholarship*. Bloomington: Indiana University Press, 1970.

Highway Beautification Act of 1965. San Francisco: Foster and Kleiser, 1965.

Hills, Patricia. *Stuart Davis*. New York: Harry N. Abrams/Washington, D.C.: National Museum of American Art, Smithsonian Institution, 1996.

Hines, Thomas S. *Burnham of Chicago: Architect and Planner*. Chicago: University of Chicago Press, 1979.

Hise, Greg. *Magnetic Los Angeles: Planning the Twentieth-Century Metropolis*. Baltimore: Johns Hopkins University Press, 1997.

Historical Statistics of the U.S., Colonial Times to 1957. Washington, D.C.: U.S. Bureau of the Census, 1957.

Honnef, Klaus. *Andy Warhol, 1928–1987: Commerce into Art*. Cologne: Benedikt Taschen Verlag, 1993.

Hopkins, F. T. *The Roadside Advertising Controversy*. Chicago: National Outdoor Advertising Bureau, 1938.

Hornung, Clarence P. *The Way It Was: New York, 1850–1890*. New York: Schocken, 1977.

Horowitz, Daniel. *The Morality of Spending: Attitudes toward the Consumer Society in America, 1875–1940*. Baltimore: Johns Hopkins University Press, 1985.

Houck, John, ed. *Outdoor Advertising: History and Regulation*. Notre Dame, Ind.: University of Notre Dame Press, 1969.

How You Can Win More Customers with Outdoor Advertising. New York: Outdoor Advertising Inc., 1959.

Howells, William Dean. *The Rise of Silas Lapham*. New York: Vintage/The Library of America, 1992.

Hower, Ralph M. *The History of an Advertising Agency: N. W. Ayer and Son at Work, 1869–1939*. Cambridge, Mass.: Harvard University Press, 1939.

Hoy, Suellen. "Municipal Housekeeping: The Role of Women in Improving Urban Sanitation Practices, 1870–1917." In *Pollution and Reform in American Cities, 1870–1930*, edited by Martin V. Melosi. Austin: University of Texas Press, 1980.

Hunnicut, Benjamin. *Work without End: Abandoning Shorter Hours for the Right to Work*. Philadelphia: Temple University Press, 1988.

Hutchison, Janet. "Building for Babbitt: The State and the Suburban Home Ideal." *Journal of Policy History* 9, no. 2 (1997): 184–210.

Huthmacher, J. Joseph, and Warren I. Susman, eds. *Herbert Hoover and the Crisis of American Capitalism*. Cambridge, Mass.: Schenkman, 1973.

Ideas and Actions: A History of the Highway Research Board, 1920–1970. Washington, D.C.: Highway Research Board, National Academy of Sciences, 1970.

Ihlder, John. "The Automobile and Community Planning." *Annals of the American Academy of Political and Social Sciences* 116 (November 1924): 199–205.

Interrante, Joseph. "You Can't Go to Town in a Bathtub." *Radical History Review* 21 (fall 1979): 151–68.

Jackson, Kenneth. *Crabgrass Frontier: The Suburbanization of the United States*. New York: Oxford University Press, 1985.

Jacob, Mary Jane, ed. *Places with a Past: New Site Specific Art at Charleston's Spoleto Festival*. New York: Rizzoli International Publications/Charleston: Spoleto Festival USA, 1991.

Jakle, John A. *The Tourist: Travel in Twentieth Century North America*. Lincoln: University of Nebraska, 1985.

Jakle, John A., and Richard L. Mattson. "The Evolution of a Commercial Strip." *Journal of Cultural Geography* 2 (spring-summer 1981): 12–25.

Jakle, John A., and Keith Sculle. *The Gas Station in America*. Baltimore: Johns Hopkins University Press, 1994.

James Rosenquist. Toronto: National Gallery of Canada, 1968.

James Van Der Zee. New York: Harry N. Abrams, 1993.

Jarvis, George Kirkham. "The Diffusion of the Automobile in the United States: 1895–1969." Ph.D. diss., University of Michigan, 1972.

Jessup, Elon. *The Motor Camping Book*. New York and London: G. P. Putnam's Sons, 1921.

Jhally, Sut. *The Codes of Advertising: Fetishism and the Political Economy of Meaning in the Consumer Society*. London: Frances Pinter, 1987.

Jussim, Estelle. *Visual Communication and the Graphic Arts*. New York: R. R. Bowker, 1983.

Kammen, Michael. *Mystic Chords of Memory: The Transformation of Tradition in American Culture*. New York: Vintage, 1993.

Karp, James P. "The Evolving Meaning of Aesthetics in Land-Use Regulation." *Columbia Journal of Environmental Law* 15, no. 2 (1990): 307–28.

Kasson, John. *Civilizing the Machine: Technology and Republican Values in America*. New York: Grossman, 1976.

Kaszynski, William. *The American Highway: The History and Culture of Roads in the United States*. Jefferson, N.C.: McFarland, 2000.

Keeping You Posted. New York: National Outdoor Advertising Bureau, n.d.

Keller, Judith. "Evans and Agee: 'The Great American Roadside' (*Fortune* 1934)." *History of Photography* 16, no. 2 (1992): 170–71.

Kerber, Linda. "Separate Spheres, Female Worlds, Woman's Place: The Rhetoric of Women's History." *Journal of American History* 75 (June 1988): 9–39.

Kern, Stephen. *The Culture of Time and Space, 1880–1918*. Cambridge, Mass.: Harvard University Press, 1983.

Kiehl, David W., ed. *American Art Posters of the 1890s*. New York: Metropolitan Museum of Art/Harry N. Abrams, 1987.

Kimball, Winfield A., and Maurice H. Decker. *Touring with Tent and Trailer*. New York: Whittlesey House, 1937.

Kirby, Lynne. *Parallel Tracks: The Railroad and Silent Cinema*. Durham, N.C.: Duke University Press, 1997.

Klein, Naomi. *No Logo: Taking Aim at the Brand Bullies*. New York: Picador, 2001.

Kling, Rob, Spencer Olin, and Mark Poster, eds. *Postsuburban California: The Transformation of Orange County since World War II*. Berkeley and Los Angeles: University of California Press, 1991.

Knutson, Anne Classen. "Breasts, Brawn and Selling a War: American World War I Propaganda Posters 1917–1918." Ph.D. diss., University of Pittsburgh, 1997.

Kouwenhoven, John A. *The Columbia Historical Portrait of New York: An Essay in Graphic History*. New York: Harper and Row, 1972.

Krausz, Sigmund. *Street Types of Great American Cities*. Chicago: Werner, 1896.

Lacy, Suzanne, ed. *Mapping the Terrain: New Genre Public Art*. Seattle: Bay Press, 1995.

Laird, Pamela Walker. *Advertising Progress: American Business and the Rise of Consumer Marketing*. Baltimore: Johns Hopkins University Press, 1998.

Larned, W. Livingston. *Illustration in Advertising*. New York: McGraw-Hill, 1925.

Lawton, Elizabeth. *Digest of Address on Billboard Campaign, Delivered at the Biennial (Los Angeles) Art Day, 1924*. New York: National Committee for Restriction of Outdoor Advertising, 1924.

——. "Regulation of Outdoor Advertising." In *Planning Problems of Town City and Region: Papers and Discussions at the Eighteenth National Conference on City Planning*. Philadelphia: William F. Fell, 1926.

Leach, William. *Land of Desire: Merchants, Money, and the Rise of a New American Culture*. New York: Vintage, 1993.

Lears, T. J. Jackson. "From Salvation to Self-Realization." In *The Culture of Consumption*, edited by Richard Wightman Fox and T. J. Jackson Lears. New York: Pantheon Books, 1983.

——. *No Place of Grace: Antimodernism and the Transformation of American Culture*. New York: Pantheon, 1981.

——. "Packaging the Folk: Tradition and Amnesia in American Advertising, 1880–1940." In *Folk Roots,*

New Roots: Folklore in American Life, edited by Jane S. Becker and Barbara Franco. Lexington, Mass.: Museum of Our National Heritage, 1988.

Lebhar, Godfrey M. *Chain Stores in America*. New York: Chain Store Publishing, 1952.

Leuchtenberg, William. *The Perils of Prosperity, 1914–1932*. Chicago: University of Chicago Press, 1993.

Levine, Lawrence W. "Progress and Nostalgia: The Self Image of the Nineteen Twenties." *The Unpredictable Past: Explorations in American Cultural History*. New York: Oxford University Press, 1993.

Lewis, Sinclair. *Babbitt*. New York: New American Library, 1961.

——. *Free Air*. Lincoln: University of Nebraska Press, 1993.

——. *Main Street*. New York: Harcourt, Brace, and World, Inc., 1961.

Liebs, Chester. *Main Street to Miracle Mile: American Roadside Architecture*. Boston: Little, Brown and Company, 1985.

Lindsay, Vachel. *The Art of the Moving Picture*. New York: Macmillan, 1915.

Linker, Kate. *Love for Sale: The Words and Pictures of Barbara Kruger*. New York: Harry N. Abrams, 1990.

Lippincott, Wilmott. *Outdoor Advertising*. New York: McGraw-Hill, 1923.

Little, Arthur D. *A Study of Human Response to Visual Environments in Urban Areas*. N.p.: n.p., n.d.

Longstreth, Richard. *City Center to Regional Mall: Architecture, the Automobile, and Retailing in Los Angeles, 1920–1950*. Cambridge, Mass.: MIT Press, 1997.

——. "Don't Get Out: The Automobile's Impact on Five Building Types in Los Angeles, 1921–1941." *Arris: Journal of the Southeast Chapter of the Society of Architectural Historians* 7 (1996): 32–56.

——. *The Drive-in, the Supermarket, and the Transformation of Commercial Space in Los Angeles, 1914–1941*. Cambridge, Mass.: MIT Press, 1999.

——. "The Forgotten Arterial Landscape: Photographic Documentation of Commercial Development along Los Angeles Boulevards during the Interwar Years." *Journal of Urban History* 233, no. 4 (1997): 437–60.

——. "Silver Spring: 'Downtown' for Metropolitan Washington." In *Streets: Critical Perspectives on Public Space*, edited by Zeynep Celik, Diane Favro, and Richard Ingersoll. Berkeley and Los Angeles: University of California Press, 1994.

Lovelace, Eldridge. *Harland Bartholomew: His Contributions to American Urban Planning*. Urbana: University of Illinois, Department of Urban and Regional Planning, 1993.

MacCannell, Dean. *The Tourist: A New Theory of the Leisure Class*. New York: Schocken, 1976.

Machor, James L. *Pastoral Cities: Urban Ideals and the Symbolic Landscape of America*. Madison: University of Wisconsin Press, 1987.

Mackaye, Benton. *The New Exploration: A Philosophy of Regional Planning*. New York: Harcourt, Brace, 1928.

The Main Street Plan or Small Town Market Coverage. New York: Outdoor Advertising, n.d.

Mandelker, Daniel, and William R. Ewald. *Street Graphics and the Law*. Washington, D.C.: Planners Press, American Planning Association, 1988.

Manual of the Outdoor Advertising Association of America. Chicago: Outdoor Advertising Association of America, 1926.

Marchand, Roland. *Advertising the American Dream: Making Way for Modernity, 1920–1940*. Berkeley and Los Angeles: University of California Press, 1985.

——. *Creating the Corporate Soul: The Rise of Public Relations and Corporate Imagery in American Big Business*. Berkeley and Los Angeles: University of California Press, 1998.

Margolies, John. *Pump and Circumstance: Glory Days of the Gas Station*. Boston: Little, Brown, 1993.

Margolin, Victor. *American Poster Renaissance*. New York: Watson-Guptill, 1975.

Margolin, Victor, Ira Brichta, and Vivian Brichta, *The Promise and the Product: 200 Years of American Advertising Posters*. New York: Macmillan, 1979.

Markets in Motion: The Wilbur Smith Study of Outdoor Advertising. Chicago: Outdoor Advertising Association of America, 1960.

Marling, Karal Ann. *The Colossus of Roads: Myth and Symbol along the American Highway*. Minneapolis: University of Minnesota Press, 1984.

Marsh, Margaret. *Suburban Lives*. New Brunswick, N.J.: Rutgers University Press, 1990.

Marx, Leo. *Machine in the Garden: Technology and the Pastoral Ideal in America*. London: Oxford University Press, 1964.

Mattelart, Armand. *Advertising International: The Privatisation of Public Space*. London: Routledge, 1991.

May, Earl Chapin. *The Circus from Rome to Ringling*. New York: Duffield and Green, 1932.

May, Lary. *Screening Out the Past: The Birth of Mass Culture and the Motion Picture Industry*. New York: Oxford University Press, 1980.

Mayer, Robert N. *The Consumer Movement: Guardians of the Marketplace*. Boston: Twayne, 1989.

McClintock, Miller. *A Traffic Control Plan for Kansas City*. Kansas City, Mo.: Chamber of Commerce of Kansas City, 1930.

McClintock, Miller, and John Paver. *Traffic and Trade: An Introduction to the Analysis of the Relationship between the Daily Habitual Movement of People and Their Trade Activities in Markets*. New York: McGraw-Hill, 1935.

Mcquiston, Liz. *Graphic Agitation: Social and Political Graphics since the Sixties*. London: Phaidon, 1993.

McShane, Clay. *Down the Asphalt Path: The Automobile and the American City*. New York: Columbia University Press, 1994.

Meggs, Philip B. *A History of Graphic Design*. New York: John Wiley and Sons, 1998.

Meier, August, and Elliott Rudwick. "The Boycott Movement against Jim Crow Streetcars in the South." *Journal of American History* 55, no. 4 (1969): 756–75.

Meikle, Jeffrey L. *The City of Tomorrow: Model 1937*. New York: Pentagram Papers, 1983.

——. "Domesticating Modernity." In *Designing Modernity: The Art of Reform and Persuasion*, edited by Wendy Kaplan. New York: Thames and Hudson, 1995.

——. *Twentieth Century Limited: Industrial Design in America*. Philadelphia: Temple University Press, 1979.

Merton, John W. "Stone by Stone along a Hundred Years with the House of Strobridge." *Bulletin of the Historical and Philosophical Society of Ohio* 8, no. 1 (1950): 3–48.

Meyer, Richard. "This is to Enrage You: Gran Fury and the Graphics of AIDS Activism." In *But Is It Art? The Spirit of Art as Activism*, edited by Nina Felshin. Seattle: Bay Press, 1995.

Miller, Angela. *The Empire of the Eye: Landscape Representation and American Cultural Politics, 1825–1875*. Ithaca, N.Y.: Cornell University Press, 1993.

Miller, David, ed. *American Iconology*. New Haven, Conn.: Yale University Press, 1993.

Miller, Perry. *Errand into the Wilderness*. Cambridge, Mass.: Harvard University Press, 1964.

——. *Nature's Nation*. Cambridge, Mass.: Belknap Press, 1967.

Mitchell, W. J. T. "An Interview with Barbara Kruger." In *Art and the Public Sphere*, edited by W. J. T. Mitchell. Chicago: University of Chicago Press, 1990.

Mock, James R., and Cedric Larson. *Words that Won the War: The Story of the CPI*. Princeton, N.J.: Princeton University Press, 1939.

Moline, Norman. *Mobility and the Small Town, 1900–1930*. Chicago: University of Chicago Press, 1971.

Monroe, Alden N. "Big Top to Bijou: The Golden Age of the Show Poster." *Queen City Heritage* (Cincinnati), summer 1984, 3–14.

Moores, Shaun. "Television, Geography, and 'Mobile Privatization.'" *European Journal of Communication* 8 (1993): 365–79.

Morrison, Ernest. *J. Horace McFarland: A Thorn for Beauty*. Harrisburg, Pa.: Commonwealth of Pennsylvania, Pennsylvania Historical and Museum Commission, 1995.

Morse, Margaret. "An Ontology of Everyday Distraction: The Freeway, the Mall, and Television." In *Logics of Television: Essays in Cultural Criticism*, edited by Patricia Mellencamp. Bloomington: Indiana University Press, 1990.

Moskowitz, Marina. "Standards Bearers: Material Culture and Middle-Class Communities at the Turn of the Twentieth Century." Ph.D. diss., Yale University, 1999.

Moton, Robert Russa. *What the Negro Thinks*. Garden City, N.Y.: Garden City, 1929.

Mott, Frank Luther. *A History of American Magazines, 1885–1905*. Cambridge, Mass.: Harvard University Press, 1957.

Mowry, Don E. *Community Advertising: How to Advertise the Community Where You Live*. Madison, Wis.: Cantwell Press, 1924.

——. *Outdoor Community Advertising*. Madison, Wis.: American Community Advertising Association, 1928.

Muncy, Robin. *Creating a Female Dominion in American Reform, 1890–1935*. New York and Oxford: Oxford University Press, 1991.

Murdock, Graham. "Blindspots about Western Marxism: A Reply to Dallas Smythe." *Canadian Journal of Political and Social Theory* 2, no. 2 (1978): 109–19.

Nasaw, David. *Going Out: The Rise and Fall of Public Amusements*. New York: Basic, 1993.

Nash, Roderick. *The Nervous Generation: American Thought, 1917–1930*. Chicago: Rand McNally, 1970.

——. *Wilderness and the American Mind*. New Haven, Conn.: Yale University Press, 1967.

National Committee for Restriction of Outdoor Advertising: What It Is and What It Seeks to Do. New York: National Committee for Restriction of Outdoor Advertising, n.d.

The National Cyclopaedia of American Biography. Ann Arbor, Mich: University Microfilms, 1967.

National Roadside Council: What It Is and What It Does. New York: National Roadside Council, 1939.

Noble, David F. *America by Design: Science, Technology, and the Rise of Corporate Capitalism*. Oxford: Oxford University Press, 1977.

Norris, Kathleen. *What Do You Want to See?* San Francisco: Standard Oil Company of California, 1929.

Novak, Barbara. *Nature and Culture: American Landscape and Painting, 1825–1875*. Rev. ed. New York: Oxford University Press, 1995.

Nye, David. *Electrifying America: Social Meanings of a New Technology*. Cambridge, Mass.: MIT Press, 1990.

Ohmann, Richard. *Selling Culture: Magazines, Markets, and Class at the Turn of the Century*. New York: Verso, 1996.

One Hundred Reformers versus 25,000 Wage Earners. New York: Outdoor Advertising Association of America, c. 1936.

Outdoor Advertising and the Agency. Chicago: National Outdoor Advertising Bureau, 1927.

Outdoor Advertising Organizations. Johnstown, Pa.: Outdoor Advertising Association of Pennsylvania, 1936.

Outdoor Advertising: A Channel of Communication in the War Effort. New York: Outdoor Advertising Association, 1943.

Outdoor Advertising: A Channel of Communication with the Public. New York: Outdoor Advertising Association, 1942.

Outdoor Advertising: General Information. Chicago: National Outdoor Advertising Bureau, 1923.

Outdoor Advertising: A Primary Medium. New York: Outdoor Advertising Incorporated, n.d.

Outdoor Advertising–the Modern Marketing Force. Chicago: Outdoor Advertising Association of America, 1928.

Outdoor 101. New York: Institute of Outdoor Advertising, n.d.

The Pacific Coast as a Market for Commodities and the Outdoor Advertising Facilities Available in This Territory. 2d ed. San Francisco: Foster and Kleiser, 1928.

Pancoast, Chalmers Lowell. *Trail Blazers of Advertising*. New York: Grafton Press, 1926.

Parsons, Frank Alva. *The Art Appeal in Display Advertising*. New York: Harper and Brothers, 1921.

Patton, Phil. *Open Road: A Celebration of the American Highway*. New York: Simon and Schuster, 1986.

Paxson, Frederic L. "The Highway Movement, 1916–1935." *American Historical Review* 51 (1946): 236–53.

Pease, Otis. *The Responsibilities of American Advertising: Private Control and Public Influence, 1920–1940*. New Haven, Conn.: Yale University Press, 1958.

Peters, Harry T. *America on Stone*. Garden City, N.Y.: Doubleday, Doran, 1931.

Peterson, Jon A. "The City Beautiful Movement: Forgotten Origins and Lost Meanings." *Journal of Urban History* 2, no. 4 (1976): 415–34.

Peterson, Theodore. *Magazines in the Twentieth Century*. Urbana: University of Illinois Press, 1956.

Pierson, George W. *The Moving American*. New York: Alfred A. Knopf, 1973.

Pollay, Richard W., Jung S. Lee, and David Carter-Whitney. "Separate, But Not Equal: Racial Segmentation in Cigarette Advertising." *Journal of Advertising* 21, no. 1 (1992): 45–58.

Poole, Caroline. *A Modern Prairie Schooner on the Transcontinental Trail: The Story of a Motor Trip*. San Francisco: n.p., 1919.

Pope, Daniel. "The Advertising Industry and WWI." *The Public Historian* 2, no. 3 (1980): 4–25.

——. *The Making of Modern Advertising*. New York: Basic, 1983.

The Poster: War Souvenir Edition. New York: Outdoor Advertising Association of America, 1919.

Pratt, Mary Louise. *Imperial Eyes: Travel Writing and Transculturation*. New York: Routledge, 1992.

Presbrey, Frank. *The History and Development of Advertising*. Garden City, N.Y.: Doubleday, Doran, 1929.

Presenting the Truth about Outdoor Advertising. Chicago: Outdoor Advertising Association of America, 1957.

President's Conference on Unemployment. *Recent Economic Changes in the United States*. New York: McGraw-Hill, 1929.

Price, Matlack, and Horace Brown. *How to Put in Patriotic Posters the Stuff That Makes People Stop–Look–Act!* Washington, D.C.: National Committee of Patriotic Societies, n.d.

Progress in 1925: National Committee for Restriction of Outdoor Advertising. New York: National Committee for Restriction of Outdoor Advertising, 1925.

Protecting Our Roadsides for Permanency or 'The Auto Graveyard'–Which? N.p.: Associated Clubs of Virginia for Roadside Development, 1941.

The Purpose of NOAB. New York: National Outdoor Advertising Bureau, n.d.

Purvis, Tom. *Poster Progress*. London: The Studio, 1938.

Radde, Bruce. *The Merritt Parkway*. New Haven, Conn.: Yale University Press, 1993.

Rae, John B. *American Automobile: A Brief History*. Chicago: University of Chicago Press, 1965.

——. *The Road and the Car in American Life*. Cambridge, Mass.: MIT Press, 1971.

Report for Outdoor Advertising Incorporated of New York, N.Y. New York: Barrington Associates, 1937.

Report of the Mayor's Billboard Advertising Commission of the City of New York, August 1, 1913. New York: M. B. Brown, 1913.

Ribbons of Gold. San Francisco: Foster and Kleiser, 1955.

The Roadside Advertising Controversy. New York: New York City Federation of Women's Clubs, 1939.

Roadside Protection: A Study of the Problem and a Legislative Guide. Washington, D.C.: American Automobile Association, 1941.

The Roadsides of California: A Survey. Washington, D.C.: American Nature Association for the National Council for Protection of Roadside Beauty, n.d.

The Roadsides of North Carolina: A Survey. Washington, D.C.: American Nature Association for the National Council for Protection of Roadside Beauty, 1930.

The Roadsides of Oregon: A Survey. Washington, D.C.: American Nature Association for the National Council for Protection of Roadside Beauty, 1930.

Robinson, Richard, comp. *United States Business History, 1602–1988*. New York: Greenwood, 1990.

Rogin, Michael. "Nature as Politics and Nature as Romance in America." *Ronald Reagan, the Movie and Other Episodes in Political Democracy*. Berkeley and Los Angeles: University of California Press, 1987.

Rose, Mark H. *Cities of Light and Heat: Domestication of Gas and Electricity in Urban America*. University Park, Pa.: Pennsylvania State University Press, 1996.

——. *Interstate: Express Highway Politics, 1939–1989*. Knoxville: University of Tennessee Press, 1990.

Rosenberg, Rosalind. *Divided Lives: American Women in the Twentieth Century*. New York: Hill and Wang, 1992.

Ross, Andrew. *Real Love: In Pursuit of Cultural Justice*. New York: New York University Press, 1998.

Rothman, Sheila. *Woman's Proper Place: A History of Changing Ideals and Practices*. New York: Basic, 1978.

Rowell, George Presbury. *Forty Years an Advertising Agent, 1865–1905*. New York: Franklin, 1926.

Rowsome, Frank, Jr. *The Verse by the Side of the Road*. Brattleboro, Vt.: Stephen Greene Press, 1965.

Sachs, Wolfgang. *For the Love of the Automobile: Looking Back into the History of Our Desires*. Berkeley and Los Angeles: University of California Press, 1992.

St. Clair, David J. *The Motorization of American Cities*. New York: Praeger, 1986.

Sams, E. C. "The Justification of the Chain Store in Our Present System of Distribution." *Annals of the American Academy of Political and Social Science* 115 (September 1924): 226–35.

Save the Beauty of America: The Landscape Is No Place for Advertising. Washington, D.C.: General Federation of Women's Clubs, Department of Art, Billboard Restriction Committee, n.d.

Samuel, Lawrence R. *Pledging Allegiance: American Identity and the Bond Drive of World War II*. Washington, D.C.: Smithsonian Institution Press, 1997.

Sann, Paul. *The Lawless Decade*. New York: Crown, 1957.

Schivelbusch, Wolfgang. *Disenchanted Night: The Industrialization of Light*. Berkeley and Los Angeles: University of California Press, 1988.

——. *The Railway Journey: Trains and Travel in the Nineteenth Century*. New York: Urizen Books, 1980.

Schlager, Ken. "On the Boards, 1894–1920." *Billboard: One Hundredth Anniversary Issue 1894–1994*. New York: BPI Communications, 1994.

Schmitt, Peter J. *Back to Nature: The Arcadian Myth in Urban America*. Baltimore: Johns Hopkins University Press, 1990.

Schultz, Quentin J. "Legislating Morality: The Progressive Response to American Outdoor Advertising, 1900–1917." *Journal of Popular Culture* 17, no. 4 (1984): 37–44.

Sears, John. *Sacred Places: American Tourist Attractions in the Nineteenth Century*. New York: Oxford University Press, 1989.

Seely, Bruce. *Building the American Highway System: Engineers as Policy Makers*. Philadelphia: Temple University Press, 1987.

Sesser, William G., and Harry Weissberger. *Solving Advertising Art Problems*. New York: Advertising Artists, 1919.

Shaffer, Marguerite S. "Negotiating National Identity." In *Reopening the American West*, edited by Hal K. Rothman. Tempe: University of Arizona Press, 1998.

——. "The Search for Identity in the Tourist Landscape." In *Seeing and Being Seen: Tourism and the American West*, edited by David M. Wrobel and Patrick T. Long. Lawrence: University Press of Kansas, 2001.

——. *See America First: Tourism and National Identity, 1880–1940*. Washington, D.C.: Smithsonian Institution Press, 2001.

Shaw, Nate. *All God's Dangers: The Life of Nate Shaw*. Compiled by Theodore Rosengarten. New York: Alfred A. Knopf, 1974.

Shedd, Peter J. *Highway Beautification: The Environmental Movement's Greatest Failure*. Boulder, Colo.: Westview Press, 1979.

Sies, Mary Corbin. "'God's Very Kingdom on the Earth': The Design Program for the American Suburban Home, 1877–1917." In *Modern Architecture in America: Visions and Revisions*. Edited by Richard Guy Wilson and Sidney K. Robinson. Ames: Iowa State University Press, 1991.

Sies, Mary Corbin, and Charles Silver, eds. *Planning the Twentieth-Century City*. Baltimore: Johns Hopkins University Press, 1996.

Sklar, Martin J. *The Corporate Reconstruction of American Capitalism, 1890–1916*. New York: Pantheon, 1984.

——. "Woodrow Wilson and the Political Economy of Modern United States Liberalism." *Studies on the Left* 1, no. 3 (1960): 14–47.

Slotkin, Richard. *Regeneration through Violence*. Middletown, Conn.: Wesleyan University Press, 1973.

Smith, Daniel Scott. "Family Limitation, Sexual Control, and Domestic Feminism in Victorian America." In *Clio's Consciousness Raised: New Perspectives in the History of Women*, edited by Mary Hartman and Lois Banner. New York: Harpers Colophon Books, 1974.

Smith, Henry Nash. *Virgin Land: The American West as Symbol and Myth*. Cambridge, Mass.: Harvard University Press, 1978 [1950].

Smythe, Dallas. "Communications: Blindspot of Western Marxism." *Canadian Journal of Political and Social Theory* 1, no. 3 (1977): 1–27.

——. *Dependency Road: Communications, Capitalism, Consciousness, and Canada*. Norwood, N.J.: Ablex, 1981.

Sontag, Susan. "Notes on Camp." In *Against Interpretation*. New York: Anchor, 1986.

——. *On Photography*. New York: Farrar, Straus and Giroux, 1977.

Spain, Daphne. *How Women Saved the City*. Minneapolis: University of Minnesota Press, 2001.

Spears, Timothy. "'All Things to All Men': The Commercial Traveler and the Rise of Modern Statesmanship." *American Quarterly* 45, no. 4 (1993): 524–55.

Spector, Nancy. *Felix Gonzalez-Torres*. New York: Guggenheim Museum, 1995.

Starch, Daniel, and Staff. *The Characteristics of Urban Outdoor Poster Readers*. New York: Outdoor Advertising Incorporated, c. 1956.

Starr, Tama, and Edward Hayman. *Signs and Wonders*. New York: Currency-Doubleday, 1998.

The State Highways: The Lesson of the Mohawk Trail. Boston: Massachusetts Forestry Association, n.d.

Steel, David. "Surrealism, Literature of Advertising and the Advertising of Literature in France, 1910–1930." *French Studies* 41, no. 3 (1987): 283–97.

Stein, Clarence S. *Towards New Towns for America*. Cambridge, Mass.: MIT Press, 1989.

Stein, Clarence S., and Catherine Bauer. "Store Buildings and Neighborhood Shopping Centers." *Architectural Record* 75 (February 1934): 174–87.

Steinbeck, John. *The Grapes of Wrath*. New York: Viking, 1976.

Steiner, Jesse Frederick. *Americans at Play: Recent Trends in Recreation and Leisure Time Activities*. New York and London: McGraw-Hill, 1933.

Sterner, Richard. *The Negro's Share: A Study of Income, Consumption, Housing, and Public Assistance*. Westport, Conn.: Negro Universities Press, 1971.

Stockett, Letitia. *America: First, Fast, and Furious*. Baltimore: Norman Remington, 1930.

Stoddard, Jacqueline L., C. Anderson Johnson, Tess Boley-Cruz, and Steve Sussman. "Targeted Tobacco Markets: Outdoor Advertising in Los Angeles Minority Areas." *American Journal of Public Health* 87, no. 7 (1997): 1232–33.

Stradling, David. *Smokestacks and Progressives: Environmentalists, Engineers, and Air Quality in America, 1881–1951*. Baltimore: Johns Hopkins University Press, 1999.

Strasser, Susan. *Satisfaction Guaranteed: The Making of the American Mass Market*. New York: Pantheon Books, 1989.

Strauss, Steve. *Moving Images: The Transportation Poster in America*. New York: Fullcourt Press, 1984.

Streeter, Thomas. *Selling the Air: A Critique of the Policy of Commercial Broadcasting in the United States*. Chicago: University of Chicago Press, 1996.

Susman, Warren. "Communication and Culture." In *Mass Media between the Wars: Perceptions of Cultural Tension, 1918–1941*, edited by Catherine L. Cover and John D. Stevens. Syracuse, N.Y.: Syracuse University Press, 1984.

——. *Culture as History: The Transformation of American Society in the Twentieth Century*. New York: Pantheon Books, 1984.

Sussman, Carl, ed. *Planning the Fourth Migration: The Neglected Vision of the Regional Planning Association of America*. Cambridge, Mass.: MIT Press, 1976.

Sutter, Paul S. *Driven Wild: How the Fight against Automobiles Launched the Modern Wilderness Movement*. Seattle: University of Washington Press, 2002.

Szczygiel, Bonj. "'City Beautiful' Revisited: An Analysis of Nineteenth-Century Civic Improvement Efforts." *Journal of Urban History* 29, no. 2 (2003): 107–32.

Taylor, Charles R., and Weih Chang. "The History of Outdoor Advertising Regulation in the United States." *Journal of Macromarketing* 15, no. 1 (1995): 47–60.

Tedlow, Richard. *New and Improved: The Story of Mass Marketing in America*. New York: Basic Books, 1990.

Thompson, George F. *Landscape in America*. Austin: University of Texas Press, 1995.

Tobey, Ronald C. *Technology as Freedom: The New Deal and Electrical Modernization of the American Home*. Berkeley and Los Angeles: University of California Press, 1996.

Tocker, Phillip. "Standardized Outdoor Advertising: History, Economics, and Self-Regulation." In *Outdoor Advertising: History and Regulation*, edited by John W. Houck. Notre Dame, Ind.: University of Notre Dame Press, 1969.

Toll Roads and Free Roads. Washington, D.C.: Bureau of Public Roads, 1939.

Trachtenberg, Alan. *Incorporation of America: Culture and Society in the Gilded Age*. New York: Hill and Wang, 1982.

——. *Reading American Photographs: Images as History*. New York: Noonday Press, 1990.

Truettner, William H., and Alan Wallach, eds. *Thomas Cole: Landscape into History*. New Haven: Yale University Press, and Washington, D.C.: National Museum of American Art, Smithsonian Institution, 1994.

Turner, Edith, and Victor Turner. *Image and Pilgrimage in Christian Culture: Anthropological Perspectives*. New York: Columbia University Press, 1978.

Updegraff, Robert R. "The New American Tempo." In *The New American Tempo*, edited by Frederick C. Kendall. New York: Advertising and Selling, 1925.

Urry, John. *The Tourist Gaze: Leisure and Travel in Contemporary Society*. London: Sage, 1990.

U.S. Department of Transportation. *America's Highways, 1776–1976: A History of the Federal-Aid Program*. Washington, D.C.: Federal Highway Administration, 1976.

Vance, Linda D. *May Mann Jennings: Florida's Genteel Activist*. Gainesville: University of Florida Press, 1985.

Van de Water, Frederic F. *The Family Flivvers to Frisco*. New York and London: D. Appleton, 1927.

Van Schaack, Eric. "Artists and Art in the Service of War and Peace." *Journal of the Picker Art Gallery* 3, no. 2 (1990–1991): 7–60.

Varnedoe, Kirk, and Adam Gopnik. *High and Low: Modern Art and Popular Culture*. New York: Museum of Modern Art, 1990.

Vaughn, Stephen. *Holding Fast the Inner Lines: Democracy, Nationalism, and the Committee for Public Information*. Chapel Hill: University of North Carolina Press, 1980.

Venturi, Robert. *Complexity and Contradiction in Architecture*. New York: Museum of Modern Art, 1966.

Venturi, Robert, Denise Scott Brown, and Stephen Izenour. *Learning from Las Vegas*. Cambridge, Mass.: MIT Press, 1972.

Vermont Federation of Women's Clubs. *Hospitality de Luxe: Pomp of Highways and Glory of Roadsides*. Burlington, Vt.: Lane Press, 1929.

Viehe, Fred W. "Black Gold Suburbs: The Influence of the Extractive Industry on the Suburbanization of Los Angeles, 1890–1930." *Journal of Urban History* 8, no. 1 (1981): 3–26.

Vieyra, Daniel. *Fill 'er Up: An Architectural History of America's Gas Stations*. New York: Collier Macmillan, 1979.

Vossler, Bill. *Burma-Shave: The Rhymes, the Signs, the Times*. St. Cloud, Minn.: North Star Press, 1997.

Warde, Walter. *Poster Design*. San Francisco: Foster and Kleiser, 1947.

Warhol, Andy. *America*. New York: Harper and Row, 1985.

Warner, Sam Bass, Jr. *Streetcar Suburbs: The Process of Growth in Boston, 1876–1900*. Cambridge, Mass.: Harvard University Press, 1978.

Weems, Robert E., Jr. *Desegregating the Dollar: African American Consumerism in the Twentieth Century*. New York: New York University Press, 1998.

Wells, Mildred White. *Unity in Diversity: The History of the General Federation of Women's Clubs*. Washington, D.C.: General Federation of Women's Clubs, 1953.

Welter, Barbara. *Dimity Convictions: The American Woman in the Nineteenth Century*. Athens: Ohio University Press, 1976.

Westgard, A. L. *Tales of a Pathfinder*. New York: A. L. Westgard, 1920.

Wiebe, Robert. *The Search for Order, 1877–1920*. New York: Hill and Wang, 1967.

Wik, Reynold M. "The Early Automobile and the American Farmer." In *The Autombile and Culture*, edited by David Lewis and Laurence Goldstein. Ann Arbor: University of Michigan Press, 1980.

Wild, Lorraine. "Europeans in America." In *Graphic Design in America: A Visual Language History*, edited by Mildred Friedman. New York: Harry N. Abrams, 1989.

Williams, Raymond. *Televison: Technology and Cultural Form*. New York: Schocken, 1977.

Wilson, William H. "The Billboard: Bane of the City Beautiful." *Journal of Urban History* 13, no. 4 (1987): 394–425.

——. *City Beautiful Movement*. Baltimore: Johns Hopkins University Press, 1989.

——. "J. Horace McFarland and the City Beautiful Movement." *Journal of Urban History* 7, no. 3 (1981): 315–34.

Wirka, Susan Marie. "The City Social Movement: Progressive Women Reformers and Early Social Planning." In *Planning the Twentieth-Century American City*, edited by Mary Corbin Sies and Charles Silver. Baltimore: Johns Hopkins University Press, 1996.

Woodruff, Clinton Rogers, ed. *The Billboard Nuisance*. Harrisburg, Pa.: J. Horace McFarland/Philadelphia: American Civic Association, 1908.

Young, James Harvey. *The Toadstool Millionaires: A Social History of Patent Medicines in America before Federal Regulation*. Princeton, N.J.: Princeton University Press, 1961.

Zabel, Barbara. "Stuart Davis's Appropriation of Advertising: The *Tobacco* Series, 1921–1924." *American Art* 5, no. 4 (1991): 57–67.

Zimmerman, M. M. *The Challenge of Chain Store Distribution*. New York: Harper and Brothers, 1931.

Zimmerman, Tom. "Paradise Promoted: Boosterism and the Los Angeles Chamber of Commerce." *California History* 64, no. 1 (1985): 22–33.

Zukin, Sharon. "Billboards Are Public Art in the Money Economy." In *Wall Power*. Philadelphia: Institute of Contemporary Art, University of Pennsylvania, 2000.

Zunz, Olivier. *Making America Corporate, 1870–1920*. Chicago: University of Chicago Press, 1990.

ILLUSTRATION CREDITS

Figures

1. *Poster* 14, no. 12 (1923): 34. Outdoor Advertising Association of America Archives, John W. Hartman Center for Sales, Advertising, and Marketing History, Rare Book, Manuscript, and Special Collections Library, Duke University (hereafter OAA/Duke).
2. Eno Collection, Miriam and Ira D. Wallach Division of Art, Prints, and Photographs, The New York Public Library, Astor, Lenox, and Tilden Foundations.
3.–4. Library of Congress.
5. Western History Collections, University of Oklahoma Library.
6. Clear Channel Outdoor, Los Angeles.
7. © Bettmann/CORBIS.
8. National Archives and Records Administration.
9. *Poster* 19, no. 3 (1928): 4. OAA/Duke.
10. *Sinclair H-C Gasoline* (New York and Chicago: Outdoor Advertising Incorporated, c. 1936), 8. Private collection.
11. *Poster* 18, no. 9 (1927): following 16. OAA/Duke. Courtesy BP America, Inc.
12. Clear Channel Outdoor, Los Angeles.
13. *Poster* 15, no. 6 (1924): facing 32. OAA/Duke. Courtesy Ford Motor Company.
14. C. O. Bridwell, *International Correspondence Schools: Outdoor Advertising* (Scranton, Penn.: International Textbook Company, 1921), 53. Courtesy Michelin North America, Inc.
15. *Poster* 10, no. 9 (1919): 24. OAA/Duke. Courtesy Michelin North America, Inc.
16. *Poster* 20, no. 6 (1929): 11. OAA/Duke.
17. *Poster* 17, no. 9 (1926): following 48. OAA/Duke. Courtesy Colgate-Palmolive Company.
18. *Advertising Outdoors: Best Posters of the Year* 1, no. 10 (1930): 66. Private collection.
19. *100 Best Posters of 1937* (New York: Outdoor Advertising Incorporated, 1937), 18. Private collection.
20. All rights reserved, The Metropolitan Museum of Art.
21. Photograph by Lee Stalsworth.
22.–23. OAA/Duke.
24. *Poster* 20, no. 7 (1929): 17. OAA/Duke. Courtesy Exxon Mobil Corporation.
25. *100 Best Posters of 1937* (New York: Outdoor Advertising Incorporated, 1937), 19. Private collection.
26. *Poster* 19, no. 9 (1928): 61. OAA/Duke. Courtesy The Goodyear Tire and Rubber Company.
27. *Outdoor Advertising: A Primary Medium* (New York: Outdoor Advertising Incorporated, 1936), 8-9. Private collection.

28. *Sinclair H-C Gasoline* (New York and Chicago: Outdoor Advertising Incorporated, c. 1936), 8. Private collection.
29. Clear Channel Outdoor, Los Angeles.
30. W. T. Warde, *Poster Design* (San Francisco: Foster and Kleiser, 1947), 13.
31. Private collection.
32. Security Pacific Collection, Los Angeles Public Library.
33. Courtesy Wm. Wrigley Jr. Company.
34. OAA/Duke.
35. *Poster* 17, no. 10 (1926): 4. OAA/Duke. Courtesy Maytag Corporation.
36. Clear Channel Outdoor, Los Angeles.
37. *OAA News* 32, no. 9 (1942): 8. OAA/Duke.
38. *OAA News* 26, no. 2 (1936): 3. OAA/Duke.
39. Clear Channel Outdoor, Los Angeles.
40. *OAA News* 26, no. 7 (1936): 1. OAA/Duke.
41. Security Pacific Collection, Los Angeles Public Library.
42. Clear Channel Outdoor, Los Angeles.
43. Security Pacific Collection, Los Angeles Public Library.
44. California Historical Society/TICOR, University of Southern California.
45. Clear Channel Outdoor, Los Angeles.
46. Outdoor Advertising Slide Library, OAA/Duke. Courtesy The Kroger Company.
47. *American Civic Annual*, ed. Harlean James (Washington, D.C.: American Civic Association, 1929), 140.
48. *Report of the Mayor's Billboard Advertising Commission of the City of New York. August 1, 1913* (New York: M. B. Brown Printing, 1913), 121.
49. *American City* 3, no. 5 (1910): 219.
50. *The Roadside Bulletin* 2, no. 4 (1933): 15.
51. *American Civic Annual*, ed. Harlean James (Washington, D.C.: American Civic Association, 1929), 136.
52. *American Civic Annual*, vol. 4, ed. Harlean James (Washington, D.C.: American Civic Association, 1932), 164.
53. Automobile Club of Southern California Archives.
54.–55. Albert Sprague Bard Papers, Box 21, Manuscripts and Archives Division, The New York Public Library, Astor, Lenox, and Tilden Foundations.
56. Library of Congress (LC-USF342-8253A).
57.–60. Clear Channel Outdoor, Los Angeles.
61. OAA News 27, no. 1 (1937): 3. OAA/Duke.
62. © Margaret Bourke-White/TimePix.
63. Library of Congress (LC-USF34-016317-E).
64. Library of Congress (LC-USF34-018619-C).
65. Clear Channel Outdoor, Los Angeles.
66. © Rondal and Elizabeth W. Partridge.
67. © Steve Kagan/Time Life Pictures/Getty Images.
68. Photograph © 1998 Quackser Fortune.
69. Outdoor Advertising Slide Library, OAA/Duke.
70. Photograph © 1988 Oren Slor.
71. Photograph by the author.
72. Clear Channel Outdoor, Los Angeles.

Plates

1. *Poster* 1, no. 8 (1910): 8-9. OAA/Duke.
2. Library of Congress (LC-USZC4-969).
3. National Archives and Records Administration.
4. OAA/Duke.

5. *Poster* 17, no. 9 (1926): following 16. OAA/Duke. Courtesy Exxon Mobil Corporation.

6. Burton Harrington, *Essentials of Poster Design* (Chicago: Poster Advertising Association, 1925), 99. Private collection. Reproduced by permission of Chevron U.S.A. Inc.

7. Clear Channel Outdoor, Los Angeles. Courtesy Wm. Wrigley Jr. Company.

8. National Archives and Records Administration.

9. Outdoor Advertising Slide Library, OAA/Duke. Courtesy The Coca-Cola Company.

10. Private collection.

11. © John Humble.

12. Clear Channel Outdoor, Los Angeles.

13. Photograph by the author.

INDEX